T·H·E
DISCIPLINE BOOK

By the same authors

The Birth Book
The Baby Book
300 Questions New Parents Ask
The Fussy Baby
Nighttime Parenting
Creative Parenting
Becoming a Father

T·H·E
DISCIPLINE BOOK

Everything You Need to Know to Have a
Better-Behaved Child — From Birth to Age Ten

WILLIAM SEARS, M.D.
AND MARTHA SEARS, R.N.

LITTLE, BROWN AND COMPANY
Boston ◆ *New York* ◆ *Toronto* ◆ *London*

First Edition

Library of Congress Cataloging-in-Publication Data

Sears, William, M.D.
    The discipline book : everything you need to know to have a better-behaved child — from birth to age ten / William Sears and Martha Sears. — 1st ed.
        p.   cm.
    Includes index.
    ISBN 0-316-77904-0 (hc)
    ISBN 0-316-77903-2 (pb)
    1. Discipline of children.   2. Child rearing.   3. Behavior modification.
I. Sears, Martha.   II. Title.
HQ770.S4 1995
649'.64 — dc20   94-3504

10 9 8 7 6 5 4 3 2 1

RRD-VA

Drawings by Deborah Maze
Designed by Jeanne Abboud

*Published simultaneously in Canada by Little, Brown & Company
(Canada) Limited*

PRINTED IN THE UNITED STATES OF AMERICA

Contents

A Word About Discipline from Dr. Bill and Martha

PARENTS STRUGGLE WITH what discipline is and how to approach it. Discipline is an integral part of your whole relationship with your child. It can't be pulled out and isolated from the rest of your family's life. At one point we intended the title of this book to be *Discipline for Life,* because our purpose is to equip children with the tools they will need to succeed in life.

This book was written on the job. Many of the stories throughout this book are from our own family, and as you will see, discipline has not always been easy for us nor have we always done it right. We could never have written this book without the many years of parenting we have under our belt. It wasn't until our kids started having kids that we fully realized the value of what we had done — and hadn't done — as disciplinarians. Besides our own experience, much of the advice in this book comes from the real experts: veteran parents of disciplined children who over the years have shared their wisdom with us.

You may feel that some advice in this book is too lenient, or that other advice is too harsh. You may feel, "I can't do that with my child." If it doesn't feel right to you, you shouldn't do it. Discipline is not a list of techniques to be plucked from a book, tried insensitively on your child, and followed rigidly. Instead, use the tools in this book to develop a *philosophy* of discipline, and use whatever tools fit your child and your family situation to create your own style of discipline.

How to read this book depends upon your needs. If you are first-time parents with a new baby, this book is a recipe for discipline, a philosophy of child rearing, and for some even a guide for living. If you are already experiencing discipline problems, this is also a repair manual, a fix-it-yourself book. Parents, we want you to realize the rewards of investing in your child's behavior. While parents should take neither all the credit nor all the blame for the person their child becomes, we believe that many of the problems society now faces — crime, violence, sexual irresponsibilities, and social insensitivities — stem from poor discipline in the child and in the adult that child becomes.

A mother in my office, desperate for direction on how she could influence society, said: "The streets are full of crime, the homes are full of violence, and schools spend more time keeping law and order than teaching. I feel powerless to make a difference, and I don't believe government knows how to change this course of events." I told this mom: "You *can* change the world, one child at a time. Do what you and no one but you can do — discipline your child."

William and Martha Sears
San Clemente, California
March 1995

I

PROMOTING DESIRABLE BEHAVIOR

How parents and child get started with each other influences the discipline relationship. Some parents will naturally ease into discipline, and some children are easier to discipline. Other parents, partly because of how they were disciplined as children, lack confidence in guiding and correcting their child. For these parents, the early chapters of this book will help you to become confident parents while giving your child the start you never got. We begin by discussing the attachment style of parenting, a way of getting connected to your child. Our journey into discipline starts by giving you the tools to get connected to your child in the early years, when the little person is under construction. We help you to build your sensitivity to your child, and your child's toward you; to know what is age-appropriate behavior; to help your child to become comfortably expressive, to handle anger, and to develop self-confidence. And from that basic relationship, loving guidance flows naturally. Attachment parenting brings rewards for parents as well as children. Putting in some extra effort at the beginning will save time and energy later on. You won't have to do as much of the repair work we discuss in Part II.

Our Approach to Discipline

HOW DO PARENTS get children to do the things they want them to do — and to *want* to do those things? This is the age-old problem of discipline, a matter not only of directing children's behavior but of motivating it. The answer is grounded not in a catalog of behavior-controlling techniques but in the parent-child relationship itself. If you know your child well and are sensitive to his needs, so that he trusts you, the ability to get him to behave well will follow naturally because he wants to please you.

Discipline is more about having the right *relationship* with your child than it is about using the "right" techniques. One of our goals in this book is to help you and your child become more sensitive persons. Our main approach to the topic of discipline can be summed up in one word — "sensitivity" — teaching parents how to understand the mind of their child, and teaching children how to consider the effects of their behavior on others. Many of today's discipline (and social) problems can be traced to one source — *insensitivity* toward oneself and others. So while we do present behavior-improving ideas throughout this book, we focus mostly on the important parent-child connection. We call this the "attachment approach."

STYLES OF DISCIPLINE

In order to better understand exactly what is different about our attachment approach, it helps to take a look at various other methods of discipline. Discipline methods fall into three categories: *the authoritarian style, the communication approach,* and *the behavior modification approach.* All three of these ways of guiding children's behavior have strengths and weaknesses. In twenty-two years of experience in handling discipline problems in pediatric practice, and in disciplining eight children of our own, we have found that all three of these approaches are useful at different times, though by themselves they are not enough.

The authoritarian style. The traditional way of disciplining, authoritarianism, focuses on parents as authority figures whom children must obey or face the consequences. As one authoritarian father put it: "I'm the dad, he's the child, and that's that! I don't need this modern psychology stuff.

If he gets out of line, I'll show him who's boss." With this style of parenting, spanking is considered appropriate, even necessary. The good part of this approach is that it makes it clear that parents must take charge of their children. Many of today's discipline problems result from adults avoiding responsibility for the behavior of their children. Children need wise authority figures in order to learn what to do and what not to do. Authority will always be an important part of the discipline package.

Yet many problems can occur with authoritarian parenting. For one, the child can fail to feel the parents' love. The child can also internalize fear of the parents' power to the point that it controls her life, even in adulthood. Most important, however, is that when it is used as the sole method of discipline, authoritarianism simply doesn't work. There are several reasons for this. First, it causes parents to focus so much on stamping out the bad in their children that they tend to overlook the good. Also, the emphasis on punishment keeps parents from learning more appropriate ways to correct their children, ways that could lessen the necessity for punishment in the first place. Worst of all with authoritarian discipline, children behave more out of fear of punishment than desire to please. As a result, they develop no inner controls. Once the controllers' backs are turned, the controllees can run wild. They may not throw their toys on the floor as adults, but they will lack the inner discipline needed to motivate and control themselves when there is no threat of dire consequences.

The authoritarian style regards discipline as something you do *to* a child, not a learning process you go through *with* a child. The newborn who cries a lot is seen as a tyrant whose noises should be squelched rather than as a little person who needs help. The toddler is a manipulator who is out to dominate the parents if they aren't careful. This sets up an adversarial relationship between parent and child, and confuses taking charge of the child with controlling the child. Authoritarianism creates a distance between parent and child, for two reasons: It is based on punishment, which can easily create anger, and thus distance the child from the parent, and it makes little or no allowance for the temper-

Discipline Is Therapeutic

Disciplining a child, especially a difficult child, brings out the best and the worst in parents. It challenges them to act like the adults they want their children to become. Thus, in disciplining your child, you discipline yourself. To fix your child's behavior, you must fix your own. As you train your child, you train yourself. Yet childish behavior also can push buttons that produce irrational reactions in parents. Understanding your child's feelings and your reactions to them can lead to greater self-understanding. Disciplining your child becomes a personal discovery in how you were parented. A mother once told us, "I notice my own mother's voice coming out of my mouth." Problems from your past may surface in your relationship with your child and infect your ability to discipline. If you had a childhood full of dysfunctional discipline, you are at risk of passing on these problems. The desire to discipline well compels you to heal the unhealthy parts of yourself so that you can be a healthy parent to your child.

ament or developmental level of the child. Wise disciplinarians become students of their children and work to know their children well. Controllers often find this consideration demeaning to their authority and therefore do not believe it belongs in their discipline package. Because authoritarian parenting is not geared to the child as an individual, this style of parenting seldom brings out the best in parents and child, even when a warm heart is behind the heavy hand.

The communication approach. This philosophy teaches that communicative rather than punitive parenting is the way to discipline. Dissatisfaction with the authoritarian/ punishment approach to discipline spawned several schools of discipline based on teaching parents how to better communicate with their children. Most of today's discipline books and classes are based on this approach. This philosophy suggests there are no bad children, just bad communication; and that children are basically good; parents just have to learn how to listen and talk to them. The good news about this "modern" approach is that it respects the child as a person whose actions result from feelings and encourages parents to delve into the feelings behind the behavior. Parents learn constructive ways to convey to their children what behavior they expect. Parents also use empathy and understanding to create a generally positive atmosphere in the home, so they can limit the use of the word "no." The communication approach emphasizes parenting skills that lessen the need for punishment. Psychology replaces punishment. Spanking is taboo.

The main problem with the communication approach is that parents tend to lose their authority, instead taking on the roles of amateur psychologist, negotiator, and diplomat. Children may end up not respecting authority because their parents do not expect them to. This lack of respect for home authority carries over into lack of respect for others, including, for example, teachers and police officers. And if it is overused, most children regard this approach as phony. The dialogue sounds like nothing more than a list of emotionally correct phrases mom and dad learned at last night's parenting class, not true communication at all. Instead of saying "Don't hit your brother," communicative parents tend to address their child's feelings: "You must be very angry with your brother." This sounds right, and to many parents feels right, but what happens if after identifying his anger the child continues to hit? What do you do then? Another problem is that parents often become so worried that they will damage their child's psyche if they don't react in the "psychologically correct" way, that they end up unwilling to take a stand. This style of discipline, therefore, runs the risk of being overpermissive.

The behavior modification approach. Behavior "mod," as it is known, teaches that children's behavior can be influenced positively and negatively according to how parents structure their child's environment. If the child continues to hit other children even after you have given him all of the psychologically correct communication you can provide, you simply remove him from the group. Most children respond well to behavior modification; some regard the techniques as contrived. Although somewhat mechanistic in its approach (it's strikingly similar to training pets), behavior modification gives parents *techniques,* such as time-out, positive reinforcement, and the teaching of natural consequences, that can be called on when the authoritarian and communication approaches are not working. Behavior modification may be especially useful for children with emotional problems or difficult temperaments who don't respond to other methods. The trainer focuses on shaping behavior, conditioning the child without judging her.

The bad news about behavior modification techniques is that sooner or later you are going to run out of them, or run out of the energy it takes to apply them consistently. The greater danger of behavior modification is that it focuses on external techniques rather than on the parent-child relationship, so that the child is approached as a project rather than a person.

The attachment approach. Parents who rely on any of the three above approaches to solve a discipline problem may find that their child's behavior improves, but only temporarily. Without a secure grounding in parent-child attachment, the other discipline approaches are merely borrowed skills, communication gimmicks, techniques that are grabbed from the rack and tried on in hopes of a good fit. None of these approaches incorporates the idea that discipline must be custom-tailored to the age and temperament of the child and to the

---

Consult the Experts

When I counsel pediatric residents about to enter practice, I tell them: "Surround yourself with wise and experienced parents, and learn from them." These are the true discipline experts. In fact, much of the material in this book comes from veteran parents in our practice who shared their successes and failures with us. In formulating our own philosophy of discipline we took note of what these wise disciplinarians did and how their kids turned out. This is what we learned: Wise disciplinarians spend time and energy keeping one step ahead of their child and setting conditions that promote good behavior, leaving the child fewer opportunities to misbehave. Wise disciplinarians

- stay connected to their children
- develop a mutual sensitivity between parent and child

- spend more time promoting desirable behavior, so they need less corrective discipline
- have a working understanding of age-appropriate behavior
- use humor to promote cooperation in the child
- are able to get behind the eyes of their child and redirect behavior

Love for your child makes you vulnerable to any advice that promises to create a bright and well-behaved child. One of our goals in this book is to sharpen your sensitivity so that you learn to discern between advice that creates a distance between you and your child and advice that draws you closer together. Pick advisers who have raised lots of children and whose kids you like. Make friends with them, watch them in action, and learn from them.

personalities of the parents. Every family, every child, every situation is different, and parents must take all these things into account when they are working to correct their child's behavior. To do this, they must know themselves and know their child.

We use the best from all of the three approaches outlined above, but only after going much deeper to construct a firm foundation: Discipline depends on *building the right relationship with a child.* With a firm grounding in a connected relationship, a parent can use the other three approaches to discipline (authority, communication, and behavior modification) in a balanced way. If your child is having discipline problems, you can use your close relationship with her to figure out what to do. Ask "What is going on inside my child, and how can I help her deal with these problems?" rather than "How can I get her to behave?" This approach helps parents and children to work together rather than clash. Picture the attachment approach as a pyramid: The

foundation is wide and strong, and it takes longer to build, but as you go up you have to use less energy and material. The structure is solid and stands forever. Other approaches may appear convenient initially, but without that broad foundation you will always be making tricky repairs later on.

Yes, you must take charge of your child, but not in a controlling way. Yes, you should communicate with your child, but in the context of a trusting relationship. Yes, you need discipline tools to help you handle real-life situations, but when these techniques don't work, you need to fall back on a deeper understanding of your child. With an attachment approach to discipline, you can have confidence that your child will (for the most part) behave well and develop the *inner controls* needed to live a happy, productive life. Where the authoritarian approach says "I'll tell you what to do," the communication approach says "What do *you* think is the right thing to do?," and the behavior modification ap-

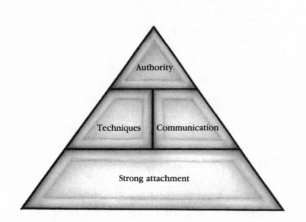

Strong parent-child connection.

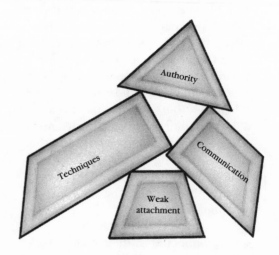

Weak parent-child connection.

proach says "If you do that, then this will happen," our suggestion is to give your child the attachment message "You can trust me to help *you* know what to do."

In the next section we will give you an overview of the attachment approach to discipline. You will see how all these other approaches fit into the total package. Remember that discipline is a package deal, and that all the separate parts must be held together by a right relationship with your child.

DISCIPLINE'S TOP TEN — AN OVERVIEW OF THIS BOOK

One day I was watching a family in my waiting room. The toddler played happily a few feet away from the mother, sometimes returning to her lap for a brief reconnecting cuddle, then darting off again. As he ventured farther away, he glanced back at her for approval. Her nod and smile said "It's OK," and he confidently explored new toys. The few times the child started to be disruptive, the mother connected eye-to-eye with him and the father physically redirected him so that he received a clear message that a change in behavior was needed. There was a peace about the child and a comfortable authority in the parents. It was easy to see that they had a good relationship. I couldn't resist complimenting them: "You are good disciplinarians." Surprised, the father replied, "But we don't spank our child."

Our understanding of the word "discipline" was obviously different. Like many other parents, they equated discipline with reacting to bad behavior. They didn't realize that mostly discipline is what you do to encourage good behavior. It's better to keep a

child from falling down in the first place than to patch up bumps and scrapes after he has taken the tumble.

Discipline is everything you put into children that influences how they turn out. But how do you want your child to turn out? What will your child need from you in order to become the person you want him to be? Whatever your ultimate objectives, they must be rooted in helping your child develop *inner controls* that last a lifetime. You want the guidance system that keeps the child in check at age four to keep his behavior on track at age forty, and you want this system to be integrated into the child's whole personality, a part of him or her. If your child's life were on videotape and you could fast-forward a few decades, what are the qualities you would like to see in the adult on the tape? Here is our wish list for our children:

- sensitivity
- confidence and solid self-esteem
- wisdom to make right choices
- ability to form intimate relationships
- respect for authority
- skills to solve problems
- sense of humor
- ability to focus on goals
- honesty, integrity
- healthy sexuality
- sense of responsibility
- desire to learn

Once you know your objectives, you can set about figuring out how to achieve them. Remember, your child is not a blank slate onto which you write your wishes. Your child's personality is *guided*, not formed, by you and other significant persons. You must take the child's individuality into account. Because children and parents have different temperaments and personalities, and families have different lifestyles, how parents guide their children will vary. Nevertheless, there are basic concepts that underlie all discipline, no matter what the characteristics of parent and child. The ten basic principles that follow should help you get started in thinking about how discipline will operate in your home. We'll discuss each of these principles fully throughout the rest of the book.

1. Get Connected Early

Discipline is grounded on a healthy relationship between parent and child. To know how to discipline your child you must first *know* your child. This kind of knowledge resides deep in parents' minds. You could call it intuition, but that term has a kind of mystique that confuses parents. ("How can I trust my intuition? I don't even know if I have any!") The term "connection" is easier to understand. With the high-touch parenting style called attachment parenting (to be explained in Chapter 2), you can build and strengthen this connection between you and your child, laying the foundation for discipline. Connected parents become *their own* experts on *their own* child, so they know what behavior to expect as appropriate and how to convey their expectations. Connected children know what behavior parents expect, and make an effort to behave this way because *they want to please* their parents. These parents and children together develop a style of discipline that works for them. In Chapter 2 we describe the tools for connecting with your baby and young child so that you can read your child's behavior and respond appropriately, and the two of you can bring out the best in each other.

Throughout the rest of the book we help you stay connected to your child and show you how to reconnect if you had a shaky start in the early years of parenting.

Unconnected parents, unsure of what is going on in their child's mind, may lack confidence in their own disciplinary skills, so they search for answers to their child's behavior from outside experts. They wander from method to method, groping for answers to problems that could have been prevented. If you and your child are having discipline problems and you feel there is a distance in your relationship, chances are the connection between you and your child needs some work. It's never too late to improve that relationship, although the earlier you connect with your child the easier discipline will be. Getting connected and staying connected with your child is the foundation of discipline and the heart of the attachment approach.

2. Know Your Child

These are the three most useful words in discipline. Study your child. Know your child's needs and capabilities at various ages. Your discipline techniques will be different at each stage because your child's needs change. A temper tantrum in a two-year-old calls for a different response than it does in a four-year-old. In later chapters we will point out what behavior is normal, what's not, and what to do at each stage of a child's development.

Know age-appropriate behavior. Many conflicts arise when parents expect children to think and behave like adults. You need to know what behavior is usual for a child at each stage of development in order to recognize true misbehavior. We find discipline to be much easier with our eighth child than it was with our first child, mainly because we now have a handle on which behaviors call for instruction, patience, and humor, and which demand a firm, corrective response. We tolerate those things that go along with a child's age and stage (for example, most two-year-olds *can't* sit still in a restaurant for more than a few minutes), but we correct behavior that is disrespectful or dangerous to the child or to others ("You may not climb on the table").

Get inside your child's mind. Children don't think like adults. Kids try crazy things and think crazy thoughts — at least by adult standards. You will drive *yourself* crazy if you judge a child's behavior from an adult viewpoint. A two-year-old who runs out into the street isn't being defiant, he just wants his ball back. Action follows impulse, with no thought in between. A five-year-old likes her friend's toy so much that she "borrows" it. An adult may stop and weigh the necessity, safety, and morality of an act, but a young child doesn't. Throughout this book we will show you ways to get behind the eyes of your child, so that you can understand what causes your child's behavior and figure out how to redirect it. We call it thinking "kid first." Here's an example.

Our Matthew at age two was a very focused child. He would become so engrossed in a play activity that it was difficult for him to let go when it was time to leave. One day when he was playing and it was time for us to depart (we were late for an appointment), Martha scooped Matthew up and carried him to the door. Matthew protested with a typical two-year-old tantrum. At first Martha had the usual "Hey, I'm in charge here" feelings and felt that she was justified in expecting Matthew to obey

quickly and be willing to leave his toys. But as she was carrying the flailing child out the door, she realized that her discipline gauge was out of balance and she was not handling things in the best way. Her actions were a result of her need to leave, but they didn't take into account Matthew's need for advance warning and a more gradual transition. She realized it wasn't in Matthew's nature to click off his interest in play so quickly, even if we did have a deadline. He was not defying her but was just being true to himself. He needed more time to let go of his activities. So she calmly took him back to the play setting, sat down with him, and together they said "Bye-bye, toys, bye-bye, trucks, bye-bye, cars," until he could comfortably release himself from the activities. It only took a couple of minutes, time that would otherwise have been wasted struggling with Matthew in the car. This was not a "technique" or "method"; this disciplinary action evolved naturally from the mutual respect between parent and child and the knowledge that Martha had about Matthew. At the end of this exercise Martha felt right because it had accomplished what she wanted — getting Matthew out of the house with the least amount of hassle. She taught him a method of releasing himself from an activity without resorting to a tantrum. That's what discipline is all about.

Realizing how much better discipline worked when we considered our children's needs in our decisions was a major turning point for us. Initially, we had to work through the fear that we were letting our children manipulate us, because we had read, heard from others, and grown up with the idea that good parents are always in control. We found, however, that considering our children's point of view actually helped us take charge of them. Knowing our children became the key to knowing how to discipline them. They knew we were in charge because we were able to help them obey. That left no doubt in their minds or ours that mom and dad knew best.

3. Help Your Child to Respect Authority

Parents, take charge of your children. That's basic in Discipline 101. But being a trusted authority figure in your child's life does not automatically come with the job of being a parent. The child who is told he must obey "or else" may behave, but he does so out of fear, not respect. "*Honor* thy father and thy mother" is the wise and time-honored teaching; not *fear* them. Honor implies both obedience and respect.

How do you get your children to respect you? An authority figure needs to be both warm and wise. First, get connected to your child. Start as a *nurturer,* a baby comforter. In so doing, you get to know your baby and your baby *trusts* you. Respect for authority is based on trust. Once your child trusts you to meet her needs, she will trust you to set her limits. One day I asked a mother why she felt so confident as an authority figure. She said, "A lot of my security comes from *knowing* my children." Because she understood her children, she was able to guide them wisely and know they would follow. Many parents confuse being in charge with being in control. Instead of directly controlling children, wise authority figures control the *situation* in order to make it easier for children to learn to control themselves. Children respond with genuine trust and respect rather than fear and rebellion.

4. Set Limits, Provide Structure

Establish rules, but at the same time create conditions that make the rules easier to follow. Children need boundaries. They won't thrive or survive without limits; neither will their parents. To learn about their environment, toddlers must be energetic and exploring. That's their job. Environmental control is the parents' job. This involves both *setting wise limits* and *providing structure,* which means creating an atmosphere in the home that makes these limits easier to respect. The limit-setting part of disciplining a toddler is to say no to an exploring child who is headed for trouble; the structure part is to childproof the home to provide busy minds and busy bodies a safe place to play and learn.

5. Expect Obedience

Your child will be as obedient as you expect or as defiant as you allow. When we ask parents of obedient kids why their children obey, they all answer, "Because we expect them to." Simple as this sounds, many parents let this basic fact of discipline slip away. They are too busy; their child is "strong-willed"; they make excuses: "It's just a developmental phase."

In the early years children don't know what behavior is acceptable or unacceptable until you tell them. One evening at a kid-friendly restaurant, we observed two families handle the same discipline situation in two different ways. The two-and-a-half-year-old in one family was incessantly climbing over the back of the booth, and she kept this climbing behavior up until it became disruptive to nearby patrons. Wimpy "don'ts" from the parents did not deter the persistent climber. It was clear this child had no idea that climbing was unacceptable behavior. She got the message "We prefer that you not climb, but we're not going to do anything about it." Another two-and-a-half-year-old got a different message and showed different behavior. The parent sat the child next to him, frequently acknowledged the child, and kept him involved in the family conversation. As soon as the toddler began to climb, the father immediately redirected him and politely planted the climber back in his seat. With a combination of creative distraction and respectful restraint, the parent conveyed to the child that he was expected to refrain from climbing because climbing would disturb the people in the next booth. The child got the message that any effort to climb the seat would not be all right. The child filed this experience into his memory bank, to be retrieved the next time they went to a restaurant, when, presumably, he would make fewer attempts to climb over the seat.

Was the parent in the second family exhibiting controlling behavior? Yes, but in the right sense of the term. Abusive control is when you forcibly impose your will upon your child, expecting her to obey, but to the detriment of your relationship. When you insist on obedience and help the child to get control of herself, you are using your power over the child in a good way that helps her develop inner controls. Remember, children want limits so that they don't feel out of control, and they want parents to stand by those limits. They keep testing the limits to see if you will uphold them. When you don't the child feels anxious that no one is strong enough to contain her. To a child, that is scary.

In the following chapters we will show you how to plant a cooperative attitude in your child so he will want to obey. Also, we will share with you tips for getting and holding your child's attention long enough to get your point across. Your child must understand your instructions in order to follow them. Expect whatever behavior makes your child a nice person to live with, and then help your child to comply. Your child will thank you later.

6. Model Discipline

A model is an example your child imitates. The mind of a growing child is a sponge, soaking up life's experiences; it's a video camera capturing everything a child hears and sees, storing these images in a mental vault for later retrieval. These stored images, especially those frequently repeated by significant persons in the child's life, become part of his personality — the child's self. So one of your jobs as a parent is to provide good material for your child to absorb.

"But I can't be perfect." Of course not. No parent is perfect. While writing this book, Martha and I would often say, "We know all this stuff and we still keep making mistakes." In fact, it's unhealthy to model perfection — a goal that neither parent nor child can meet (though many are crippled by trying). It's the *overall impression* that your child receives that counts, not the occasional blunders or outbursts. If a parent is habitually angry, anger becomes part of the child's self. The child learns that this is the way people deal with life. If a parent models happiness and trust, with an occasional angry tirade, the child sees a healthier model: People are happy most of the time, but sometimes, difficulties make you angry. You handle the situation and go back to being happy.

Parents, you are the first people your child knows. You are the first caregivers, authority figures, playmates, male and female. You set the standard for your child's attitude toward authority, her ability to play with peers, and her sexual identity. Part of yourself becomes part of your child. Yes, much of a child's behavior is genetic. More than one parent has been known to remark, "He came wired that way," but much is also influenced by the child's behavioral models. Throughout this book we will show you how to provide your child with a disciplined model.

7. Nurture Your Child's Self-Confidence

A child who feels right acts right. In the first part of this book we will show you how to help your child like herself. The growing person with a positive self-image is easier to discipline. She thinks of herself as a worthwhile person, and so she behaves in a worthwhile way. She is able to forgo some willful misbehavior to maintain this feeling of well-being. When this child does misbehave, she returns more quickly to the right path, with less need for punishment.

Not so the child with poor self-image. The child who doesn't feel right doesn't act right. His parents don't trust him, so he can't trust himself. No one expects him to behave well, so he doesn't. The bad behavior cycle begins: The more misbehavior, the more punishment, which intensifies the child's anger and lowers his self-esteem, producing more bad behavior. This is why our approach to discipline focuses primarily on promoting inner well-being in the child from the beginning. Throughout life your

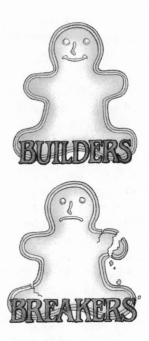

Builders and breakers.

child will be exposed to people and events that contribute to his self-worth and to others that chip away at it. We call these *builders* and *breakers*. We will help you to set the conditions that expose your child to many more builders than breakers, and, of course, to become a builder yourself.

8. Shape Your Child's Behavior

A wise parent is like a gardener who works with what he has in his garden and also decides what he wants to add. He realizes he cannot control the characteristics of the flowers he has, when they bloom, their scent and color; but he can add those colors that are missing in his garden, and he can shape it to be more beautiful. There are flowers and weeds in every child's behavior. Sometimes flowers bloom so beautifully that you don't even notice the weeds; other times the weeds overtake the flowers. The gardener waters the flowers, stakes the plants to help them grow straight, prunes them for maximum bloom, and keeps the weeds in check.

Children are born with some behavioral traits that either flourish or are weeded out, depending on how the children are nurtured. Other traits are planted and vigorously encouraged to grow. Taken altogether, these traits make up a child's eventual personality. Your gardening tools as a parent are techniques we call *shapers,* time-tested ways to improve your child's behavior in everyday situations. These shapers help you weed out those behaviors that slow your child down and nurture those qualities that help him mature.

The goal of behavior shaping is to instill in your child a sense of what is "acceptable behavior" and to help him have positive feelings about it. The child learns to behave, for better or for worse, according to the response he gets from his authority figures. When a child gets encouraging responses to desirable behavior, he is motivated to continue it. When a child gets unpleasant responses to desirable behavior, it dies out. However, when a child gets lots of attention, positive or negative, for undesirable behavior, it may continue, especially if that's the only behavior that gets a response. Be careful which behaviors you reinforce and how you do it.

Most shaping of a child's behavior is a *when-then* reaction. (When Billy's room is a mess, Mom says "No more playing outside until it's cleaned up.") Eventually, the child internalizes these shapers, developing his own inner systems of *when-then,* and in so doing learns to take responsibility for the consequences of his actions. ("When my

room is a mess, it's no fun to play there, so I better clean it up.") He learns to shape his own behavior.

At each stage of development, your shaping tools change, depending on the needs of your little garden. In the pages ahead, we give you gardening tips to help you confidently shape your child's behavior and make his personality work to his advantage. He will be a more likable person who contributes to the garden of life.

9. Raise Kids Who Care

Being a moral child includes being responsible, developing a conscience, and being sensitive toward the needs and rights of others. A moral child has an inner code of right and wrong that is linked to his inner sense of well-being. Inside himself he knows that "I feel right when I act right, and I feel wrong when I act wrong." The root of being a moral child, and one of the main focuses of this book, is sensitivity to oneself and to others, along with the ability to anticipate how one's actions will affect another person and to take that into account before proceeding. One of the most valuable social skills you can help your child develop is empathy — the ability to consider another person's rights and feelings. Children learn empathy from people who treat them empathetically. One of the best ways to turn out good citizens is to raise sensitive children.

Besides teaching children responsible behavior toward others and toward things, also teach them to take responsibility for themselves. One of the most valuable tools for life you can give your child is *the ability to make wise choices.* You want to plant a security system within your child that constantly reminds him: *Think through what you're about to do.* By learning to take responsibility for their actions in small things, children prepare to make right choices when the consequences are more serious. Our wish for you is to raise *kids who care.*

10. Talk and Listen

Throughout each chapter we will point out ways to communicate with your child so she doesn't become *parent deaf.* The best authority figures specialize in communication with children. Oftentimes rephrasing the same directive in a more child-considered way makes the difference in whether a child obeys or defies you. (See "Discipline Talk," pages 162–163.) Wise disciplinarians know how to open up a closed-off child and consider the Golden Rule: Talk to your children respectfully, the way you want them to talk to you.

Besides learning how to talk to a child, it is equally important to learn how to listen. Nothing wins over a child (or adult) more than conveying that you value her viewpoint. Being in charge of your child doesn't mean putting her down. In Chapter 8 we will show you how to help your child recognize and appropriately express her feelings. Once she is able to manage her own feelings she is more likely to become *sensitive* to the feelings of others.

Each of these discipline points depends on the others. It's hard to be an authority fig-

The balance of love and limits.

ure, a good model, a behavior shaper, and an obedience teacher if you and your child aren't connected and you don't know your child. You may know the psychological principles of behavioral shaping, but shapers won't work if you can't communicate with your child. And even a connected relationship doesn't guarantee a disciplined child if you fail to convey your expectation that your child obey you. These ten interdependent building blocks form the foundation of the approach to discipline advocated throughout the rest of this book. Put them all together, and you have a blueprint for raising children who are a joy to be with now and who will make you proud in the future.

2

Birth to One Year: Getting Connected

WHY ARE SOME CHILDREN EASIER to discipline? It took us more than twenty years of parent and baby watching to answer this question. Our conclusion is: *The deeper the parent-child connection, the easier discipline will be.* To help you appreciate the relationship between connecting to your child and disciplining your child, in this chapter we will share with you our observations of thousands of parent-child pairs, our experience in connecting with our own eight children, and what other researchers have observed about the relationship between parent-child attachment and discipline.

What we observed. We noticed three features of connected kids that made them easier to discipline:

- They want to please.
- They are willing to obey.
- They are more self-controlled.

These are the kids you like to be around.

We also noticed these features of connected parents:

- They respond sensitively to their child's needs.
- They respond appropriately, neither giving too much nor too little.
- They know their child. They are observant of age- and stage-appropriate behaviors.
- They are in charge of their child in a guiding, not controlling, way.

What others observed. In addition to our own observations, we read the most credible research that attempted to answer the age-old question What can parents do that most affects the way their children turn out? These are known as *attachment studies.* Attachment researchers use the term "securely" attached children (we call them connected kids) or "insecurely" or "anxiously" attached children (we call them unconnected kids). The striking conclusion that we can make from these studies is that, in addition to our genetic wiring, *how we become who we are is rooted in the parent-child connection in the first few years of life.* Attachment researchers found that connected kids shine in nearly every area of competence and behavior. The summary of their observations is shown in the chart on page 31.

Modern research is finally concluding what savvy mothers have always known: A healthy attachment in infancy is likely to turn out a healthier adult. How a mother and infant spend the first year together makes a difference, probably for the rest of their lives. The basis for discipline at all ages is being connected to your child. The earlier you get connected, the more successful your discipline will be. To guide your child you have to know your child, be able to read your child's body language, and give age-appropriate responses. For your child to receive your discipline, your child needs to be able to read and trust you. This mutual connection allows discipline to flow naturally from you to your child, and prepares your child to want your guidance. As rational as this sounds, there are many families where this doesn't happen. Our purpose in this chapter is to show you how to let this connection happen, right from the very beginning.

MARTHA AND MATTHEW — HOW THEY GOT CONNECTED

We love reading teacher's reports about our nine-year-old Matthew: "He's so focused." "He's so well-behaved." Our friends give us compliments about Matthew: "He's such a joy to have around." "He's a good influence on my son." During a toy squabble between Matthew and a friend, an observing parent said, "Matthew is incredibly sensitive to other children." A new mother watching Martha discipline a conflict between Matthew and a sibling remarked, "How did you know what to do?"

How did Matthew come to be this way?

Is he afraid of being punished, or is he just naturally "good"? Where did his self-control come from? How can one subtle look from Martha pull him back from the brink of trouble? How did this pair get so well connected? The story of disciplining Matthew goes all the way back to the day of his birth.

Immediately after birth Martha gathered up Matthew and cuddled him to her breast. As Matthew lay skin-to-skin, no longer enclosed in the warmth of her womb, he found a new place where he fit. As he nursed from Martha's breast, snuggled against her chest, nested in her arms, he found a new "womb." When he opened his eyes, he found Martha's eyes gazing adoringly into his. Matthew arrived knowing where he belonged and feeling that this was a warm and comfortable place to be. Matthew felt right. Though no longer connected by the cord, the pair stayed connected by the hormonal high of new motherhood and the ability of a newly born baby to make his needs known. No distance — physical or emotional — developed between them. During the day Martha held Matthew close to her or wore him in a baby sling, nursed him on cue, and responded sensitively to his needs. At night they slept side by side, Martha providing security and comfort to Matthew.

This connection, the beginning of discipline, continued through Matthew's baby days. When Matthew cried, Martha responded, and Matthew learned that his distress was followed by comfort. Because Martha gave Matthew a consistent response, Matthew learned to *trust* that his mother was responsive to him. Never mind that Martha did not always give the "perfect" response (Matthew may have wanted a change of scenery, but Martha offered to feed him). The important point is that she responded. Even though this was our sixth baby, Martha had to learn to read Matthew as an individual. With time and patience and through hundreds of rehearsals, Matthew and Martha worked at their communication until they got it right most of the time. As time progressed, Martha learned to anticipate Matthew's needs. When a grimace appeared, a cry was sure to follow. So she responded to the grimace before a panic cry had a chance to develop. Mother and baby were comfortable and happy together.

As I watched this pair grow together (and did what I could to support them), I noticed that while Martha's initial responses to Matthew's cues involved some trial and error, they quickly became more intuitive. There was harmony to their relationship, a flow of cue-giving and caregiving between a little person with big needs and a mother motivated to meet those needs. This led to an inner feeling of well-being that is characteristic of a connected mother-baby pair. The same sparkle was in the eyes of both mother and son. We enjoyed being with him, and he enjoyed being with us. Because Matthew was connected, he felt *valued* — the beginning of a child's self-worth, the basis of disciplined behavior. Matthew's smiles and contentment made Martha feel valued as well, the beginning of parental self-confidence.

I saw a *mutual sensitivity* develop between Matthew and Martha. When Matthew was upset, Martha knew what he needed, almost as if she could get inside his mind. Martha seemed to feel what Matthew was feeling and vice versa. When Matthew's behavior deteriorated or when he was not feeling well, her sensitivity went up a notch. She clicked into motherly overdrive, with a higher level of acceptance and a

higher level of giving. Matthew also became sensitive to Martha. When she was having a bad day, Matthew became less sparkly and more clingy. By the time Matthew was a year old, we were well on our way to having a disciplined child. *We knew our child, and Matthew felt right.*

Once we put the initial investment of time and energy into getting to know Matthew, meeting his needs, and anticipating his behavior, his entry into toddlerhood did not worry us. When Matthew drifted into undesirable behavior, it was not difficult to rechannel his actions. He was willing to be redirected because he knew we respected his need to hatch. His sense of self was blossoming. (Bill's connection to Matthew is described in Chapter 6, "Fathers as Disciplinarians.")

ATTACHMENT PARENTING — THE KEY TO EARLY DISCIPLINE

Martha's style of parenting is called attachment parenting, a style that brings out the best in parents and baby. Attachment parenting begins with being *open* to the cues and needs of your baby, without fretting about spoiling or being manipulated. It gets discipline off to a good start by helping you get to know your baby. Alternatively, parenting styles that place the emphasis on parents getting their babies on a set schedule, under control, are likely to keep you from connecting with your baby and can undermine the development of true discipline.

By knowing your child you learn her needs and preferences at each stage of development. You are able to understand why she behaves a certain way, what situations promote desirable behavior, and which ones produce undesirable behavior. You help her feel right by setting conditions that promote the best behavior. The child who feels right acts right. She operates from an inner sense of well-being and so is less impulsive, less angry, and less likely to misbehave. Attachment parenting will help you reach two goals: *to know your child* and *to help your child feel right.* These two goals form the cornerstone of a strong disciplinary relationship with your child. Six features of attachment parenting that will help you get connected and shape the relationship between you and your baby are: responding to your baby's cues, breastfeeding, wearing your baby, spending time playing with your baby, sharing sleep, and being a facilitator. Here's how each of these attachments contributes to discipline.

1. Respond to Your Baby's Cries

Before you actually hold your baby in your arms you will wonder, "How will I ever know what my baby needs?" You will learn quickly because your baby will tell you. The key is to listen and observe. Babies are born with *attachment-promoting behaviors* (APBs). These behaviors are baby's earliest language, cues that he uses to communicate his needs. You will find them irresistible; they're designed to be that way, to penetrate parents to the core, demanding a response. The strongest APB is baby's cry. Responding to your baby's cries is Discipline 101. When your baby cries, pick him up and comfort him. Don't waste your time wondering, "Should I pick him up?" "Is he trying to manipulate me?" "Will I spoil her?" Just do it.

Don't worry whether you've given the correct response. If your baby is hungry and you try to comfort her by holding and singing rather than feeding her, she will let you know she wants to be fed instead by gnawing on her fists or searching for your breast. With practice, you and your baby will work out the correct cues and responses. Your baby will learn to give you specific cues to specific needs, and you will learn to read body language that signals a specific need. Your response will become less calculated, more intuitive and natural. For some mothers this comes easily; others may need to overcome uncertainty or preconceived fears that their baby will control and manipulate them. At some time near the beginning of your parenting career you are likely to hear the advice "Let your baby cry it out" (meaning leave your baby to cry alone). Don't do it! A baby's cry is his language — listen to it. A baby's cry is designed to ensure that his needs for food, holding, rest, and social interaction are met. His cry also develops his mother's parenting skills. Responding to your baby's cries is your first exercise in teaching your baby to trust you. It's an exercise in disciplining your baby.

We do not mean to imply that it is your responsibility to make your baby stop crying. Only baby can do that. It *is* your job to help him stop crying. Yet there will be times when baby does keep crying because even your holding or feeding doesn't help, and you'll have some research to do.* The difference is he's not being left to cry alone. You continue to hold, rock, bounce, jiggle, take a walk outside — do whatever it takes

---

*We discuss each of these attachment tips in greater detail in *The Baby Book* (Boston: Little, Brown, 1993). We treat them here in briefer form to show how they lay the foundation for discipline.

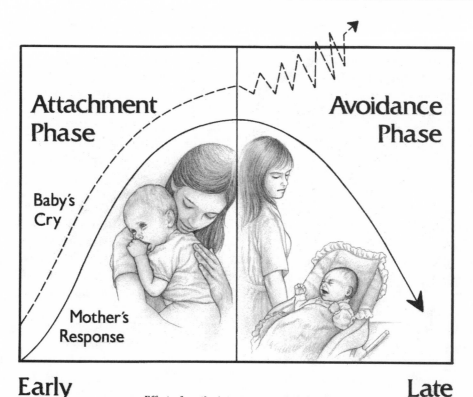

Effect of mother's response on baby's cries.

to help him. Just being with him helps, and you'll learn as you go. Keeping baby in arms as much as possible helps him cry less and feel supported when he does cry. The cry is baby's first communication tool. Listen to it.

After the first four to six months, your response to your baby's fussing will seem to become intuitively less immediate. Baby gradually learns he can wait a bit and anticipate your holding. He can do this because he has learned to trust you and is familiar with that right feeling he gets when you respond to him. You're in the midst of an activity you want to complete when baby wakes up or decides he's tired. Instead of rushing over to tend to your baby's cry you say, "Mama's right here..." which can be enough to satisfy baby for a minute or two.

Baby develops the ability to wait because he knows you always come. You develop an ear for knowing how urgently he needs you to come.

Teach your baby to cry better. Responding to a baby's cries is not only good for the baby and the parents, it's also good for the relationship. Some babies have ear-piercing cries that distance them from their parents. These cries shatter nerves and provoke anger, diminishing parents' enjoyment in being with their baby. Yet immediate responses can help mellow this kind of cry. The opening sounds of baby's cry are not so aggravating. Instead they have a quality that strikes an empathetic chord in the mother and elicits a nurturing and comforting response. This is the attachment-promoting phase of a baby's cry. We have noticed that babies whose early cries receive a nurturant response learn to cry better — their cries mellow and do not take on a more disturbing quality. Mothers call these "nicer cries." But a baby whose cries do not receive an early nurturant response begin to cry in a more disturbing way as she grows more angry. These cries can make the mother angry, promoting an avoidance response. As these babies learn to cry harder, a distance develops between mother and baby. Mothers who follow the advice to let their baby cry it out soon begin giving their babies negative labels, such as "difficult baby" or "fussy baby." These babies, because their cries go unanswered, use the attachment-promoting phase of the cry less, and the more irritating avoidance-promoting sound more and more. This relationship is at high risk for discipline problems because mother and baby are not communicating well.

The ultimate in crying sensitivity happens when you become so fine-tuned to your baby's body language that you read and respond to precry signals and intervene before crying is necessary. Baby soon learns he doesn't have to cry hard (or sometimes at all) to get what he needs. A very attached and nurturant mother who was well on her way to becoming a good disciplinarian told us, "My baby seldom cries. She doesn't need to."

2. Breastfeed Your Baby

There is a special connection between breastfeeding and discipline. Promoting desirable behavior requires that you know your child and help your child feel right. Breastfeeding helps you get to know your

baby and provide the response that helps him feel right.

Discipline benefits to mother. *Breastfeeding is an exercise in baby-reading.* Learning about your baby's needs and moods is an important part of discipline. Part of learning how to breastfeed is learning to read your baby's cues rather than watching the clock. You learn to read her body language so that you can tell when she needs to feed, when she's had enough, and when she just wants to nurse for comfort. One veteran disciplinarian told us, "I can tell her moods by the way she behaves at the breast." Baby gives a cue asking for food or comfort, and you respond by offering to nurse. After hundreds of these cue-response practice sessions, your responses become completely natural. What was initially a mental exercise ("Is she hungry? Restless? Upset? I wonder what she needs") eventually becomes an intuitive response. A flow of communication develops between the little person in need and the big person who is in a position to meet those needs. You get in *harmony* with your baby.

This harmony is especially helpful if you need to overcome preconceived fears of spoiling that restrain you from naturally responding to your baby. Jan, a first-time mother whom I talked with at a prenatal interview, had a lot of hang-ups from her past that threatened to interfere with her enjoyment of motherhood. She had been on a rigid schedule as a baby, and control was the big issue in her childhood. Jan was now entering motherhood feeling that her main task as a parent was to be sure that her baby did not control or manipulate her. She feared that picking up the baby whenever she cried would result in spoiling. As part of her parenting plans, she was going to train her baby to soothe herself by letting her cry it out. She also planned to put the baby on a feeding schedule, called parent-controlled feeding, and she felt this would be easier to do if she bottle-fed. She thought this would ensure that she would be in charge, and not the baby. I explained that in order to be "in charge" of her baby she had to get to know her baby and become intuitively responsive. Jan changed her mind and decided to give breastfeeding a try. I'm happy to report it not only

worked very well for baby but was therapeutic for Mommy.

The right chemistry. Breastfeeding stimulates your body to produce prolactin and oxytocin — hormones that give your mothering a boost. These magical substances send messages to a mother's brain, telling her to relax and make milk. The levels of these substances go up during breastfeeding and during other motherly activities such as looking at and caressing the baby. They may

The Body Chemistry of Attachment

Good things happen to the hormones of mothers and babies who are attached. Hormones regulate the body's systems and help them react to the environment. One of these hormones is *cortisol.* Produced by the adrenal glands, one of its jobs is to help a person cope with stress and make sudden adjustments in threatening situations. For the body to function optimally, it must have the right balance of cortisol — too little and it shuts down, too much and it becomes distressed. Cortisol is one of the hormones that plays a major part in a person's emotional responses. In reviewing attachment-chemistry studies, we conclude that a secure mother-infant attachment keeps the baby in hormonal balance. Insecurely attached infants may either get used to a low hormonal level, and so they become apathetic, or they may constantly have high stress hormones, and so they become chronically anxious. The securely attached infant seems to be in a state of hormonal well-being, and because the infant is used to that feeling, he strives to

maintain it. Scientists are confirming what mothers have always known: Mother's presence is important for keeping baby's behavioral chemistry in balance.

Besides attachment parenting helping the baby's hormones, it also helps the mother's body chemistry. Maternal behaviors, especially breastfeeding, result in an outpouring of the hormones prolactin and oxytocin. These "mothering hormones" act as biological helpers, giving moms motherly feelings. They may, in fact, be the biological basis of the concept of mother's intuition. Prolactin levels increase ten- to twenty-fold within thirty minutes after mother begins breastfeeding. Most of it is gone again within an hour. Prolactin is a short-acting substance, so to get the best response a mother must breastfeed frequently — which is what babies want anyway. Hormones are biological helpers that improve the behavior of the baby and the caregiving of the mother. Your choice in parenting style can make them work for you.

form a biological basis for the term "mother's intuition." Your reward for spending time touching and enjoying your baby and breastfeeding frequently is a higher level of "feel-good" hormones. A prominent psychotherapist we interviewed revealed her observation that "breastfeeding mothers are better able to empathize with their children."

Discipline benefits to your baby. Baby's cues for food and comfort are met, so naturally baby learns to trust. Because he spends many hours each day at the breast, he feels valued and "in touch." Baby feels right, and this inner feeling of well-being translates into desirable behavior. Over my twenty-two years in pediatric practice I have observed how mellow breastfeeding babies are, especially toddlers who nurse through their second year. A nursing toddler seems to be at peace with himself and with his caregivers. Although in the last century of Western culture we have learned to think of breastfeeding in terms of months or even weeks, historically, in most cultures, babies have nursed for at least two or three years. The behavior-improving effects of breastfeeding have been known for millennia. You will find breastfeeding particularly useful as a discipline tool when a toddler is going through the stage where he is easily frustrated or when his newfound independence frightens him. We knew a secure and independent two-and-a-half-year-old child who after experiencing a setback such as a toy squabble would come to his mother for consolation saying, "Nursie 'bout it."

"But won't prolonged breastfeeding spoil a toddler? He needs to become independent." Actually the reverse is true — children who are not weaned before their time are more independent. Premature weaning

breaks a connection before the child is equipped to make other connections. Extended nursing, rather than encouraging a child to stay dependent, creates conditions that encourage independence. Offering a familiar connection (breastfeeding) during tumultuous toddlerhood gives the child an anchor from which he can explore the unfamiliar.

The idea of nursing past your child's first birthday may seem strange to you, but we believe that it is important that children not be weaned before they show signs of readiness. Weaning is a part of growing up. It should take place gradually. We have noticed that children who have been weaned too early show what we call diseases of premature weaning: aggression, anger, more tantrum-like behavior, anxious clinging to caregivers, and less ability to form deep and intimate relationships. Breastfeeding seems to mellow out the aggressive tendencies of toddlers and restores balance into their behavior. In 1990, former surgeon general Dr. Antonia Novello, after extolling the benefits of breastfeeding, added, "It's the lucky baby, I feel, who continues to nurse until he is two." (See "Weaning from Attachment," page 55.)

Can a bottle-feeding mother achieve the same degree of closeness with her baby as the breastfeeding mother?

We believe she can, but she has to work at it harder since she is not part of a natural feedback loop enjoyed by the nursing baby and mother. The bottle-feeding mother is more likely to schedule her baby's feedings, because formula-fed babies are easier to schedule (artificial baby milks take longer to digest). Bottle-feeders tend to worry more about spoiling their babies. A bottle-feeding mother does not have the benefit of the hormonal boost that happens with breastfeeding or the intimate skin-to-skin connection. Holding her baby lovingly in the breastfeeding position, caressing her baby during feeding, and giving a nurturing response to cries can stimulate her mothering hormones, yet the effects are not as great as with breastfeeding. By carrying her baby a lot, responding to her baby's cries, and making feeding time a nurturing interaction, a bottle-feeding mother can achieve a level of sensitivity and knowledge of her baby closer to what comes with breastfeeding than if she didn't add these attachment boosters. We realize there are mothers who would be deeply unhappy breastfeeding. It's important for a mother to choose a method of feeding that reflects a happy mother to her baby. Perhaps as inner conflicts are explored she'll want to breastfeed her next baby.

Babywearing helps you know your infant.

3. Wear Your Baby

Beginning in the early weeks, hold or wear your baby in a baby sling for as many hours a day as you and your baby enjoy. Since 1985 we have been studying how babywearing improves behavior. Parents would come into our office exclaiming, "As long as I wear our baby he's content." Research has validated this parental observation: Babies who are carried more cry less. For centuries parents have known that motion calms babies, especially the rhythmic motion of parents' walking. Carrying modifies behavior primarily by promoting quiet alertness — the state in which babies behave best.

Babywearing also improves the way babies feel. The carried baby feels like a part of the parents' world. He goes where they go, sees what they see, hears what they hear and say. Babywearing helps the baby feel included and important, which creates a feeling of rightness that translates into better behavior and more opportunities for learning. The brain is stimulated through motion, increasing the baby's intellectual capacity, a forerunner to the child's ability to make appropriate sensory-motor adaptations in the future.

Wearing improves the sensitivity of the parents as well. Because your baby is so close to you, in your arms, in constant contact, you get to know him better. Closeness promotes familiarity. Because your baby fusses less, he is more fun to be with and you tend to carry your baby more. The connection grows deeper.

Like breastfeeding, babywearing promotes eye-to-eye contact. As I watch babywearing pairs parade through my office, I notice that not only are these babies and mothers physically connected, they are visually in tune. What a wonderful way to learn to read each other's faces. As you will learn throughout this book, the ability to read and respond to each other's "looks" is a powerful discipline tool. Over the years I have observed that "sling babies" become children who are easier to discipline.

4. Play with Your Baby

What does playing have to do with discipline? you may wonder. Play helps you know your baby's capabilities and age-appropriate behaviors at each stage of development. It sets the stage for you and your baby to enjoy one another. It opens the door to a valuable discipline tool you will need at all stages of your child's life — humor. To smile, laugh, and giggle your way through a situation sidesteps a conflict, gets the child's attention, opening his mind to your discipline. You want your baby to grow up to be a happy person, so it follows that you want him to have lots of practice being happy. And nothing makes a baby happier than to play with mom or dad. If the child is used to following instruction during play, he is likely to listen to you during correction.

Playing together gives your baby the message "You are important to me," a valuable feeling for growing self-esteem. Peek-a-boo, stacking blocks, doing puzzles, playing pretend helps you get behind the eyes of your child and view things from her perspective — a valuable discipline tool for you to learn. Play brings discipline down to earth. With the proliferation of parenting classes and the overemphasis on "techniques" of modern discipline, it's easy for parents to get caught up in the science of discipline yet overlook the simplicity. Much of discipline is just being with your baby enjoying the simple things of life.

5. Share Sleep with Your Baby

Nighttime is scary for little people, but our usual Western custom is to separate parents and babies at night. We would like you to consider nighttime not as a block of time for you to finally get away from your baby but a special time when you can strengthen your connection. Every family needs to work out a sleeping arrangement where all sleep best, and we believe the nighttime environment that can best strengthen your parent-child attachment allows for baby sleeping near you — a style we call *sharing sleep.*

Our observations over more than twenty years, our examination of studies of mother-infant sleep-sharing pairs, and our own studies on one of our babies lead us to conclude that a baby's overall physiological system works better when baby sleeps next to

Play is part of discipline.

mother. The cardiorespiratory system is more regulated, less stressed; therefore, baby is less stressed and thrives better.

Besides these physical benefits, there are emotional benefits to the sleep-sharing pair. Babies show less anxiety. They feel right at night, just as they do during the day. The connection continues. Sleep-sharing babies get the message "I'm just as valuable to be next to at night as I am during the day. I belong to someone twenty-four hours a day." For a mother who responds to her baby's cues, breastfeeds, and wears her baby, sleep sharing naturally becomes part of the attachment package. Our daughter-in-law Diane, who is a new and very attached mother, said, "I can't imagine us sleeping away from each other. Nighttime with Lea is our special time to be together without interference."

The time in your arms, at your breasts, and in your bed lasts a very short while in the life of a growing child, but the messages of love and security last a lifetime.

6. Become a Facilitator

At each stage of development, a child needs significant people who care about him and whom he cares about. These people act as facilitators, helping the child learn how to conduct himself in the world. A facilitator is like a consultant, a trusted authority figure who provides emotional refueling to the child, a person to lean on who helps the child both develop his skills and take advantage of the resources around him with a view toward becoming self-sufficient. The facilitators don't tell the child what to do, they help the child learn what to do. They don't give commands; instead they take cues from the child and weave their wishes into the child's wants. The child says "I do

Babies need facilitators.

it myself"; the facilitator says, "Yes, you can!" The facilitator watches for teachable moments and takes advantage of them. A wise disciplinarian in my practice describes her role as facilitator: "My job is to help my child glean from life's experiences lessons he might not otherwise glean for himself."

You have been functioning as a facilitator ever since the moment of birth. You positioned your baby at the breast to make it easier for her to feed. You held the chair steady to make it safer for the beginning cruiser to keep his balance. You arranged child-sized furniture, utensils, and cups to make it easier for your child to have a snack. A facilitator structures the environment so a child doesn't waste energy. She helps the child focus on important tasks.

There needs to be mutual trust between the child and the facilitator. They are interdependent (see meaning of "interdependence," page 53). The child relies on the helper's availability and the helper is sensitive to the child's needs, taking cues from the child and filling in the missing steps to help the child complete a task. The facilitator anticipates what the child needs at each stage of development in order to thrive. Thinking of yourself as a facilitator keeps you from hovering over and smothering your child with overprotection. Being on standby as needed helps you and your child negotiate an appropriate level of independence. When your child is going through a healthy independent stage you stay connected, but at a distance.

Expect discipline problems to occur when the child lacks a facilitator. A child forced to function on his own will become frustrated and discouraged. I've watched children try to function without the help of a parent or someone else to act as a facilitator: The child seems angry, as if he senses that he is missing out on the help he needs. He will either withdraw out of insecurity or, if gifted with a persistent personality, make himself noisy enough to get help. Either way, his emotional and intellectual development are compromised. One of the main features I have noticed among attachment-parented children and their facilitator parents is these children know how to use adult resources to their advantage, and the parents know how to respond appropriately. Ideally, for two years, the facilitator is mainly the mother and then gradually both of the parents as the father helps the child move away from "mother only." As children grow they may latch on to additional facilitators: grandparents, teachers, coaches, scoutmasters, and so on. It's the parents' job to monitor these persons of significance in their child's life. Behavior often deteriorates when a child

must function without these special persons. Throughout this book you will find many suggestions to help you become a facilitator.

HOW ATTACHMENT PARENTING MAKES DISCIPLINE EASIER

You probably never thought of these attachment tools as being acts of discipline, but they are. Attachment parenting is like immunizing your child against emotional diseases later on. Here are other ways this style of parenting improves the behavior of your child and the way he experiences life. Gina, an attached mother of three, told us: "Knowing my children empowers me." This kid knowledge becomes like a sixth sense enabling you to anticipate and control situations to keep your kids out of trouble. Our daughter-in-law Diane describes her experience with this style of parenting: "I know Lea so deeply at every stage of her development. Attachment parenting allows me to put myself in her shoes. I imagine how she needs me to act."

Attachment parenting promotes mutual sensitivity. At six years of age Matthew would come to me with a request, "Dad, I think I know the answer, but . . ." Because our mutual sensitivity and trust is so high, he knows when to expect a yes or a no answer. He tests me, but knows my answer. The connected parent and child easily communicate each other's feelings. Once connected to your child you will be able to read his body language and appropriately redirect behavior, and your child will be able to read your desires and strive to please. As one connected parent put it:

An Exercise in Sensitivity

Because of misguided teachings from "experts," some mothers have to go through "deprogramming" before they can let themselves respond naturally. Try this exercise: When a baby cries (yours or someone else's), examine the first feeling that comes over you. Does the cry bother you in the right way, prompting an irresistible urge to lovingly pick up and comfort the baby? Or does the baby's cry trigger insensitivity: "I'm not going to let this little person control me." If you have a less than nurturing response, you are at risk for a disappointing disciplinary relationship with your child, and you need to learn more about the needs of tiny babies and to rethink the giving end of parenthood.

A mother I counseled in my office during a prenatal interview was worried that she wouldn't be a good mother. I asked her how she feels when she hears babies cry. She responded, "I just can't stand to leave a baby crying. I want to rush over and pick that baby up. It bothers me to see other mothers ignore their babies' cries." I assured this woman that she was very likely to be a good mother because she had the quality of sensitivity. Cries bother sensitive women — and men too. Cries are supposed to bother us.

once said, "Men who can't cry scare me." Many of the world's problems can be traced to one group of people being insensitive to the needs and rights of another group. One of the mothers in my practice arranged a talk for a group of attachment mothers, and she invited one of the survivors of the Holocaust to come and tell her story. Commenting on the social benefits of sensitive parenting, the survivor concluded her talk, "Because of children like yours, this tragedy will never happen again."

"Often all I have to do is look at him disapprovingly and he stops misbehaving."

Attachment parenting produces people who care. General Norman Schwarzkopf

Attachment parenting organizes babies. To understand better how attachment parenting organizes infant behavior, think of a baby's gestation as lasting eighteen months — nine months inside the womb, and at least nine more months outside. The womb environment regulates the baby's systems automatically. Birth temporarily disrupts this organization. Attachment parenting provides a gentle, sensitive, external regulating system that takes over where

Synthetic Substitutes

Soothing babies has become big business. There are vibrating beds, lullaby-singing teddy bears, battery-operated swings, and bottle holders. These synthetic sitters are snapped up by tired parents in hopes of making life with baby easier. While many parents need a break, and artificial soothers can provide this occasionally, a steady diet of synthetic subs will sabotage your discipline. Using your own resources when the going gets tough boosts your creativity, your patience, and your confidence — all of which you will need to discipline your child. And if the use of artificial substitutes gets out of balance, your baby is at risk of learning to be comforted by things rather than people. As you browse through baby stores, hold on to your credit cards. Relying too much on synthetic help early on may set you up for later disappointment when you realize there are no substitutes for disciplining your child.

and stimulation receiving predictable responses, the attachment-parented baby is physiologically better off. A 1993 study from Virginia Tech compared sleep-wake patterns and heart rates of breast- and bottle-fed babies. The breastfed babies showed more energy-efficient heart rates and sleep patterns. They were more organized. The researchers concluded that a baby who isn't breastfed is like an engine out of tune.

Attachment parenting promotes quiet alertness. Both research and our own experience have demonstrated that attachment-parented babies cry much less. So what do they do with their free time? They spend much of it in the state of quiet alertness. During waking hours, babies go through many types of behavior: crying, sleepy, alert and agitated, and quietly alert. Babies are most attentive to their environment in the state of quiet alertness. By not fussing and crying, they conserve their energy and use it for interacting. The result is

the womb left off. When a mother carries her baby her rhythmic walk, familiar from the baby's time in the womb, has a calming effect. When the baby is cuddled close to his mother's breast, her heartbeat reminds him of the sounds of the womb. When baby is draped across mom or dad's chest, he senses the rhythmic breathing. Being kept warm and held close calms him and helps him control his reflexes. This high-touch style of parenting, with its emphasis on keeping the baby comfortable, has a regulating effect on the infant's disorganized rhythms. Baby knows where he belongs. With his needs for food, warmth, comfort,

Connected Kids Are Less Accident-Prone

Securely attached children do better in unfamiliar situations because they have a better understanding of their own capabilities. In parent parlance, they are less likely to "do dumb things"! The organizing effect of attachment parenting helps to curb their impulses. Even children with impulsive temperaments tend to get into trouble less if they are securely attached to a primary caregiver. A child who operates from internal organization and a feeling of rightness is more likely to consider the wisdom of a feat before rushing in foolishly. This may be because connected kids are not internally angry. Anger adds danger to impulsivity, causing a child to override what little sense he has and plunge headfirst into trouble. In essence, connected kids are more *careful.* Also, connected parents are naturally more vigilant and are more likely to keep on the heels of their toddler when visiting homes that are not childproofed.

that they are more pleasant to be with. And because a responsive parent takes time to enjoy the baby when he is in this state, the baby is motivated to stay quietly alert for longer.

Attachment parenting promotes trust. Being in charge of your child is an important part of discipline. Children need to know that they can depend on their parents not only to meet their needs but also to keep them on the right path. Authority is vital to discipline, and authority must be

based on trust. It is crucial for baby to trust that he will be kept safe. An attachment-parented baby learns to trust the one person who is strongly connected to him. When an infant can trust his mother to meet his needs, he will also look to her to help him behave.

Attachment parenting promotes independence. If you are wondering whether attachment parenting will make your child clingy and dependent, don't worry. Attachment parenting actually encourages the right balance between dependence and independence. Because the connected child trusts his parents to help him feel safe, he is more likely to feel secure exploring the environment. In fact, studies have shown that toddlers who had a secure attachment to the mother tended to play more independently and adapt more easily to new play situations than less attached toddlers. (To read more about how attachment fosters independence, see pages 51–52).

Between one and two years of age, an infant perfects a cognitive ability called *person permanence* — the ability to recreate mentally the image of a person, even when that person is out of sight. A baby who is securely attached to his caregiver carries the mental image of that caregiver into unfamiliar situations. Even when mother is not physically there, she can be there in the child's mind, and this gives the child further confidence to explore. Attachment parenting helps the child build a mental image that is loving and dependable, which helps the child feel confident and capable. A child who is pushed into independence before she is ready to maintain this mental image will be either anxious and clingy or she may register no concern whatsoever. Much of her exploring energy will be diverted to

The Unconnected Child

Suppose parents, for fear of spoiling their baby or letting her manipulate them, restrain themselves from responding to her cries and develop a more distant, low-touch style of parenting. What happens then? The baby must either cry harder and more disturbingly to get her needs met or give up and withdraw. In either case, she finds that her caregiving world is not responsive. Eventually, since her cues are not responded to, she learns not to give cues. She senses something is missing in her life. She becomes angry and either outwardly hostile or else withdrawn. In the first case, the baby is not very nice to be around, and parents find ways to avoid her. In the second case, the baby is harder to connect with, and again, parents and child enjoy each other less. Either way, this child will be difficult to discipline. She comes to believe that safety and security depend on no one but herself. Problems in relationships develop when a child grows up thinking she only has herself to trust in. Since the parents don't allow themselves to respond intuitively to their baby's cues, they become less sensitive and lose confidence in their parenting skills, another setup for discipline problems.

You can tell the unconnected baby by his expression — or lack of one. He does not seek eye contact and he does not evoke the warm feelings so evident with connected babies. "He looks lost" is a comment we once heard about an unconnected baby. You can also tell an unconnected baby by the way he holds himself stiff as if conformed to his baby seat rather than to soft shoulders.

As the unconnected child gets older, much of his time is spent in misbehavior, and he is on the receiving end of constant reprimands; or he tunes out and seems to live in his own separate world. This child becomes known as sullen, a brat, a whiner, a spoiled kid. These undesirable behaviors are really coping strategies the child uses in search of a connection. The unconnected child doesn't know how to regain a sense of well-being because he has no yardstick to measure attachment. He has difficulty finding a connection because he isn't sure what he lost. This scene results in patch-up parenting, with perhaps much time spent in counselors' offices.

The unconnected child is less motivated to please; he's less of a joy to be around. As a result, unconnected parents don't find job satisfaction on the domestic scene, so they seek fulfillment in professions and in relationships not involving their child. Parent and child drift further apart. Unlike the connected child who is a joy to be around and keeps making healthy friendships, peers may shun the unconnected child. He even puts off people who can help him form connections. The emotionally rich get richer, the emotionally poor get poorer.

With professional counseling, children and parents can begin connecting and settle into a style of discipline that brings out the best in each other. It will require a lot of energy to accomplish this at a stage past when it naturally is designed to happen. Newborns are more into being held than six- or nine-year-olds. The best chance for staying connected later on is to get connected early. (See "How to Raise an Expressive Child," pages 106–113, and "Getting a Handle on Anger," pages 118–120.)

Growing Up Connected*

Behaviors and Competencies	Connected Kids	Unconnected Kids
Behavior as infants and toddlers	Secure, settled, trusting, interdependent; inner sense of well-being, learn early how people treat other people	Clingy, anxious, distant, angry, dependent, disorganized, impulsive
Obedience	Open to redirection, expect to behave, want to please, feel guided	Closed; protest redirection; oppositional, devious, defensive; don't know what behavior is expected; feel controlled
Getting along with peers, making and keeping friends	Sociable, considerate, cooperative, sympathetic, trusting, popular, more willing to share; deep lasting friendships; mixes well with all age groups	Aggressive, manipulative, selfish, unwilling to share, bullying or easily victimized; withdrawn, isolated, distant, distrusting, unpopular; shallow friendships
In preschool setting (observations of 3½ year olds)	Social leaders, curious, eager to learn	Hesitant, less curiosity to learn
Empathy, caring	Sensitive, empathetic; consider others in decision making; help friends	Selfish, insensitive, unsympathetic
Problem-solving capabilities	Enthusiastic, persistent, positive, less frustrated, responsive to instruction, adaptable	Highly frustrated, negative, give up more quickly, less adaptable
Self-worth, confidence	High; realistic self-appraisal; confident	Low; lack confidence
Show of emotions	Appropriately expressive, transparent, affectionate	Stuff feelings; uncontrolled anger; react inappropriately; either overreact or clam up
Use of adult resources (facilitators)	Expect help, use facilitators wisely, confident in conversation with adults; eye contact	Distrust; don't seek help; avoid eye contact
Sense of right and wrong	Sincerely feel wrong when acting wrong; healthy guilt; innate sense of right and wrong	Don't feel remorse; confused sense of right and wrong
Adult outcome	Morally mature, more likely to have fulfilled marital relationships, less prone to addictive habits, more psychologically stable	Morally immature; risk of violence and sociopathic behaviors; problems wiith intimacy; less likely to be fulfilled in marital relationships; prone to addictive behaviors

*The studies on which this table is based compared the quality of mother-infant attachment during the first two years with later outcome. These are statistical correlations only; there was not always a perfect correlation between how children were parented and the persons they later became.

Reconnecting

What if, due to medical problems, domestic changes, or just bad parenting advice, you weren't able to connect with your infant during the first two years, and now you are having discipline problems with your child? The beauty of human nature is its *resiliency,* the ability to bounce back from a poor start and have a happy ending. Yet reconnecting can be complicated by developmental mistiming. If you connected early, you were bonding when your baby wanted to bond. Trying to connect with the older child is more difficult because you are trying to bond when the child is working on breaking away. Still, it's never too late to get attached. If you are having discipline problems with your child, no matter what your child's age, step one on the road to recovery is to examine the depth of your parent-child connection. If it is weak, strengthen it. Remember, a child's attitude wasn't built in a day, and behavior doesn't change overnight. You may need to devote six to twelve months to the reconnection process. This time may include drastic lifestyle changes, involvement in your child's projects, a high frequency of focused attention, and lots of time just having fun with your child. One parent we know home-schooled her six-year-old for a year; another father took his seven-year-old with him on frequent business trips. One parent described his reconnecting process with a difficult child: "It was like camping out with our five-year-old for a year." Whatever you need to do to shorten the distance between you and your child, do it; and discipline will follow naturally.

Timing is important. Developing children take two steps forward when they need to act and feel independent. The child may be generally negative; "I do it myself." During this stage parent-child conflicts are likely to occur. Then they take one step backward, a positive stage when they return to home base for some needed emotional refueling. During this stage, the child is most open to reconnecting. Watch for openers: The child sits next to you on the couch while you are reading; stop reading the magazine and read your child. Your older child reappears for the nighttime story to the toddler and hints for "one night" sleeping in your room; honor this request. When your child shadows you, take the opportunity to reconnect. If you try to bond while your child is trying to break, you are likely to meet resistance.

handling these feelings instead of into learning.

Attachment parenting enables intimacy. Attachment-parented kids have a look about them. You can spot them in a crowd. They are the persons looking intently at other persons. They seem to be genuinely interested in other persons. I love to engage these children in visual contact because they are so attentive. The reason these kids will look you straight in the eye is that they have grown up from birth being comfortable connecting to people, and they connect

Building Better-Behaved Brains

The developing brain of an infant resembles miles of tangled electrical wire called neurons. At the end of each neuron tiny filaments branch out to make connections with other neurons, forming pathways. This is one of the ways the brain develops *patterns of association:* habits, and ways of acting and thinking; in other words organization. Attachment parenting creates a behavioral equilibrium in a child that not only organizes a child's physiology but her psychological development as well. In a nutshell, attachment parenting helps the developing brain make the right connections.

The unconnected child, however, is at risk for developing disorganized neurological pathways, especially if that infant has come wired with even more than her average share of disorganized pathways. This child is at risk of developing behavioral problems later on, namely hyperactivity, distractiblility, and impulsivity — features of one of the most increasingly prevalent "diseases" in childhood and now adulthood — attention deficit/hyperactivity disorder (ADHD). A person's brain grows more in the first three years than anytime in life. Could the level of nurturing during those formative years affect the way the behavioral pathways in the brain become organized? We believe it does, and we also believe that research will soon confirm that many later child and adult behavioral problems are really *preventable* diseases of early disorganization. (See related topic, "Disciplining the Hyperactive Child," pages 267–281.)

---

appropriately. Their gaze is not so strained or penetrating as to put off the other person, or so shallow as to convey lack of interest. It's just the right visual fix to engage people and hold their interest.

Much of a child's future quality of life (mate and job satisfaction) depends on the capacity for intimacy. Therapists we interviewed volunteered that much of their time is spent working with persons who have problems with intimacy, and much of their therapy is aimed at reparenting their patients. Because connected kids grow up learning to bond with people rather than things, they carry this capacity for intimacy into adulthood. Many a night I watch two-year-old Lauren inch over and snuggle next to Martha in bed. Even at this young age

Lauren is learning a lifelong asset — *the capacity for feeling close.*

Attachment parenting helps you discipline the difficult child. This style of parenting is especially rewarding in disciplining kids we call *high-need children.* Sometimes parents don't realize until their child is three or four years of age that they have a special child who needs a special kind of discipline (for example, a hyperactive child, a developmentally delayed child, or a temperamentally difficult child). By helping you shape your child's behavior and increase your sensitivity to the child's special needs, attachment parenting gives you the right start that increases your chances of having the right finish. Connected parents have a headstart in disciplining high-need children because they are sensitive to their child's personality. The connected high-need child is easier to discipline because he is more responsive to his parents. One of the reasons temperamentally difficult children are difficult to discipline is they are disorganized. As we discussed earlier, attachment promotes organization. In fact, studies comparing the long-term effects of early parenting styles on a child's later development show that attachment parenting (or the lack of it) most affects the character trait of *adaptability* (the ease with which a child's behavior can be redirected to the child's and parents' advantage). Adaptable children are better prepared to adjust to life's changing circumstances. They learn to accept correction from others and eventually correct themselves. Some children are born puzzles. Attachment parenting helps you put the pieces together.

Attachment parenting encourages obedience. The real payoff of attachment parenting is obedience. This style of parenting, besides opening up parents to the needs of their baby, also opens up the baby to the wishes of the parent. The universal complaint of parents is "My child won't mind." Think about this term "to mind." What does it mean? As a child normally goes from dependence to independence and searches for an identity, the child minds his *own* mind.

So, your child *is* minding, but he's minding his own mind and not yours. How compliant your child is depends upon his temperament, which you can't control, and the depth of your parent-child connection, which you can influence. Because your minds mesh, the connected child is more open to accept your perspective and switch from his mind-set to yours, to listen to you instead of being closed to you. The connected child trusts that parents know best. *The attached child wants to please.*

Even the iron-willed child bends to the will of the mother or father who operate on the parenting principle "The stronger my child's will, the stronger must be my connection." It is this connection that gives parents confidence. Wanting to please and trying to obey are the behavioral trademarks of the connected child. Nancy, the mother of a high-need baby, who is now a strong-willed four-year-old volunteered: "Initially attachment parenting took more energy and was less convenient. Now caring for Jonathan is easier because discipline flows naturally between us. I'm finally beginning to cash in on my investment."

For more benefits of attachment parenting and discipline, see: Chapter 3, "Understanding Ones, Twos, and Threes"; Chapter 7, "Self-Esteem: The Foundation of Good Behavior"; Chapter 8, "Helping Your Child Express Feelings"; and the special feature "Inner Peace," page 118.

3

Understanding Ones,
Twos, and Threes

HOLD ON TO YOUR HAT — THE
FUN BEGINS. Babies turn into
toddlers, and their new skills
add challenges to being a parent.
As a child's physical and mental world
grows, parents begin to think about how to
shape his behavior to help him learn yet
keep him out of trouble. This is an important learning period for parents as well.
To understand how to discipline a toddler,
it's helpful first to understand toddlers and
their behavior. Let's get into the mind and
behind the eyes of the typical toddler to
learn why this fascinating little person is so
challenging.

HOW TODDLERS ACT —
AND WHY

At each stage developmental skills dictate
behavior. To cope with toddler behavior it
helps to remember the basic principle of
development discipline: *The drives that babies have in order to develop are the same
ones that create discipline challenges.* Babies need a strong desire to explore so they
can learn, yet these ventures can lead them
into uncharted territory. By understanding

what skills click in when, you can be prepared for the actions that result and channel them into positive behaviors. From one
to two years of age a baby gets a lot of
what he needs to be more independent —
"wheels" to roll on and a "horn" to blow.
With these tools he feels ready to travel the
roads of the world — or at least the immediate neighborhood. Here are the changes
you can expect.

Wheels to run on. Imagine how it must
feel to learn to walk! Baby can see all those
tempting delights around the room, and he
finds ways to get his hands on many of
them. Once the developmental skill of walking appears, children have an intense drive
to master it. So toddlers toddle — constantly. And they can toddle into unsafe situations. Walking progresses to running, and
climbing a few stairs turns into scaling
kitchen counters.

Hands as tools. Along with learning how
to get things, the year-old baby develops
hand skills to manipulate what he gets.
Doors are to be opened, knobs turned,
drawers pulled, dangling cords yanked, and
waste cans emptied. Everything within

Growing Out of It

How often have you heard, "Oh, just wait, he'll grow out of it"? Though partially true, this lame excuse for not bothering to correct certain behaviors shows an incomplete understanding of child development. Growth and development used to be pictured like clothing sizes. The child outgrows an outfit, discards it, and puts on a bigger one that fits better. In reality, it's not that simple. Children don't always discard behaviors from one stage of development when they grow into another. Misbehavior that is not corrected at one stage may linger into the next. On the other hand, don't get too excited or worried when you see "good" or "bad" behavior in your children. It may be a onetime thing that children try on for size and quickly discard when it doesn't fit.

A child's behavioral development is like a trip by elevator through a department store. The doors open and two children get off to find what they need on each floor. One child gets no sales help. He explores freely, puts on a bunch of new clothes, and gets back on the elevator to go to the next floor. When he gets there he realizes that he still has the old clothes on underneath, and his new ones don't fit that well. But he keeps going up on his own, putting new clothes over the old ones, carrying more and more excess baggage to each new floor. Soon he is weighed down with layers of clothing that he should have discarded earlier.

Eventually, there is less and less room for new stuff.

The other little shopper gets the help of a wise and experienced disciplinarian. She has seen many children get off that elevator and knows just what he needs. "Let me help you try on some new clothes," she offers, adding, "but we'll have to figure out what to do with your old clothes. Some seem to fit you just fine, so we'll keep them. They'll be useful to you later. Let's get rid of the ones that aren't nice to make room for the ones that fit you better." The disciplined child goes to each new floor not only with better clothes that fit but without excess baggage slowing his progress.

Which behaviors will children outgrow on their own and which need your attention? Behavior that is linked to specific needs, tasks, or limitations of a certain developmental stage are probably best left alone; for example, thumb-sucking in a toddler, negativism in a two-year-old, shyness with strangers in a four- or five-year-old. Behavior that may be understandable at a certain age but is nevertheless obnoxious should be worked on; for example, throwing food from the high chair, teasing the family dog, aggression toward parents. Children need limits that help them grow up to be polite, thoughtful, and caring. Your job as parents is to arm your children with the self-control tools that will help them make the transition from one developmental stage to the next.

Guiding Little Hands

Exploring hands are always looking for things to handle, so give the young explorer word associations to help him sort out what he may touch. Try "yes touch" for safe things, "no touch" for objects off-limits, and "soft touch" for faces and animals. To tame the impulsive grabber, try encouraging "one finger touch." Other words ("hot touch," "owie touch") will come to mind as you discover the world of touch together.

walking and grabbing distance is fair game, or so he figures. To the inquisitive adventurer, the whole house is an unexplored continent, and he intends to leave no stone unturned.

Out of the mouths of babes. The development of language — verbal and body — makes parenting a bit easier. Baby can now begin to tell you what she needs with words. This new skill is a mixed blessing. While baby words are entertaining, they can also be frustrating as the parents struggle to understand just what "da-boo" means. Toddlers like to try on different noises to hear how they sound and how they affect their audience. They screech and squeal, yell and jabber. Sometimes their little baby words are pleasing to your ears, at other times they are nerve-wracking. Language also gives expression to feelings; a feisty "No" from your formerly agreeable child can raise your eyebrows.

A mind of their own. Toddlers think, but not logically. Just as motor skills take off during the first half of the second year, to-

ward the last half mental skills blossom. The one-year-old plunges impulsively into activities without much thinking. The two-year-old studies her environment, figuring out a course of action in her head before venturing forth with her body. But *a baby's desire to do something often precedes the ability to do it successfully.* This developmental

Respecting Little Grabbers

Your toddler has a jar of olives, and you have visions that there will soon be a mess to clean up. You hastily snatch the jar from her clutches. And within a millisecond you have set off a protest tantrum. You've saved yourself a mess to clean up on the floor, but now you have an emotional mess to care for.

Grabbing a prized object from a child for whatever reason is not socially appropriate: It violates the personhood of the child. And it's not good discipline — you're teaching your child the very thing you tell her not to do. "Don't grab," you say, as you grab back what was grabbed. Snatching the jar away from her is bound to anger her, as well as reinforce the grabbing mentality.

There is a better way. For a young toddler, make eye contact and divert her attention to something else she'd like. For an older toddler, tell her you'll help her open the jar so she can have an olive, and point to where you want her to put it. This is simply an exercise in politeness and respect, and "adult-in-charge" approach. Children need adults to communicate and model the behavior adults expect.

quirk drives toddlers into trouble and care-givers to the brink. Even though you know that baby hasn't mastered a skill yet, your explanation won't stop him from trying. For example, one morning our son Stephen insisted on pouring his own juice. He had the ability to maneuver the cup and pitcher but lacked the wisdom to know when the cup

was full. He did not want us to pour it for him. So we let him stand at the sink and pour water into cups while we poured the juice at the table. After a pouring party at the sink he accepted my hand on his hand and followed my nudge about when to stop pouring.

During the second year your baby's temperament will become more apparent. "Bubbly," "daredevil," "determined," "cautious," and "adventurous" are labels toddlers acquire. Children come wired differently, and different kinds of children need different kinds of discipline. Matthew, a relatively cautious toddler, seemed to think out a task carefully before attempting it. And if he got himself in too deep he would not protest being rescued. Our two-year-old Lauren came wired with a different program. She sees an enticing gadget on top of the kitchen counter and she is willing to risk life and limb to get it. Because of her personality, we don't often let her out of our sight. Her drive helps her keep going, to get up after falling, to persist after being told "no," to struggle with words to make her needs known. It also inspires her to climb higher if the cookie jar has been promoted to the top shelf. The parents' task, in the words of one frazzled toddler manager, is to "keep my child from breaking his neck, and yet encourage him to learn."

Thinking "Kid First"

Kids do annoying things — not maliciously, but because they don't think like adults. You are likely to have a miserable day if you let every kid-created mess bother you. As you enter the kitchen, you see your two-year-old at the sink splashing water all over the floor. You could sink into a "poor me" mind-set: "Oh, no! Now I have to clean up the mess. Why does she do this to me?" Here's a healthier choice. Instead of first considering your own inconvenience, immediately click into your child's viewpoint: "This is fun. Look at all the different things you can do with dishes and water." You'll remember that what she is doing is developmentally appropriate. She's exploring and learning. You'll also realize that because two-year-olds get so engrossed in their activity, she is likely to throw a tantrum if you try to remove her. If you wait a few minutes, she'll go on to something else; and, besides, water cleans up easily anyway; no big deal. She won't do this anymore when she's six. You'll find yourself smiling. Getting out of yourself and into your child saves mental strain. You don't have to clean up the mess in your mind along with the water on the floor.

TALKING WITH TODDLERS: WHAT THEY CAN UNDERSTAND, WHAT THEY CAN'T

Even though toddlers don't say much, that doesn't mean that they don't comprehend what you are asking. As a general guide, take what you imagine your toddler understands and *double it.* She is probably picking up at least that much.

Follows directions. Around age fifteen months toddlers can begin to follow one-step directions: "Go get the ball." By two years they can follow two-step directions: "Please find your shoes and bring them to me." Prior to eighteen months toddlers seldom follow verbal warnings unless accompanied by action. Shouting "Don't pull the cat's tail" is meaningless unless you get up, cross the room, pry his fingers loose from the cat's fur, and *show* the child as you tell him: "Pet the cat. Be gentle to the cat. Don't pull the cat's tail." By two, children can follow most verbal commands without physical help.

A one-year-old baby can understand that "no" or "stop" means that she should stop what she is doing, and that is about the limit of her understanding. But that doesn't mean that you don't offer an explanation: "Stop. Don't touch," you say as you pull her hands away. "Hurt baby." As time goes by, make your explanation more complex: "Stop. Don't touch. Hurt baby. Stove hot!" Parents can usually tell how much of their explanation sinks in by their child's reaction. For the toddler, keep explanations simple and brief. Better to spend your creative energy devising alternatives to a misbehavior than defining terms.

A useful developmental fact that parents need to remember is that toddlers think concretely. *They cannot generalize concepts.* An eighteen-month-old can learn that your stove is hot (usually by experiencing it solo — the hard way — or by some supervised exploration), but when he goes to Grandmother's house, don't rely on his knowing that all stoves are hot. This ability to generalize develops around age four.

Discipline through talking. A toddler's growing receptive language skills (what she understands) make discipline easier. Between eighteen months and two years, children may say little, but they understand all. (All brief, simple sentences, that is.) Capitalize on this developmental achievement by announcing what you're going to do before you do it: "Daddy's going to change your diaper." Rather than catching your toddler by surprise, a prior announcement at least gives daddy a fair chance of getting the child's cooperation. (See related feature, "Discipline Talk," pages 162–163.)

Baby's expressive language skills (what she says) also make discipline easier. Not only can she now understand what you want her to do, she can tell you what she wants: "Off" means she wants her diaper off. Here's when your wise investment in responding to your baby's cues begins to pay off. A baby who trusts that her signals will be responded to learns to give more readable signals.

Between eighteen and twenty-four months of age another developmental perk makes discipline easier, *the ability to think before acting.* How consistently a toddler does this depends more on temperament than intelligence. Impulsive children often rush into a feat instead of first figuring out the consequences and plotting an alternative course. Just watching your child play will teach you where he is in his developmental thought processes. At fifteen months Lauren used to drive us bananas by trying to go up a flight of steps carrying a bowl of cereal. To prevent the inevitable spills, we didn't allow this activity. At nineteen months Lauren grabbed a bowl of cereal and started for the steps. She stood at the bottom, looked up, turned around, and handed the bowl of cereal to Martha before

Developmental Discipline

Think "age-appropriate behavior" and you'll be able to give age-appropriate direction. Here are some helpful reminders that will help your discipline be developmentally correct.

Some challenging behaviors are developmentally correct. In the normal course of development those same behaviors the child needs to exercise in order to move on are the very ones that can get him into trouble. As a child goes from dependence to independence, he will often merit labels like "defiant," "won't mind," "bossy," "sassy," and "impulsive." Some of these behaviors are simply a by-product of the child's need to become an independent individual. And the "stubbornness" that keeps your child from "minding" is the same spunk that helps him get up after a fall and try again.

Get in "phase" with your child. Developing children take two steps forward and one step backward. In each stage of development, they bounce back and forth from equilibrium to disequilibrium. While they're stepping forward into uncharted territory, finding new friends, trying new things, expect discipline problems due to the anxiety that tags along with experimenting. In each stage, expect the calm to come after the storm. The same child who spent two months in a snit may act like an angel for the next three. This developmental quirk can work to the child's advantage and yours. Spot which phase your child is in. If he's trying to move away and grow up a bit, let out the line. During this phase, your child may seem distant from you; she may even answer back and defy you. Don't take this personally. This phase will soon pass. The child is just in the "do it myself" phase and needs some space and coaching (including correcting) from the sidelines. One day soon, as sure as sunrise follows nightfall, you'll find your child snuggling next to you on the couch asking for help with tasks, suggesting activities you can do together. You may even wake up one morning and discover your six-year-old nestled next to you in bed. This child is now in a *reconnecting phase,* a pit stop in the developmental journey when your child needs emotional refueling. Take advantage of this intermission. It's time to patch up breaks in communication, cement your relationship, and recharge your child and yourself for the next unsettled phase.

When parents and child are out of harmony, discipline problems multiply. If your child is trying to break away when you are trying to bond, you are likely to overreact to what may be normal behaviors of independence. If you are too busy while your child is in the reconnecting phase, you miss a window of opportunity to strengthen your positions as comforter, adviser, authority figure, and disciplinarian.

Developmental Discipline (continued)

Respect negative phases. When your child is developmentally negative don't take it personally. This is hard sometimes because life does have to go on. This is why a project such as toilet training should not be undertaken during a negative phase. To do so would just frustrate you and give your child more to say no about. Another way to respect negativity is not to punish behavior that a child is developmentally incapable of (such as saying "yes" during a negative phase). Use nonpunitive methods of directing developmental negativity. Above all, *do not punish for any aspects of toilet learning.* As with food discipline, it's your child's body. Trust him to learn its natural functions.

Plan ahead. Discipline problems are likely to occur when a child is making the transition from one developmental stage to another, or during major family changes: a move, a new sibling, family illness, or so on. I recently counseled a family whose previously sweet child had turned sour. The mother had started a new job, and at the same time the child started a new school. If possible, time major changes in your life for when a child is not going through major changes herself.

What is "normal" may not be acceptable. "I don't care what the book says, Bobby and Jimmy, fighting is not going to be normal in our home," said a mother who knew her tolerance. Part of discipline is learning how to live with a child through different developmental stages, and the child's learning how to live with you. A child's early family experience is like boot camp in preparing for life. A child must learn how to get along with family members in preparation for future social relationships. He needs to be adaptable, to learn to adjust his behaviors to a particular family need. Billy is boisterous by temperament. Yet Billy is expected to play quietly for a few days because mommy is recovering from an illness and has a headache. It is healthy for the child to learn that the sun rises and sets on other people besides himself. Children must learn to adapt to house rules to prepare them to adjust to society's rules.

Disciplining in a developmentally correct way does not mean becoming lax. While it is necessary to tailor your discipline to the temperament and stage of your child, widen your acceptance when the going gets tough, *there is no excuse for not expecting and helping your child to obey.* It is easy to pass off behavior by saying "He's just going through a stage" or "That's just part of his temperament," yet it's important to keep a balance between the child's need to develop and the family's need for well-being.

taking off up the steps. Reaching the top, she turned around and reached out for Martha to bring the bowl of cereal up to her. She now had matured enough to figure out the consequences of her action and develop creative alternatives using her adult resources for help. These improvements in language and cognitive skills also decrease the likelihood of tantrums, since the child is less frustrated and better able to figure out alternative ways to get what she wants.

CHANNELING TODDLER BEHAVIORS

Paying attention to your toddler's emotional needs and understanding his developmental level are the first steps in disciplining a toddler. Once you realize how and why toddlers act the way they do, it will be easier for you to tolerate behavior you *shouldn't* change and change the behavior you shouldn't tolerate.

When your baby learns to walk he officially becomes a toddler. This and other developmental milestones, mental and motor, bring a new set of challenges. Your role as disciplinarian expands from simple nurturing to providing a safe environment in which your toddler can explore and learn. Have realistic expectations for normal toddler behavior: Toddlers are curious, driven, strong-minded. They need these qualities to learn, to persist, to bounce back in spite of life's little setbacks, to get up and try again. Toddlers also begin to think of themselves as individuals separate from Mommy. This is both exciting and frightening: The toddler is ready to shed the restrictions of being a baby but not ready to leave behind the security.

The lessons an attachment-parented baby learns during his first year help him cope with the ambivalence of toddlerhood. Because he is used to feeling right he is less likely to get himself into situations that make him feel wrong. Because he enters toddlerhood *trusting* in himself and in his caregivers, there is a *balance* in what he does and how he acts. There is a *purpose* to his actions that make him fascinating to watch. The attachment mother reads her child like a book and anticipates what will happen on the next page. She will learn specific ways to channel her toddler's behavior.

Offer redirectors. A baby's mind is filled with hundreds of word associations. One pattern of association we noted in Matthew's developmental diary was that when I would say "Go" to sixteen-month-old Mat-

---

Distract and Divert

Your one-year-old is toddling toward the lamp cord. Instead of scooping him up and risking a protest tantrum, first get his attention by calling his name or some other cue word that you have learned will stop him in his tracks long enough to distract him pleasantly. Then, quickly divert him toward a safer alternative. For example, when Lauren was younger (and it still works now sometimes), as soon as she would head for mischief we'd call out "Lauren!" Hearing her name took her by surprise and caused her to momentarily forget her objective. She'd respond "Yeah?" Once we had her attention, we'd quickly redirect her interests before she'd invested a lot of emotional energy into her original plan.

thew he would get the baby sling and run to the door. We used this ability to associate for distraction discipline: When we saw Matthew headed for major mischief we'd say "Go." This cue was enough to motivate his mind and body to change direction. We filed away a list of cue words to use as "redirectors" ("ball," "cat," "go," and so on). Of course, you must carry through and go for a walk or play ball or find the cat; otherwise your child will come to distrust you and you will lose a useful discipline tool. Toddlers from fourteen to eighteen months need lots of energetic catering to. Past eighteen months you can start saying things like "Not now. Maybe later." (See other discussions of redirectors, pages 65 and 178.)

Our strong-willed Lauren, at seventeen months of age, was stubbornly bent on going into the next room and finding her mother, who was trying to write. As I put out my arm to stop her she angrily pushed it away and began to throw a tantrum. I conveyed to her that she must stay with me, but I decided to make a game of it. Instead of physically restraining her, I let her play with my arm while using it to keep her from getting by. This turned into a "Give Me Five" game; and then, as she used her hand to push my arm away, I would take her hand and show her how to stroke my whiskers and she would laugh about it. Soon Lauren forgot her strong desire to go into the other room, deciding it was fun to stay and play with daddy. It took time and extra effort to distract Lauren, but it saved a lot of wear and tear on both of us. Instead of getting into an unpleasant father-daughter power struggle, I was able actually to improve our relationship. The stronger the will of the child, the more creatively a parent has to work at steering the child into good behavior.

Distract and substitute.

Set limits. Much of your discipline depends upon your ability to set limits. Humans need limits, and the younger the human the more defined should be the limits. Boundaries provide security for the child whose adventurous spirit leads him to explore but whose inexperience may lead him astray. Consider the classic experiment: After a schoolyard fence was removed, the children, who previously roamed free all over the yard, huddled toward the center of the grounds, reluctant to explore the formerly fenced-in corners. Limits do not really restrict a child but rather protect the curious explorer and his environment, freeing him up to function better within those confines. For example, your toddler doesn't want to hold your hand as you cross a street or parking lot together. You firmly set a limit: Street or parking lot crossing is *only* done while holding hands. There is no option.

We worked hard to achieve the right balance between freedom and constraints for our toddlers. It was not easy. We wanted them to learn about their environment and about themselves, but not at the expense of harming themselves or others. They liked having rules and knowing how to apply them. When a rule needed applying they would often recite the rule to us just to hear it and see if it still applied.

Limit setting teaches a valuable lesson for life: The world is full of yeses and nos. You decide what behavior you cannot allow and stick to that limit. This will be different for every family and every stage of development. Setting limits introduces a new level of frustration, which every child must experience on the home front before he is hit with it in the world outside the door. You decide you don't want your toddler to throw trash around, so you keep the lid on or the door closed. You keep the door to the pantry closed because you don't want the shelves mindlessly emptied. You make him stop pulling the dog's fur and teach him to pat nicely. Scissors and sharp knives are off-limits. You learn to keep them out of reach, and you firmly "distract and substitute" when the inevitable happens. Setting limits helps the whole family. The toddler needs to learn how to share the house with the whole family, and parents need to be realistic about their tolerances. As one mother put it, "I know my child's limits — and *mine*."

Some parents fail to set limits because they can't stand to see their baby frustrated. Healthy doses of frustration help a baby have just the right amount of resistance to keep him reaching for his full potential. No frustration, no growth. All frustration, no life. Be sure you model the healthy way to handle frustration. Adults have limits, too. If you know how to deal with your limits, you'll know how to provide limits for your baby. Attachment parenting doesn't imply you won't have parent-child conflicts, yet it prepares you to better handle them.

Toddlers *want* someone to set limits. Without limits the world is too scary for them. They intuitively know they need the security that limits bring. When they test the limits they are asking you to show them how dependable you and your limits are.

Take charge. As each of our babies graduated into toddlerhood, we had to examine our roles as authority figures — what that meant and how we would maintain that status. We wanted to be clearly in charge of our toddlers so that they would feel safe and secure with someone standing between them and the dangers of the big world, with a place to go for help. We didn't want to control them like puppets so that we ourselves could feel powerful. And contrary to the opinion of some theorists, we did not believe that our toddlers wanted to control us. It was themselves that they wanted to learn to control. We helped them in two ways: by letting them know by our tone of voice and our actions that we are mature adults, and by being available as a safe and secure home base that they could leave and return to at will, exploring the world then returning for comfort and reassurance when needed. In this way we could help them develop their own *inner controls.*

We gave our toddlers chances to mess up. They learned from their parent-supported failures. When Stephen insisted on having juice in an open cup with no help from Martha, she let him try it, and he spilled it all over himself. The cold juice running down his body startled him. For

Helping Your Child Play Alone

Part of self-discipline is the ability to enjoy playing alone. Before eighteen months of age, a baby will do this only in short spurts and will be eagerly checking in with mother frequently, either physically coming to her or finding her with his eyes. Attachment-parented babies may prefer to be in touch with mother almost constantly, and this is healthy. It seems as though allowing the baby to have his fill of mother's presence as an infant and young toddler prepares him for time on his own. He will know how to manage himself and won't need to be entertained as much as the baby who is not well connected.

The time between the ages of fourteen and eighteen months is very hard for mothers. The high-energy toddler wants to do everything, but he still needs mother involved "big time." Mothers of one-year-olds need to gear up for this marathon spurt of giving, because the tendency is to think "Ah, now he's one — I'll be able to ease off." You will eventually, but not yet. Hang in there through age eighteen months, then be alert for signs that your toddler is trying to make space between you. Some mothers might tend to hover and smother and continue to hang on, but remember, the one-and-a-half-to-two-year-old needs to become his own person. You will see these efforts

more and more. At first you won't believe your eyes. Your toddler will do what he sees you doing. She will tend doll babies, get out pots and pans, want to play at the sink, dig in the dirt with spoons. You name it — the possibilities are endless. She'll want you to pretend with her a bit. It's fun to be a dog or a lion, but she really only needs you to get her started. Pretend tea parties or picnics where you gobble up everything she hands you don't require much involvement from you.

By age three, a child's imagination and creativity will allow him to be able to have fun with anything. Keep toys simple and basic — building blocks, balls, dolls and blankets, cars and trucks (no batteries please). A four-year-old alone in a room with nothing to play with will figure out how to use shoes and socks as cars and people or as cradles and dolls.

By the time your child is six, you will have reached what one psychologist we talked to calls "planned detachment." Your child will check in for breakfast, be out the door, check in for lunch, and be gone again. You'll say "You're looking well, dear," you'll write a note to remind him of chores, and finally at dinner you'll get to talk some. After dinner some card playing, singing, or other family-oriented activity reconnects you with this individual who used to stick to you like Velcro.

the next sip he was willing to be less impulsive; he listened closely to Martha's advice to tip the cup "slowly." Because of the mutual trust and sensitivity that we developed during their first year, it was easier for our

toddlers to respect us as authority figures. We were able to convey to them what behavior we expected, and their actions often showed that they wanted to *please themselves by pleasing us.*

Once we reach that level of discipline, we feel tremendous job satisfaction. This is really what discipline is all about. It is not what we are doing to our children, it is what we are doing *for* and *with* them, and what they are doing for themselves.

PROVIDING STRUCTURE

When your child reaches one year of age, another title is added to the parenting job description: architect of your child's environment. By taking on this job you steer the child's energies toward enjoyable learning experiences and away from harm. You create structure, which does not mean being inflexible, repressive, or domineering. On the contrary, what we mean by "structure" is setting the conditions that encourage desirable behavior to happen. Structure protects and redirects. You free the child to be a child and provide the opportunity to grow and mature. Structure creates a *positive* environment for the child. By a bit of preplanning you remove most of the "nos" so that a generally "yes" environment prevails.

Structure changes as the child grows. At all developmental levels restructuring the child's environment is one of your most valuable discipline strategies. When your infant reaches the grabby stage, you are careful to set your coffee cup out of his reach. When your toddler discovers the toilet, you start keeping the lid latched or the bathroom door closed. The preschooler who fights going to sleep at night gets a relaxing bedtime routine. The nine-year-old struggling to keep up with her homework gets a quiet, enticing place to work in, as well as firm restrictions on school-night television. Structure sets the stage for desirable behaviors to override undesirable ones.

Create a toddler-friendly, toddler-safe environment. Toddlers get frustrated easily trying to live in a house furnished only for bigger bodies. Your role as designer of your child's environment involves making your house safe *for* your toddler and safe *from* your toddler. Toddlers are full of interest. Your job is to facilitate that interest safely. This is much easier to do at home, of course. When a child sees something enticing and sparkly, he will naturally want to touch it. It's the parent's job to get down and help the child explore that object without damaging it, or himself, and then redirect the child's attention.

Putting away the breakables and the family heirlooms in your home is not a capitulation to toddler power; it is simply a way to avoid having to be constantly on guard and having to always say no to your child, causing a buildup of frustration and anger in both of you. This is a much better alternative to being ever watchful and protective, or punitive toward a natural urge to explore. You, as the adult, have the maturity to put your own things aside (up or away) for a while until your child has the maturity to respect adult valuables. Keep in mind that this is only for a short time. We found that when our babies mastered crawling, we had to remove all our plants from floor level. Six months later we put the plants back down and the babies completely ignored what had been irresistible before. When your child starts to crawl, take a tour of your house from his perspective to discover what needs childproofing. There are many inexpensive products available that will help you make your home safe for your child (toilet seat latches, doorknob covers, drawer and cabinet latches, electric outlet and plug covers, and so on). These and some ingenuity will enable you to protect your little scientist. Effort spent baby-proofing your home will pay off in less conflict with your toddler. Plus, you will be more relaxed parents. Childproofing also provides your young explorer with guidance from the controlled environment itself. Here's a room-to-room guide to start with:

Living room/family room:

- Cover electrical outlets.
- Secure lamp cords so lamps can't be pulled down.
- Anchor floor lamps, or remove them.
- Cover controls on the television, stereo, VCR.
- Cushion sharp corners on coffee tables, piano benches, hearths.
- Display breakables out of baby's reach, or put them away for a few years.
- Reorganize bookshelves (toddlers love to empty these, tearing covers and dust jackets).
- Move plants.

Dining room/eating area:

- Push chairs all the way up to the table to prevent climbing.
- Install latches on drawers or cabinets holding breakable dishes.
- Push items on the tabletop to the center.
- Fold tablecloth corners under and up, out of grabbing distance.

Bathroom:

- Keep medicines, razors, pins, mouthwash, cosmetics, perfume, nail polish and re- mover, scissors, and other dangerous objects out of reach.
- Keep medicine cabinet latched.
- Pad tub faucets.
- Place a nonskid mat in the tub.
- Use rugs with nonskid backings.
- Keep the toilet seat down and latched.
- Empty the tub after use. Don't leave children unattended in tub.
- Use plastic, not glass or ceramic, cups and soap dishes.
- Keep the bathroom door shut.

Kitchen:

- Store knives out of reach.
- Unplug small appliances. Don't leave cords dangling.
- Store cleansers, solvents, bleaches, dishwasher detergent, and other poisons out of baby's reach in a latched cabinet.
- Cook on the back burners, and turn pot handles toward the back.
- Cover the stove controls, or remove them.
- Store breakables, things your baby can choke on, and other dangerous objects out of reach. Remember, that toddlers can climb onto kitchen counters.
- Use unbreakable dishes when your baby is around.
- Store plastic bags and plastic grocery bags out of reach.
- Hold hot drinks where your baby can't grab them, and keep them away from the edge of tables or counters.

Windows and doors:

- Keep sliding glass doors closed, or keep the screens locked.
- Place decals at toddler eye level on glass doors.

- Lock windows and be sure the screens are secure.
- Shorten the cords on draperies and blinds to get them up out of children's reach.
- Use netting to enclose the rails on balconies or porches so that your baby can't squeeze through.

Miscellaneous:

- Don't forget the garage, with paint thinners, antifreeze, gardening tools, supplies, insecticides, and other hazards.
- Use a safety gate at the top and bottom of stairs, especially if they are steep and unpadded. Some parents choose instead, if their stairs are carpeted and not too steep, to let the baby learn to crawl up and back down and keep a close eye on the ungated stairs for the few weeks it takes baby to learn.
- You can move an adjustable safety gate from doorway to doorway to keep your child away from temptation when you can't be right on his heels to supervise. Being able to block off the kitchen, for example, can save a lot of wear on mom and dad — you may not want the Tupperware cupboard emptied at *every* opportunity. It's safe, but sometimes mom can only take so much.

Once you have the "don't-touch" items out of the way, consider positive steps you can take to encourage good behavior in your toddler. Give him his own drawer in the kitchen, filled with interesting items to pull out, sort, and study, things like measuring spoons, plastic dishes, a potato masher. Provide things of his own around the house that he can push, pull, turn, and manipulate. Give him a safe outlet for climbing. Let him experiment with pouring water in a dishpan outside or in a tub, or at the sink under your supervision. Uncooked rice or oatmeal are easy-to-clean-up indoor substitutes for pouring sand.

Placing child-sized furniture around the house encourages the busy toddler to sit still longer and "work" at her own special table. A step stool will help her reach the kitchen sink for hand washing, tooth brushing, and for "helping" in the kitchen.

Toddlerhood is an exciting time in a child's life. It can be great fun just to watch your little one play. Being observant will also help you know when to step in and help out and when to let your child work out a problem on his own. A safe environment allows him to do this.

Program your day to fit your child. It's easier to shuffle your daily schedule around a bit than to change the temperament of your toddler. Do not set yourself up for impossible struggles. You know your own child best, and you will learn by trial and error what works. Try these tips:

- *Use wisdom when shopping.* When you shop with a toddler, be sure you are both well rested, well fed, and be ready with a nutritious snack to keep his mind off the cereal boxes, lettuce, and egg cartons. Be prepared to have it take twice as long — take your baby sling along, let baby ride in the cart, have fun and a short list. If you're in a hurry, feeling distracted, or stressed, shop without baby. (See "Supermarket Discipline," pages 197–199).

- *Plan ahead.* Know your child's up and down times of the day. Most toddlers behave their best in the morning, their worst in late afternoon or just before naptimes. Plan outings during what we call "easy times." Martha finds mornings one of the easiest times of the day to get our children to fit her agenda. During "tough times" of the day, our toddlers stay at their home base.

- *Anticipate your child's moods.* Provide snacks, lunch or supper, before he gets ravenous. Sit down to share some quiet activity before he's so wound up he can't fall asleep at night.

- *Provide regular routines.* You don't have to be a slave to a schedule, but toddlers need predictability: breakfast first, then get dressed; put on socks and shoes, then go bye-bye; supper, quiet play, bath, brush teeth, then bedtime stories. Routines give a child a sense of mastery.

Program your child to fit your day.
While children are not machines set to behave according to the design of the parent engineer, there are simple ways to channel little minds and bodies to make your day run smoother:

- *Rested mind and full tummy.* If you have no choice but to take a toddler to a place where it's difficult to be a two-year-old, plan ahead. Suppose you have a meeting with your older child's schoolteacher at four o'clock and you have to take along your two-year-old. Encourage your child to take a one-and-a-half- to two-hour nap at one-thirty, give a snack just before leaving home, and take along some quiet but fascinating toys. Be sure your child has had sufficient attention earlier in the day. This may help him behave better while you concentrate on the meeting. Invite him to sit on your lap while you talk.

- *Provide workable playtimes.* Life with a toddler can seem like a roller-coaster ride unless you know what sets off the highs and the lows. Note what prompts desirable behavior, and cut out what stirs turmoil. Some play environments foster good behavior in your child and fewer hassles for you. Seek out the ones that work; avoid the ones that don't. It may be a who, when, and how-many-playmates decision. Recognize who your child has the most fun with (this may not be the child of your best friend) and the time of the day he plays best. Does he play better one-on-one or beside two or three other mates? Most toddlers do best playing alongside a carefully selected playmate with a compatible temperament. Many children under three are not developmentally ready to play together cooperatively. Play groups for toddlers work well when the mothers are willing to be present and observant, able to be involved as the toddlers learn the social "ropes." An alternative to same-age playmates would be four-to-six-year-old playmates for your two-year-old. The older ones like playing with "babies" and they won't end up fighting.

Eliminate high-risk toys. Plastic bats are great for solo play but a disaster in a group. Select age- and temperament-appropriate toys. An impulsive thrower needs soft toys, not metal cars that he can use as projectiles. If a toy habitually excites squabbles among playing children, shelve it. Children under three do not yet have the developmental capacity to share. (See "Sharing," pages 249–255.)

Busy the bored child. A bored child is a breeding ground for trouble. Let your child be busy with you, sometimes have things to do on his own, and sometimes play with him yourself. The fourteen-to-eighteen-month-old will need you a lot. After that, a toddler is more and more able to self-stimulate.

The bored child with a busy parent is a high-risk mismatch. An attachment-parented child who has been connected well from birth will always be able to make her own fun by age four. Until then, count on the old standby: "Want to help Mommy?" Her "help" may slow you down, but this is less time-consuming than dealing with an "un-busy" child.

GOING FROM ONENESS TO SEPARATENESS: BEHAVIORS TO EXPECT

During the last half of the first year babies begin a developmental process known as *hatching.* Baby realizes there is a whole wide world out there apart from mother. Throughout the second year, your baby's understanding of himself matures from a feeling of "Mommy and me are one" to "me different from mommy" to "me" as an individual. Words like "my," "me," and "mine" show a struggle for identity apart from the mother. Besides an intellectual desire to be "me," the little individual now has the motor and language skills to help him be himself. How a baby develops this concept of "me," and how the parents discipline the behaviors that naturally go along with this "me" stage, are vital to the emotional health of the child. Child and adult psychologists believe that pleasant separation experiences in early life act as a sort of psychological vaccine against the anxiety of stressful separations that come in later childhood and adulthood.

The infant who was never connected

misses the healthy "Mommy and me as one" stage. This infant will have more difficulty transitioning into the healthy "me" stage. The infant who is pushed into the "me" stage prematurely is also likely to develop a shaky self-image, leading to insecurity, withdrawal, and anger. Finally, parents who misinterpret the normal behaviors that go along with this oneness-to-separateness process are likely to have the most problems with discipline.

Certain behaviors happen along the way in the child's journey from oneness to separateness. Some of these behaviors that help him become more independent are the very ones that may get him into trouble. By understanding why these occur and how you can help, discipline becomes easier.

Ambivalence. Baby wants and needs to separate, but she is not certain how soon or how far. Baby is constantly testing what is a comfortable distance from you. One minute she's a clinging vine, a few minutes later she's happily playing across the room. This requires moment-by-moment parenting decisions. Baby is up and down from floor to arms like a yo-yo. If you're relaxed, amused, and unhurried you may hardly notice. If you're bored, hurried, or feeling needy yourself it will drive you crazy.

Stranger anxiety. Independence has its price. Anxiety in the presence of strangers begins in the last half of the first year. This is where being connected to your baby once again pays off. The connected baby relies on parents to assess the security of a situation. In an unfamiliar social situation, baby rates strangers by your reaction. She sees strangers through your eyes. If you are anxious, baby is anxious. As the "stranger" approaches, baby will notice that you re-

The ability to create a mental image of mother helps baby to separate from her.

right into a happy-to-be-here dialogue with me, baby often clings less to mother and cooperates with me, sensing that I am a "mom-approved" person.

Separation anxiety. The fear of separating from mother is another normal development beginning in the last half of the first year. Understanding this stage helps parents cope with separation anxiety and not inflict separation when the baby is clearly saying it would make him anxious. It used to be thought that if a mother got too attached to her baby during the first year she would spoil her baby and the baby would cling to her forever. Many people still believe this, even though attachment research has shown the opposite to be true. The babies who are the most connected early on are the ones who later separate with less anxiety.

The physical and mental presence of the connected mother during play situations acts as an anxiety regulator, giving the baby the message "It's OK to explore." The connected infant has such a rich storage file of mental images of his mother that he is able to take mother with him mentally even when he no longer has a visual connection to her.

When encountering a strange play situation with mother, an infant has to balance the desire to explore a novel situation against the need to remain attached to the familiar caregiver. This is why even secure infants, upon entering a strange situation, initially cling to the mother before beginning to explore. Attachment parenting helps babies develop a balance between clinging and exploring. Infants check in with mother periodically for reassurance while they explore the strange situation. Mother's presence seems to add energy to the child's

flect an "It's OK, there's no need to be anxious" attitude in your body language. In the cautious mind of the baby if the stranger is OK to you, she is OK to baby. Hopefully, the "stranger" will also have enough knowledge of baby development to allow time and space for this evaluation to occur. A baby knows it is inappropriate just to barge into his personal space and will react strongly against the intrusion. The parent can act as a buffer in this situation.

Some babies are more stranger sensitive than others. When I see a new baby in my office, I've noticed that the baby often reacts to me the way the mother reacts. If the baby initially clings to the mother and the mother clings to the baby, often adding an anxious "He won't hurt you," she reinforces the anxiety and baby clings harder. But if mother relaxes her grip and clicks exploration. Since the infant does not need to waste effort worrying about whether mother is there or might leave, he can use all his energy for exploring. In time he will cling less and comfortably explore the environment, increasing his distance from the maternal home base, though checking in from time to time for emotional refueling. If you watch toddlers in play groups, you'll notice that they periodically run over to their mother, sit on her lap, and get a reassuring cuddle or even a brief chance to nurse — an emotional pit stop before darting off again to play.

Insecurely attached babies have more difficulty developing this balance. They are likely to spend more time clinging or may withdraw from both mother and the play situation. The late British psychologist Dr. John Bowlby, one of the most influential researchers of attachment theory, stated, "A child with no confidence does not trust that his attachment figures will be accessible to him when he needs them. He adopts a clinging strategy to ensure they will be available. He is uncertain of the mother's availability, and thus is always preoccupied with it; this preoccupation hinders separation and exploration, and therefore his learning." Attachment parenting acknowledges the developmental principle that an infant must go through a stage of healthy dependence before she can comfortably handle independence. (See related feature "Becoming Interdependent," page 53.)

Some babies are more separation sensitive than others; so one of your discipline goals in the second year is to find out in what situations, how often, and how long baby can comfortably separate from you. Some infants are anxious separating from their mothers because their mothers are anxious about them separating. The health-

ier the connection between you and your baby the first year, the more willingly your toddler may separate from you between the second and third year.

Every baby has his own separation timetable. Around two years of age our toddlers would usually happily wave "bye-bye" to Martha if I or a sibling were with them for connection. By three-and-a-half our "big kids" were happy to be on their own in Sunday school; and by four, they could securely spend the night at a close friend's house.

Tantrums. Baby's desire to have it all gives way to the realization he can't. His desire for bigness and power gives way to the frustration that he is not all-powerful. Tantrum

---

Leaving a Baby the Right Way

A highly attached, separation-sensitive baby has a hard time if mother leaves. The clue here is intuitively to know when your older baby can handle short absences (not counting the hour or so you may leave her with daddy now and then). In times past, grandmothers, aunts, even a neighbor lady were so intimately involved in a family's life that baby would feel secure with one of these familiar people for three or four hours at a time. If you don't have such a person in your life, look for a friendship you can cultivate — spend time together several times a week with another mother and child your toddler enjoys. Play and work together and be consistently in one another's home. This mutual attachment will give you and your friend "the perfect babysitter" with a similar parenting style.

Becoming Interdependent

Many child-rearing theories teach that a prime parenting goal is to get the child to be independent. This is true, but gaining independence is only part of becoming an emotionally healthy person. A child must pass through three stages:

- *Dependence:* "*You* do it for me." The infant under one year of age is totally dependent on his parents.

- *Independence*" I do it *myself.*" During the second year, the exploring toddler, with the encouragement of parents, learns to do many things independent of parents.

- *Interdependence:* "*We* do it." This is the most mature stage. The child has the drive to accomplish a feat by himself but has the wisdom to ask for help to do it *better.* For a child to have the best chance of becoming an emotionally healthy person, she should be encouraged to mature through each of these stages gradually. Getting stuck in the dependent stage is as crippling as being forced out of it too soon. Remaining in the independent stage is frustrating. Maturing into interdependence equips children with the ability to get the most out of others, while asking the most of themselves.

Interdependence means the parent and child need each other to bring out the best in each other. Without your child challenging you as he goes through each stage, you wouldn't develop the skills necessary to parent him. Here's where the connected pair shines. They help each other be the best for each other.

Learning interdependence prepares a child for life, especially for relationships and work. In fact, management consultants teach the concept of interdependence to increase productivity. The ability to know when to seek help and how to get it is a valuable social skill that even a two-year-old can learn: "I can do it myself, but I can do it better with help."

Throughout all stages of development a child goes from being solitary to being social, from wanting to be independent to wanting to be included. In fact, going back and forth from oneness to separateness is a lifelong social pattern among interdependent people. You want your child to be comfortable being alone and with other people, and which state predominates depends on the child's temperament. Interdependence balances children who are predominantly either leaders or followers. The independent individualist may be so tied up in himself that he misses what the crowd has to offer. The dependent child is so busy following the crowd that he never gets a chance to develop leadership.

Learning to be interdependent ties in with the child learning to be responsible. When children get used to seeking help from other persons, they naturally learn to consider the effects of their behavior on others. Truly happy and healthy persons are neither dependent nor independent; they are *interdependent.*

behavior is a natural by-product of the normal determination that is needed in the development of a healthy self. (See Chapter 5, "Taming Temper Tantrums," for an understanding of why tantrums occur and how to help your toddler through them.) It's important not only to structure the toddler's environment to lessen the need for tantrums, but also to allow and support the child's need to express feelings.

Between ages two and three a child's inner life becomes more transparent. Feelings children cannot express in words they communicate through *symbolic play*, giving you a clue to what they are feeling by how they act. Mary "nurses" her doll while mommy nurses the new baby. She's feeling like a little mommy. Jimmy pounds his teddy bear to show he's angry when things don't go his way.

Defiance. Understanding why your toddler says no helps you not to be threatened by this toddler behavior. Your toddler is not actually being defiant or stubborn. He is not saying "I won't"; rather, he is saying "I don't want to." Often he will give you two or three nos before he says "OK." Or he is experimenting, thinking, "What happens when I say no?" He is thinking, "I am into my thing now. This is my time, my space, and I have a right to it." He is "minding" his own mind. This behavior is a normal part of your toddler's struggle to develop a sense of self.

Around two, we would be met with a "No!" when we tried to remove a toddler from mischief, as if he perceived we were encroaching on the territory he had staked out. He was trying to see what power he had to enforce that right. During this stage, both parents and their toddlers need to learn a vital developmental lesson: the abil-

ity to give and take "no." When a parent feels threatened by a toddler's "no," harsh words are likely to come: "Don't you say that to me." A confident parent will not perceive this as a threat to authority but rather as a healthy stage all toddlers need to go through. A mature adult does not react anxiously or punitively when the attachment-parented toddler says no. Instead, the parent calmly takes each situation as it comes and guides according to his or her wisdom.

HELPING A TODDLER EASE INTO INDEPENDENCE

The child needs to break from the mother in order to learn about his environment and about himself; the mother needs to let her child go and learn how to maintain their connection over a longer distance. As with so many aspects of discipline, it's a question of balance, giving the child enough slack to become independent, yet keeping the connection. Mother does not let the child go off entirely on his own, nor does she keep him hanging on to her apron strings because of her own fears or need for his continuing dependence. Throughout the second year, parents may feel they are walking a fine line between being overrestrictive and being negligent. One way carries the risk of hindering a baby's development, the other of allowing the baby to hurt himself or others or damage property. Here are some ways of keeping connected while helping your baby separate.

Play "out of sight" games. Beginning around nine months of age or earlier, play peek-a-boo and chase around the furniture with your baby. As you hide your face with

Weaning from Attachment

Weaning means a child is ripe — the needs of one stage of development are filled so that the child is ready to take on the challenges of the next stage. The key to weaning is that it be *gradual* because weaning is a process, not an event. In the process of gradual weaning, the parent sees to it that the child is filled with one set of competencies as she becomes ready to take on the next set. Consider the close connection achieved by practicing the baby basics: being responsive to baby's cries, breastfeeding, and babywearing. These are natural discipline tools that can lessen the anxiety of toddlerhood, freeing up this little person to tackle challenges smoothly. A toddler who still breastfeeds, spends some time being worn in a sling, and gets responsive parenting continues to get the attachment tools that equip him to become gradually independent. This process cannot be rushed. When the baby inside the toddler stays connected, the toddler has the self-assurance he needs to separate.

Many toddlers I see in my practice are not like some I read about. These infants, who are not prematurely weaned, are *positive* kids, not at all the negative persons or the terrible twos commonly portrayed in baby books and child magazines. In my twenty-two years in pediatric practice I have noticed that *the most well-behaved children are those that were not weaned before their time.*

But won't prolonged attachment spoil a child? Yes, if mother is possessive — holding on to her toddler to fulfill her own needs for attachment at the expense of her child moving on. No, if the mother allows a weaning from each attachment stage as mutually agreed upon by mother and toddler. Contrary to the popular belief that extended attachment hinders independence, we notice that babies who are not prematurely rushed through any attachment stage and weaned before their time actually become more independent. And many attachment studies support our observation.

Mothers who wean early believe they may gain some freedom. Possibly, yes, but there is a trade-off. With early weaning you lose a valuable discipline tool. Attachment mellows toddler behavior. We believe that much of toddler misbehavior, such as anger and aggression, and behaviors that are passed off as "normal twos" are really *behaviors of premature detachment.* We pay a price for precocious independence. Early weaning from the breast, from primary caregivers, and from the home is a norm in Western society. A great deal of confusion about discipline methods is also characteristic of this same society. Any connection? The best way to build age-appropriate discipline into your parent-child relationship is to allow the child to separate from the parent instead of the parent prematurely separating from the child.

your hands or you hide your body on the other side of the couch, the baby has the opportunity to imagine that you exist even though you're out of sight.

Separate gradually. Best odds for a baby developing a healthy sense of self is for the baby to separate from the mother and not the mother from the baby. Discipline problems are less likely to occur when baby separates from mother *gradually.* When the baby inside the toddler remains connected, the toddler part of this growing person feels more secure to go off on his own. The connected child takes a bit of mother with him for comfort and advice during his explorations. It's like having the best of both worlds — oneness, yet separateness. We learned to appreciate this feeling during our family sailing adventures. Because our sailboat was fitted with an electronic homing device that kept us "connected" to a radio control tower on land, we felt secure venturing farther out into the ocean. Connection provides security.

The problem with many of the modern theories about discipline is that they focus so much on fostering independence that they lose sight of the necessity for a toddler to continue a healthy dependence. Try to achieve the delicate balance between maintaining the connection and encouraging self-reliance.

Take leave properly. Our eighteen-month-old grandson Andrew has very polite parents. Bob and Cheryl are careful to let him know when one of them plans to "disappear" into the next room. Because Andrew is separation-sensitive, he taught them to do this from a very early age. Especially important is saying "Good-bye!," "See-ya," and "Daddy's going to work." Andrew is able to

handle even his mother's leave-taking because there have never been any rude surprises. Including your child in your leave-taking helps him know what the score is at any given moment. He can trust his parents to keep him posted.

Be a facilitator. Children will naturally become independent. It is not your job to make them independent but rather to provide a secure environment that allows them to become independent. As your child is struggling for a comfortable independence, you become a facilitator. You are like a battery charger when the little dynamo needs emotional refueling. One moment he is shadowing you, the next moment he is darting away. How much separation can he tolerate and does he need? How much closeness? The child needs to maintain the connection while increasing the distance. Toddlers who behave best are those that find the balance of attaching and exploring as they go from security to novelty. Your job as facilitator is to help the child achieve that balance. That's the partnership you and your toddler negotiate.

Substitute voice contact. If your young toddler is playing in another room out of your sight and starts to fuss, instead of immediately dropping what you are doing and rushing to baby's aid, try calling to him instead, "Mama's coming!" Maintaining a dialogue with a toddler outside the shower door has prevented many a separation protest.

Shift gears if separation isn't working. Sometimes even a baby who was "easy to leave" suddenly becomes a toddler who is separation-sensitive. If baby isn't taking well to your absences, you might try more creative ways of staying happy yourself that don't involve leaving your baby. What you may perceive as a need to escape may actually be a need for you to give yourself more nurturing.

Provide "long-distance" help. Exploring toddlers get stuck in precarious places. The protector instinct in all parents makes us want to rush and rescue the stuck baby. Sometimes it's good to encourage from the sidelines and let the young adventurer get herself out of the mess. While writing this section, I observed two-year-old Lauren trying to negotiate her doll buggy down a short flight of steps. Halfway down, the buggy got stuck and Lauren began to protest. Instead of immediately rushing to help her, I offered an encouraging "Lauren do it." That was all she needed to navigate her buggy down the rest of the steps. Encouraging toddlers to work themselves out of their own dilemmas helps them develop a sense of self-reliance.

Watch for signs of separation stress. There are times when toddlers still need to cling, some more than others. On days when your usually fearless explorer won't leave your side, honor his wishes but try to figure out why he is staying so close. Does he feel ill? Have you been distracted or too busy to attend to him? Has he had more separation then he can handle lately? Refuel his connectedness "tank" with some time together, and he'll be off on his own again soon.

Have "just being" time. Take time to let your toddler just be with you, on your lap cuddling and talking, if he wants, at various times throughout the day. Says Martha: "First thing in the morning is a favorite time

for our Lauren to want this, especially if she's slept in her own bed that night, or if I got up before her and we miss that snuggle time in bed. If I let her 'be' until she calls a halt, she charges herself for a nice long stretch of independent time. It's not always easy for me to sit still long enough to let this happen, yet I'm always glad when I do."

Encourage relationships with other significant adults. Grandparents, family friends, a substitute caregiver you use regularly can help your older toddler learn to depend on adults other than his parents. Invite significant others into your child's life so that as he separates from you he learns that he can depend on a variety of people for help.

Remember, children's behaviors are more challenging to deal with when they are making the transition from one developmental stage to the next. By easing the transition, you lessen the discipline problems that tag along.

FROM TWO TO THREE

Not only is "the terrible twos" a terrible term, it's unfair. Though admittedly challenging, the twos (and threes!) are also terrific. The big transformation that takes place in a child's abilities is in the area of language. The toddler has fairly good receptive language — he understands most of what you say. The child of two can make himself understood much better; expressive language blossoms. This two-way verbal communication makes discipline easier. Language lets the two-year-old use adult resources to his advantage and helps him feel "big." Of course, there will be frustrating moments when your two-year-old struggles to make himself understood or discovers that he can't make the world fit all his expectations.

Fitting into family. The two-year-old begins to have an awareness of the balance of power within the family. This little person begins to size up limits, how far he can go with mom, dad, brothers and sisters, and familiar caregivers. He is more in control of his home environment and can make things happen there. He has explored every nook and cranny and has conducted independent research on every room in the house. He sees himself as king of the domain. He claims all for himself. To older sibs, he becomes imperious: "*My* mommy" (not yours). Two-and-a-half-year-old Lauren summed it up the other day when she spotted some cut flowers Hayden had just received from a boyfriend. She assumed what was obvious to her and blurted out, "Oh, Brandon, is this for *me?*"

Advance notice. Twos don't make transitions well. They get so engrossed in their own agenda that they don't easily conform to someone else's. When it's three o'clock and time for your daughter to leave the play group, she won't want to go. Respect this developmentally appropriate quality of engrossment, and give your child *advance warning* of departure. (For practical departure tips, see page 9.)

Fixed mind-sets. Twos and threes thrive on rituals and routines. The drive for organization at this stage makes them intolerant of changes that seem trivial by adult standards. If you get into the mind of a growing child and see how it operates, you'll understand this developmental thinking. In the

early years a child stores thousands of *patterns of association* in the mind. These patterns help the child make sense of the world, but some children greet any variation from the pattern with a protest. For example, when Matthew was three, the jelly had to be on top of the peanut butter in the sandwich. That is what he was used to and that was the pattern fixed in his mind. If we forgot and spread the jelly first, he fell apart. This did not mean he was being stubborn or unreasonable; the new way just didn't fit his expectations.

Order in the house. This may not be readily apparent, but twos and threes actually behave better in an orderly environment. A disorderly environment invites disorderly conduct. Young children's developing nervous systems are searching for organization. Heaps of clothes and toys can bring out a frenzy of flinging in children. Instead of toy boxes, try toy shelves. Low shelves with one-foot-square compartments, each containing one or two treasured toys, are much better than a pile of toys in a big box. This makes it easier to choose something to play with. Too many piled-up toys confuse a child and give the message that care is not needed. Rotate toys frequently to keep interest high.

Besides creating an ordered environment, giving your child a place for her belongings encourages a sense of responsibility. Show your child how to use eye-level pegs or plastic hooks for hanging clothing, and have a special place for shoes. One of the most frustrating moments of a parent's day is not being able to find a child's shoes — or worse, finding only one shoe when it's time to go out. Show your child how always to place shoes together (or when older, tie them together) "so that they will be easy to find in this special shoe place." Children will be as messy as we let them be, or as neat as we help them to be. Living in a world that is chaotic disturbs children at a stage of their development when they are trying to put order in their lives.

Threes have the mental ability to follow directions, and they retain the memory of familiar places. They can remember where things in the house go, and they begin to realize that each toy has its place. Capitalize on this mental maturity by giving your child credit for knowing this. Instead of "Put the book in the bookshelf," try "Please put your book where it belongs."

Social chairman. Your child's job at this age is to learn social skills, to learn to play cooperatively, and to be sensitive to others' needs and feelings. Your job as disciplinarian is to set the conditions that allow your child's social skills to mature. This job description includes seeking out well-matched playmates, refereeing squabbles, and, if necessary, selecting appropriate day care or preschool. Weaning from you as the primary playmate and from playing alone to other children is a mixed blessing. The good news is your child learns developmental skills in the company of other children. The bad news is he may learn behaviors you don't want him to learn. This is why one of your main jobs as disciplinarian for the two- and three-year-old is to structure the child's social life to work to her advantage.

Beginning manners. Two- and three-year-olds are ready to learn manners. It helps to understand just how far a child is mentally and emotionally capable of carrying out these social graces at this stage. A true understanding of sharing and politeness is based on the ability to get into other people's minds and appreciate their viewpoint. This level of understanding seldom clicks in prior to age five. Also, children under five think in particulars, not generalities. You can teach your child to say thank you when grandma gives her a cookie. But she may say thank you without prompting only when grandma gives her a cookie, not when you do. Around five years of age the child develops the ability to generalize "thank you" and discovers that it is the appropriate response anytime anyone gives her anything. Even so, it is still good to establish the habit of politeness in a child's growing mind, even if the child is polite mostly for the sake of parental approval and to get what she wants. It is easier for the meaning of manners to take hold in the child's mind if the custom has already been stored there.

Children learn manners by how mannerly you are toward them. At two-and-a-half, Lauren learned that if she tacked on the word "please" ("pees") to her request, it got her a very gracious and usually positive response. Twos soon learn which social charms give them a richer life. Expect and model politeness toward adults and toward other children, yet keep in mind that a two-year-old's abilities to cooperate with others are limited. (See "Sharing," pages 249–255.)

"I do it myself." Yes, your child can, with a little help from a friend. Expect this normal show of independence to bloom fully between ages two and three. Take advantage of this opportunity to foster responsibility and self-help. Allow plenty of time whenever you can to wait for your child finally to fit that foot in that shoe. Then when you are in a hurry you can matter-of-factly say without guilt, "Not this time, Mommy wants to hurry."

Says Martha: "I remember two-year-old Lauren, watching her four-year-old brother hop out of the car seat and car himself, deciding that she didn't want my help once her restraint strap was off. She was ready for a change in the routine but hadn't notified me ahead of time. As I reached for her she stiffened and resisted my lifting her out, yelling 'no' and 'me.' I knew intuitively she wasn't being defiant. It was her first 'do it myself.' It took three times as long as it would have if I had scooped her up as usual, but I put on my brakes and called up patience and good humor, seeing this as a time for her to try out being big. Once again, a toddler is teaching me to slow down and enjoy life."

DISCIPLINE GETS EASIER

Threes are easier to live with. The three-year-old now has the language skills that let two-way communication become real conversation. She is a more settled person, having spent a whole year refining her language skills. You can take Three shopping and actually enjoy it.

Internalizing. "I've told my eighteen-month-old over and over not to pull the cat's tail." Sound familiar? Mothers find themselves saying things over and over and over to their toddlers, and "it's as though he never heard it." Many directives don't sink in; not because your child is being defiant but because *most* children under two don't yet have the cognitive ability to remember and reflect on prior instructions. You'll just have to keep saying things — that's how he learns at this age. One day

you'll realize you haven't warned him about the cat's tail for a week. Between two and three years children begin to *internalize* what you say to them. They pay more attention to directions and store them in their memory bank as part of their own operating code. When you say "No street" to an eighteen-month-old, he may act like he never heard it before. When you say the same thing to a three-year-old, he seems to reflect, "Oh, yes, I remember." The ability to make instructions part of himself makes discipline easier.

Sharing emotions. The three-year-old is less egocentric and realizes there are people in the world who are as important as himself. This budding sensitivity can work to a caregiver's advantage or disadvantage in discipline. While Two notices her parents' emotions, Three gets involved with them. An entry from Matthew's baby journal noted this event: Martha asked three-year-old Matt to pick up his wooden blocks as part of our daily kids pick-up time. Matt balked and then was slyly letting his older sister do all the work. Because she was irritated at the moment, Martha yelled that she was unhappy with his not obeying but then realized Matt needed time to reconsider his position. She backed off for a few minutes, and Matthew then willingly did his job. As he was picking up his blocks he said, "Do you still love me?" Martha reassured him, "Even when you cry and yell and disobey, I love you." Matt persisted, "Do you like me?" Martha answered, "Yes, I like you, but I don't like it when you don't listen and help. I like it when you make the right choices." Job done, Matthew came over, hugged Martha, and said "I'm sorry, Mommy." Martha hugged him back and said, "I'm sorry for yelling." A few minutes later he said, "Are you happy to me?" This is the depth of emotional exchange you can expect between three and four years of age. They really want to make you happy. You will find living with children much easier if you give them many opportunities to please.

Three becomes more satisfied with her*self* or him*self*. Three begins to praise "self." One night our three-year-old Matthew announced, "I turned on the Christmas tree all by myself." We acknowledged his triumph by exclaiming, "Wow!" He said, "I'm so happy to myself."

House rules. Three is often described as the "absolute mother's dream" stage, mainly because threes are obedient. The nos of Two becomes yeses for Three. "OK, Mom" comes more quickly and willingly. While disagreements still happen, you can now breathe easier knowing that you are likely to meet a willing Three rather than a negative Two. While Two thinks no one else's agenda could possibly be as important as her own, Three considers the needs of others. Expect her to come when asked, put away toys when asked (usually), and generally want to please, though these changes will not come overnight.

Three understands house rules and consequences for breaking them, and he begins to internalize parents' values. You can gradually expand your explanations of what you expect according to your child's mental maturity. While Two still operates on an association of act and consequences ("I hit, I get put in the time-out chair"), Three can now understand why he shouldn't ride his tricycle into the street. Threes are beginning to think before they act; but don't count on it. When they do think about the consequences of their act, they do not yet

have the ability to consider the rightness or wrongness of the action; they just click into what you have taught them — ride the trike into the street and it gets put away in the garage. Discipline at this age involves *conditioning the child* to act a certain way rather than teaching him to make moral judgments. (The concept of right and wrong develops around ages six or seven.) Discipline techniques that were marginal for Twos, work better at three. Parents wonder how much their three-year-old actually understands. As a rule of thumb, at all ages, estimate how much your child understands and double it. The out-of-control Three can understand time-out as a time in the "quiet corner" to regain control.

Choices, choices, choices. Threes thrive on choices. Sharing in the selection process makes them feel important, and they are more likely to cooperate. Share your choice making with Three. ("Which dress should Mommy wear, the blue one or the red one?"). Children with persistent personalities ("power kids") need choices. (Be sure you like all the alternatives you offer.) Most kids do best with *two* choices; more may overwhelm them. Don't feel you have to be psychologically correct all the time. In some situations you just have to pull rank and give your child a matter-of-fact command.

Vivid imagination. This is the stage where children spend much of their time immersed in pretend play. They create imaginary scenes for their own personal enjoyment. The ability to live in a make-believe world helps children learn about the real world. They role-play endlessly: pretending to be animals, mommy and daddy, doctor and patient, truck drivers, teachers, and princesses. Share in your child's imaginative play ("Who will come to your tea party?"). Your child's pretend play is a wonderful window into what's going on in her mind.

Try using your child's imagination to get him to cooperate. Here's how one mother taught her three-year-old to brush his teeth: "On Brandon's toothbrush there is a little picture of Oscar the Grouch, so I become the voice of Oscar the Grouch. I say 'Is there any trash in your teeth? Let me come in and see.' He immediately opens his mouth for Oscar to come in and look at his teeth and eat up the trash that's in there. Then we talk about having clean teeth, and how we don't want to leave trash in our teeth. Brushing Brandon's teeth has not become a big issue because I help him cooperate."

The mind of the preschool child is rich with fantasy. To three-year-olds Big Bird and Barney are real. They don't waste energy separating real from pretend; they sit back and enjoy. While parents may feel it's their disciplinary duty to purge their child's gullible mind of things unreal, resist this urge. Strike a balance. Let the child enjoy his fantasies, and as his thought processes become more sophisticated he will accept that these fictitious characters are only pretend. You don't have to manipulate his environment in order to maintain the fiction, the way some parents do to keep a child believing in Santa or the Easter Bunny. Just enjoy these games for what they are — pretend. Santa at best is a jolly, benevolent figure, not a punishing one. Everyone enjoys fantasy, and even for adults it's therapeutic. Use your child's behavior as a barometer of whether his imaginary experiences are helpful or harmful. The same imaginative mind that creates the fantasies also creates fears. We make sure our children know it's Mommy and Daddy who give them gifts at Christmas. We've never agreed with telling children that "Santa Claus" is watching to see if they're good. Be especially vigilant about cartoons. (See "Helping Your Child Handle Fears," pages 296–300.)

Saying No Positively

PARENTS SPEND THE FIRST NINE MONTHS SAYING YES. From nine to eighteen months you'll do a lot of distracting and redirecting. Baby will be introduced to frustration gradually as your responses to his wants and needs become less and less immediate. After that the nos become more direct. "No" is a power-packed word, quick on the lips, easy to say; it gets results if you expect it to and say it without being abusive. Your child will hear this word often from you; you will hear it from your child as well. Here's how to use this negative little word to teach positive messages.

THE IMPORTANCE OF SAYING NO

It's necessary for a parent to say no to a child so the child can later say no to herself. All children — and some adults — have difficulty delaying gratification. "I want it now" is a driving desire, especially in toddlers. Learning to accept no from someone else is a prelude to saying no to oneself. What gets children (and adults) into trouble is a knee-jerk, impulsive reaction to a want — an immediate yes — without taking time to run it through their internal sensor and consider the necessity of saying no to themselves.

Strike a balance. Too many nos and too many yeses cripple a child's self-discipline. It's important to achieve the right blend of yeses and nos in a child's environment. If you rarely say no to your child, the few times that you do he'll disintegrate because he is not used to being frustrated. If his whole day is full of nos, the child believes the world is a negative place to be and will grow up a negative person. The real world will always be full of yeses and nos. In many homes, children soon learn who is the "yes" parent and who is more likely to say no. Even the Ten Commandments have dos and don'ts. As the child gradually learns this lesson of life, she's on her way to having a healthy, balanced personality.

Nos grow too. The art of saying no develops along with your baby. During the first year, a baby's needs and wants are the same, so that you are mainly a "yes" parent. During the second year, baby's wants are not always safe or healthy, so you become a "yes" and "no" parent. From nine to four-teen months, no-saying is straightforward. We call them "low-energy nos." Between fourteen and eighteen months, as babies click into overdrive, they get easily frus-trated and are likely to protest being steered in a direction other than the one they want to go. This is when you will need both high-energy nos and very creative al-ternatives, such as the distraction and sub-stitution approach, which is intended to minimize wear and tear on you and your child. By eighteen months, no-saying can begin to be more matter-of-fact. Parents can begin to convey an attitude of "that's life, and I'm confident you can deal with it." By two years of age toddlers become infatuated with saying no themselves. (See "Defiance," page 54.)

CREATIVE ALTERNATIVES TO "NO"

One morning when she was eighteen months old our daughter Lauren, who was going through an impulsive phase, was flit-ting around the house climbing on and get-ting into everything. She was endangering herself and trashing the house. After the twentieth "No," I was tired of hearing that word and so was Lauren. On the wall in one of our children's bedrooms I noticed a poster of a kitten stuck out on a limb at the top of a tree. The caption read, "Lord, pro-tect me from myself." I realized that Lauren needed rescuing from her impulsive self. She needed a change of environment. We spent the rest of the day outside. Parks and play yards provide space and a "yes" envi-ronment in which to roam and climb. If you find yourself isolated with a curious toddler who is flitting from thing to thing,

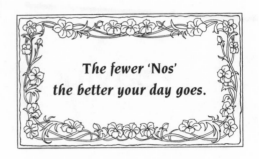

The fewer 'Nos' the better your day goes.

and you're chasing him around the house saying no, consider changing to something more fun. Go outside; take along a good book and plant yourself in a safe location to let him run.

Teach stop signs. Even in the early months, teach your baby to recognize body language that means stop. Your baby needs to be exposed to "stop" body language long before hearing the no word. The first nip on Mother's nipple during breastfeeding will invoke an "ouch" sign on your face; the first time your baby reaches for something dangerous, your face will register alarm. You are likely to get best results from your stop signs if your baby has been so used to positive body language that any change makes him sit up and take notice. Your "nos" will be more meaningful during tod-dlerhood if your baby sees a lot of "yes" body language: looks of pride and approval, gestures of delight and pleasure, eye-to-eye contact, hugs, tickles, and a sparkly face that says "I love you. You're great!"

We have noticed that attachment-parented children, because they spend hours a day in their parents' arms and in face-to-face contact, easily learn to read par-ents' faces and body language. Having lots of face-to-face contact in the early months makes face-to-face communication easier in the months and years to come. Some children are so impressed by body language that you can get your point across without saying a word. An expressive mother of a connected two-year-old told us: "Usually all I have to do is glance at her with a slight frown on my face, and she stops misbehaving."

Teach stop sounds. Often a change in your mood or body language is not enough to redirect impulsive actions. Words are needed. Children soon learn which discipline words carry more power and demand quicker response than others. And children soon learn which tone of voice means business and which allows for some latitude. Arm yourself with a variety of "stop-what-you're-doing" sounds so that you can choose one that fits the occasion. Tailor the intensity of the sound to the gravity of the behavior. Save the really big sound for the true danger.

Create alternatives to the n-word. Constantly saying no causes this word to lose its power. Since stop sounds are used mainly to protect, try using more specific words that fit the situation. Consider this example: When a toddler is about to reach into the cat's litter box your first reaction is to say "No!" but you follow it up with an explanation, "Dirty! Make you sick." Next time the child goes for the litter box (and he will do it again), instead of no, say "Dirty! Make you sick." That and a disgusted expression on your face will help the child learn the why as well as the what of good behavior, and the litter box will lose its attraction. (We are assuming here that the litter box is kept in a location well away from the toddler's beaten path. Litter,

---

Mastering "The Look"

You can often correct a child without saying a word. I have noticed that master disciplinarians use a look of disapproval that stops the behavior but preserves the child's self-image, a type of "I mean business" look. Martha, after disciplining eight children, has mastered "the look": head turned a bit, eyes probing, just the right facial gesture and tone of voice to convey to the child, "I don't like what you're doing, but I still feel connected to you. I know that you know better." Remember, your eyes will disclose what you are really thinking and feeling. If you are feeling anger or contempt toward your child, that's what she will read in your eyes. If one or both of you recognize this is happening, you will have to apologize for the harshness of the feelings communicated toward her person by "the look." Be sure that stop signs and stop sounds stop the behavior and not the growth of self-worth in your child. Your child should understand that you disapprove of the behavior, *not the child.* Follow the look with a hug, a smile, or a forthright explanation: "I don't like what you did, but I do like you."

---

like sand, is irresistible to babies.) Babies start reaching for "no-nos" around six months. A good phrase to use early on is "Not for Madelaine." By the time baby is a toddler this phrase will be familiar and matter-of-fact.

Coincidentally, one day while we were writing this chapter, two-year-old Lauren came prancing into our study clutching a

"The Voice"

Besides mastering "the look," reserve a special tone of voice for those occasions when you must get your point across vocally. A veteran disciplinarian shared her secret with us: "I am an easy-going mommy, but my children know just by my tone of voice when they have crossed the line. One day our two-year-old was misbehaving and our four-year-old said, "Don't mess with Mommy when she talks like that!"

bag of peanuts. Instead of grabbing the peanuts from her and shouting "No!" (they are on our chokable food list for children under three), Martha looked Lauren straight in the eye and calmly said, "Not for Lauren." Her tone of voice and concerned look stopped Lauren in her tracks. Martha picked Lauren up (still clutching the peanuts) and headed off for the pantry, where they found a safer snack. By using our standard "not for Lauren" phrase and giving her a safe alternative, she didn't have time to consider throwing a fit, which a no surely would have produced. (For more alternatives to no, see discussions of redirectors, pages 42–43 and 178). In any family there will be items that are "not for" the little one. When you use this phrase calmly and consistently from early on, the toddler understands you are protecting him.

"No" is so easy to say. It requires no thought. It's knee-jerk automatic, yet irritatingly oppressive. Saying "cannot" communicates more, and you'll use it more thoughtfully, reserving it for situations where baby truly cannot proceed. You're respecting his mind as you protect his body. In our experience, babies respond to

"Stop!" better than to "No!" It gets the child's attention, and stops behavior long enough for you to plan other strategies. "Stop" is protective rather than punitive. "No" invites a clash of wills, but even strong-willed children will usually stop momentarily to evaluate a stop order, as if they sense danger ahead. Strong-minded children often ignore "No" if they've heard it a thousand times before. Even "Stop" loses its command value if overused.

Give positive subs. Present a positive with your negative: "You *can't* have the knife, but you *can* have the ball." Use a convincing expression to market the "can do" in order to soften the "can't do." "You can't go across the street," you say with a matter-of-fact tone of voice, then carefully state, "You can help Mommy sweep the sidewalk." There is a bit of creative marketing in every mother.

Avoid setups. If you're taking your child along with you to a toy store to buy a birthday present for your child's friend, realize that you are setting yourself up for a confrontation. Your child is likely to want to buy everything in the store. To avoid the inevitable "No, you can't have that toy," *before* you go into the store tell him that you are there to buy a birthday present and not a toy for him so that he is programmed not to expect a toy.

RESPECTFULLY, NO!

Each stage of development has it yeses and nos; the stakes just get higher as children get older. Learning how to give and receive a no is part of maturity and part of discipline.

The Humor of "No"

One afternoon Martha walked into the TV room and saw Matthew and his friend watching a video that the older children had rented and watched the day before. (Later we found out Matthew had also watched it at that time.) She took one look at the movie and realized she would have to ask him to turn it off. Besides, it was the middle of the day and the boys should have been playing outside. As she stood watching the movie for a few moments, planning her course of action, Martha caught the flavor of the character in the movie and in a spurt of inspiration decided to use humor to say no. As she clicked off the TV, she spun around on her heels and launched into a monologue using the character's facial expressions, accent, and hand gestures. She must have done a good job of impersonating this actor because both boys sat staring at her wide-eyed as though they couldn't believe a mom was capable of such improvised insanity. They both jumped up and headed out the door as the voice of this character told them to find something better to do. They were still laughing.

"No" is a child's word too. Prepare yourself to be on the receiving end of "No." Your two-year-old has just run out the door. You ask her to come back. She yells, "No!" Your first reaction is likely to be, "This little pipsqueak is not going to talk back to me that way. I'll show her who's boss. . . ." (In our family, being disrespectful is a real "no-no.") Understanding what's behind that two-year-old and that two-letter word will help you accept this normal toddler behavior. Don't take "No" personally. Saying no is important for a child's development, for establishing his identity as an individual. This is not defiance or a rejection of your authority. (See the meaning of defiance, page 54.) Some parents feel they cannot tolerate any nos at all from their children, thinking that to permit this would undermine their authority. They wind up curtailing an important process of self-emergence: Children have to experiment with where their mother leaves off and where they begin. Parents can learn to respect individual wishes and still stay in charge and maintain limits. The boundaries of selfhood will be weak if the self gets no exercise. As your child gets older, the ability to get along with peers in certain situations (stealing, cheating, drugs, and so on) will depend on her ability to say no.

By eighteen months Lauren had surmised that "No" meant we wanted her to stop what she was doing. One day she was happily playing with water at the kitchen sink. As she saw me approaching, and in anticipation of my stopping her play, she blurted out an emphatic "No, Dad!" Lauren had staked out her territory, and she had concluded she had a right to do this. Her "No" meant she was guarding her space. I verbalized what I thought her "No" meant: "You don't want me to stop you. You want to play with the water. Go ahead, that looks like fun." If I had wanted her to stop I would have said, "Sorry, not now. How about a squirt bottle with water in it?"

Personalize "No." We are convinced Lauren is destined for public relations. Her "No, Dad" was the diplomatic way to say no. By adding "Dad" she *personalized her message.* Rather than giving a dictatorial

"No," we add the child's name. If you tend to shout, personalized address at least softens the sound and shows respect for the listener. Some parents confuse respecting the child with granting him equal power, but this is not a power issue. The person with the power should respect the person taken charge of. That consideration holds true in parenting; it holds true in other relationships as well.

Be considerate. When you have to stop a behavior, there is no reason to be rude. For example, your baby discovers the tape dispenser someone left out. This is a wonderful toy. Instead of descending on him and snatching it from his hands, causing him to wail pitifully as you carry him off, you can take a few moments to explore it with him. Then you say "bye-bye" to the tape and hand him a decent length of the fascinating stuff to compensate for not getting the whole roll as you turn his attention to a perhaps less interesting but more age-appropriate activity.

When you say it, mean it. Follow through on your directives. For months we said to Lauren that in order to have bedtime stories she had to submit to toothbrushing. And for months it worked, sometimes easily, sometimes with a certain amount of coaxing and saying, "OK, no stories . . ." One night she decided to test Martha. She could tell by the set of Lauren's jaw and firmly shut lips that she finally was "calling our bluff." So rather than proceed with coaxing and humoring, Martha calmly said, "OK, no stories!," turned off the lights, and carried her to bed. She fussed a bit as Martha lay there with her because she realized Martha had called *her* bluff and now the lights were out — the irreversible sign that

the next step was to go to sleep. After that, toothbrushing went unchallenged and stories were reinstated.

MAKING DANGER DISCIPLINE STICK

Your toddler reaches for the handle of the soup pan on the stove. Instead of shouting "No!" try "Stop!" As soon as baby stops in her tracks, issue a quick follow-up — "Hurt baby." As you firmly grab her exploring hand (thinking next time you'll keep the handle turned in and use the back burner), look into her amazed big eyes and continue your serious look: "Hot. Hurt. Don't touch what's on the stove. Ouchie!" You've made your point without saying no. Follow up with a hug, especially if you found yourself speaking harshly. Reconnect with your child so that one incident doesn't ruin your child's whole day. ("Hot" is another helpful stop word, especially once your child has some personal experience with the sensation. Carefully hold her hand where she can feel the heat so she understands the connection.)

As young parents with our first few children, we believed that spanking was appropriate in life-threatening situations, such as toddlers running out into the street. We reasoned it was necessary to make a lasting impression on mind and body to prevent the child from running into the street again. At the time we concluded that safety comes before psychology. But as we learned more about discipline, we realized there are better ways than spanking to handle even danger discipline. And we realized toddlers don't remember from one time to the next, even with the "physical impression." Here's what worked for us:

Negotiate or Hold Your Ground?

Children, especially those with a strong will, try to wear their parents down. They are convinced they must have something or their world can't go on. They pester and badger until parents say yes just to stop the wear and tear on their nerves. This is faulty discipline. If, however, your child's request seems reasonable after careful listening, be willing to negotiate. Sometimes you may find it wise to change your mind after saying no. While you want your child to believe your "No" means no, you also want your child to feel you are approachable and flexible. It helps to hold your "No" until you've heard your child out. If you sense your child is uncharacteristically crushed or angry at your "No," listen to her side. Maybe she has a point you hadn't considered or her request is a bigger deal to her than you imagined. Be open to reversing your decision, if warranted. Make sure, though, that she knows it was your fairness and not her "wear down" tactics that changed your mind.

Our daughter Erin seems destined to become a trial lawyer; she pleads her case with logic and emotion. It's even harder to say no to her when she raises those eyelashes you could paint a house with. Eventually we learned to say no without discouraging Erin's creative persistence. When Erin wanted a horse, we said no (we had too many dependents already). Erin persisted. By trial and error we had learned that any big wish in a child, no matter how ridiculous, merits hearing the child's viewpoint. We listened attentively and empathetically while Erin presented her horse wish. We countered, "Erin, we understand why you want a horse. You could have a lot of fun riding and grooming a horse, and some of your friends have horses." (We wanted Erin to feel we understood her side.) "But we have to say no; and we will not change our minds. Now let's sit down and calmly work this out." (Letting the child know her request is nonnegotiable diffuses the child's steam and saves you from getting worn down.) "You are not yet ready to care for a horse." (We enumerated the responsibilities that went along with the fun of owning a horse.) "When you have finished another six months of lessons and you show us that you can be responsible for a horse, we'll talk about it then." Nine months later Tuffy was added to our list of dependents. Erin got her horse and she learned two valuable lessons in life: how to delay gratification and that with privileges come responsibilities.

Danger "No." When a toddler was in the driveway, Martha watched him like a hawk. If he ventured too close to the street, she put on her best tirade, shouting "Stop!! Street!!" and she grabbed him from the curb and carried on and on, vocalizing her fear of his being in the street. She was not yelling at him or acting angry. She was expressing genuine fear, giving voice to that inner alarm that goes off in every mother's heart when her child could be hurt. It was very important that he believe her, so she didn't

Mothers Who Can't Say No

In their zeal to give their children everything they *need,* some parents risk giving their children everything they *want.* Mothers who practice attachment parenting risk becoming totally "yes" mothers, with "no" being foreign to their parenting style.

It is important for the mother to feel comfortable saying no to her little one from the very beginning. In fact, it begins when she teaches her newborn to latch on to the breast correctly. It is the mother's first discipline situation — to show baby how to latch on properly so that he can get fed sufficiently and she can avoid sore nipples. (Some mothers cannot do this. They are afraid to be assertive for fear of causing baby to cry. They would rather let the baby do it wrong and put up with the pain.) She says no early on when she stops him from yanking her hair or biting her breast while nursing. By telling him to stop because it hurts her, she is beginning to teach boundaries. Serious no-saying comes with toddlerhood. Besides the literal word "no," there are many ways to communicate that

something is not safe or appropriate. Whether she says "Stop that" or "Put it down" or "Not safe," or physically redirects her toddler's activity, she is consistently and gently redirecting behavior and teaching boundaries. Whatever the terminology, saying no is not a negative thing. It is a way of giving, and it takes a lot of effort. Mothers who can't say no have a big problem on their hands down the line. They become the moms that we see getting yanked around like puppets by their preschoolers.

When mothers begin saying no — confidently, firmly, and lovingly — at the appropriate times, it does not threaten the child. It might wrinkle him for a few minutes, because he doesn't like hearing "Stop" or "Wait" or whatever the word might be that you pick. But he has had the foundation of attachment and he trusts the parent. Limit setting is not the big undoing that some think it might be, and mothers cannot wait until the preschool years to start. It needs to happen very naturally, very confidently, and intuitively, and very early on.

hold back. And it worked! He acquired a deep respect for the street and always looked for permission, knowing that Mom would take his hand and they would cross together. A few times Martha had to reinforce this healthy fear by issuing a loud warning sound. She saves this sound for times when an immediate response is needed for safety. This sound is hard to describe in writing, but it is a very sharp, forceful "Ahhh!" Once she had to use it

from a distance of about two hundred feet at a park where Stephen had wandered off and was about to step into the street. To her intense relief, he stopped in his tracks and looked back at her, giving her time to get to him. She never uses it casually, and doesn't use it often. Day-to-day, moment-by-moment situations need to be handled more normally.

Any "danger" situation still requires constant adult supervision — no amount of spanking will danger-proof a child when the adult is not there to administer the blows. Any after-the-fact hitting will just be confusing — he won't know why he's being hit. Your job as a disciplinarian means keeping your child away from situations in which his ignorance or impulsiveness could get him into real danger.

Instant replay. Our four-year-old, Stephen, was headed for the street. I immediately ran to his side and began our danger-preventing tirade (see above). Then we played the *rewind game*. Ten times we reenacted the scene. We ran toward the street, stopped at the curb, and looked both ways: "Look this way, no car; look that way, no car, and then we walk across the street to your friend's house." By graphic repetition, I hoped to imprint in Stephen's mind the habit of automatically looking both ways for the car as soon as he approaches the curb, and then crossing the street. Eight-year-old Matthew was running on a slick, wet sidewalk and slipped and fell. I used "rewind" to prevent this accident from occurring again. We both ran toward the puddle, stopped, walked around it, and then carried on, replaying this scene ten times. By using "rewind," you provide your child with a script to follow when the same situation arises later.

Have a "Yes" Day

Jill, mother of five-year-old Andrew, confided to me, "I don't like what's happening to me. I want to enjoy being a mother, but our whole day is spent in conflict with each other. Andrew won't mind when I ask him to do even the simplest things. I'm becoming a cranky person, and I want to be a happy mother." I advised her, "Tell Andrew exactly what you want. Say 'I want to be a happy Mommy, not a cranky Mommy. To help me be a happy Mommy, we're going to have "yes" days. First, make a chart so we can keep track of yeses and nos. Every time I ask you to do something and you say "Yes, Mommy," put a "yes" on the chart. At the end of the day if there are more yeses than nos, that's a "yes" day, and we'll do something special together.'" Soon Andrew will realize that the happy Mommy is more fun to be with than the cranky Mommy, which will motivate him to continue having "yes" days.

Taming Temper Tantrums

WHEN YOUR CHILD is between the ages of one and two years, you'll want to be ready for tantrums. Nearly all babies throw fits, some more than others. Learning how to prevent and survive toddler outbursts is one of the many challenges in disciplining a young child.

WHY TANTRUMS?

You're already late for work, but you can't find your shoe. As you search your closets, you mutter that your day is ruined. Your irritation escalates and objects fly as you search frantically for the missing footwear. In a huff you storm out of the bedroom looking for someone to blame, slamming open the door so that the knob hits the wall forcefully. Just as you are ready to start yelling, your mate appears with the missing shoe, found under the bedspread that you tossed aside in your fury. You're embarrassed. You peer at the dent in the wall made by the doorknob, a permanent reminder of your tantrum. Sound familiar? Pressure gets to us if we let it. As adults we're supposed to know how to keep our peace in the midst of frustration.

Now take an impulsive little person whose desire to do something far exceeds his capabilities, a little person who cannot yet reason about the wisdom or safety of an action. Mix these things together with an authority figure saying no and applying a firm hand to pull the child back from his goal, and you have the ingredients for a tantrum, especially if the no is shouted and the pull is actually a yank.

Temper tantrums are a normal by-product of infant development. Babies operate on the "just do it" principle. Their desires are a step ahead of their mental and motor competence. That's how they keep going. Their strong will helps them get up and try again. They need persistent personalities to motivate them to master new situations. Tantrums are the price children — and their parents — pay for growing and learning.

Tantrums also result from this fact of infant development: Mental and motor skills develop more quickly than language. A child knows what he wants and how he feels long before he is able to talk about it. Because he does not yet have the language skills to express frustration, he does so in

---

Toddler Power

Words give power over feelings and frustrations. Parents who talk with their babies and toddlers, teaching them language in the daily flow of living, are equipping them to handle the moments of frustration and strong feelings. If a toddler can be given a word or two to say in a moment of conflict, he will often be able to cooperate with you because saying that word himself gives him mastery over the concept he's struggling with.

---

actions — tantrums. Irrational thinking also contributes to tantrums. Babies cannot reason through the consequences of their actions. They want to put square pegs in round holes, to pile cubes on top of spheres, to get the dog to return the cookie offered (and eaten) a moment before. They think differently from adults: "If Mommy has so much fun with the big knife, why can't I use it?" When these intentions are thwarted, all the emotional intensity a toddler pours into his experiments explodes.

The tantrum-prone child. Some kids are more inclined toward tantrums than others. Babies with high needs and children with strong wills and who have trouble controlling their emotions are more likely to fall into tantrum behavior. They have more difficulty achieving equilibrium, an inner emotional balance that helps people bounce back from life's many setbacks and regain composure. They have problems emotionally in two ways: They are more prone to blow their lid, and they are less able to put the lid back on once it has blown.

Some of the traits that make children more prone to tantrums, such as sensitivity, persistence, determination, and creativity, can be very beneficial to a child's intellectual and social development. One of your tasks as a parent is to channel these qualities to happier ends. Now that you appreciate why your usually sweet baby occasionally turns sour, here is how to head off tantrums and deal positively with them when they occur.

PREVENTING TANTRUMS

Our theme throughout this book is that the best way to discourage undesirable behavior is to encourage desirable actions. This principle applies to tantrum prevention. Discourage those conditions that contribute to emotional upsets and encourage those that promote emotional stability.

Practice attachment parenting. We have noticed that infants who are carried a lot and whose cues are sensitively responded to are more mellow, less prone to tantrums, and are able to ride the waves of emotional upsets without falling apart so drastically. Because they operate from an inner peace, they are less prone to impulsive behavior or angry outbursts. Children, however, who are parented with less attachment are less able to recover from emotional storms. Attached parents can read their child so well that they naturally create conditions that minimize tantrum behavior. Practice as many of the attachment styles of parenting as you can, as often as you can (see "Attachment Parenting — The Key to Early Discipline," pages 17–26). Making it easier to deal with temper tantrums is one of the immediate payoffs of attachment parenting.

Identify the trigger. Tantrums usually occur at the worst time for parents: You are on the phone, at the supermarket, busy with your agenda. Think about it. The very circumstances that make a tantrum inconvenient for you are what set the toddler up for a tantrum. Wise parents avoid situations that lead to emotional overload in their children. Keep a tantrum diary, noting what sets your child off. Is he bored, tired, sick, hungry, overstimulated? Prepare a behavior chart. Making this chart will help you analyze what you know and observe about your child. Behavior charts also help you create conditions that encourage calm behavior. You may discover that tantrums occur most often before naptime or bedtime, or when parents are busy making dinner. They may happen when you return home from an all-morning play date at a friend's house. The chart may show that the child behaved during meal preparations when he was allowed to help and nibble. Learn from this bit of childhood history so that you don't have to repeat it. When you discover a tantrum prevention technique that works, use it again.

Even with your best efforts, tantrums will still erupt from time to time. Try to diffuse them early. Know your toddler's pre-tantrum signs — body language that signals the coming storm. Our Lauren has a short fuse. Setbacks can cause her to fall apart. When she is trying to retrieve a stuck toy from beneath the couch, we stand by and watch as she pulls on the toy, murmuring some angry sounds, her face getting red. We intervene early, after only one or two unsuccessful attempts on her part to retrieve the toy. Once those murmurs begin, she can no longer think straight. With others of our children who had more patience at that age, we would stand in the background and let them work on their problem alone a bit longer. In parenting the tantrum-prone child you must learn to strike a balance, knowing when to stand by and let the child work through the difficulty on her own, and when to intervene. Be careful, though, not to protect your child from ever being frustrated. It would be possible for parents to arrange life so nicely for a child who is already of a mild temperament that he would not be getting a healthy share of frustration. Then he'll enter the next stage not knowing how to say no to himself or handle frustration. A child will not learn how to solve problems unless he has problems.

Know yourself. Some toddlers' behaviors push parents' anger buttons a lot, and some parents have very sensitive buttons. The combination of the tantrum-prone child and

My Child Behaves Best When:	My Child Behaves Worst When:
I'm attentive	Shopping in the afternoon
She's well rested	I'm too busy too long
He's held in a sling	There's too much commotion
She's busy	She's bored

a parent with a short fuse is at risk for major conflicts. You'll learn quickly how a mature respone to your child's tantrum can mean the difference between your child raging totally out of control and your child being normally frustrated. Identify which behaviors cause you to blow easily; you'll then know when to leap to your feet to save both of you from each other. Assess how you react to your toddler. If you typically regress to tantrum behavior yourself, seek professional help to get your buttons reset.

WHAT TO DO WHEN THE VOLCANO ERUPTS

Even after you do your best to create an attitude within your child and structure the environment in your home to prevent tantrums, they still occur. Don't take them personally. Normal tantrums are a result of your child's development and temperament, not of your parenting. Here's what to do when the little volcano blows, at home, in public, or at grandma's house.

Tantrums are due to frustration (your toddler is trying a complicated engineering feat and howls when it goes wrong), so don't ignore this need for help. Take this tantrum as an *opportunity to connect*: By helping your child out of a tight spot, you build authority and trust. Offer a helping hand, a comforting "It's OK," and direct his efforts toward a more manageable part of the task (for example, you slip the sock halfway onto the foot, and then he can pull it on all the way).

Sometimes children just need to blow off steam. You can help your child by verbalizing for him what he can't say himself: "You

---

Speak Your Child's Mind

As a connected parent, you usually know what's going through your child's mind. When you see a tantrum start, put it into words. A child who is losing it (or is about to) can calm down remarkably fast when she hears her *exact feelings* coming from your mouth. When this happens the tantrum ceases to be needed. For example, your child wants something (a story, the toy someone else has, to go outside...) *right now*. As the tantrum kicks in you calmly say "It's hard to wait. You wish we could do it [or get it, or go] *right now*." Hearing feelings being put into words is the best way for your child to learn how to put feelings into words.

---

are mad that Mommy won't let you have candy." Other times, when children have lost control, they want someone bigger and wiser to take hold of them lovingly and securely take charge. Try: "You're angry and I'm going to hold you until you get control of yourself because I love you." Soon the tantrum will fizzle and you will feel your flailing child melt into your arms as if thanking you for rescuing him from himself.

Feel your way through the tantrum. Avoid forceful restraint. If holding makes your child furious and escalates the tantrum, loosen your hold or quit holding. Your child needs support, not anger. (Forcefully holding on to your child when your child needs to release from you is controlling too much.)

The tantrum-throwing child under age two will most often need the holding approach. He can't talk about his problems.

Your strong arms in place around him give the message that since he's out of control you have stepped in to help him hold himself together. You may or may not be heard, but you can speak softly near his ear reassuring phrases like "Mama's here. I'll help you. Show me what you need," and so on. Don't coddle and don't allow his kicks and flails to hurt you. If you can't contain him enough and he does hurt you, calmly put him down next to you and stay as close as you can without letting him hurt you. When to hold the child and when to just be on standby is a tantrum-by-tantrum call.

Time-out the tantrum. If neither ignoring the tantrum nor comforting it seems appropriate, remove the child from the triggering circumstance and call for a time-out. For example, if your child throws a tantrum in the supermarket, calmly pick him up and retreat to a corner in the store or head for the car. (See "Time-out When You're Out," page 167.)

For tantrums at grandma's (often the ones that embarrass parents the most because it is in the presence of their own parents and in-laws that they feel the most scrutinized), it helps if you are able to share your tantrum strategy ahead of time so grandma knows not to sabotage your approach, and also so she knows you really *are* in charge of her grandchild and she can just relax and watch you parent. If might be similar to what she did when she was a younger mom, or it might be very different. But it will help your perspective on things if she says to you something like, "He's just like his dad. I had lots of days like this, and we both survived." Then you can both share a laugh and you may get to hear some wisdom from one who's been there.

HANDLING AND PREVENTING TANTRUMS IN OLDER CHILDREN

As a child nears three years of age, tantrums lessen because he now has the language to express himself, and he's busy developing in areas other than individuation (for example, his imagination is blossoming and he has more fears, therefore he *needs* the "giants" to keep him safe). Tantrums may reappear at age four with a surprising twist. A four-year-old is smarter, stronger, louder, and more adept at pushing parents' buttons. The child realizes he has come into his own power in the family, and that can be threatening to some parents. It is important not to squelch an emerging person by overreacting.

Give a positive message. Give your child a clear message of what you expect. Be positive and specific in your instructions: "I expect you to be polite at Grandma's. We can show her your new books and maybe she'll read one to you. After lunch, we'll go home." This is more meaningful to a child than "I won't tolerate tantrums, and I expect you to be good." You can't reason with a child during a tantrum, but you can before it occurs.

Give your child other outlets for emotional overload other than tantruming: "Use your words instead of your body to get what you want." Help him use his body positively — give him lots of opportunity for large motor activities and outdoor play. (Get an old mattress or a mini-trampoline to *bounce* on all day long.) Play lively music to dance to and have jumping contests. Encourage him to draw what he feels on a "tantrum tablet." After a tantrum, ask him to "draw angry pictures" about what he feels. You can do this yourself when you're angry and talk about what you're doing: "I'm drawing angry lines and angry faces!" What really helps is for your child to see you manage *your* temper tantrums. When you're angry, try lying facedown on your bed, kicking and hitting the bed. Or say "We're going on an 'angry walk.' Get in the stroller." If you are beginning to realize this is a problem area for you, now that you have little eyes and ears soaking up your every move, you will want to get help on managing your anger. Having children forces adults to take stock of their own emotional maturity. We've all been there to one degree or another, so don't be embarrassed to admit, even to yourself, that there are changes you would like to see take place in you, so you can be a calmer parent.

Don't reinforce tantrums. Don't let your child use a tantrum as a means to an end. If he knows that as soon as he gets within grabbing distance of the candy at the checkout counter in the supermarket all he has to do is pitch a fit and you'll give in to quiet him down, then he's already conditioned to begin his act as soon as you approach the counter. Next time, before you enter that high-risk area, explain, "We are not buying any candy, so it won't do any good to fuss. You can help Mommy put the groceries on the counter. Remember, we're buying frozen yogurt to have at home." A friend tells us she handles private and public out-of-control tantrums differently. In private, she becomes so bored by the tantrum that it soon stops. In public, she says sternly to the child, "You may not embarrass me" — and the child believes her.

Ignore it? Whether or not you ignore a tantrum should depend on what you think the cause is. If you judge that the child is pitching a fit to gain your attention, ignore it. By you not reinforcing tantrums, your child will get the message that this behavior is not acceptable: "It gets me nowhere, I might as well be my nice person." (Then be sure to reinforce the nice person.) If you're going to ignore the tantrum and walk away, leave your child with the message that you are available: "Eric, you must really be

Screaming

The part of a tantrum that bothers parents the most (and causes them to give in or get angry) is screaming. The key here is to not take the screaming personally. Take it for what it is — a verbal expression of explosive feelings. Screaming that is given into quickly turns into a tool for manipulation. We made a house rule: "You can only scream on the grass." A friend taught her toddler to do this by going outside with him and showing him how. Seeing his mother "screaming on the grass" made a lasting impression!

Nighttime is an especially vulnerable time for parents to feel powerless against screaming (for example, your two-year-old wants to nurse for the third time and you've decided to let dad take over). We tell parents they don't have to protect the child from his own screaming. He is choosing to scream and he can choose to stop. As long as the child is not left to scream alone, he has your support without your capitulation. He'll figure out how to stop the screaming.

angry. When you calm down, I will try to help." Then you walk away, though not far, and allow the child to regain his composure. Shouting "Shut up" and storming off closes the door to communication and escalates a tantrum.

Instead of walking away from the tantrum, you could try the home-base approach. Stay nearby the scene and keep busy: Read a book. Don't get drawn into the tantrum or start arguing. If the tantruming upsets your harmony or the child wants to get physical, you need to walk away. Remember, a tantrum will go on as long as it can hold an audience. Big audience reactions will be rewarded with encores. Sometimes, announcing "I'll be here when you're ready to calm down and talk" is enough to motivate the child into changing characters.

When a two-year-old goes out of control, you can usually physically take charge. This is not so with the four-year-old or older. He is now big enough to hurt you. You may feel like locking him in his room, but a safer option would be for you to lock yourself in your room until he is able to calm down. If you feel angry enough to hit your child, get

yourselves separated however you can. Some mothers have put a child in his room and have found that the child destroys property. If he destroys toys, remember they are his toys, and you will not be replacing them. If he destroys parts of the room (breaks a window, dents walls, and so on), he will be shocked at his own angry power the first time it happens. It will most likely not be repeated because it is so scary. He should be required to work off what it costs you for repairs. If this destructive behavior does happen again, you will need professional help to sort it all out. There is just too much anger there. A sudden onset of tantrums is a clue to put on your detective hat. There is likely to be a problem going on in your child that needs solving.

One mother we talked with, who is also a psychologist, said she had realized her large part in escalating tantrums. She'd keep talking, keep engaging the child in battle. What she learned was that she should have stopped talking and just done something, as suggested above, to bring the tantrum to a close.

6

Fathers as Disciplinarians

THE BASIC PRINCIPLES OF DISCIPLINE can be used equally by both moms and dads, but I have noticed that fathers and mothers approach discipline differently. Perhaps this is as it should be. This difference provides a balance in child rearing. The stereotypes are less defined today than in previous decades. Still there are specifically male traits that affect how fathers discipline children.

BECOMING A DAD: BILL'S STORY

Dads, let me share with you how I blew it as a disciplinarian with our first three children. Our first two came at a time when I was learning to be a doctor, and the third as I was getting a practice started. I bought into the philosophy of putting career pursuits far ahead of everything. Having grown up without a father, I had no model to show me the importance of the father in child rearing. Besides, Martha was such a good mother. I felt I didn't need to be available. As with many fathers, I planned to get involved when the boys were old enough to throw a football. Big mistake!

When one of our children misbehaved, I would either overreact or underreact, but Martha knew just what to do. Most of the time she reacted in the right way and got results. She had a handle on disciplining our children; I didn't. And because I didn't, she had to become the full-time correction officer as well as the chief nurturer. I realized also that she was a sensitive disciplinarian because she knew the children so well. She knew them because she was in touch with them. She nursed them, carried them, and responded sensitively to their cries. Not only did she know them, but they knew her too, and respected her wisdom. "How did you know that they were about to get into trouble?" I would ask Martha. "I just knew," she would reply. The light went on: "Not only does the parent develop the child, but the child develops the parent. Our children had helped Martha develop her sensitivity toward them. Meanwhile, I was losing at both ends. I wasn't around my children enough, so they didn't respond to me.

Lesson number one for fathers: In order to discipline your children, you have to *know* them. And to know them, you have to spend time with them. Except for breastfeeding, there is nothing about baby care

High Priority — High Yield

I once attended a seminar on time management where the speaker advised trimming obligations down to those that were high-priority, high-yield. After the seminar, I told the speaker he had just described the juggling act of parenting. Rid your agenda of low-priority, low-yield tasks that suck up your energy yet yield little return. Instead, concentrate on those tasks that give a good return on your investment of time.

that father can't be involved in. I came to realize that our babies needed what I had to offer as their father. Just being available to them as Dad, and to Martha as husband, would help.

But being available takes time. What about my profession? The turning point in my fathering came after several older fathers (on their second marriages) came in to my office with their wives for their newborns' checkups. Many expressed regrets that they hadn't been involved in their older children's lives. Now they had the time for these children, but the children didn't have the time for them. I wanted a "no regrets" old age. I imagined how I would feel when I was fifty and my children were grown. (At the time I didn't know that at age fifty I would still be fathering babies.) I didn't relish the idea of feeling "I should have done this" or "I should have done that." I decided to change. At first, I feared my career would stall, but then I realized that in my profession I could go back and restart the tape at any point, but the tape of parenting and childhood goes in only one direction — forward. Kids pass through each stage only once.

My children needed me, not my resume. They wanted and needed a father to wrestle with them and play with them. They needed a father's deeper voice to read them to sleep, not just to say a dutiful "good night." I turned my attention toward being a father — and a husband. I not only had to connect with my children, I had to reconnect with my wife. I freed up weekends and more evenings by turning down the position I had been offered of Chief Resident of Pediatrics at the Hospital for Sick Children in Toronto, Canada. We went camping a lot. We took up sailing. I got to know and enjoy our three boys and managed to convince Martha finally that we could have another baby. I was more involved this time, and it was better.

Then came our first daughter, Hayden, whose birth would change my life. This bundle of energy came wired differently from our other children. She craved being held, shunned any attempt to schedule feedings, and cried when put down. She inspired us to coin the term *high-need baby*. Father involvement with Hayden wasn't a choice, it was a necessity. Because she strongly objected to being put down, Martha needed me to be available to play "pass the baby." She was in our arms by day and in our bed by night. There were days when she nursed constantly. She craved skin-to-skin contact and sometimes fell asleep on my fuzzy chest and gave Martha a break. (We had not yet discovered "babywearing.") I grew to know her, and she grew to trust me. A paternal sensitivity was developing in me that I had never had before. This newfound sensitivity carried over to my relations with the other children and with my wife. When the father is doing what is needed, the whole family functions better. My being around and involved provided the framework for family discipline. By the time Hayden was three I realized what it takes for a father to become a disciplinarian: *A dad must first know his child before he can set limits for his child.*

There is an important difference between mothers and fathers, and our children profit from that difference. One of the myths of modern fatherhood is that fathers are portrayed as mere substitutes for mothers, pinch-hitting while mom is away. There is nothing optional about father involvement, nor is dad just a hairier version of mom. The father's input into his children's lives is different from the mother's; not less, different. Babies and families thrive on this difference. We thrived and added number five, Erin.

With baby number six, I made my fathering motto the U.S. Army slogan "Be all that you can be." Beginning at his birth, Matthew gave me the opportunity to be all that I could be as a father. Our birth attendant didn't make it to the birth in time, so I got to catch Matthew — an experience greater than being quarterback at the Super Bowl. That first touch from my quivering hands Matthew may never remember, but I shall never forget. I was hooked! We were buddies from birth.

Because we thought Matthew would be our last baby, I didn't want to miss anything. A few months after Matthew was born, I moved my pediatric practice temporarily into our home. (Actually, we turned part of our large garage into a pediatric office. My teenage patients called it "Dr. Bill's Garage and Body Shop.") This allowed me to be around Matthew when I was between patients. Sometimes after Martha had nursed Matthew I could "father-nurse" him by simply holding him or by carrying him around in a baby sling — opportunities to be close

When Kids Are Driving Mom Crazy

A sensitive husband once told me he made sure his wife kept herself happy so she didn't drive the kids crazy. Another dad said, "I try to keep my wife wrinkle free." Be tuned into when your wife needs help. For fear of shattering the supermom myth, women seldom confide their needs to their husbands. If "lose it" days are becoming more frequent for the queen of the castle, plot together to make some changes.

Get help for the queen. Hire a young teenager to help out during after-school hours and holidays. Teens are tolerant, cheap, and able to put on goofy acts that hold children's attention. This takes some of the pressure off mom. Give your children a clear view of what is expected of them. And follow through on what you expect. A little marriage training early on works nicely here: "I expect you to be kind to the woman I love." (See also "Holding a Family Meeting," page 179.)

to Matthew that it took me six children to discover. I knew that Matthew sensed my body was different. As he lay in the "warm fuzzy" position, his ear was over my heart, his chest and tummy were draped over mine, and his body moved rhythmically up and down with my breathing while my hands embraced his soft little body. My breath warmed his scalp as he nestled under my chin; he was discovering a warm corner in this different "womb."

As I practiced these male touches, Matthew got used to my body: the different breathing, sound, walk, touch, and deeper voice. In fact, in the "neck nestle" position, fathers have the edge over mothers in that their voice box structures vibrate more noticeably, and babies can feel these vibrations against their head. These touches are not better than mothers', just different. Matthew thrived on that difference. He liked being in my presence, like a child given two nicely different desserts. Matthew's response to my fathering and my amazement at my own feelings helped me discover a new level of fathering and new value in my contribution to parenting.

Not only was my newly discovered aptitude for fathering good for Matthew and me, it was good for Martha. In the past, because I had not hung out enough to learn baby comforting, Martha would get exhausted from doing it alone. Now, as I became available as a baby comforter, she was more willing to release him to me. She liked watching me with Matthew — she sensed that my tenderness toward Matthew underlined my commitment to her. She liked having little breaks every now and then to care for herself. This helped her to be a better mother for all our children and a happier wife for me. Even our sex life improved.

After a year, I closed my home office and moved into a nearby medical building. But even though I worked outside the home, my priorities were inside the home. When away from Matthew, I thought about him. When we were together, we were truly together. My bond extended naturally to the other children and forced me to put balance in my life, giving priority to my family above the demands of my pediatric practice, teaching, and writing. When outside commitments competed for my time, I felt stretched. But my attachment acted like a

Salvaging a Bad Situation

Kids make inconvenient and costly mistakes, and many of these are beyond parental control. But you can control your reactions to these misdeeds. A week after Peter started driving, he stepped on the gas pedal instead of the brake and demolished part of the garage door frame and the car fender. My first reaction was to think of the cost and inconvenience. Peter saw my anger, which further saddened an already dejected child. In order to salvage some of his feelings, I told Peter how happy I was that he wasn't hurt and that he'd had his first accident in the garage rather than on the highway. Three years later Hayden took out the frame on the other side of the garage door. But this time I was a bit wiser and was able to look at a negative situation in a positive light. Instead of focusing on the damage, I focused on her, saying, "I'm just glad you weren't hurt. . . ." Seeing that her father was more concerned with her than the damage reassured her about what was more important to me. After all, the damage was already done. I couldn't change that, but I did get something in exchange for my $250 insurance deductible: self-respect and a stronger relationship with my daughter. And both children were helped to appreciate the fine art of maneuvering a vehicle by paying for half the repairs.

strong rubber band pulling me back home. The rubber band could not break because I never allowed it to be stretched that far. It's amazing how one little kid can change a grown man.

Matt and I are still incredibly close. He is nine years old at this writing. The attachment continues. As Matt develops from one stage to another, my development as a parent — and as a person — goes up a notch. When he began Little League, I wanted to be involved, so I signed on as coach. When he entered scouting, I volunteered to be the scoutmaster. These are roles that I might not have found the time for if I hadn't been hooked on my kids. And my career hasn't stalled one bit.

My kids are not finished with me yet. We have added two more children to the Sears family pack. My eight children are training me to be a better person and father — because I'm there for them. Attachment fathering pays off; in disciplining children, we become disciplined persons.

Discipline comes more easily to an attached father. It seems less strained and more intuitive. I can guide our children because I know them. They obey me because they trust me. My learning process as a dad has convinced me that many fathers have a tough time with discipline because they are not connected to their kids. Unconnected kids may obey out of duty or fear, but they don't have a dad to be close to and trust.

Attachment fathering *opens up* a dad to his child and vice versa. I notice a difference in disciplining Matt. We connect during each interaction. For example, when I ask him to do something, he looks me straight in the eye and says, "Yes, Dad" (occasionally "Aww, Dad"). The combination of eye contact and direct address personalizes his response. This reflects a mutual

trust between us. Matt trusts that my request is right, and I trust he will obey. Matt wants to please me. When I'm correcting him, he understands the authority in my body language and tone of voice. Harsh words and heavy hands are never necessary to correct Matt. How much of this is his temperament and how much is due to our right start together I will never know. But what I do know is this style of fathering gives me a handle on discipline I did not have before. As Matthew progressed from "Dada" to "Daddy" to "Dad," our relationship grew more valuable.

I realize that because family and career situations are variable, many dads are not able to rearrange their lives around their children. But whatever path you take, take time to get connected with your baby. Disciplining your child will be much easier.

EIGHT TIPS TO HELP FATHERS BECOME DISCIPLINARIANS

Fathers become disciplinarians in much the same way that mothers do — by knowing their child. The more we are exposed to both well- and poorly behaved children, the more we realize that fathers don't start becoming disciplinarians early enough.

1. Start early. Spending time with your baby will pay off as the years go by. Get connected to your baby, and disciplining the child she becomes will follow naturally.

2. Start at the bottom. Most men who climb the corporate ladder work their way into a position of authority by beginning at the bottom. Fathering works the same way. "But what has diapering to do with disci-

A Surprise Cleanup

Dads, here's a tip for easier living — with your children and with your wife. Your children are watching television after dinner. You sit down next to them and offer a suggestion: "Mom needs a break, so she's going for a walk. How about if we all work together and clean up the kitchen while she's gone? If everyone helps, we can finish quickly and surprise her." Everybody benefits from this plan: Your wife gets a clean kitchen, and the kids and you get a chance to spend some time together and share the fun of pleasing mom.

pline?" you may wonder. Baby care helps you learn more about your baby. Change your baby, bathe your baby, dress your baby, play with your baby. Every interaction with your baby helps you learn to read her. Over the first two or three years your baby will need around five thousand diaper changes. If you change diapers 20 percent of the time, that's a thousand chances to interact with your baby. Initially, even with Matthew, managing a squirmy body and smelly bottom was not my thing. Eventually, I discovered that diapering could be a learning experience for the baby and me. I was starting "at the bottom." I had to come up with connecting ways to hold baby's attention and learn to convey softly a "father in charge" message.

3. Be trustworthy. In giving talks on discipline, I have noticed that dads seem to have more concerns and more problems with discipline than do moms. One evening I was giving a talk on discipline to a group of new dads. When I asked what they most

wanted to learn about discipline, they responded, "To be an authority figure in our home. I want my child to look up to me with respect and obey me." I agree that fathers should be authority figures. But just because you're the man of the house doesn't automatically mean you are going to get the respect you want. Some dads believe that a child must obey simply because "I am the dad, you're the child." It's not that simple. A child will obey people he trusts. But trust doesn't come automatically with the title of father. It has to be earned. With true authority, a child obeys because he *wants* to, not just because he *has* to. To whom would you be more loyal, the boss you trust or the boss you fear?

So how do you get a child to trust you as an authority figure? It took me several kids to learn this basic principle of discipline. *Before I could become an authority figure, my*

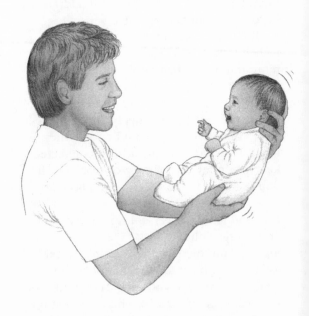

Playing with your baby helps you get to know your baby.

Emotional Abuse Turnaround

Kandis was a high-need baby from birth. She cried a lot, was hard to console, became irritated at the slightest setback, and withdrew from cuddling by arching her back. She was a restless and unpredictable sleeper, and she resisted any attempts at scheduling. Not only was she a tense baby, but her irritability infected her parents' marriage so that they became increasingly irritated at each other. Mark, the father, would make comments such as, "Yeah, she sure isn't my favorite child." Or he would call her "cry baby." He seldom held her and would never kiss her or even talk to her in a positive manner. It was all negative attention. Mark never smiled or laughed with her, and when exasperated, he would sit her on the couch and angrily tell her to "shut up." By the time Kandis was two, she was a difficult child, yet her nurturing and patient mother had hung in with her the whole time. It's unfortunate that she didn't call a halt to the abusive treatment sooner.

I met with Mark for a father-to-father rap session and impressed upon him how high-need babies are ultrasensitive and pick up the prevailing vibrations coming from their parents. Because Mark interpreted Kandis's behavior as negative, he reflected this back to her and she became more negative in his presence. I suggested that for the next two weeks he should try giving her nothing but positive attention. Mark was skeptical, but he agreed that something had to change. Here is the progress report I received from his wife: "His efforts were strained at first. I could tell it wasn't easy for him. But Kandis picked up on it right away and returned the positive attention. Believe me, the change in her happened almost overnight, from whining, lethargic, and sickly to happy, bubbly, laughing, silly, and healthy. She gained almost three pounds in one month. People would say things like, 'Does she do anything else besides smile all day?' or 'She sure is a happy kid.' The good feelings snowballed. The more Kandis smiled at Daddy, the more sincere and affectionate Daddy became. Kandis sure loves her daddy now and Daddy definitely loves her. Mark is actually a sensitive man. He thought he was doing the right thing by being tough. He doesn't like to admit he was wrong, but now he knows the loving approach is better."

children first had to trust me to be available to them. This means I had to get to know them — touch their needs, share their triumphs. By becoming an involved father you begin teaching your baby to trust you.

4. Provide structure. From nine months to two years, babies' drive to explore exceeds their mental ability to contain themselves. Impulsive behaviors, such as yanking lamp cords, darting into streets in pursuit of a ball, and climbing up on counters to explore cabinets are all part of the normal behavior of growing toddlers. Father helps provide the framework that contains a child's impulsive behavior. Children want

Qualities Desired in Child	How Do You Model These Qualities?
• trust	Keep the promises you make to your child.
• sensitivity	Show you care when little bodies or feelings get hurt.
• honesty	"Yes, Officer, I was speeding."
• healthy sexuality	Be kind to your child's mother.
• respect for authority and elders	(See "honesty," above) — "Grandmother, can I help you?"
• self-control	"I can wait a year for that new car."
• sense of humor	Laugh at your own mistakes.

and need limits set by a person whom they trust, one in authority. When you provide structure in a child's life, the child feels more secure because you channel her energies in a meaningful direction. As former Philadelphia Eagles coach Dick Vermeil once said concerning why some players show more discipline on the field than others, "Coaching begins at home."

5. Be a role model. Dads, remember, you are bringing up someone else's future husband or wife, mother or father. The attitudes you instill in your baby and child are the building blocks for the adult that person will become. Children learn by example. The best way to build character is to model the qualities you want to see in your children. I found it helpful to list those qualities that I wanted to model for my children. When I made such a list, I realized that there were flaws in the model I presented to my children. I couldn't model what I didn't do. As I went down the list of values and related these to an average day with my children, I realized how often I didn't reflect these attitudes myself. This re-

alization taught me a valuable lesson: *In order to discipline my children, I had to discipline myself.*

6. Become involved in your child's activities. Dads, to know and enjoy your child, join your child's team. Don't be a distant dad, be a dugout dad. Volunteer to coach your child's favorite sport, or try a stint as a scoutmaster. "But sports are not my thing," you say, "and I don't know anything about scouting." You don't have to be an expert, you just have to be there. Besides, you're guaranteed to be smarter and more skilled than the kids. Through my experiences as a Little League baseball coach and as a scoutmaster, I've learned more about kids in general, and my child in particular, than I did in all the psychology lectures I attended in medical school.

Consider what your child learns in a team sport: success and failure, strikeouts and home runs, pulling up a mate, pulling himself up after a put-down (or put-out), teamwork, starting at the bottom and working his way up the batting order, how to deal with his own and someone else's mis-

Daddy-Daughter Date

Fathers, if you have a preteen daughter, the adolescent years are soon to come. Those will be years when your daughter will gravitate toward her friends and away from you. Yet they will also be a time when she will need your support. To prevent a distance from developing between you, try this preventive medicine: When your daughter is around ten years of age (or even younger), start a custom I call a daddy-daughter date. Have an occasional "date" with your daughter, time together where she feels special and has your undivided attention. This is a time for one-on-one communication and shared enjoyment. Be sure to use this time strictly for being together and not for correction. This is a time to laugh, to listen, and to connect with your daughter, especially if the two of you have become distant. In fact, these special times work well for any child at any age.

Dads, a word of caution: Don't let a daddy-daughter date substitute for day-to-day come-what-may activities with your daughter. It's an addition to, not a substitute for daily fathering. The date won't work if it's the only time you want to "really talk." Spend some time with your daughter: Go to parks, play catch, play board games, play dolls, wash the car, shop and run errands, get gifts for Mom together. You will get used to relating closely with a female child, and she with a quality male.

Daddy-daughter date.

Gender Differences in Discipline

Mothers and fathers often approach discipline differently — not better or worse, just differently. If used wisely, this difference is good for kids. Moms and dads should complement each other's discipline, not compete to be "right." It's a question of balance.

When toddlers begin to explore their environment, mothers tend to be protectors, and fathers become encouragers. Dad offers a challenging "Climb higher." Mom adds a protecting "Be careful." When toddler wakes up at night (for the third time) Dad suggests letting her fuss for a while to try to resettle herself, while mother goes to comfort her. Dads encourage independence, moms ease fears. (In some families, these roles may be reversed.) Tracey and Tom are aware of these differences and work hard to make them an asset in their family. They realize that they need each other's balance, as does their child. Their three-year-old, Nathan, is an adventurous child whose desires to accomplish a feat exeed his capabilities. He is always getting stuck in precarious situations and fussing for

help. Tracey and Tom found themselves disagreeing on when to help Nathan and when to let him work himself out of his predicament. Finally, they agreed that when Nathan was stuck they would ask him, "Do you need me?"

Mothers delve into their children's feelings, trying to understand their children's viewpoint. When a child has a problem, moms are geared toward understanding the process that led to the problem; dads want to rush in and fix it. Mothers tend to ramble and repeat; fathers are more concerned with results, use fewer words in discipline requests, and are quicker to pull rank when psychology isn't working. I witnessed this example: Kyle was riding his bike without a helmet. Mother sat down next to him and launched into a long explanation of why it was unsafe not to wear a helmet. Father, seeing that this dialogue was getting nowhere, walked up to Kyle and respectfully yet authoritatively said, "Kyle, you know the helmet law. You didn't wear your helmet. Now put away your bike for a week."

---

takes, how to win and lose gracefully, and how to get along in a group. This is baseball. This is discipline. This is life.

7. Model healthy sexuality. Dads, the first male your son or daughter meets is you. In fact, studies suggest that fathers, more than mothers, affect a child's attitudes toward sexuality. Babies and young children identify readily with mother from birth, but *how* they experience their relationship to

father is crucial to the development of sexual identity.

Boys need a father who is involved in order to value their own masculinity. A father who is available and who enjoys being a man gives his son a healthy sexual role model to follow. Studies show that a boy needs to perceive his father as an active disciplinarian and family decision maker in order to develop a healthy male identity. Paternal behavior that is macho without showing tenderness is associated with non-masculine behavior in sons. And remember, dads: It isn't how involved *you* feel that counts — it's how your son *perceives* you. You have to show and tell your love.

Paternal nurturance is also important for your daughter. It contributes to her enjoying being a woman. Fathers give daughters their first experiences relating to the opposite sex. When father is "out of the loop," passive, insensitive, and uninvolved in family life, the daughter misses out on early lessons about balanced male-female relationships. She won't feel comfortable talking with boys or, later, young men, and they will sense her discomfort. She is at risk for problems in relationships with men. In her search for love, she may enter a promiscuous or abusive relationship or an unhappy marriage. Dads, remember that your daughter will at some time in her life seek out a male model. Be that model for her.

One of the most powerful influences on children's sexual identity is the way they perceive the relationship between their parents. If a man is loving toward his wife, supportive, and available, the daughter is more likely to value her own femininity and the mothering role. She feels, "Dad respects Mom for being a woman and a mother." Dad's attitude toward his wife also shapes his son's attitude toward women. As one woman whose marriage was disintegrating said bitterly, "Our marriage is failing because my husband's father didn't do his job." (See also Chapter 18, "Building Healthy Sexuality.")

8. Be a father *and* a provider. For most men, being a good provider is crucial to their masculinity and feelings about themselves as dads. This is what drives them to work long hours, even if their families

---

Dad's Traveling — A Survival Guide

Parenting is a two-person job. Single parents survive by having a support system in place. In a two-parent family children often misbehave when one parent is away. Because the family equilibrium is upset, children will tend to be defiant and show mood swings and sleep disturbances. Poor behavior occurs because the parent in charge is unsupported and the children pick up on the anxiety. Children who are the most sensitive to change are the ones most likely to misbehave when dad (or mom) is away. To help your children thrive and the at-home mate survive, have a contingency plan for these times. Give "special" responsibilities for which there will be special rewards. If you have a strong-willed child, capitalize on this trait by putting him in charge of some extra daily duties. The parent traveling can phone home each day to monitor the children's behavior. To help the at-home parent cope, plan ahead for fun things to do — time at the park and other out-of-home activities. Inviting friends over provides adult companionship for the at-home parent, easing the stress of overload.

---

would be happier with more of *them* and less of *things.* (A note to wives: It may help bring your husband home more if you tell him this in a tactful, loving way.) Men who are the sole wage earners in the family may feel heavy pressure, especially when double-income families are the neighborhood norm. (This may be changing. A 1994 study showed that for the first time in thirty-three years, the *single-income household* is the fastest-growing group in the U.S. population. Lower interest rates have made this possible for many families, together with the growing realization that it does make a difference to have one parent at home full-time.) If you must work long hours, try to incorporate your fathering into your work. Do some of your work at home. Take your child to work. It's healthy for her to learn about your work, and when she understands what you are doing while you're away from home, it is easier for her to accept your absence.

The media has typically portrayed fathers as economic providers who are inept, bumbling, and optional around their home and family. Even though some of these images are still around, I now see television commercials and cartoon strips showing fathers bathing babies and taking charge of households. The media is enhancing Dad's image in the nineties. I believe that fathers finally are realizing the rewards of investing themselves in their children.

Fathers Provide Balance

Dads, to help you understand why your wife may have difficulty saying no to your toddler, consider this analogy. Suppose your wife is browsing in a "parenting store" and she finds an elixir called Attachment Parenting Tonic that, if used properly, will make parents sensitive, giving, and intuitive toward their baby. So you both take this tonic and become very giving persons. But there is a warning label on the bottle that says: "When used, some parents, especially mothers, may develop side effects after the first year that include: overgiving leading to burnout, and inability to say no, especially in circumstances that the toddler finds particularly pleasurable, such as frequent night nursing."

Treatment consists of father sharing baby care when his wife is overgiving, especially during high-need times, and becoming a wise no-sayer when mother is in over her head and exhausted. Yet don't worry; side effects are more common with the first child, and less so with subsequent children. Besides, these side effects are temporary and easily remedied. The effects of not using this elixir are much more difficult to deal with, and the effects on the child can last a lifetime.

Self-Esteem: The Foundation of Good Behavior

SELF-ESTEEM IS YOUR CHILD'S PASSPORT to lifetime mental health and social happiness. It's the foundation of a child's well-being and a key to success as an adult. At all ages, how you feel about yourself affects how you act. Think about a time when you were feeling really good about yourself. You probably found it much easier to get along with others and feel good about them.

Self-image is how one perceives oneself. The child looks in the mirror and likes the person he sees. He looks inside himself and is comfortable with the person he sees. He must think of this self as being someone who can make things happen, who feels good much of the time, and who is worthy of love. Parents are the main source of a child's sense of self-worth. One of your jobs as a disciplinarian is to nurture your child's positive self-image and help it grow so that he can tackle life's setbacks as well as appreciate its joys.

Lack of a good self-image very often leads to behavior problems. Most of the behavioral problems that I see for counseling come from a poor sense of worth in parents as well as children. Why is one person a de-

light to be with while another always seems to drag you down? How people value themselves, get along with others, perform at school, achieve at work, and relate in marriage all stem from the strength of their self-image.

Healthy self-esteem doesn't mean being narcissistic or arrogant; it means having a realistic understanding of one's strengths and weaknesses, enjoying the strengths and working on the problem areas. Because there is such a strong parallel between how a person feels about herself and how a person acts, helping your child build self-confidence is vital to discipline.

TEN WAYS TO HELP CHILDREN BUILD SELF-CONFIDENCE

Throughout life your child will be exposed to positive influences (builders) and negative influences (breakers). Parents can expose their child to builders and help him work through the breakers.

Putting Humpty-Dumpty Back Together Again

You spend the early years building your child's self-confidence. You spend the later years protecting it. Many thin-skinned children need protection from situations they find overwhelming. I was examining five-year-old Thomas for his school-entry physical. Thomas was a sensitive child whose mother had spent years helping him build a strong sense of self-esteem. We were engaged in a philosophical discussion of the long-term benefits of attachment parenting, and Thomas was understandably bored. He began hanging on my scale — an expensive scale that is built into the top of the examining table. My first thought was for the safety of my table. To me, it was more at risk than Thomas, so I asked rather firmly, "Thomas, would you please stop hanging on the scale?" Just as Thomas was about to crumble from my unintended put-down, his mother interjected a saving ". . . because you're so strong." She knew how to get behind the eyes of her child.

1. Practice Attachment Parenting

Put yourself in the place of a baby who spends many hours a day held in her mother's arms, worn in a sling, breastfed on cue, and having her cries sensitively responded to. How do you imagine this baby feels?

This baby feels loved; this baby feels valuable. Ever had a special day when you got lots of strokes and were showered with praise? You probably felt like queen for a day, and hopefully you behaved accord-

ingly. The infant on the receiving end of this high-touch style of parenting develops self-worth. She likes what she feels.

Responsiveness **is the key to infant self-value.** Baby gives a cue, for example, crying to be fed or comforted. Mother responds promptly and consistently. As this cue-response pattern is repeated thousands of times during the first year, baby learns that her cues have meaning: "Someone listens to me; therefore, I am worthwhile." A stronger self emerges.

Of course, you can't always respond promptly or consistently, and you will have days when you are short on patience or self-esteem. It's the predominant pattern that counts. Babies pick out the prevailing parenting style and form impressions. As your baby grows older it actually becomes important for her development to learn to deal with healthy frustration, as that will teach her to accommodate change. The important thing is that you are there for her; that's the message on which your baby will build her sense of self.

The confidence-building aspects that result from attachment parenting pay off especially with high-need babies. Because of these infants' more intense demands, they are at higher risk of receiving negative responses. When attachment parenting produces sensitivity between connected parents and high-need babies, the babies learn to see themselves in a good light.

Because of responsive nurturing, the connected baby knows what to expect. He feels that he has control over his environment. The unconnected baby, on the other hand, is confused. If her needs are not met and her cues unanswered, she may feel that signals are not worth giving. This leads her to conclude, "I'm not worthwhile. I'm at the mercy of others, and there's nothing I can do to reach them."

We emphasize the importance of early nurturing because during the first two years the brain is growing very fast. This is the period when a child develops *patterns of associations* — mental models of the way things work. The developing mind is like a file drawer. In each file is a mental picture of a cue given along with the expected response. After a certain interaction, the mind stores a mental image of what happened. For example, a baby raises her arms and a parent responds by picking her up. Repetition deepens these patterns in the baby's mind, and eventually emotions, positive or negative, become associated with them. A file drawer full of mostly positive feelings and images leads to a feeling of "rightness." A sense of well-being becomes part of the baby's self.

Infants who get used to the feeling of well-being they get from attachment parenting spend the rest of their lives working to keep this feeling. Because they have so much practice at feeling good, they can regain this right feeling after temporary interruptions. These secure persons cope better with life's setbacks because they are motivated to repair their sense of well-being, which has become integrated into their sense of self. They may fall down a lot, but they always wind up back on their feet. This concept is especially true for a child who is handicapped or who seems to come into this world relatively short-changed in natural talents. Children who do not have this early sense of well-being struggle to find it, but they are unsure of what they are looking for because they don't know how it feels. This explains why some babies who get attachment parenting in the early years manage well despite an unsettled childhood

because of family problems. Consider the famous case of Baby Jessica, the two-year-old who was taken from the familiar and nurturing home of her adopting parents, whom she had known since birth, and given to her biological parents, who were strangers to her. She is likely to thrive because she entered this situation with a strong sense of well-being created by good early nurturing. She will spend the rest of her life maintaining that feeling despite the trauma she endured.

Playing catch-up. "But what if I didn't practice all those attachment styles of parenting?" you may wonder. Don't be too hard on yourself. Babies are resilient, and, of course, it's never too late to start building up your child's self-image. This kind of nurturing cements together the blocks of self-esteem and can also repair them. Still, the earlier the cement is applied, the smoother it goes on and the stronger it sticks. (See "Reconnecting," page 32.)

2. Improve Your Own Self-Confidence

Parenting is therapeutic. In caring for your child you often heal yourself. A mother with a high-need baby in our practice once declared, "My baby brings out the best and the worst in me." If there are problems in your past that affect your present parenting, get psychological help and confront them.

Heal your past. A child's self-esteem is acquired, not inherited. Certain parenting traits and certain character traits, such as anger and fearfulness, are learned in each generation. Having a baby gives you a chance to become the parent you wish you had had. If you have a poor self-image, especially if you feel part of the cause is how

To Tease or Not to Tease

Fairly often I referred to our oldest daughter as "our live-in help." I thought this teasing was cute. Hayden didn't. I meant it as light family humor; Hayden took it as a heavy put-down. Since the humor was directed at Hayden, her feelings counted more than mine. Hayden finally had to tell me, "Dad, you've said this many times, and each time I let you know I don't like it. Please stop." When you think you are joking around, be sensitive to which lines are fun and which ones touch a nerve or aggravate a child. Don't persist with something that's not funny to both of you. It's rude and hurtful.

While you can't (and shouldn't) protect your child from all the bombardments to his self-esteem, you can make your home a *safe zone.* Don't allow siblings to tease each other. Older brothers can be ruthless toward the youngest who happens to be a girl. Act as a buffer against adults and neighborhood kids who come into your home and, by teasing with words or tone of voice, make your child feel small inside. Establish the reputation in the neighborhood that teasing is not allowed at your house. (See related section on handling put-downs, page 205.)

you were parented (it usually is), take steps to heal yourself and break the family pattern. Try this exercise (therapists call this "passing on the best, discarding the rest"): First, list the specific things your parents did to build your self-image. Second, list what, in the parenting you received, may have weakened your self-image. Now resolve to emulate the good things your parents did and avoid the rest. If you find it difficult to follow through with this exercise on your own, get help from a professional. Both you and your child will benefit.

Don't be too hard on your parents. They probably did the best they could given their circumstances and the prevailing advice of the times. I remember once hearing a grandmother say to a mother, "I was a good mother to you. I followed exactly the schedule the doctor gave me." This new mother felt that some of her present problems stemmed from the rigid scheduling that she endured when she was a baby. She was determined to learn to read her baby's cues. I reminded her not to blame her mother because the prevailing parenting practice at the time was to follow the "experts'" advice on child rearing. The mother of the nineties, however, is more comfortable becoming the expert on her own child.

Polish your mirror. No one can put on a happy face all the time, but a parent's unhappiness can transfer to a child. Your child looks to you as a mirror for his own feelings. If you are worried, you can't reflect good feelings. In the early years, a child's concept of self is so intimately tied up with the mother's concept of herself that a sort of mutual self-esteem building goes on. What image do you reflect to your child? She will see through a false facade to the troubled person beneath. Matthew, on a fill-in-the-blanks tribute to his mother, wrote: "I like being with my mother most when *she's happy.*" Children translate your unhappiness with yourself to mean unhappiness with them. Even infants know they are supposed to please their parents. As they get older, they may even come to feel responsible for their parents' happiness: "If

*Each day remind yourself,
What my baby needs
most is a happy mother.*

my parents are not content, then I must not be good (or good enough)." If you are experiencing depression or anxiety, seek help so that you can resolve these feelings before they affect your child.

Martha notes: *Shortly after the birth of our eighth child, I was overwhelmed with two babies in diapers and the needs of four older children at home. My stress was reflected in my face; I was often not a happy person. Fortunately, I recognized what I was showing of myself to my children. I did not want my children growing up believing that mothering is no fun or that they caused me to be unhappy. I sought help, fixed my inner feelings, and polished my mirror so that my children could see a better image of themselves.*

3. Be a Positive Mirror

Much of a child's self-esteem comes not only from what the child perceives about herself but from how she thinks others perceive her. This is especially true of pre-schoolers, who learn about themselves from their parents' reactions. Do you reflect positive or negative images to your child? Do you give her the idea that she's fun to be with? That her opinions and desires matter to you? That her behavior pleases you?

When you give your child positive reflections, he learns to think well of himself. He will also willingly rely on you to tell him when his behavior is not pleasing. This becomes a *discipline tool.* "All I have to do is look at him a certain way, and he stops misbehaving," said one mother. She had saturated her child's self-awareness with positive feelings, and the youngster was used to the way he felt, being on the receiving end of these strokes. When the mother flashed a negative reflection, the child didn't like the feeling it produced. He changed his behavior quickly to regain his sense of well-being.

Be realistic. You can't be up and smiling all the time and still be human. Your child should know that parents have down days, too. Children can see through fake cheerfulness. Your sensitivity toward him will increase his sensitivity toward you, and someday he may be the one lifting your self-confidence. (See chart on page 96.)

4. Play with Your Child

You will learn a lot about your child — and yourself — during play. Playtime gives your child the message "You are worth my time. You are a valuable person." Children learn through play. Instead of viewing playtime as a chore (and sending your child that message), use it to make an investment in your child's behavior.

Let your child initiate the play. A valuable learning principle that parents should keep in mind is this: *An activity initiated by the child holds the child's attention longer than one suggested by the adult playmate.* More learning takes place when the child chooses what to do. Child-initiated play also increases self-esteem:

Positive Reflections	Negative Reflections
sustained eye contact, smiles, holding and cuddling baby	short glances, frowns, preoccupation with your own thoughts
wearing baby	leaving baby to lie alone for long periods
having fun with diaper changes	disgust at diapering
feeding on cue	rigid feeding schedules
napping and sleeping with baby	leaving baby to fall asleep alone
reading stories to baby	preoccupied with having a perfect house
baby in arms or parent on floor, laughing with the child	uninterested holding patterns, too serious, sullen
continual hugs and kisses as child grows	discourage show of affection
verbal encouragement	distant toward child, verbal put-down
frequent passing-by touches	infrequent physical contact
always using eye contact to connect	unable to make eye contact
What Child Feels When She Receives Positive Reflections	**What Child Feels When She Receives Negative Reflections**
I'm valuable.	I'm not important.
I'm fun to spend time with.	I'm boring.
I'm glad I'm me.	What's wrong with me?
My caregiver likes me.	My caregiver would rather do something else.
Mom and Dad are glad to have me around.	I'm on my own, I'm not good enough.
I'm excited about life.	I'm lost and terrified.

"Dad likes to do the things I do!" Of course, you may be thinking, "Oh, no, not the block game *again!*" or "We've read that story twenty times!" That's the ordeal of parenting. You'll get bored with *The Cat in the Hat* long before your child does. If you want to bring something new to the same old play activity, add your own new twists as the play continues. Stop to talk about the book: "What would you do if the Cat in the Hat came to our door?" Or look for an alternative way of seeing an old toy: "Let's turn this block tower into a parking garage."

Make your child feel special. During play, focus your attention on your child. If your body is with your child but your mind is at work, your child will sense that you have tuned out, and neither one of you benefits from the time together. Your child loses the value of your being with her, and she concludes that she is not important. You lose the opportunity to learn about and enjoy your child — and to relearn how to play. I remember the fun six-month-old Matthew and I had in our "play circle." I sat him in front of me facing me with a few favorite toys (mine and his) and made a circle around him with my legs. This space contained him and provided support in case he, as a beginning sitter, started to topple sideways. Matthew had my undivided atten-

tion. He felt special and so did I. Making all those goofy baby noises is fun.

Parents need play. As a busy person, I had a hard time getting down to a baby's level and enjoying unstructured, seemingly unproductive play. After all, I had so many "more important" things on my agenda. Once I realized how much we both could benefit, this special time became meaningful. Play became therapeutic for me. I needed some time away from my adult preoccupations to focus on this important little person who was, without realizing it, teaching me to relax. Play helped me to get to know Matthew, his temperament, for instance, and his capabilities at each stage of development. The child reveals himself to the parent — and vice versa — during play; the whole relationship benefits greatly. Playtime puts us on our child's level, helping us

---

Do You Owe Your Child Self-Esteem?

No discipline book would be worth its price without a section on self-esteem. Yet we fear that parents misunderstand the meaning of this concept and feel that this is one more thing they are required to give their child along with regular meals and a warm winter jacket. They guard against anything that may undercut self-esteem — to the point where it becomes ridiculous. ("Oh, Billy, you don't really sing flat. You're just tonally challenged.") They measure self-esteem daily, as one might take a temperature. ("Julie's self-esteem is low today. Her big brother beat her at checkers last night.")

Every infant whose needs are met has self-esteem built in. Like an arborist

caring for a tree, your job is to nurture what's there, do what you can to structure your child's environment so that she grows strong and straight, and avoid whittling away at the tender branches. You can't build your child's self-esteem compliment by compliment, activity by activity. Parents are already overloaded with guilt because they may not be doing enough to foster their child's self-worth. You don't need a degree in psychology to raise a confident child. Much of parenting is easy and fun. Hold your baby a lot, respond sensitively to her needs, enjoy your baby. Then sit back and enjoy the person whose self-esteem is developing naturally.

get behind the eyes and into the mind of our child. Take time to enjoy the simple pleasures of play.

Play is an investment. You may feel that you are "wasting time" stacking blocks when you could be "doing something" instead. Many adults struggle to let go of their grown-up agenda. Of course you don't have to play all day long; nor will your child want you to. After eighteen months your child will need you less and less. Think of it this way: You are doing the most important job in the world, raising a human being. What may seem like a meaningless activity to you means a lot to your baby. Consider playtime one of your best investments. The more interest you show in doing things with your baby early on, the more interest your child will have in doing things with you when he's older. As your child grows, you can involve him in your play and your work, since being with you is the best reward. (See related topic, "Helping Your Child Play Alone," page 45).

5. Address Your Child by Name

What's in a name? The person, the self — little or big. I can still remember my grandfather impressing on me the value of using and remembering peoples' names. This lesson has proved profitable. One year I was a premed student competing with a bunch of marketing majors for a summer sales job. After I landed the job I inquired why I, though less qualified, had been hired. "Because you remembered and used the names of all of your interviewers," I was told. Addressing your child by name, especially when accompanied by eye contact and touch, exudes a "you're special" message.

Beginning an interaction by using the other person's name opens doors, breaks barriers, and even softens corrective discipline.

Children learn to associate how you use their name with the message you have and the behavior you expect. Parents often use a child's nickname or first name only in casual dialogue: "Jimmy, I like what you are doing." They beef up the message by using the full name to make a deeper impression, "James Michael Sears, stop that!" One child we've heard about refers to his whole name as his "mad name" because that's what he hears when his parents are angry at him. We have noticed that children with self-confidence more frequently address their peers and adults by name or title. Their own self-esteem allows them to be more direct in their communication with others. As I am writing this section, two-year-old Lauren dashes by my desk chirping "Hi, Dad!" The addition of "Dad" impressed me more than an impersonal "Hi!" A school-age child who is comfortable addressing adults by name will be better able to ask for help when needed.

6. Practice the Carryover Principle

As your child gets older, encourage her talents. She can do well at something, whether as a two-year-old who packs exceptional pretend picnics or as a ten-year-old who loves ballet. Over the years, we've noticed a phenomenon we call the carryover principle: Enjoying one activity boosts a child's self-image, and this carries over into other endeavors. One of our sons is a natural athlete, but he wasn't interested in academics. Operating on the carryover principle, we encouraged his enjoyment of athletics while supporting him as he worked on the academics. The schoolwork improved, so his overall self-confidence increased. Recognize your child's special talents, and help her build on them. Then watch the whole person blossom.

7. Set Your Child Up to Succeed

Helping your child develop talents and acquire skills is part of discipline. If you recognize an ability in your child that he doesn't, encourage him. Yet be careful that you don't load him down with an assignment that is wrong for him but makes you look good. Strike a balance between pushing and protecting. Both are necessary. If you don't encourage your child to try, his skills won't improve, and you will have lost

---

Wall of Fame

In our Sears family gallery of accomplishments, our walls display Hayden's cheerleading trophies, Erin's horse ribbons, Matthew's Little League pictures, and other evidence of our children's pursuits and achievements. Every child is good at something. Discover it, encourage it, frame it, and display it. If your home is missing this wall, your child is missing his moment of fame. If you have a child who is not athletic, try scouting. With Boy Scouts and Girl Scouts everyone wins and everyone gets lots of badges. As older children walk by their showcase, they can see at a glance years of achievement. This gives them a lift, especially during times when their self-esteem is faltering.

---

a valuable confidence builder. If you don't protect your child from unrealistic expectations, his sense of competence will be threatened.

Beware of value-by-comparisons. Children measure their own value by how they perceive others value them. And in our measuring-and-testing society, children's skills — and therefore their value — are measured relative to others. Your child may bat an exceptional .400 on the softball team, but she will feel inadequate if her teammates are batting .500. *Be sure your child believes you value her because of who she is, not for how she performs.* Do this by giving her plenty of eye contact, touching, and focused attention. In other words, give of yourself regardless of how the game or the achievement test turns out.

Don't expect your child to excel in sports or music or academics just because you did. The one thing your child can excel in is being herself. She must know that your love for her does not depend on your approval of her performance. That's a tough assignment for a parent who may have been raised to perform for love and acceptance.

8. Help Your Child Be Home-Wise Before Street-Smart

Sometime during your parenting career you may run into the idea that a child should be exposed to children with different values so that he can choose for himself. This may sound good, or at least politically correct, but it just plain doesn't work. It's like sending a ship to sea without either rudder or captain. Only by remote chance will that ship reach a desirable destination. Children are too valuable to be left to chance.

Arm your child against intruders into his self-esteem. By attachment parenting during the first three years and staying connected to your child thereafter, you give your child a firm grounding in your values about home, family, and interpersonal relationships. She develops a conscience and respect for parental wisdom so that she can safely enter the street jungle without getting eaten alive. This connected child is equipped with the tools to build her own road and stay on it. Even if she experiments a bit, as nearly all children do, this child finds her way again.

Screen your child's friends, at least in the preteen years. The child's values and self-concept are affected by *persons of significance* in his life — relatives, coaches, teachers, religious leaders, scout leaders, and friends. It's up to parents to screen out those who pull down their child's character and to encourage those who build it. Keep a watchful eye on your child's friendships. First, let your child choose his own friends and monitor the relationships. At the end of a play experience, examine your child's feelings. Is he at peace or upset? Are the children compatible? Coupling a passive person with a strong personality is all right if the stronger child pulls your child up rather than knocking him down. More often than not attachment-parented children will wisely seek out compatible playmates on their own. Depending on your child's temperament it may be helpful to *set up your child* by purposely exposing him to appropriate peers. Some groups of children just naturally seem to get along well. If your child's group does not seem to have the right chemistry, it would be wise to intervene. By being a monitoring mom, Martha was able, many years ago, to come to the rescue of one of our children, who was being intimidated and blackmailed into stealing money from us. A junior racketeer in the neighborhood was busted because Martha became suspicious of certain phone calls and she listened in one day. Our frightened seven-year-old was in way over his head and was greatly relieved when we intervened.

The roots of a young child's self-concept come from home and from nurturing caregivers. After six years of age, peer influence becomes increasingly important. The deeper the roots of home-grown self-confidence, the better equipped kids are to interact with peers in a way that builds up self-worth rather than tearing it down. They know how to handle peers who are fun to play with and those that give them problems. When children are attachment raised, they are better equipped to manage different environments (home, neighborhood, grandparents, preschool) with different rules. For healthy social development, a child first must be comfortable with himself before he can be comfortable with others.

Keeping a Kid-Friendly Home

Make your home inviting to your child's friends. Yes, you will have more messes to clean up, but it's worth it. Hosting the neighborhood helps you monitor your child; it gives you the opportunity to observe your child's social style and generally learn more about your child's personality, which social behaviors are appropriate and which need improving. You'll be able to make on-the-spot disciplinary interventions, either with your child in a private lesson or in group therapy if the whole pack needs some redirecting.

Clinging to home base. In normal development a child moves out from the known into the unknown. She tries out new experiences in much the same way that an attached baby learns to separate from her mother. It is quite normal for a child to retreat periodically into the comfort of the known (her home and family) as she progressively ventures into the jungle of the unknown. It is important for all children to have a strong attachment base. Some more sensitive kids may need an extra dose of confidence so that they can follow their own inner compasses in adjusting to new situations and relationships. Parents often wonder what degree of clinging to home base is normal. Look at the problem over the course of an entire year. If you see no change in the child's willingness to venture out, that may be an unhealthy sign. But if you see some gradual moving out, then your child is simply a cautious social developer, which is characteristic of sensitive children, who may form a few meaningful and deep relationships, rather than numerous superficial ones.

9. Monitor School Influences on Your Child

Some schools can be hazardous to a child's emotional health. School choice (if you have one) needs to be carefully considered. The connected child who enters the school arena with peers from various upbringings and degrees of attachment will have a set of expectations that he may not find fulfilled at school. If a child is securely attached to his caregivers and armed with a strong self-image, he may not be disturbed by the dif-

---

Lose Labels

"I'm asthmatic," seven-year-old Greg proudly said to me when I inquired why he came to my office. Indeed, Greg did have asthma, but the physical problem was much easier to treat than the emotional side effects of his label. A few puffs of a bronchial dilator and his wheezing cleared, but his label persisted. I mentioned privately to Greg's mother that there are two issues to address in any child with a chronic illness: the problem itself, and the child's and family's reactions to the problem.

Every child searches for an identity and, when found, clings to it like a trademark until it wears down and is replaced by a more attention-getting identity. "Asth-matic" had become Greg's label, and he wore it often. His whole day revolved around his ailment, and his family focused on this part of Greg instead of on the whole person. Instead of feeling compassion, Greg's brothers and sisters had become tired of planning their lives around Greg's asthma. They couldn't go on certain trips because Greg might get too tired. It became a family illness, and all, except Greg, were put into roles they didn't like.

To take away Greg's label would be to take away Greg's self-esteem. So, we made a deal. I would treat Greg's asthma; the family would enjoy Greg, and we all worked at giving "the asthmatic" a healthier label to wear.

ferent behaviors he finds in the new social group. He may stick cheerfully to his own style of play; or he may be frustrated, creating stress on his emerging personality. If his self-confidence is shaky, a child may view aggressiveness or bullying as normal and make these behaviors part of himself or allow himself to be victimized.

Around age six, when your child begins elementary school, other adults become influential in her life. These are people who are around your child enough to influence her behavior and model values. Once upon a time persons of significance in a child's life came primarily from within the extended family, but in today's mobile society a child is likely to have a wider variety of peers and persons of significance. This means that today's parents need to be vigilant as to who is modeling what behavior to their children. Here is where there is confusion in the ranks of parents as disciplinarians. There are two extremes. On the one side are the parents who feel it's healthy for children to experience a lot of different value systems while growing up so that they will be more open-minded as adults. On the other side are parents who want to protect their child from all outside influences and any ideas that may differ from their own beliefs; the child grows up in a bubble-like atmosphere.

Somewhere between these two extremes is the right answer for your child. Throwing a child into the melting pot of diverse values at too young an age, before she has any of her own values, may produce a child who is so confused that she develops no conscience and no standing value system. Parents who overprotect may end up with a child who cannot think for herself, leaving her vulnerable to challenges or so judgmental that she condemns anyone with different

beliefs. Somewhere in the middle is the parent who grounds the child in a firm value system and guides her as she encounters other value systems. The child, because she has a strong value system to begin with, is better able to weigh her parents' value system against alternatives and develop her own firm code of values. It may be different from the parents'. It may include many of the parents' values with a sprinkling of alternatives learned from peers or teachers. But the important thing is that the child has a value system from which to operate. He is not a leaf hurried downstream in the river that takes the path of least resistance, overflows its bounds, and eventually drains into a large sea of uncertainty. Many children flounder, sometimes for the rest of their lives, searching for values that should have been formed in infancy and early childhood.

Parents, don't be misled by the complacent term "latent" applied to middle childhood. This is not the time to sleep and get careless. This is the age in which your children build consciences and learn your value system. In fact, it's the only time in their entire life when they unquestionably, at least early in that stage, accept their parents' value system. Slowly they form their own standards through interaction with peers, other families, and teachers, and through neighborhood relationships and church/synagogue friendships. They discover a larger world with a variety of beliefs and behaviors. As they talk (endlessly) and observe and experiment in a variety of situations, they learn about how they will choose to act and react. Trying belatedly to impose your values on a teenager whose main developmental task at this stage is to identify his own values is difficult. The best way to get your values across is to "walk your talk" by living your values.

10. Give Your Child Responsibilities

Children need jobs. One of the main ways children develop self-confidence and internalize values is through helping maintain the family living area, inside and out. Giving children household duties helps them feel more valuable, besides channeling their energy into desirable behavior and teaching skills. Try these tips:

Enter the work force early. Beginning around age two, children can do small jobs around the house. To hold a child's interest, choose tasks the child has already shown an interest in. Our two-year-old, Lauren, had a thing about napkins, so we gave her the dinnertime job of putting napkins at each place. A mother in our practice told us: "I couldn't keep our three-year-old away from the vacuum cleaner. So I gave him the job of vacuuming the family room. He kept busy and I got some work out of him." Starting between ages two and four, a child can learn the concept of responsibility to self and to parents and for his personal belongings. Once he learns a sense of responsibility for these things, a sense of responsibility to society will come naturally in the next stage of development.

By three years of age, a child can be taught to clean sinks and tubs (using a sponge and a small can of cleanser). Young children love to scrub. Threes and fours love to sort laundry into dark and light loads. At five, the child can be doing dishes every night. Teach him exactly how you want them handled (for example, garbage in the disposal or waste container, dishes rinsed, and then put in the dishwasher). Be sure to use unbreakable cups and plates and put messy pans on the stove or in the oven to be cleaned later by an adult.

By seven, a child can be cooking at least one meal a week from start to finish. Teach her how to fix her favorite meal and let her learn how to pick out the ingredients at the market. Encourage school-age children to make their own lunch. Besides giving them a sense of responsibility for their own nutrition, they are more likely to eat what they make. Once taught, the child can be left alone in the kitchen — no hovering mother. Relax and talk to Dad.

Give special jobs. Call a job "special" and it's more likely to get done. Whatever magical ring the word "special" has, it sure gets results. Perhaps a child infers, "I must be special because I get a special job." A four- to five-year-old can have preassigned chores, with reminders, of course. To put some order in our busy house we announce: "It's tidy time." Try assigning one room for each child to tidy up. Children at all ages suffer a bit of work inertia, especially as tasks wear on and lose their fun appeal. But sometimes children need to learn that work comes before play. To get them started, work *with* them.

Create job charts. Make this a creative activity for a family meeting. List the jobs to be done, and let each child choose and rotate if they want. We divide jobs into paying, extra-credit jobs they can earn money for, and nonpaying, those that are naturally expected of the children for the privilege of living in the home. Expect to pay a higher price on the most unwanted jobs. Best is to pay immediately after the work is responsibly done, since children are immediate-reward oriented. Between five and ten years, children can make the connection that with increasing privileges come responsibilities. When we decided to get a family cottage, the deal was that Saturday mornings would be family fix-up time at the cottage, and only after the work was completed would the recreation begin.

Plant a family garden. Planting a garden teaches children that they reap what they sow. During our family garden phase, our children learned a lot about commitment, just as we were learning about parenting: Water the plants and they grow nicely; keep the weeds away and the flowers bloom better.

Other jobs boys and girls love and do well when first taught alongside a parent include washing the car, sweeping outdoor living areas and sidewalks, gardening, vacuuming, dusting, and baby tending. By seven or eight they can put in a load of laundry, and by ten they can be doing their own laundry. When children have jobs in the home, not only are parents relieved of some of the busywork, but children feel they are contributing to a cause. They feel useful and needed. And the energy they spend on the home becomes an investment they are making in the value system of the home.

Helping Children Like Their Bodies

"You're fat," eight-year-old Emily teased her five-year-old sister, Laurie. "I'm not," retorted Laurie, bursting into tears as she ran to the bathroom mirror. Some of her body reflected in the mirror came from Laurie's genes. Yet there are ways that parents can help children have healthy, attractive bodies. Most importantly, model healthy dietary and exercise habits in your family. Next, tell your child you like his body: "I love to see you run," "You dance so gracefully," "You look terrific." Avoid comparisons, such as: "Your sister has nice long legs," "Your brother is so strong." If your child has a body part she is sensitive about, turn her negative feelings toward positive ones. One mother had two daughters; one felt her feet were too big, the other thought her feet were too small. This wise mother channeled the perceived liability into an asset. To the large-footed daughter, she said, "Your feet will really help you in swimming." To the daughter with the petite feet, she encouraged, "Your feet will help you in skiing."

Never tease a child about a body part she can't change. Don't allow kids to criticize other kids' bodies. Be sure they know body-teasing is not allowed. Remember, children perceive themselves by how they believe others perceive them. It is best to avoid negative body opinion words like "short," "gangly," "tall," "skinny,"

"buxom," "big-nosed," "clumsy," "klutzy," and so on.

Most kids go through a sloppy stage when they don't seem to care about appearance or hygiene. This will pass, especially if you model, rather than preach, neatness. Many pre-teens, even kids whose parents are slim, go through a "dumpy" stage. When adolescent growth hormones click in, the body stretches, and you wonder if the pictures of the ten-year-old and the fourteen-year-old are of the same child.

Fat children are at a terrible emotional and social disadvantage. They don't like themselves, are often depressed, and compensate by being the class clowns. Sometimes children as young as nine years old begin anorexic or bulimic dietary practices to overcome poor self-image and gain control of their bodies. If a child is seriously overweight or bulimic/anorexic, seek professional counseling for the whole family. These are danger signs. Healthy children will eat just what they need to maintain their active lifestyle. Best odds for children liking the body they see in the mirror is to start them liking their bodies before they begin school. Attachment-parented infants feel valued; a complimented toddler feels special; a wisely fed four-year-old feels physically and emotionally secure.

8

Helping Your Child Express Feelings

ONE OF THE GOALS OF DISCI-PLINE is to teach children to be sensitive to others. Yet in order to understand others, children must first be sensitive toward themselves. They must recognize their own deep feelings and feel comfortable expressing them when appropriate. This is the starting point for building good relationships with others and for being able to keep one's emotional balance as an adult.

FEELINGS: EXPRESSING OR STUFFING?

Expressing feelings does not mean the child is free to explode at every emotional twinge, but rather that she develops a comfortable balance between expressing her feelings and keeping them to herself. She should eventually be able to keep a lid on her emotions when needed, but not so tightly that she can't remove the lid in a "safe" setting, such as when exercising (for example, running like mad to blow off steam) or with a trustworthy friend. Gaining control over the expression of feelings is a sign of maturity. A child with unbridled

emotions is a brat. A person who never expresses emotion is flat. Too much control or too much emoting will both produce problems in adult life.

Stuffing feelings doesn't do any good for the child, the parents, or the relationship. Expecting a child to deny his feelings tells him that you are threatened by his feelings or gives him the message that you don't care to understand his feelings. The child decides that the feelings that accompany the ups and downs of his daily life are not worthwhile. According to a child's logic, if his feelings are not worthwhile, he is not worthwhile. If this unfeeling pattern happens over and over, the child quickly learns both to suppress the feelings and especially to hide them from his parents. Eventually, the child becomes less tuned in to himself, and parent-child communication becomes difficult.

Even more devastating than being uncaring is responding to a child's feelings with anger messages: "I don't want to hear any more bellowing about that stupid dead fish!" Or, even worse, "I'll give you something to cry about." The *fear* of parents' reactions to her feelings turns a child into a feelings stuffer. Insensitive parents can take

Stuffing Feelings		Releasing Feelings	
Child's Expression	Parents' Reaction	Child's Expression	Parents' Reaction
"My necklace from Grandma broke."	"It's only a necklace."	"My necklace from Grandma broke."	"I'm sorry. You feel sad, don't you?"
Sob! Sob!	"We'll get another necklace."	"Yeah, it was special to me."	"I know Grandma is special to you."
"I don't want another one. I want the one Grandma gave me."	"Come on, pull yourself together." "Why weren't you careful with it?"	"She picked it out specially for me."	"When you really care about something it's hard to lose it."

this stuffing dialogue one step further by imposing blame ("I told you not to feed that fish too much!"), loading the child with guilt and inner hurt he won't dare express or setting him up for an explosion of anger. Changing this pattern of responding is challenging for parents who were raised with insensitivity.

On the positive side, picture what happens when a child feels free to express herself, and a parent accepts her feelings. Consider this example: "Daddy, the necklace Grandma gave me for my birthday broke." Dad stops what he is doing and focuses on his child, looking into her eyes and placing his arm around her shoulder. He says, "I'm sorry. That was such a special necklace." Both his verbal and his body language convey: "I am available to you; your feelings are important to me. You are important to me." Dad's reaction frees the child to tell him more about her feelings and to work through them by talking to him. Instead of retreating into her shell or erupting into a tantrum, she has been given

a way to express her sadness. And he has boosted her self-esteem by accepting her feelings, which are a reflection of herself.

HOW TO RAISE AN EXPRESSIVE CHILD

Raising an emotionally expressive child is one of the biggest challenges of parenting for those of us who weren't allowed to express our feelings as children. We need to learn how to accept and understand our children's feelings as well as our own.

Practice attachment parenting. A baby who can express needs becomes a child who can express feelings. This is why in the first part of this book we emphasized the importance of being responsive to your baby's cues. A one-month-old cries to express his need for food or holding. Parents pick up on these cues and respond sensitively. Baby learns that these impulses within himself have meaning. His cries bring comforting responses. Expressing his needs leads to good things. By being open and responsive to their baby's cues, parents affirm their baby's self-expression. When you anticipate needs by recognizing subtle pre-cry signals, your baby learns a greater variety of ways to express himself and seldom has to cry to get what he needs. This makes him a joy to have around, which ensures that his parents will continue to be responsive to his needs. The connected baby becomes a child who is capable of recognizing and showing deep feelings.

Not so the unconnected infant. A baby who is dutifully scheduled, left to cry it out, and whose well-meaning parents fall prey to fear-of-spoiling advice learns early that the caregiving world is not responsive to his needs. He learns to stop asking. This baby learns to shut down and stuff his feelings at an early age. He learns neither to identify nor to express them. On the surface, this little person is a "good" baby; he doesn't bother anybody. He adjusts to the inflexible schedule, sleeps through the night, and is convenient to have around. This "good" baby, seemingly so "well disciplined," is at risk for becoming a withdrawn child and an internally angry, depressed adult. Other unconnected infants cry harder when they receive no response, becoming obnoxious and openly angry. These babies become children who are very hard to manage. They carry these feelings into adulthood and, like the "good" baby, are at risk of ending up in the psychologist's office. (This "good" baby or "obnoxious" baby is different from the temperamentally easy baby or difficult baby.)

Not approachable: "Don't bother me about that stupid dead fish."

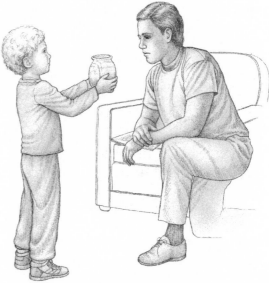

Approachable: "You really miss Snappy, don't you?"

Encourage toddler feelings. The expressive baby and responsive parent bring a winning combination into toddlerhood. Because her cues were listened to and decoded in the first year, the toddler is better able to express herself. The infant who learned to express her needs becomes the toddler who is in touch with her feelings. Some mothers tell us, "My toddler doesn't have many words yet, and it drives me nuts trying to understand him." We tell them to watch their toddlers' eyes. Martha has gotten very adept at reading toddlers' eyes. When she's not sure what the toddler is telling her, she can get a clue from the expression in his eyes. The toddler knows exactly what he is telling you, and his eyes often speak more eloquently than his tongue. Intently watching the eyes as your toddler "bares his soul" will often help the garbled words suddenly make sense.

Be approachable. Toddlers are little person with big needs who have limited ability to communicate these needs. Help them. Meet your toddler at eye-to-eye level when he is talking to you. Be attentive even when you don't understand what your toddler is trying to say. Give body language cues (nodding your head, eye-to-eye contact, hand on shoulder) that you want to understand his viewpoint. When you can't stop what you are doing, you can at least make voice contact with your child. He isn't mature enough to understand why your needs are more pressing than his at this moment, but hearing you talk to him ("Tell Mama what you want. . . .") will help him feel that you care about him.

Lauren, our two-year-old, hurts her finger. She holds her hurt finger up to me. "Daddy, kiss owie." I know she's not badly hurt, because she'd be crying in pain if she'd pinched her finger hard. I could dismiss this and get back to my important agenda, but my heart looks behind the eyes of my child. I realize that this very healthy-looking finger is not the issue. The fact that Lauren feels her finger is hurt is the issue. Lauren learns she can tell me her feelings and get my attention and my empathy. By showing interest in her plight, I help her continue expressing. "Show me where it hurts," I respond. I look into her eyes and sensitively examine her finger. "Let's make it better." I put a bandage on her finger or show her how to go to the freezer for the "boo-boo bunny" (a cloth container for ice cubes). I hold her on my lap for a few minutes until her attention is diverted to something new. The inexperienced parent may hesitate to make such a fuss over "nothing." The veteran realizes how sensitive little children are to "owies." From a child's viewpoint, the tiniest pinprick represents a hole in his body, and he needs the bandage to repair the "leak."

Avoid feeling stuffers. Children can be exasperating when they react (we sometimes think "overreact") to life's little setbacks. Children are like that. Nevertheless, these "small" events are important to them.

Don't try to get a child to stuff her feelings. When a child is upset, give her time and space to express herself. Resist the urge to unload anger, judgment, or logic. Your child is not in a receptive frame of mind to receive any of these. Sometimes children express themselves in ways that really push buttons, and so parents squelch automatically. Feeling stuffers give the child the message that you are not accepting of her emotions, and they cause the child to clam up. It's a lose-lose situation. The child loses the ability to express herself, and you become an unaccepting parent whose child learns not to open up to you. A distance develops between parent and child.

Instead of lashing out with feeling stuffers:

- "Stop that horrible crying."
- "There is nothing wrong with you."
- "You're being a baby."
- "You're overreacting."
- "It's not a big deal."
- "You don't need a bandage."
- "Quit bothering me."
- "You're not cold" (or hungry, or thirsty, and so on).

Try helping your child identify her feelings:

- "Do you think you were bad?"
- "That made you angry."
- "Ouch! That must hurt."
- "Does that make you sad?"
- "What a happy feeling!"
- "That really hurt your feelings, didn't it?"
- "Scraping your knee hurts a lot."
- "I'll bet you feel good."

Past age six, a child can take more responsibility for keeping harmony in the household. If your seven-year-old is glaring at you with hateful looks and seems bent on wallowing in turmoil, resisting your invitation to communicate, you can calmly request that she go into another room where the foul mood will not affect your harmony.

Match mind-sets. Early in our parenting careers I learned a valuable approach to children's feelings by observing how Martha reacted to our children's emotional outbursts. For example, when a child came running to us with a "boo-boo," I would immediately click into my doctor role and make an objective assessment of the situation. I was so caught up in analyzing the external appearances of the boo-boo and making judgments about it that I was out of sync with my child's emotions. While he was expressing his feelings, I was mired in a mental exercise about how significant the scrape was.

Martha, on the other hand, was able to match the child's emotions with her own. Instead of locking into her own adult mind, she would click into the child's view of the problem. She would first match the child's emotional state. If the child's emotions registered a "10" on the boo-boo rating scale, Martha's empathy would rate a "10." She was using the oldest negotiating trick in the world: First, meet people where they are, and then carry them where you want them to be. Martha would gradually begin lessening her worry signals, which would help the child wind down into the realization that the scrape was not the end of his life. He would realize that if the hurt was no big deal in Mommy's eyes, it was not worth

Please Help Me!

Every child needs to know how to ask for help. Asking for help is not only necessary for learning, but it's also a way of drawing closer to the helper. Model this when asking your child to help you with tasks by explaining to her that even you need help. Helping makes a child feel needed, therefore valued, and plants the idea that helping each other is what families naturally do. Children whose parents help them gladly will be more likely to ask for help from adults like teachers, coaches, and other grown-ups in their lives.

wasting energy on, and he would go back to his play, happily sporting a Band-Aid.

"How hurt am I?" Wait for the child to initiate the call for help. Many a time when we see a child go splat we brace for the tears, but the child picks himself up and then steals a glance in our direction. If we look worried and rush forward, the child takes his cue from us and disintegrates. If we stay calm, the child will often ignore the owie and continue his play.

Be an empathetic listener. Preparing for a family trip, we had carefully chosen a seat on the airplane for our eleven-year-old daughter Erin so that she could have a good viewing place for the movie. When we got on the plane she was upset about her seat because she wasn't sitting next to us. Instead of jumping into a tirade about her ingratitude, we listened to her reasoning and her explanation of why she was upset. We listened, then tried to get her to realize that if she sat next to us she wouldn't have a good view of the movie. As she continued to plead her case, we saw her start to discover that she had a better deal after all. So we took the discussion out of the realm of conflict by simply stating, "You can sit whichever place you like." Given the face-saving opportunity to make a choice, she chose the original seat. Children, and adults, often need to express their negative feelings before they can solve their problem. Watch masterful negotiators. They first try to un-

---

Read Between the Lines

Andrew and Mary had practiced attachment parenting with their child, Michael, now three. Mary relates this example of how being connected to their child helped their discipline: "One night Andrew returned home late from work, as he had been doing all week. We put on a favorite video of Michael's, *The Sound of Music,* and we all sat down together to watch it. Michael, for only three, is incredibly communicative, but there are days when he can't say what he needs and wants to say. After a few minutes of the movie, Michael said rather angrily, 'Turn it off!' We were surprised and said, 'But you love this movie. What's wrong?' To which he replied, 'Turn it off!' and proceeded to toss some toys around where he was standing. So I suggested, 'Michael, why don't you go sit on the couch with Daddy to watch the movie.' He then said, 'No, I don't want a daddy.' Andrew and I looked at each other puzzled; Michael adores his father. So as much as we wanted to see the movie, we turned off the VCR and questioned Michael while he was still upset. We asked him if there was anything about the movie that upset him. He answered no. Then we asked him why he wouldn't sit with Daddy on the couch, but Michael responded even more angrily: 'No, I don't want a daddy.' Michael was on the verge of a tantrum. He was next to Andrew, on the floor, kicking the couch as if wanting Andrew to tell him to stop. So instead of getting furious at Michael's negative behavior, Andrew said, 'How would you like to help Daddy fix some of his tools?' Michael's whole face lit up. 'Yes, I would like that.' Then Andrew said, 'I thought you didn't want a daddy.' Michael replied, 'I do want a daddy;

derstand the other side's viewpoint rather than making judgments about it. Next, they let the other person present her whole argument before offering a solution. Use similar strategies for helping a child work through her feelings. Give her the opportunity to present her whole story. Listen attentively and match emotions with her. Don't jump right in with advice or solutions. If you are busy constructing your own arguments while the child is talking, she'll know it. You won't get her viewpoint and you won't be able to help much. Knowing when to speak and when to hold back helps you be a good listener — and a good disciplinarian.

Avoid playing amateur psychologist.
"And how does that make you feel?" Older children, especially teenagers, sense when someone is fresh out of Psychology 101 or has just finished the latest discipline class. They may resent your trying some outsider's methods on them; at best, they may find it embarrassing, at worst, infuriating. Personalize your approach; if you do use tips from this book or another outside source, ease into them. Make them your own. Use your own words and your own style of communicating.

Avoid cover-ups. Shallow people shy away from deep relationships. If you are blessed

---

Read Between the Lines (continued)

I want my daddy so I can be with him.'

"We realized that this was the first night all week that Andrew had come home when Michael was still awake. How could Michael possibly say what an adult would say, 'Excuse me, Daddy, would you mind watching this movie another time? I haven't seen you all week, and I really need some time with my father.' Of course he couldn't, but he was trying.

"Michael helped his daddy with his tools for the next two hours. Michael was attentive and cooperative. Toward the end of the evening Michael began getting tired, and as he drifted easily off to sleep he said, 'Thank you for being with me, Daddy. I love you.'

"The evening changed because we invested time in getting to the bottom of Michael's behavior. We came close to punishing him or just brushing him off

for being 'fresh,' but we sensed that his behavior required the investment of time and energy to find out why. Just as we had programmed ourselves to respond to his cues as an infant, we needed to find out the reasons behind his cues right now. We would have failed a crucial parenting test. We realized that even though we may have applied the ideas of attachment parenting in Michael's baby days, the need for it continues, and our parenting principles must always be reapplied to the new features of his development. Had we not looked beyond Michael's behavior that night, we would have planted a seed of broken communication, of not caring. This is more than a simple, airy, modern approach of trying to elicit emotion from a child and talk about 'how he feels'; there can be no phony attempt at caring, and the child knows it."

Feeling Puppets

Ideally, the way for children to deal with fears and feelings is to talk to you. In reality, children often clam up when asked "How do you feel?" Yet they will tell how they feel to some go-between, such as a puppet or a favorite doll. Take one puppet yourself and give another to your child. The friend puppet asks your child's puppet what he is feeling, and often your child will release his feelings through his puppet. These stand-ins are less threatening to your child if he worries that you might pass judgment on his feelings.

with a deep-feeling child and you offer shallow responses, a distance is likely to develop between you. One day Erin's bunny died. She was heartbroken, but she shared her tragic discovery with me when I was busy. I should have focused first on her feelings, second on the bunny's death, and third on my inconvenience. Instead I offered a lame "We'll get you another bunny." That was a *cover-up,* a refusal to deal with deep feelings. Instead of addressing Erin's sorrow, I offered an economic remedy, as if acquiring a new bunny would help. Besides encouraging her to stuff her feelings, this cover-up modeled a shallow attitude: We live in a disposable society where broken relationships can be quickly healed by buying new ones. It turned out that Erin's sorrow was laden with guilt because the bunny didn't have any water when he died, and giving him water had been her responsibility. (Later she shared this with Martha during a bedtime talk and prayer.) It took some careful listening and empathetic counseling to help her work through these heavy feelings.

Use empathy before explanations. Empathy is part of the *sensitivity* that is at the heart of attachment parenting. True empathy means getting into the mind of your child, looking at the world from his viewpoint, trying to feel what he feels. Empathy is not the same as sympathy. Sympathy is feeling *with* a person. Empathy is feeling *like* the person. Logical responses will not take the place of empathy. Children are not logical. You can say that there is no such thing as a monster in the closet, but as long as the fear is real to your child, the logical explanation will do no good. Deal with the feelings first, to encourage your child to trust you, and then work in your logical adult wisdom. This approach is valuable for both younger and older children. Before you can get through to them, they first have to believe that you truly understand (though not necessarily agree with) their point of view. Nothing bugs a preteen (or teenager) more than sensing that a parent does not understand her viewpoint. Try this method for being an empathetic listener:

- Acknowledge the child's feelings. (*Instead of:* "You don't have to be afraid of that big dog," say: "That dog sure is big, and big dogs can be scary. Did his bark make you jump?")
- Mirror your child's feelings with empathetic facial expressions.
- Listen empathetically while the child tells his feelings (but not when he screams or kicks or bites or criticizes).
- Draw out the child's explanation of why he feels the way he does.

The ability to get into the mind and behind the eyes of your child is a valuable tool for discipline. It starts early in infancy, as child and parent learn to understand each other's body language. Being empathetic toward your child will give him the skills he needs to be empathetic toward others. Being able to read and understand interpersonal cues is the key to successful social living.

Making Anger Work for You

"I HATE YOU, MOMMY!" Have you ever been devastated by such ungracious outbursts from your children? Understanding why parents and kids get angry and how to handle anger makes family living much smoother.

WHY KIDS GET ANGRY

Anger is normal. Anyone with a heartbeat will get angry. The colicky infant shows angry outbursts. The beginning walker gets angry with her frequent falls. The tantrum-throwing two-year-old rages when the glass vase is rescued from his exploring hands. The four-year-old has a fit because you won't buy him candy. The eight-year-old can't believe you won't let him see the blockbuster horror movie. Children are most anger-prone when moving from one developmental stage to another. That's when desire precedes capabilities and frustrations peak. That's a good thing. This motivates a child to keep trying.

Why some kids get more angry. Some children are more easily frustrated. The

sooner parents pick up on this tendency, the easier it is to smooth out the wrinkles. A baby's low tolerance for frustration is due partly to her temperament. Easy babies and compliant children have high levels of tolerance for frustration. They can accept not being held all the time and being fed on a schedule; they comply when asked not to grab the cat's tail and sail through toddlerhood on relatively smooth waters, leaving their parents delighted with their "terrific" two-year-old, satisfied that they must be doing everything right.

On the other hand, the high-need baby — soon to become the strong-minded child — has strong needs and an intense emotional style that makes those needs and feelings known to parents. This baby fusses when you try to put him down and will be angry a lot if you keep trying to put him down. (Both types of baby need a lot of holding — the type who is easily frustrated has the temperament to keep protesting if he doesn't get it.) He fumes when left with a substitute caregiver, flails wildly as parents snatch him back from the brink of disaster, and frazzles parental nerves as he motors through his tumultuous twos.

Don't Take it Personally

"You are so stupid! You are the worst mom!" That's what I heard our ten-year-old daughter, Erin, shout at her mother after Martha reasonably denied her request to go see a certain PG-13 movie. My first reaction: "No child of mine will get away with talking to her mother like that. Is she going to get it!" Next, I internalized my anger: "Where did we go wrong? This child was carried constantly, breastfed for years, and given an incredible amount of her parents' energy, and this is what we get? Plus, we've written twenty books on parenting!"

Martha, in the wisdom that comes from mothering eight children, calmed me down and helped me understand why a child reared as Erin had been could say something like that. Martha didn't take this affront personally. She considered the source. As a preteen, Erin is going through a lot of changes. This had been a bad week for her. She was dealing with pressures at school and from moviegoing friends, and Erin wanted to unload. The only person in the whole wide world she could safely dump on was Mom. Mom is always forgiving, and she will love unconditionally. I had not realized that Erin's whole week had involved a series of nos and that one more no had pushed her over the edge.

Martha's insight kept me from launching into my "You ingrate . . ." tirade against Erin. I decided to sit back a few minutes and let the drama unfold. I could see that Erin's outburst left her crushed, although it did not bother Martha. Erin needed to be rescued from her feelings rather than be put down by me. Martha began to help her work through all the tension accumulating in her life, and we ended with this exchange:

"You must feel awful telling your mother she's the worst mom," I offered.

"Yeah, and I didn't mean it."

"I know you didn't, Honey," Martha reassured her.

The scene ended with a hugging, eye-dabbing, apologetic Erin melting in the arms of her forgiving mother. I realized how therapeutic an understanding mom can be.

HOW ADULT ANGER AFFECTS PARENTING — AND DISCIPLINE

Inappropriate anger blocks your ability to parent appropriately. If anger rises up in you whenever your baby cries a lot, or won't sleep, or keeps getting into things, or is otherwise "dominating your life," you are in danger of harming your baby psychologically or physically. Your anger will cloud your response to your baby, and he will sense your anger and, sadly, apply it to himself. Or worse, your anger will cause you to be abusive: hitting or shaking your child. If this is happening to you, realize you owe it to your baby and to yourself to get professional help.

Anger that is expressed inappropriately blocks your ability to discipline wisely. For example, your four-year-old does something stupid. She covers the dog with spaghetti sauce, and the dog bounds off into the living room, leaving orange-red paw prints on the pale beige carpeting. This may seem like the perfect time to blow your top. Yet the more aggravating the deed, the more you need a clear head to evaluate your options in handling the misbehavior. Being in a state of rage clouds your thinking. Your unthinking expressions of anger cause the situation to escalate. You hit the dog (which causes him to run through more rooms, leaving more sauce behind); you spank the child and send her to her room (which leaves you, still seething, to clean up the mess alone). By the time the episode is over everyone feels abused. An approach less draining on everyone requires a level head and a dose of humor: quickly grab the dog and head for the bathtub, calling for your child to come along (in the most cheerful voice you can muster) to help de-sauce the dog and then the rug. Your child learns how you handle a crisis and how much work it is to clean up a mess. A temper tantrum from you can't undo the childish mess. It can only add to it.

Anger puts up a barrier between parents and child. Our children taught us this lesson. We saw a distance developing between us and our seventeen-year-old, Peter. We weren't communicating comfortably with each other. Our then fourteen-year-old daughter said, "He stays in his room to escape the yelling. He knows you'll get angry and start yelling." We hadn't thought of ourselves as an angry, yelling family, but Peter felt we were, and so he recoiled from family interaction to preserve his peaceful self. This quote from Hayden explains in a nutshell why anger creates distance, especially in a child like Peter, who has a laid-back temperament. Hayden's openness prompted us to reevaluate our show of emotions. We called a family meeting, acknowledged that yelling seemed to be a problem we needed to deal with, apologized for this failing, and discussed how that would change.

Also, we wanted our children to feel comfortable approaching us, no matter what they had done or how they felt. So we set about eliminating the fear factor: "Here's the deal. We will listen calmly to anything you tell us. We will not yell." This did not happen overnight, and we still "blow it" from time to time. When this happens, we apologize and move on. Displays of anger scare children and put them on the defensive. They will either retreat into a protective shell or grow to have an angry personality themselves. Once we removed the barrier of fear, Peter came out of his room. And we continue to work on our communication. We've learned to say calmly, "I get angry when you . . ." Children and spouse need to know what makes you angry. Yet they don't need to have your anger spewed all over them.

Small children are devastated by the sight of big, scary, out-of-control Daddy or raging Mommy. They fear that the parent will stop loving them, hurt them, or leave. You don't want your child to have to squelch the flow of his feelings because he's frightened of what he might set off in you. Adults must be responsible for controlling themselves. The child should not be put in a position where he starts to feel responsible for causing or managing your rage. This sets up very dysfunctional patterns as your child grows. If your anger gets out of control, seek help! You need to learn that it is not wrong to feel angry, even as an adult (remember — you have a heartbeat). Unfortunately, many of us were taught as children that anger is bad, sinful, or very frightening. Anger itself is not right or wrong. It's what we do with anger that can be very wrong. Staying calm in the face of any feeling (anger, fear, even love) is a measure of emotional maturity. Your child will learn how to handle his anger by watching you. Our goal is to acknowledge and communicate our feelings (so our children know we are real people) and at the same time model to them the kind of real people we want them to become.

If you and your child have a healthy relationship, you don't have to worry that an occasional emotional outburst will harm your child. In fact, it's healthy for a child to know you're annoyed or angry. Honest communication sometimes requires honest anger that does not frighten or shame the child. Here is how one mother (she and her child have a healthy attachment) used healthy anger to get through to her child:

When my son was three, I was totally exasperated with his behavior one day. He was in what my husband and I call "a dip" — a temporary low spot in maturity and judgment on his life road. He was being exceptionally testing that day, and after repeated time-outs, which apparently meant nothing to him, exile to his room was the next step. I sat him on his bed. He raced me to the door. I tried it again a bit more firmly (as though there was some sort of adhesive on his pants that wasn't working properly). He did the same thing again (of course). I sat him on the bed again, a little too firmly, and was angry at myself now. I sat on the bed too, and was angry clear through, so I said very loudly,

Laughter — The Best Medicine for Anger

Humor diffuses anger and keeps trivial upsets from escalating. Our kids love spaghetti — the messier the sauce, the more they love it. Once at dinner we left the older kids in charge of the two- and five-year-old, who were dawdling over their messy meal. As often happens in large families, the oldest child delegated responsibility to the next oldest and so on down the line: "You watch the kids. . . ." Lauren and Stephen were ultimately left unsupervised, and a spaghetti frenzy ensued. When we discovered the stringy mess we scolded the older kids for allowing it to happen. While we yelled at them, they yelled at each other. Lauren and Stephen peered up at their angry elders, sauce covering their cheeks and foreheads, spaghetti in their hair. We all began to laugh, and worked together, in good spirits, to clean up the kids and the mess. Now when we delegate authority, we're more careful to be sure the appropriate-aged child really is on duty.

"Listen! Do you think this is a fun game for me? It isn't! In fact, I HATE IT! Do you know why I am here? Do you know why I'm going to keep it up until you get it right? Because I love you, and I'm not just going to stand by and watch you grow up and act like a jerk!" I was livid and couldn't even stop myself from shouting the words "I love you" in total anger.

But when Sammy heard the word "jerk," he laughed. It wasn't a nervous what's-going-to-happen-to-me-now kind of laugh. It was a sincere giggle at something funny.

I realized then that he had never heard the word "jerk" before. What did he think it meant? Taken literally, I suppose it must have conjured up a pretty comical mental picture. This little levity, though, gave us the needed opportunity to talk calmly and resolve the issue with quiet "I love you's" and hugs. Then he completed the required time-out in his room, followed by more love and hugs.

My point in relating this story is that you can read all you want about how to teach your children what is right, but in the heat of the battle, when your wits are at their end, you're going to revert to just being yourself and saying what you think on a gut level. This is risky, of course, and potentially damaging if it gets out of hand. Yet when your relationship with your child is based on a solid attachment, letting yourself go will most often work to your advantage. Sometimes sincerity is the only thing that will penetrate even the toughest brick wall that stubborn children set up.

GETTING A HANDLE ON ANGER

While no person or no family will be, or can be, anger-proof, there are ways you can make emotions work for you.

Help your child have inner peace. Research has shown, and our experience supports the observation, that connected children and their mothers get angry with each other less often. The connected child, growing up with a sense of well-being, has peaceful modeling. He will get angry, but he learns to handle the anger in such a way

---

Inner Peace

Many adults spend much of their life trying various philosophies, religions, self-help books, support groups, and therapies, or they turn to drugs and other addictions in a quest to achieve the inner peace they never had while growing up. They may not find it because they are not sure what they are looking for. Attachment-parented children who grow up with inner peace know how it feels. If, through life's inevitable setbacks, they temporarily lose this feeling of rightness, they are able to recover it because they know what they are looking for. They have the emotional skills necessary to find inner peace, create it within themselves, and be open to further spiritual insight as they mature.

---

that it does not take over his personality. Connected parents know their children well, so they are less likely to create situations that provoke themselves and their children to anger. Attached parents know they don't have to be harsh to be in authority.

The unconnected child operates from inner turmoil. Down deep this child feels something important is missing in his self and he is angry about it. (The feeling may continue into adulthood, by the way.) This void is likely to show itself in angry behavior toward himself and his parents, placing everyone at risk for becoming an angry family.

Don't let your child stuff anger. Encourage your child to recognize when he is angry, starting when he is a toddler. Be an attentive listener, helping your child talk about feelings. Given a willing audience that shows empathy rather than judgment, children will often talk themselves out of their snits. Our eight-year-old, Matthew, insisted on watching a certain TV program. I disagreed, and he became angry. Matt felt that he absolutely had to watch the program. I felt that the program content was harmful to his growing self and to family harmony. I listened attentively and nonjudgmentally while Matt pleaded his case. *After* he had made his appeal, I made mine. With calm authority, I made my own points, while conveying to Matt that I *understood* but did not agree with his viewpoint. I let him know that since I am the dad and it's my job to decide what he watches on TV, the decision would stand. We talked about what we could do instead. Gradually Matt realized that this program was not worth getting so worked up about. As the dialogue continued, his eyes dried and his reddened

The "Angry Kid"

The habitually misbehaving child is usually an angry child. If your child seems "bad" all the time or you "don't know what else to do" or your child seems withdrawn, search beneath the surface for something that is angering your child. In counseling parents of these children, I have found two causes: Either there is a lot of family anger — mother and/or father is on edge all the time and the child incorporates these feelings as part of himself; or the child feels angry because his sense of well-being is threatened. Helping children who misbehave repeatedly or seem "bad" more than "good" usually begins with a total family overhaul. Take inventory of the influences in your child's life. What builds up his self-esteem? What wears it down? What needs are not being met? What inner anxiety is at the root of the anger? Anger is only the tip of the iceberg, and it warns of needs to be dealt with beneath the surface.

Inner anger often causes a child to withdraw. In a struggle to ward off attacks on a shaky self-image, this child puts on a protective shell. On the surface he may seem calm, but underneath a tight lid is a pressure cooker of emotions needing to be channeled or recognized. To keep the lid on, the child withdraws, avoiding interaction that might set him off. This is why we advise getting behind the eyes and into the mind of your child — things may look different from that perspective.

It's devastating for a child to feel that she is a "bad kid." Unless that feeling is reversed, the child grows up acting the part. To get the "bad" feeling out of your child, intervene with a reassuring "You're not bad, you're just young, and young people sometimes do foolish things. But Daddy is going to help you stop doing them so you will grow up feeling like you are the nice person I know you are." This sends a message to your child that you care enough to find the child beneath the bad behavior.

face relaxed. I'm sure his pulse rate was coming down too. We ended this encounter with a chuckle about how he had let

---

Lighten Up the Perfectionist

Children need to learn that it's all right to goof. You can lighten up the uptight child by modeling ways to handle mistakes. If you spill your coffee, try laughing it off: "I guess I win the Mr. Messy award today." Don't rant and rave when you leave the shopping list at home. Children learn that adults mess up too. It's all right to mess up and it's normal not to be perfect. This is especially true of the perfectionist who may feel that approval — and therefore his value — depends on error-free living at home and at school. We realized that Matthew was very hard on himself when he didn't get a task done perfectly. We realized he was picking up on our tendency to become angry at our own mistakes. Once he saw us lightening up on ourselves, he lightened up on himself. Mistakes *are* a good way to learn, and we do a lot of learning in our family. When one of us makes a mistake, someone is sure to comment: "Now, what can we learn from this situation?" If the anger button gets pushed this won't work. Be careful not to react in an angry way when someone spills his milk or tears his pants. Just say, "Now what can we learn from this?" Then, maybe even have a laugh over it. The laugh part will take a lot of work, though, if you were punished angrily for every mistake you made as a child.

---

such a stupid program upset him. We went out and played catch instead.

PEACE FOR PARENTS

To help your child have inner peace, you must have inner peace. We feel that this concept explains how some adults seem to move into the parenting role so smoothly, while others struggle. The feeling of rightness fostered by attachment parenting is not enjoyed by everyone. If you did not experience a secure attachment as a child, you probably struggle with a lack of inner peace as an adult. Even attached children as they grow into adulthood must pursue spiritual truth to find their purpose in life and the deep inner peace we all need. This is a lifelong journey that is exciting and exacting, demanding and delightful. One way to start this journey is to take a look at your past so you can see where you need to go.

Heal your angry past. Parenting can be therapeutic. It can show you where your problems are and motivate you to fix them. If your past is loaded with unresolved anger, take steps to heal yourself before you wind up harming your child. Studies have shown that children whose mothers often express anger are more likely to be difficult to discipline. Identify problems in your past that could contribute to present anger. Were you abused or harshly punished as a child? Do you have difficulty controlling your temper? Do you sense a lack of inner peace? Identify present situations that are making you angry, such as dissatisfaction with job, spouse, self, child. Remember, you mirror your emotions. If your child sees a chronically angry face and hears an angry voice, that's the person he is more likely to become.

Keep your perspective. Everybody has anger buttons. Some parents are so anger-prone that when they explode, the family dog hides. Try this exercise: First, divide your children's "misbehaviors" into *smallies* (nuisances and annoyances), which are not worth the wear and tear of getting angry about, and *biggies* (hurting self, others, and property), which demand a response, for your own sake and your child's.

Next, *condition* yourself so that you won't let the smallies bother you. Here are some "tapes" to play in your mind the next time you or your child spills something: "I'm angry, but I can control myself." "Accidents happen." "I'm the adult here." "I'm mad at the mess, not the child." "I'll keep calm, and we'll all learn something." Rehearse this exercise over and over by playacting. Add in some lines for you to deliver: "Oops! I made a mess." "I'll grab a towel." "It's OK! I'll help you clean it up." You may notice a big contrast between this and what you heard as a child. You may also notice it won't be as easy as it sounds.

When a real-life smallie occurs, you're more conditioned to control yourself. You can take a deep breath, walk away, keep cool, plan your strategy, and return to the scene. For example, your child smears paint on the wall. You have conditioned yourself not to explode. You're naturally angry, and it's helpful for your child to see your displeasure. You go through your brief "no" lecture firmly, but without yelling. Then you call for a time-out. Once you have calmed down, insist the child (if old enough) help you clean up the mess. Being in control of your anger gives your child the message, "Mommy's angry, and she has a right to be this way. She doesn't like what I did, but she still likes me and thinks I'm capable enough to help clean up after myself."

We find going into a rage is often harder on us than the child. It leaves us feeling drained. Oftentimes, it's our after-anger feeling that bothers us more than the shoe thrown into the toilet. Once we realized that we can control our feelings more easily than our children can control their behavior, we were able to keep our perspective on these annoying stages of childhood, and life with our kids became much easier. And when we do get mad at a child, we don't let the anger escalate until we become furious at ourselves for losing control.

The Cycle of Anger

Mad at child

Mad at self

Mad at being mad

More mad at child for causing you to get mad at yourself

You can break this cycle at any point to protect yourself and your child.

Make anger your ally. Emotions serve a purpose. Healthy anger compels you to *fix* the problem, first because you're not going to let your child's behavior go uncorrected, and second because you don't like the way the child's misbehavior bothers you. This is helpful anger. I have always had a low tolerance for babies' screams. At around age fifteen months our eighth child, Lauren, developed an ear-piercing shriek that sent my blood pressure skyrocketing. Either my tolerance was decreasing or my ears were getting more tender with age, but Lauren's cry pushed my anger button. I didn't like her for it. I didn't like myself for not liking her. It might have been easier to deal with the shrieking if I had not been feeling angry. But because I was angry and realized it affected my attitude toward Lauren, I was

impelled to do something about her shrieking, which I believed was an unbecoming behavior that didn't fit into this otherwise delightful little person. So instead of focusing on how much I hated those sounds, I focused on what situations triggered the shrieks. I tried to anticipate those triggers. I discovered that when Lauren was bored, tired, hungry, or ignored, she shrieked. She shrieked especially when harassed by her brother Stephen. She is a little person who needs a quick response, and the shriek got it for her. My anger motivated me to discover things about Lauren and to be more alert to monitoring the little ones. I've become a wiser parent. Lauren has become nicer to be around. That's helpful anger.

Anger becomes harmful when you don't regard it as a signal to fix the cause. You let it fester until you dislike your feelings, yourself, and the person who caused you to feel this way. You spend your life in a tiff

Children do childish things.

"I expect you to clean up the mess you made. Here's how."

over smallies that you could have ignored or biggies that you could have fixed. That's harmful anger.

Quit beating yourself up. Anger flares inwardly as well as outwardly over something that you don't like. After a lot of energy is spent emoting, you may come to realize that the situation as it stands now is actually better for everyone concerned. This "hindsight" keeps you humble and helps diffuse future flare-ups. Our motto concerning irritating mistakes is: "Nobody's perfect. Human nature strikes again."

Beware of high-risk situations that trigger anger. Are you in a life situation that makes you angry? If so, you are at risk for venting your anger on your child. Losing a job or experiencing a similar confidence-breaking event can make you justifiably angry. But realize that this makes it easier for otherwise tolerable childish behaviors (smallies) to push you over the edge. When you're already angry, smallies easily become biggies. If you are suddenly the victim of an anger-producing situation, it helps to prepare your family: "I want you all to understand that daddy had a bad day. I've just lost my job and I'm angry about it. I will find another job, and we'll all be OK, but if I yell at you sometimes, it's not because I don't love you. I'll try to stay peaceful." If you do blow your top, it's wise to apologize to your children (and expect similar apologies from them when they lose their tempers): "I'm sorry for being rude. You don't deserve being yelled at. It's not your fault. I'm not mad at you." It also helps to be honest with yourself, recognize your vulnerability, and keep your guard up until the anger-causing problem is resolved. There will always be problems in your life that you cannot control. As you become a more experienced parent — and person — you will come to realize that the only thing in your life that you can control is your own actions. How you handle anger can work for you or against you — and your child.

10

Feeding Good Behavior

WHAT YOU EAT AFFECTS HOW YOU ACT. The child who eats right is more likely to act right. Proper nutrition, or the lack of it, can profoundly affect a child's behavior. While some children fill their tolerant little tummies with all sorts of junk and act no differently, other kids go berserk after one jelly bean. By putting the right food into your child, you are more likely to get better behavior out of him. Here's how.

Do some foods bother your child's behavior? While scientists claim there's no relationship between what children eat and how they behave, mothers disagree. A 1994 study compared the behavior of forty-eight children aged six to ten years who were fed sugar diets with those who were fed a non-sugar diet and found no difference in the children's behaviors, even though twenty-three of these children had been reported by their parents as sugar sensitive. Despite the failure of science to prove a cause-and-effect relationship between food and behavior, some parents definitely notice a correlation in some children. It could be

that it is not the sugar itself, but what the sugar is derived from that causes a problem. Is your child vulnerable to certain foods? Everyone seems to notice a difference between "feel good" and "feel bad" foods. Just because a study didn't confirm this doesn't mean parents should totally relax about what they feed their children. "Feel bad" foods should be identified. Try this checklist.

☐ Does your child show sudden unexplained emotional outbursts repeatedly within a half hour of eating or drinking certain foods?

☐ Do some foods make your child aggressive, fidgety, or belligerent?

☐ Do some foods seem to make your child irritable? Does he have difficulty sleeping?

☐ Does your child become distant or inattentive for a few hours after eating or drinking certain foods?

Grazing for Good Behavior

Just as what you eat affects how you behave, so does how you eat it. I have learned to believe in the *wisdom of the body,* an age-old concept of nutrition. It means that if you make a variety of healthful foods available and present them attractively, the child will eat the right amounts of the foods that are necessary for his individual well-being. In our large and busy family, we don't have time or energy to fuss with picky eaters. Here's a trick from the Sears family kitchen.

To encourage good eating habits and good behavior for your toddler or preschooler, *prepare a nibble tray.* Use an ice-cube tray, muffin tin, or a compartmentalized plastic dish to arrange small portions of nutritious and colorful foods. Keep extras in the refrigerator so they'll stay fresh. Give these bits of nutrients attractive names, such as avocado *boats* (a quarter of an avocado sectioned lengthwise), banana or cooked carrot *wheels,* broccoli *trees,* cheese *blocks,* little *Os* (O-shaped cereal), *canoe* eggs (hard-boiled eggs cut lengthwise in wedges), *sticks* (strips of whole wheat bread), *moons* (peeled apple slices, maybe thinly spread with peanut butter), or *shells* and *worms* (different shapes of pasta). Be sure to reserve a compartment in the tray for one of your child's favorite nutritious dips, such as guacamole or yogurt.

Let your child help you put the nibble tray together. (Children are more likely to eat their own creations.) Place the trayful of goodies on the child's table in the eating area or on a low shelf in the refrigerator in a space reserved for the child. Encourage the child to graze from this tray all day long. As the busy explorer makes his rounds throughout the house, he is likely to make frequent nutritional stops for refueling. Don't allow running around the house with food (a practice that is unsafe and messy for the child under three).

Be a healthy grazer yourself and share with your kids. Grazing minimizes the ups and downs of blood sugar and the resulting behavior swings that occur when children go without food for several hours. Children need between-meal snacks. Day-care and preschool caregivers (and mothers, too) have long noticed that children's behavior deteriorates in the late morning and late afternoon. This behavioral plunge can be prevented by a nutritious midmorning and midafternoon snack. Smart moms learn to take along a grazing bag on family shopping trips. Best odds for best behavior is to stick to good-behavior foods and encourage your child to eat nutrient-dense foods (foods that yield a lot of nutrients in a small volume) such as: avocado, whole-grain pasta, nut butter, and some cheese.

Grazing from a nibble tray.

FOODS THAT BOTHER BEHAVIOR

While any food may bother a particular child, there are a few ingredients that are well known for changing behavior. The most notorious ones, according to parent reports, are sugars and food additives.

Bad-behavior sugars. Some sugars are quickly absorbed into the bloodstream. There is a quick burst of energy, but the sugar in the bloodstream also triggers a sudden release of the hormone insulin, which causes the child's blood-sugar level to plunge. When the child's blood sugars are low, she may be moody, distant, or impatient. To compensate for the low blood-sugar levels, the body releases stress hormones that have good and bad effects on the body. They bring the blood sugar back up by releasing stored sugar from the liver, but at the same time they can rev up the whole system, causing the child to feel anxious, "hyper," and irritable. Too much sugar can also make it hard for a child to concentrate, even make him sleepy. Bad sugars go by many names and can be found in many foods: glucose, sucrose, dextrose, granulated sugar, brown sugar. These are the sugars that sweeten candy, frosting, ketchup, soft drinks, many cereals, frozen treats, and so on. If you read labels carefully, you may discover more than one of these in some highly processed foods, adding up to a powerful sugar "hit." While these sugars provide a quick source of energy, in vulnerable children the foods they are in seem to produce wide swings in mood and behavior.

Better-behavior sugars. Sugars that take longer to digest are *fructose,* found in fruit and honey, and *lactose,* found in dairy products. These sugars do not enter the bloodstream as rapidly, but still provide a steady source of energy for the child. They do not excite the hormonal roller coaster, unlike the bad-behavior sugars mentioned above. One of our children wants ketchup with everything, so we are glad there are fruit-sweetened varieties available in nutrition stores. We have also found a big difference in fructose derived from fruit and "high-fructose" corn syrup. One of our children used to have full-blown tantrums until we stopped all corn syrup. She gets a headache from popcorn, so we surmise a connection. Three years ago she binged on marshmallows and "went nutsy." Corn syrup is often in sweetened foods along with sugar.

Best-behavior sugars. Complex carbohydrates are another type of sugar. Grandma called them "starches." These sugars have longer molecules, and it takes time for the digestive system to break them down, like a time-release capsule of energy. These super sugars provide gradual, steady energy, leave you feeling full longer, and do not trigger bizarre behavior. Examples are bread and crackers (whole-grain are best), unsweetened cereal, pasta, and potatoes.

Other food offenders. *Caffeine* is another culprit that causes up and down behavior in children and some adults. While caffeine may act as a beneficial stimulant to a tired adult, it can overstimulate a vulnerable child. Common sources of caffeine are soft drinks (colas, Mountain Dew, Jolt, some brands of root beer), chocolate, coffee, and tea.

Food colorings. Strange as it may sound, red and yellow dyes have been implicated

Scheduling Feedings for Discipline

You may be led to believe that putting your baby on a feeding schedule is disciplining your baby. Wrong. Decades of experience and years of research have shown that fixed scheduling for breastfed babies actually undermines discipline. Formula-fed babies schedule easier. The whole concept of scheduling evolved from having babies fed on artificial baby milk. While some babies do well on a predictable feeding schedule, most need flexible feedings to nourish their frequent growth spurts.

Rigid schedules work against the very foundations of good discipline: knowing your child and setting the conditions that make it easier for him to behave. Picture what goes on when parents try to impose a three- or four-hour feeding schedule on a breastfed newborn baby — a scientifically unsound method sometimes called Parent Controlled Feeding. The baby awakens and cries. Is he hungry? The mother consults the clock; it's been only two hours since the beginning of the last feeding, so she wrongly concludes that the baby can't possibly be hungry. She picks him up, but he continues to cry. He's hungry *now,* but Mother has determined he isn't. Hunger is overwhelming to this tiny, newly born person who has never experienced this feeling before birth. He can't wait, he has no concept of time. He only knows how he feels at this moment, and no one is responding. He gets frightened, and after enough episodes like this he no longer trusts his own feelings or his mother.

Mother, meanwhile, is becoming increasingly frustrated. She doesn't know why her baby cries so hard. She can't comfort him since she's holding off on feeding him. She can't stand the noise, so she puts him down in his crib, where he finally falls asleep, too exhausted to wake up and feed when the clock says it's time. Eventually, the schedule "disciplines" the baby because he has no choice but to learn to wait. Some learn more slowly than others. Many babies will keep trying to convince Mom they do need to eat and spend much of their infancy crying to be fed, and being not just a little angry. The mothers with the faster learners (who give up or who are of an easy temperament) will think schedules are wonderful and will try to convert every mother they meet.

Contrast this with the mother who feeds her baby "on cue" and lets him set his own schedule. This mother and baby work out their own communication system, without the intervention of that enemy of mother's intuition, the clock. They trust each other and themselves, sowing the seeds of a parent-child relationship in which discipline will be relatively easy later on. Mother knows her child well and almost always knows how to handle him. Eventually, a flexible but predictable pattern develops; but because it arises from the baby's own needs and temperament, and not from some outside source, it is easy for the baby to behave well for this mother. Her consistent, sensitive responses reinforce this peaceful behavior.

Food Discipline

Many children are raised in homes where food is an emotionally charged issue. Often food becomes a substitute for love or power. Here is a collection of bits of food wisdom we've gleaned over the years.

- Don't become upset over food. You've spent "hours" shopping and preparing healthy, organically grown squash for your baby, and proudly present her with a few chunks. She turns up her nose at "your hard work," and minutes later you find her nibbling out of the cat dish. Relax, eat the squash yourself and don't even *think* about being angry or disappointed. She'll probably eat it the next time, and if not squash, she'll appreciate some other lovingly prepared dish from mom.

- Don't use food as a control tool. Never push food on babies or children. If they want it, they'll either open wide or pick it up themselves. It's your job to provide healthy, nutritious food. It's your child's job to eat it. Never chase your child with a spoonful of anything. Never use the threat of "no dessert" to get a child to finish his main course. ("If you don't eat your peas, you can't have pie.") Don't even talk about how well or poorly a child has eaten. Zip your lip. It's his stomach.

- While feeding picky eaters does require some salesmanship along with a knowledge of good nutrition, you don't have to be a short-order cook and cater to every whim of your child's taste buds. When a child in our family doesn't like what we are eating, we point him in the direction of the refrigerator.

- Give choices. "Do you want broccoli or peas for dinner tonight?" Either way, your child is eating vegetables. Let your children help you prepare food. By seven, children can fix whole meals on their own. What they make they'll eat. Let your child make a list of food preferences and help you shop. Or, you make a list of healthy foods and let your child check off which ones he wants.

- "But my child will eat only crackers." Remember, you're the adult and you buy the groceries. You have two

in causing behavior problems in some children. Though few studies have found a direct cause-and-effect relationship between food additives and behavior, I have known astute mothers who have traced their children's behavior swings to food colorings.

The threshold effect. Some children don't seem bothered by small doses of one or more bad-behavior foods, but put a bunch of these offenders together in the same food or increase the portion size, and you'd better fasten your child's seat belt lest he take off. A candy bar or soft drink can contain large doses of sugar, caffeine, or food coloring, and children react differently. What is one child's energy source or thirst-quencher is another child's mind-meddler.

If your child has a sweet tooth but goes nuts after eating a piece of store-bought choices: Either don't buy crackers or buy nutritious whole-grain crackers and add a nutritious spread.

- There are two approaches to eating in the home. According to the control approach, the adults are the only ones allowed to hand out food. Children are not allowed to open the refrigerator or the pantry themselves. This approach works well with people who don't want to take responsibility for having only good-food choices in their home or for people who want to be in control all the time. The self-help approach is what we have chosen. Because our pantry is stocked with healthy snacks, our children can help themselves. We enjoy seeing our two-year-old helping herself in our pantry because everything in there is OK to eat. This gives her a way to be independent and eat when she's hungry, not just when we tell her she's hungry.

- Don't use food to fix emotional or physical hurts or to diffuse fights: "If you stop your toy squabbling I'll get you both a cookie." One exception to this would be comforting your toddler at the breast. The breast is not just for the delivery of food. Use similar caution in the use of food for reward. The "M&M" technique may motivate the reluctant toilet trainer, but withdraw the food reward once the training is under way. Creating healthy attitudes is one way to prevent eating disorders later.

- Do recognize that hungry children or children who have been nibbling on junk food or sugary treats find it harder to behave well. Late-morning or late-afternoon tantrums can often be forestalled by serving a meal or a nutritious, substantial snack.

- Saying no to food indulgence helps the child learn a valuable lesson in life — how to delay gratification. If you always have a double-scoop ice cream cone, he'll want the same. Save double-scoops for special treats, and model your delayed gratification by having a single scoop yourself, usually. (Better still would be to bypass the ice cream shop altogether and have a piece of fresh fruit.) Saying no to food indulgence helps a child say no to other unhealthy impulses as well.

cake, he doesn't have to give up sweets altogether. Make his favorite dessert, but instead of granulated or brown sugar use good-behavior sweeteners such as fruit concentrate or sweeteners derived from fruit and honey (date sugar is wonderful for baking). Additives and preservatives are not needed in homemade sweets, and you know exactly what ingredients are in your creations.

Nutrition first. Sweets need to be limited in younger children so that they will want to eat "the food that makes you grow." Plant this habit now so it takes root early and will be established by the time you have less say in what your child eats. Don't give sweets on an empty stomach, especially not as breakfast. Be aware that most children's cereals are sweet enough to qualify as desserts. "Sugar cereal is not what you are going to start the day with" is a hard-and-fast rule in our house. (One exception: For a special treat the birthday child gets to pick the cereal he's dying to try and he can serve it to his sleep-over guests for breakfast.) One of the fastest ways for our children to get a requested food item vetoed is for them to tell us they saw it advertised on TV. Instead of establishing the dessert habit, it's better to have some nutritious cookies or fruit a couple of hours after dinner so that the digestive process is not hampered by adding a sugar-laden layer to the "food that makes you grow" already in the stomach.

TRACKING DOWN FEEL-BAD FOODS

Food may indeed be a factor in your child's undesirable behavior, and the effort it takes to track down the culprit may be well worth it. Beware of the temptation to blame food for problems that actually have other sources. It's easier to blame sugar than to deal with disturbing family issues or change your parenting style. Try to be an objective detective when you track down offending foods. Here is a step-by-step approach:

Step 1. Record what your child eats for a week. The child over five can often help you write down everything she eats at each meal (at home and away), between meals, and at what time she eats it.

Step 2. Record how your child behaves. Pick out those behaviors that most concern you and note when they occur. Ask your child to record changes in how she feels and the time she has these feelings.

Step 3. Look for connections. Do similar problem behaviors crop up daily after eating or drinking the same food or groups of foods? If your child throws a tantrum at four o'clock every afternoon and she habitually indulges in a three o'clock Twinkie, you've nabbed your culprit. Ask your child what food she thinks might be bothering her. (If she says "broccoli and spinach," you should know that vegetables rarely affect behavior.)

Step 4. Eliminate the suspect. For at least a week keep the suspected food out of your child's diet and note whether or not the offensive behavior subsides.

Step 5. Challenge your discovery. To test your findings, reintroduce the suspect food into your child's diet and see if the behavior reappears. If it does, either totally eliminate the food or, if it's a favorite, lessen the amount until you figure out how much your child can tolerate.

As with so many exercises in discipline, you will find that eating to feel good is just common sense.

Sleep Discipline

INFANTS AND YOUNG CHILDREN spend a large portion of their twenty-four-hour day sleeping. But this is not just time when they disconnect from their caregiving world. During sleep a child still learns much about caregivers, about self, and about life. Nighttime discipline means more than just getting your child to go to sleep and stay asleep; it means helping your child to develop healthy sleep habits to carry into adulthood. How a child spends the night matters.

WHAT EVERY PARENT SHOULD KNOW ABOUT BABIES' NIGHTTIME NEEDS*

Sleep, or the lack of it, affects the behavior of children and parents. Parents and children need to get enough sleep. A tired parent cannot discipline wisely, and a tired child is not open to being disciplined. Be careful not to waste your time doing other things when you could be getting the sleep you need. Understanding the unique nighttime needs of children will help you arrive at a nighttime discipline approach that works for you.

Babies go to sleep differently from adults. Adults go from being awake into a deep sleep relatively quickly compared to babies. Babies and toddlers go through a lengthy period of lighter sleep before they drift into deep sleep. Getting them to settle through the light sleep phase until deep sleep arrives is often a challenge. This fact of normal sleep physiology explains why it's unrealistic to expect babies and even most two-year-olds to lie down and go to sleep when you want them to without assistance. Lesson for parents: *Babies and toddlers need to be parented to sleep, not just put to sleep. Teach them to relax into sleep.*

Babies naturally wake up more often than adults. Because babies and many children under three have shorter cycles of light and deep sleep, they are physiologically programmed to wake up more often than adults. Each time a person moves from deep sleep into light sleep he enters a vul-

---

*In *The Baby Book* we thoroughly discuss the uniqueness of babies' sleep patterns and how to deal with night waking. We present only the highlights here to help the reader understand nighttime discipline.

nerable period for night waking. Infants can have twice as many vulnerable periods as adults. Lesson for parents: *Little ones often need to be parented back to sleep.*

Nighttime is a scary time for little people. Younger children do experience separation anxiety when they awake and find themselves alone. Children also have difficulty sorting out dreams from reality and reorienting themselves when awakening. They are less able than adults to handle nighttime upsets. Lesson for parents: *Children need parents to be available during the night.*

Children's sleep habits result more from their temperaments than your nighttime parenting style. Some infants are born sleepers; some high-need babies carry their high-energy daytime style into waking at night. So if your neighbor brags that her baby sleeps through the night, and yours doesn't, don't blame yourself. It's possible her baby came wired that way, and yours didn't. "Good sleepers" are partly born and partly made. It's also possible she's ignoring her baby at night and he has shut down, if he really is "sleeping through the night."

PRINCIPLES OF NIGHTTIME DISCIPLINE

There is no right way to put every child to sleep and no right place for every child to sleep — only the right one for your child. Lesson for parents: *Be open to trying whatever nighttime parenting style fits the sleep temperament of your child and helps you all sleep best.*

Consider your primary goal in nighttime

Causes of Night Waking in the Older Child*

Some night waking is inevitable in childhood, and you will sometimes have to juggle your need to sleep with your midnight visitor's need for attention. Yet incessant night waking is neither normal nor healthy. Rather than becoming a nighttime martyr, search for the cause of night waking the way you would search for the cause of a fever. Here's a checklist to get you started.

☐ fear of sleeping alone
☐ family upsets: move, divorce, illness
☐ change of school
☐ one parent away
☐ emotional disturbances in a family member
☐ depressed child
☐ scary television, movies, books
☐ problems with peers or siblings
☐ environmental irritants and allergens: smoke, dust, animal dander
☐ medical causes: intestinal worms, respiratory allergies, food sensitivities, ear infections

*For causes of night waking in babies and toddlers, see *The Baby Book.*

---

discipline to be *helping your child develop a healthy sleep attitude, and an understanding that sleep is a pleasant state to enter and not a fearful state to remain in.* Here's how to build this healthy sleep attitude in your child, beginning with creating a healthy sleep attitude in your infant.

Develop a nighttime philosophy. "Is your baby sleeping through the night?" How many times have you heard this, either from people who care about the rest you're getting or from people who somehow equate this behavior with good parenting. Expecting babies and even young children to sleep through the night is unrealistic. Beware of sleep trainers who package directions for getting babies and children not to bother parents at night. They are all variations of the same tired theme: Let your baby cry it out. Use caution about succumbing to this advertised quick-fix cry-it-out method. It not only creates a distance between parent and child, but it keeps you from finding out why your baby is restless and what you can do about it. Every situation is unique, and there are no easy answers to complex sleep problems. We have observed that parents who insensitively persist in using the cry-it-out method are more likely to have more problems disciplining their children.

We advise alternatives to the "close the door, plug your ears, and leave your baby to cry" approach and modified versions thereof. Children should acquire healthy attitudes about sleep — and about life — in the first two years. If the infant has been nursed to sleep at mother's breasts or parented to sleep in a caregiver's arms, the child develops the attitude that sleep is a pleasant state to enter. If the infant sleeps close to the parents and the parents sensitively respond to the crying baby during night waking, the infant learns that sleep is a secure state to remain in. So, nighttime attachment parenting lays the foundation for healthy sleep attitudes.

If your older child has troublesome sleep problems, and you practiced a less-sensitive nighttime parenting style during infancy, don't despair. It is never too late to reconnect with your child. Develop whatever high-touch responsive style of nighttime parenting that teaches the two lessons of nighttime discipline: Sleep is a pleasant state to enter, and it is a safe state to remain in.

Choose the right bedroom. Many first-time parents ask where their baby should sleep. The right answer is wherever all of you sleep the best. Some infants will sleep well in their own room, some better in their own bed in their parents' room, some best in their parents' bed. The key is to be open to juggling various sleeping arrangements until you find one that works for your family; the sleeping place may change with each stage of your child's development. The bed-sharing infant may become the solo-sleeping toddler, or vice versa.

In looking at the nighttime parenting practices of families we've encountered during twenty-two years in pediatric practice, we've made a number of observations: Veteran parents often welcome their infants into their bed because they have, by experience, learned that it's easier on their baby and themselves. They are more confident in their own intuition about their baby's nighttime needs and are less influenced by outside advice. Novice parents tend to encourage separate sleeping because they have not yet discovered the importance of nighttime closeness to their baby. They are more influenced by neighborhood norms and sleep gurus who warn of terminal dependency if you dare to let your baby into your bed. Also, we have found that in general, separate sleepers (mainly those who are not attachment parented) tend to have more behavior problems than babies who share sleep with their parents.

Just how important to attachment is

sleep sharing? The answer to that question lies in another question — How responsive do you want to be to your baby? — and in how well your baby sleeps on her own. Some parents naturally gravitate toward sleep sharing from the first day. They know that this closeness is best for their baby. They are excited about it and don't mind making the lifestyle changes this will entail. Some of these changes actually make life easier for the new mother anyway. One mother states that although she was happy that her first baby slept well on his own, she realized she had gotten him "bonded to his bed." By sharing sleep she got the next two babies bonded to her.

Other parents take a wait-and-see attitude — take it one night at a time. If their baby sleeps well in her bassinet next to their bed or even in her crib in another room (with a monitor on so they can hear her easily), they are comfortable with that arrangement. Yet they are open to the possibility that babies' sleep patterns may change and will reevaluate things if it becomes obvious that she needs to be closer to them at night.

This is how we stumbled onto sleep sharing. Our first three babies slept in their cribs, but we did not ever leave them to cry alone. When our fourth child let us know loud and clear that she needed to spend the night close to mom, we listened. In 1978 that was a pretty daring thing to do, since the prevailing advice then predicted dire consequences (spoiling, child will never leave your bed, ruined sex life) if we let our baby sleep with us. But we were more concerned about the consquences of leaving her to cry (loss of trust and connection) or of Martha's continuing to get up with her four or five or more times a night (exhaustion and total collapse). Once we

started listening to what the frequent night waking meant (this baby's need for closeness and security in order to *relax* off to sleep), we all started sleeping much better. We now wonder whether our first three babies would have preferred sleeping with us but, being easy-temperament babies, they didn't persist at telling us so.

Once we found how well this worked, we carried out this wonderful nighttime tradition with our next four babies. It just plain made life easier for Martha because she got more rest and we both came to enjoy the extra time this gave us with our baby. The main reason we did it is that we believe babies need a warm body to sleep next to. We didn't worry about how long our babies stayed in our bed any more than we worried about how long they would breastfeed. People are partly right when they warn, "He'll *never* want to leave." As long as the need is there, baby/toddler will want to continue this arrangement. Can you blame him? The key is not to worry. As I explained to a flight attendant/mother, "When a person is used to flying first class, he doesn't like flying coach." Toddlers can sense when they are being hurried developmentally in any area, and the more pressured they feel, the more they will resist. Around age two, many sleep sharers naturally begin toying with the idea of separate sleeping. By three, they are usually ready to have their own special mattress on the floor at the foot of your bed, or a real bed in their own (or a sibling's) room.

This is testimony from a mother who achieved perfect nighttime harmony with her eighteen-month-old:

Our eighteen-month-old still sleeps with us, and he still nurses at night, and most of the time I don't even wake up. We have a different attachment at night than during the day. During the day, he's so busy playing. He needs me, but for different reasons. Daytime, he's my little boy. At night, he's my little baby. Nighttime is a chance for him to get back in touch with me.

I didn't have this nighttime harmony, nor did I share sleep, with our first child, and I definitely notice a difference. Jason is more willing to do what I ask. I'm important to him, therefore he doesn't do much to upset me. And if I have to reprimand him, he responds in seconds and apologetically. My daughter took a half hour to respond. I understand him better than I understand my daughter. We walk in the same path. He mumbles, and I know what he needs and what he is saying. My husband will ask me, "How did you know what he said?" I just know. I don't want to sound psychic, but it seems like we're on the same brain wave. Jason likes to go to bed because he likes how he's going to spend the night. For my daughter, going to bed was a struggle. I sleep better now too.

The turning point for me was when I let Jason take the lead and found that was easier for me. When I went with what he needed instead of what I thought I needed, my night life went much more smoothly. I did not feel that he was controlling; it just worked for us. Actually, I feel more "in charge" with Jason than I did with my daughter because I understand him better and he respects me more. Because I'm so tuned in to him at night, I feel better tuned in to him during the day, so that discipline is much easier.

Just like healthy weaning from the breast, weaning from the parents' bed will happen gradually, perhaps two steps forward and one step back. Expect steps back during times of high stress or illness (how good it is to know you can give this extra closeness at high-need times). When a new baby joins the family, the older one can "graduate" to his own space in whatever way is not threatening. We are officially down to just one child in our room now. Three-year-old Lauren sleeps in her own special little bed next to ours, and some mornings she's still there when we wake up.

Children's nighttime habits often reflect their daytime struggles. A child who feels good during the day is more likely to be sleeping well at night (and vice versa, of course). Ever notice that when you've had a good day you're more likely to have a good night? If your previously good sleeper becomes restless at night, consider whether there is some disturbance in his overall environment: a new developmental stage, starting preschool or day care, stress in sibling or marital relationships. Like most behavioral problems, sleep problems improve when your child's overall internal comfort improves. Even older children may suffer from sleep disturbances when problems at school or with peers threaten their confidence.

HANDLING COMMON NIGHTTIME DISCIPLINE PROBLEMS

Teaching a child to go to sleep and stay asleep is the task of nighttime discipline, along with helping the child develop a healthy sleep attitude. Here are some common nighttime discipline problems that parents have consulted us about.

Sleep Time, Make-up Time

Don't let the sun set on your anger. This advice is as valuable for disciplining a child as it is for living with a mate. When you and your child have a day of locking horns in conflict, bedtime provides an opportunity to make up. The child who is going off to sleep is more receptive to what you have to say, and the quiet nighttime environment is more conducive to healing. A mutual apology, a hug, and a reaffirmation of your love for each other clear the air of hard feelings, allowing both parties to begin the next day feeling good about each other.

The Sleep Fighter

Our three-year-old fights going to bed. It's always a battle getting him to sleep before 10:00 P.M., and by that time I'm more tired than he is.

Parents usually wish their children would go to sleep earlier than the children need to. Sleep is not a state you can rush a child into. It is better to create an environment that allows sleep to overtake the child. First, be sure your child is tired. You may have to omit or shorten the afternoon nap or let him take it earlier. Replace before-bed activities that rev up a child (for example, scary or stimulating TV, wrestling, sugary snacks) with wind-down interactions (for example, a warm bath, stories, quiet games, or a nutritious snack). Reasonably consistent bedtimes are healthful for children of all ages, and a sanity saver for tired parents. The child over three can understand the con-

cept of bedtime. Children under five usually can't understand actual time but can relate time to events: "When the story is over." "After you've had your bath and a snack." If you don't take charge of your child's bedtime, it will often drag on until midnight.

Bedtime routines are helpful in getting younger children to sleep without much fuss, assuming they are tired. It should be a fairly simple routine, such as: have a snack, brush teeth and put on pajamas, hear some stories, say a prayer, and snuggle down with mom or dad. This requires a commitment from you, but it's well worth it to know that in thirty minutes, more or less, your child will be asleep.

Remember, children want to have fun. If it's more fun to stay up, they'll fight sleep. They don't want to miss anything. In our family, going to sleep is a pleasure, not something to fight. Make bedtime special and fun — in a quiet way. Reserve favorite stories just for bedtime, with the condition that you will tell the story only if your child is in bed at the appointed time. Alternate homemade stories with those in books. The most sleep-inducing stories are those that involve *counting or repetition* and lull the child to sleep. Take your child's favorite story characters and spin a long tale: Winnie-the-Pooh and Tigger went fishing, and they caught one blue fish, two red fish, three green fish. Of course, don't just count — embellish each "catch" with the sequence of getting into the boat, getting out the bait or lures, baiting the hook, casting the line, and so on. Pooh and Tigger will be lucky if they catch more than a half dozen fish before your child is asleep.

A bedtime ritual conditions children to form a mental picture that sleep is soon to follow. The ritual helps them *relax* and get used to the idea. Before you begin the story, tell your child that he has to lie still for you to start the story. (Be sure he is tired already.) Special bedtime rituals come with strings attached. "No backs rubbed after nine o'clock." Use whatever enticement your child likes. Nighttime obedience has its rewards.

Martha notes: During the writing of this book, we realized that one way to deal with our little night owl, Lauren, is to respect her state of unreadiness for sleep. While we try for consistent nighttime routines, sometimes Lauren just isn't tired at her usual bedtime. She's ready enough to get into bed for stories, *but after four or five, I can sense that sleep is the farthest thing from her mind. She'd be happy to lie there for an hour and listen to stories, then have the light out, hear lullabies, and flop around. (I fall asleep first on those nights.) If I don't wish to spend my time that way, we get back out of bed and I give her the message that she's welcome to play quietly if she stays out of trouble. Then I get to spend an hour working on the book while waiting for Lauren to be ready to go to sleep quickly.*

The Procrastinator (The Sleep Fighter, continued)

It takes me an hour to parent our four-year-old to sleep. She finally goes to sleep, but by this time I'm too exhausted to get anything else done.

The more children we raised, the more we observed that children do what they do in order to meet their needs. Unless they are angry or have a distant parent-child relationship, kids don't use bedtime ploys deliberately to annoy parents. First, take your child's bedtime attachment to you as a compliment. She likes being with you and doesn't want to give up the delights of the day. Get behind the tired eyes of your child. The before-bed hour may be the only time in the whole day she has your focused attention. If so, relax and enjoy it with her. Bedtime procrastination is especially common in children who don't get much focused attention from their parents during the day. When both parents work outside the home, children normally regard prolonged bedtime rituals as their birthright. This is prime quality time, and they don't want to be shortchanged.

Consider whether your child needs more attachment rituals during the day. Children seem to recognize that they benefit from a certain amount of touch time each day in order to thrive. They learn very quickly that bedtime gives them this opportunity. Try to give your child the attention she craves at other times during the day.

On nights when you feel low on patience, videos may be helpful to wind down the child who fights sleep or to pacify the bedtime procrastinator. Choose a calming video that you can enjoy together. Then you can snuggle up together, giving your child bedtime closeness without expending much energy. Many nights when Matthew was three to four years old, we snuggled together in a bean bag chair, and he dozed off to *Lady and the Tramp.*

When a Parent Is Away

My husband travels a lot, and when he's away, our three-year-old is restless and often comes into my room in the middle of the night. How can I get her to sleep better during these times?

When one parent is away, children usually sense a change in atmosphere, especially if

The Nighttime Psychologist

Bedtime is a good time to fix childhood problems. The child who clams up during the day often pours out her soul at night. Be alert for cues that a child may need to unload daytime baggage in order to enter sleep a settled person. Set the stage for your child to open up. A relaxing back rub is a winner. Then, without prying, give your child an opener to encourage her to talk: "Honey, I sense something is troubling you. If you want to tell me, I'll try to help."

you are a closely attached family. Upsetting the family harmony often leads to disturbed sleep. Even children younger than one can sense when a parent is away.

Your child's security may be threatened. To ease this nighttime insecurity, put a futon or sleeping bag at the foot of your bed. Market this as a "special bed" to be used when daddy is away. The fun of sleeping in a special place will help her forget her fear, as will the closeness to you. Be open to this arrangement even when dad is home. If he's gone a lot, this nighttime closeness for the whole family could be a way to make up for lost time.

Separation anxiety can cause a child to become restless when fathers or mothers travel a lot. The child under four may not understand that mommy or daddy will be back in two days. When one or both of us must travel, we ease the separation by helping our children understand when we will come back. We take them to the airport and let them see planes taking off. While we're gone we call every day, and then we have our substitute caregiver bring the chil-

dren to the airport to see our plane land and watch us deplane. Your child may not comprehend the concept of "two days," so use concrete terms she can understand: "Today, we'll go to the store and visit Grandma and then go to sleep. Tomorrow, we'll play with your friends. One more bedtime, and then Daddy will come home." Make a chart or a picture and cross off the events as they happen. Also, ask dad to make a tape recording of him reading the child's favorite stories and bedtime songs.

The Midnight Visitor

Our three-year-old sometimes comes into our bed in the middle of the night and I wake up with his cold feet on my back. I don't want him in my bed. That's my space and I don't sleep well with him there.

During high-need times expect little midnight visitors. That goes with the parenting package. Nighttime discipline involves giving your child two messages: (1) Nighttime is for sleeping, and (2) If you have trouble sleeping, I will help you. Take charge of your nighttime by establishing bedroom rules. Teach your child to respect your need to sleep. Put a futon at the foot of your bed and call it a "special bed." Or if your child needs a more enticing substitute for your bed, try a child-sized sleeping bag decorated with Winnie-the-Pooh or whoever is the current favorite. Lay down the rules: "Mommy and Daddy need to sleep because if we don't we will be grouchy tomorrow. If you are scared and need to come into our room, we'll leave the door open for you, but you have to tiptoe in as quietly as a mouse and climb quietly into your 'special bed,' fall asleep quietly,

Tuck Me In, Dad

Little minds are in a receptive state at bedtime. Bedtime stories can reflect on the day and neatly tuck in a little teaching. Your growing-up years can make some great stories. Surround your child with pleasant thoughts and admirable values as she drifts off to sleep. Do this night after night and these bits of wisdom will be filed away in her library of experiences. Years later these bedtime lessons will be an important influence in her life. Bedtime prayers are a time-honored tradition effective for smoothing out the wrinkles of life and for passing on parental values and beliefs.

A word of advice: Even though their eyes are closing, children's ears are very keen to follow a story. A seven-year-old friend of ours instructs his mother to "Keep reading — I can still hear you even when I'm sleeping."

dling with him, especially as we all fall asleep, he's an after-midnight kicker, and we'd spend most of the nights he was with us crossing our arms over our sensitive body parts. So we made a deal. We told Josh that we loved sleeping with him, but now that he was bigger, we didn't sleep well when he was in our bed all the time, and this made us tired and grumpy parents. We further explained that we could probably handle feeling that way once a week. So we made up a chart and told Josh that if he stayed in his own bed all night Monday through Saturday, he could sleep with us all night on Sunday. Now Josh is eager to sleep "well" on his own so that we can all enjoy our Sunday night snuggles.

Night Waking After Mother Returns to Work

I've recently returned to full-time employment. Since then our toddler wakes up in the middle of the night and climbs into our bed, and she seems more reluctant to go to bed in the first place. Any connection?

This nighttime behavior is common and normal after mothers return to work outside the home. Yes, everyone needs to sleep, but children have nighttime needs. You could take the hard line here and either lock your door or lock your child's door, but this insensitive approach ignores the fact that your child has needs as pressing as your need to sleep. (It is never appropriate to lock your child in his bedroom or even to lock your own door at night except temporarily to ensure privacy for sex.)

By her nighttime behavior, your child is trying to tell you she misses you during the

and not wake us up." This stage will pass. If he still wakens you, matter-of-factly lead him to the futon and lie with him till he settles. If he refuses to go along with the routine, calmly escort him back to his room. Soon he will either stay in his room or come into yours quietly, keeping his cold feet to himself. (You could also have him wear socks at night and teach him to lie quietly next to you.)

Here's how creative parents we know solved the problem of the midnight visitor:

After we moved, our four-year-old Josh wanted to sleep with us all the time. Even after he fell asleep in his own bed, he'd creep in with us at about three o'clock in the morning. Even though we enjoy cud-

day and she needs you more at night now. Take this as a compliment to your parenting. Try lengthening the bedtime ritual to give her more attention. Put a futon or sleeping bag at the foot or side of your bed and, if your child is old enough, lay down the conditions mentioned in the preceding paragraphs under the heading "The Midnight Visitor." If you child is still in a crib, try the *sidecar arrangement:* Place your child's crib adjacent to your bed and remove the near-side rail. Be sure the mattress is flush against your own. The sidecar arrangement respects both your bed space and that of your child yet provides a nighttime closeness that your chld seems to need. If these alternatives do not satisfy your little person, try letting her sleep in your bed — if all sleep well in this arrangement. This nighttime closeness can make up for some of what your child is missing now that you are gone all day.

"But I'm being had. Isn't she manipulating me?" you may wonder. Consider this from another perspective. A sensitive disciplinarian respects her own needs and those of her child, as you would in a relationship with another adult. This is discipline based on love, not power. It leaves a lasting impression.

Here is another thought to consider: Now that both parents are working outside the home, early bedtimes are not realistic. Otherwise, the only daily interaction would be that "happy hour" before dinner when a tired child is at his worst behavior. Instead, have your caregiver give your child a later nap so that she is well-rested and sociable when you arrive home from work. Expect a longer bedtime ritual and later bedtime to give your child a greater quantity of quality time.

Waking Up Too Early

Our three-year-old wakes up at 5:00 A.M. to play. He's bright-eyed and bushy-tailed and ready to go, but I'm not.

Here's where your need to sleep takes precedence over your child's desire to play. Enforce the rules: Nighttime is for sleeping, not playing. "You may not wake Mommy or Daddy up unless you are sick, scared, or need help. We need to sleep, otherwise we can't be a fun mommy or daddy the next day." If your child awakens ready to play and doesn't seem tired the next day, perhaps he's ready to awaken. Try putting him to bed later.

Here's a nighttime technique we have used with occasional success: When your child wakes up and comes into your room ready to play, take him into your bed, and try to go back to sleep. Cuddle up to your child to settle him. You may be able to get him back to sleep. If he wriggles away, feel free to just drift off, hoping that the little intruder will leave you alone and amuse himself until the alarm rings.

Give your child alternative activities that he can do on his own if he does awaken ready to play. Put easily available snacks in his room to satisfy early-morning hunger and tide him over until breakfast. Role play: "If you wake up, play quietly *in your room* like this." Show him how to play with quiet toys like noiseless blocks and those made of foam rubber. "When we wake up we will come right into your room and see what you made."

Nighttime Fathering

I get stuck putting our two-year-old to bed every night. We both still enjoy breastfeed-

ing off to sleep, but sometimes I'd like a break. She won't go to sleep for her father.

It's normal for children to prefer one or the other parent to put them to bed. But night after night of the same ritual can exhaust even the most committed mother, and it deprives the child of experiencing different ways of being parented to bed. This problem could be avoided by dad getting used to comforting and bedding down the toddler. It's helpful and often necessary for babies and children to get used to the unique bedtime rituals of both parents (for fathering to bed suggestions, see pages 81 and 136). *Mothers, the reason your toddler "needs" you to get to sleep is because nursing is how she relaxes into sleep.* (Dad can help her relax, too. Long stories, back rubs, going for a walk or a ride, whatever it takes to help your child relax.) Arrange to be away occasionally at bedtime. If mom is around, some children won't settle for dad. Children may fuss at first at not getting their preference, but once reality hits, they settle down to their second choice and extract every ounce of what dad has to offer. Avoid the tendency to hover around your husband, ready to step in at your child's first protest. Give daddy and child time and space to work out their own bedtime ritual.

Refusing to Nap

Our three-year-old refuses to nap. I know he's tired, and by late afternoon he's a bear. How can I get him to nap?

Many children need an afternoon nap (or parents need them to nap) up to age four. Naps have restorative value, allowing the child to unwind, rest, and recharge to go on with the day. Part of discipline is to help a child develop habits that make his (and the family's) life run more smoothly. When your child's behavior no longer deteriorates late in the afternoon, he has outgrown the need to nap.

Sometimes the resistant napper just won't succumb to any sleep marketing. Announce "special quiet time." Set the time of the day your child needs a nap, and lie down with him, closing your eyes for effect. Mothers often need a rest as much as the children and find this midday rest therapeutic. Don't succumb to the temptation common to a busy parent and think, "Now I can get something done." Gradually your child may fall into a predictable nap time without your presence.

To entice resistant nappers, allow them to nap anywhere in the house. When, where, and how is up to the child. Make a "nap nook," a special place in a corner, on a mat, under the table, or in a little tent made up of blankets. Try a large cardboard box with an opening like a cat door that the child crawls into when he is tired. This capitalizes on children's natural desire to create their own little retreats in all the nooks throughout the yard and house.

Our "very busy" two-year-old couldn't relax enough to nap if we just lay with her. So Martha started a routine of going for a stroller ride at the right time, and this lulled her off for an hourlong snooze in the stroller parked in the front hall. Another predictable way of getting her to sleep is to wait until carpool time and let her fall asleep in her car seat, then carry her into the house.

Condition your child to nap. Set a consistent nap time. While you can't force the resistant napper to sleep, you can create an environment that allows sleep to overtake him: lunch, a story, a dark room, and quiet music. Don't expect these conditions to result in sleep every time, or you will set yourself up to feel angry when those little eyes won't close. He may be weary but not sleepy — he can be irritable without having "bed" shoved at him and perceived as a punishment. If your child is not ready to nap, he may need another hour to play before he truly needs and can accept sleep. Or he may simply need a brief "down" time of quiet play while resting in his room. By age three, some children are ready to go without a nap and have an earlier bedtime. This transition will take a while — several months of napping every other day, then napping once or twice a week. In the meantime remember that mothers at home with young children often function in a different zone from their prechild days. Appreciate this difference while it lasts, because it will pass. Think of it as functioning at half-power — you lower your expectations for those days when weariness but not sleep is your reality. Getting angry about it makes this hard to do.

One final thought: Early afternoon naps and early bedtimes are not realistic when one or both parents arrive home late from work. Encouraging the child to nap early in the afternoon "so he'll be tired and go to bed early and we can finally have some time to ourselves" deprives parents and child of prime time together. But it is no fun to be with a tired child. We have found that later naps work better for us. When I come home from work, I like to be greeted by a rested and playful child. With later bedtimes you do give up some child-free time together, but once you have a child, your night life won't be the same for a long time anyway.

Letting Your Child Cry It Out

I've tried every way to get our eighteen-month-old to stay asleep, but every night he wakes up and screams in his crib until we go in and comfort him. We thought he would sleep through the night by this age. My friends suggest that I just let him cry it out, but that doesn't feel right to me.

If it doesn't feel right, don't do it. Letting the child cry it out desensitizes you to your child's needs, and when you begin going against your intuition, you are weakening yourself as a disciplinarian. This insensitive method of sleep training keeps you from appreciating the real reason for your child's behavior. And it is likely to create a distance between you and your child. If you are trying the cry-it-out method and you are feeling increasingly uneasy, this method is not for you. Don't persist with an experiment that is not working. It takes two of you to fight. If you give up the war he'll give up, too.

Besides not benefiting parents, the cry-it-out approach may harm the child by causing him to lose trust and become angry. The reason this advice is so popular is because it's easy to give. (No wonder busy pediatricians tend to like this method.) Up to age three or so, crying once or twice at night is not uncommon. Everyone wakes during the night — when a child wakes and cries it may mean he is experiencing separation anxiety. Here is a more sensitive approach to a child's night waking.

- Be sure your child gets plenty of physical activity during the day, outdoors when possible. As bedtime approaches, and your child is tired, use your winding-down rituals. Sleep psychologists insist

Letting baby cry it out risks losing sensitivity.

settles down, you aren't needed. If things escalate, setting off your sensitivity alarm, attend to your child matter-of-factly, by whatever means helps him resettle (no lights on, no playing, limit talking).

- **Help him learn to put himself back to sleep.** When you attend to your child have him hug his favorite teddy bear or whatever transitional object is necessary to help him resettle. When parenting your child to sleep, use the same association. Place the teddy bear in his arm and let him snuggle it off to sleep so that when he does wake up, the teddy bear might substitute for the parent. Be aware that you are helping him bond to things. Some children fall for the furry sub, but other more discerning kids won't settle for anything but a live body. One tired but creative parent, fearing her child would learn to bond to things, not her, left a continuous recording of herself singing a lullaby, so when her child awakened he would hear his mother's voice and resettle.

that if a child always associates you with going to sleep, he will not be able to resettle without your help when he wakes up. This sounds rational, but to advise a parent to put a crying child down in a crib and walk out of the room is inhumane, and few sensitive parents would do it anyway. How would you like to go to sleep on such a negative note every night? Wouldn't you be *more* likely to wake up if you were distraught when you fell asleep?

- After parenting your child to sleep, the first time he arouses, instead of rushing in, give him time to resettle on his own. Don't put time limits on how long you wait. Instead, use your sensitivity as a barometer of your response. If he quickly

- As you ease your child out of nighttime dependence, increase your degree of daytime attachment: more holding, more playtime together. As you are weaning your child from you at night, use your child's daytime behavior as a barometer. If all is well and you both remain sensitive and trusting, continue with this nighttime weaning. If, however, you sense changes in your baby's daytime behavior — clinginess, anger, tantrums — or you find a distance developing between you and your child, increase your nighttime responsiveness until you get your sensitive self and child back. Allow trust to build back up before trying again in about two weeks. The difference in this more sensitive way of dealing with night waking is that your child becomes a partner in this approach, and you use both your own sensitivity barometer and that of your child as an index to whether it is working.

Nighttime responsiveness sends your child the message: We care about you at night, just as we care about you during the day. If the above sequence of training sounds tedious to you, you could consider having your child sleep with you. Often this solution brings immediate relief to everyone. Sometimes, however, when sleep sharing is tried later in a baby's life it may take a few weeks for all three of you to adjust.

II

CORRECTING UNDESIRABLE BEHAVIOR

In Part I we discussed how to get connected to your child and help your child have a positive attitude so she wants to please. Yet even the most connected children misbehave. One of the reasons for correcting misbehavior is to help your child be pleasant to live with. This means that you are able to get her to stop doing things that are annoying to others. Also, children need to learn what is acceptable behavior, and they won't know unless you tell them. In Part II we discuss techniques of discipline, ways of shaping your child's behavior so that good conduct becomes part of her self. We also help you learn to live with bothersome habits and behaviors that are a normal part of growing up. Correcting undesirable behaviors inappropriately can create distance between you and your child. Appropriately correcting undesirable behavior draws you closer to your child, and she learns to appreciate you as a valuable resource. As you will see, our focus is not to control the child by external force but to help children develop inner controls to correct themselves.

Spanking — No? Yes? Sometimes?

PARENTS STILL HIT THEIR KIDS, despite hundreds of studies showing that spanking harms rather than helps behavior. Spanking rarely works, yet this method of behavior control persists. Parents justify, "We don't hit our kids, we spank them." What's the difference? When an adult strikes another adult we call it hitting; when a child strikes another child we call it hitting; but when an adult strikes a child, parents soften the description to "spanking." Spanking persists among parents who as children were treated that way and among parents who don't know better alternatives.

TEN REASONS NOT TO HIT YOUR CHILD

1. Hitting Models Hitting

There is a classic story about the mother who believed in spanking as a necessary part of discipline until one day she observed her three-year-old daughter hitting her one-year-old son. When confronted, her daughter said, "I'm just playing mommy." This mother never spanked another child.

Children love to imitate, especially people whom they love and respect. They perceive that it's OK for them to do whatever you do. *Parents, remember you are bringing up someone else's mother or father, wife or husband.* The same discipline techniques you employ with your children are the ones they are most likely to carry on in their own parenting.

The family is a training camp for teaching children how to handle conflicts. Studies show that children from spanking families are more likely to use aggression to handle conflicts when they become adults. Spanking demonstrates that it's all right for people to hit people, and especially for big people to hit little people and stronger people to hit weaker people. Children learn that when you have a problem you solve it with a good swat. A child whose behavior is controlled by spanking is likely to carry this mode of interaction into other relationships with siblings and peers, and eventually a spouse and offspring.

But, you say, "I don't spank my child that often or that hard. Most of the time I show

Verbal and Emotional "Hitting"

Physical hitting is not the only way to cross the line into abuse. Everything we say about physical punishment pertains to emotional/verbal punishment as well. Tongue-lashing and name-calling tirades can actually harm a child more psychologically. Emotional abuse can be very subtle and even self-righteous. Threats to coerce a child to cooperate can touch off his worst fear — abandonment. ("*I'm leaving* if you don't behave.") Often threats of abandonment are implied (such as when the way you stalk off gives the child the message that you can't stand being with her) or threats smack of emotional abandonment (by letting her know you are withdrawing your love, refusing to speak to her, or saying you don't like *her* if she continues to displease you). Scars on the mind last longer than scars on the body.

him lots of love and gentleness. An occasional swat on the bottom won't bother him." This rationalization holds true for some children, but other children remember spanking messages more than nurturing ones. You may have a hug-hit ratio of a hundred to one in your home, but you run the risk of your child remembering and being influenced more by the one hit than the hundred hugs, especially if that hit was delivered in anger or unjustly, which happens all too often.

Physical punishment shows that it's all right to vent your anger or right a wrong by hitting other people. This is why the parent's *attitude* during the spanking leaves as great an impression as the swat itself. How to control one's angry impulses (swat control) is one of the things you are trying to teach your children. Spanking sabotages this teaching. Spanking guidelines usually give the warning never to spank in anger. If this guideline were to be faithfully observed, 99 percent of spanking wouldn't occur, because once the parent has calmed down he or she can come up with a more appropriate means of correction.

2. Hitting Devalues the Child

For a child to act right, he has to feel right. The child's self-image begins with how he perceives that others — especially his parents — perceive him. Even in the most loving homes, spanking gives a confusing message, especially to a child too young to understand the reason for the whack. Parents spend a lot of time building up their baby or child's sense of being valued, helping the child feel "good." Then the child breaks a glass, you spank or scream at him, and he feels "I must be bad." This is the obvious conclusion since to the young child you are always right. Another obvious conclusion to the child is that the glass he broke is more valuable than he is. Of course the reason you hit is because you are angry, but your child will not enter that fact into his equation: Mom hit me equals I am bad. You rationalize that he needs to learn to be careful. He is learning, but not what you think. He is learning that he deserves to be hit because he is bad.

Even a guilt-relieving hug from a parent after a spank doesn't remove the sting. The child is likely to feel the hit, inside and out,

Slapping Hands

How tempting it is to slap those daring little hands! Many parents do it without thinking, but consider the consequences. Maria Montessori, one of the earliest opponents of slapping children's hands, believed that children's hands are tools for exploring, an extension of the child's natural curiosity. Slapping them sends a powerful negative message. Sensitive parents we have interviewed all agree that the hands should be off-limits for physical punishment. Research supports this idea. Psychologists studied a group of sixteen fourteen-month-olds playing with their mothers. When one group of toddlers tried to grab a forbidden object, they received a slap on the hand; other toddlers did not receive physical punishment. In follow-up studies of these children seven months later, the punished babies were found to be less skilled at exploring their environment. Better to separate the child from the object or supervise his exploration and leave little hands unhurt. (For alternatives to slapping, see pages 42–43.)

long after the hug. Most children put in this situation will hug to ask for mercy. "If I hug him, Daddy will stop hitting me." When spanking is repeated over and over, one message is driven home to the child: "You are weak and defenseless."

Joan, a loving mother, sincerely believed that spanking was a parental right and obligation needed to turn out an obedient child. She felt spanking was "for the child's own good." After several months of spank-controlled discipline, her toddler became withdrawn. She would notice him playing alone in the corner, not interested in playmates, avoiding eye contact with her. He had lost his previous sparkle. Outwardly he was a "good boy." Inwardly Spencer thought he was a bad boy. He didn't feel right — he didn't act right. Spanking made him feel smaller and weaker, overpowered by people bigger than him.

3. Hitting Devalues the Parent

Parents who spank-control or otherwise abusively punish their children often feel devalued themselves because deep down they don't feel right about their way of discipline. They feel more powerless. Often they spank (or yell) in desperation because they don't know what else to do but afterward feel more powerless when they notice it doesn't work. As one mother who dropped spanking from her correction list put it, "I won the battle but lost the war. My child now fears me, and I feel I've lost something precious."

Spanking also devalues the role of parent. Being an authority figure means you are trusted and respected but not that you are feared. Lasting authority cannot be based on fear. Parents who use spanking to control children enter into a lose-lose situation. Not only does the child lose respect for the parent, but the parents also lose out because they develop a spanking mind-set and have fewer alternatives to spanking. The parent has fewer preplanned, experience-tested strategies to divert potential misbehavior, so the child misbehaves more, which calls for more spanking. This child is not being taught to develop any inner control — another loss for the child.

Hitting devalues the parent-child relationship. Corporal punishment puts a *distance* between the spanker and the spankee. Our society already places too many obstacles between parent and child. This distance is especially troubling in home situations where parent-child relationships may already be strained, such as single-parent homes or blended families. While some children are forgivingly resilient and bounce back without seeming to have a negative impression on mind or body, for others it's hard to feel loved by the hand that hits them. The parent-child relationship suffers, affecting other relationships in the family as well.

4. Hitting May Lead to Abuse

Punishment can escalate. Once you begin physically punishing a child "a little bit," where do you stop? A toddler reaches for a forbidden vase. You tap the hand as a reminder not to touch. He reaches again; you swat the hand. After withdrawing his hand briefly, he once again grabs grandmother's valuable vase. You hit the hand harder. You've begun a game no one can win. The issue then becomes who's stronger — your child's will or your hand — rather than the problem of touching the vase. What do you do now? Hit harder and harder until the child's hand is so sore he can't possibly continue to "disobey"? The danger of beginning corporal punishment in the first place is that you may feel you have to bring out bigger guns: Eventually your hand would become a fist, the switch would become a belt, the folded newspaper would become a wooden spoon. What began seemingly innocently escalates into child abuse. Physical punishment sets the stage for child abuse. Parents who are programmed to spank set

themselves up for punishing harder, mainly because they have not learned alternatives and click immediately into the punishment mode when their child misbehaves.

5. Hitting Does Not Improve Behavior

Many times we have heard parents say, "The more we spank, the more he misbehaves." Spanking makes a child's behavior worse, not better. Here's why. Remember the basis for promoting desirable behavior: The child who feels right acts right. Spanking undermines this principle. A child who is hit feels wrong inside and this shows up in his behavior. The more he misbehaves, the more he gets spanked, the worse he feels. The cycle continues. We want the child to know that he did wrong, and to feel remorse, but still to believe that he is a person who has value.

The Cycle of Misbehavior

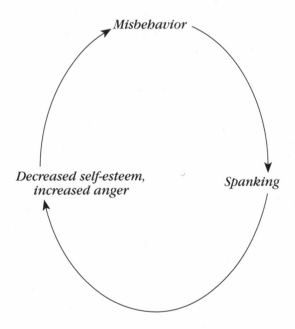

Misbehavior

Spanking

Decreased self-esteem, increased anger

One of the goals of disciplinary action is to stop the misbehavior immediately, and spanking may do that. But it is more important to create the conviction within the child that he doesn't want to repeat the misbehavior (that is, to promote internal rather than external control). One of the reasons for the ineffectiveness of spanking in creating internal controls is that during and immediately after the spanking, the child is so preoccupied with the humiliation of the physical punishment (and the degree of it he's getting) that he "forgets" the reason for which he was spanked. Sitting down with him and talking after the spanking to be sure he's aware of what he did can be done much better without the spanking part. Alternatives to spanking can be much more thought- and conscience-provoking for a child, but they may take more time and energy from the parent. This brings up one main reason some parents lean toward spanking — it's easier.

6. Hitting Is Actually Not Biblical

Don't use the Bible as an excuse to spank. There is confusion among some people of Judeo-Christian heritage who, seeking help from the Bible in their effort to raise good children, believe that God commands them to spank. They take "spare the rod and spoil the child" (which is not found in the Bible) seriously and fear that if they don't spank, they will commit the sin of losing control of their child. In our counseling experience, we find that these people are devoted parents who love God and love their children, but they misunderstand the concept of the rod.

Rod verses — what they really mean. The following are the biblical verses that have caused the greatest confusion:

> "Folly is bound up in the heart of a child, but the rod of discipline will drive it far from him." (Prov. 22:15)

> "He who spares the rod hates his son, but he who loves him is careful to discipline him." (Prov. 13:24)

> "Do not withhold discipline from a child; if you punish him with the rod, he will not die. Punish him with the rod and save his soul from death." (Prov. 23:13–14)

> "The rod of correction imparts wisdom, but a child left to himself disgraces his mother." (Prov. 29:15)

At first glance these verses may sound pro-spanking. But you might consider a different interpretation of these teachings. "Rod" (*shebet*) means different things in different parts of the Bible. Our Hebrew dictionary defines it as a stick, whether for punishment, writing, fighting, ruling, walking, or other activities. While the rod can be used for hitting, it is also used to protect vulnerable sheep. Shepherds don't use the rod to beat their sheep — and children are certainly more valuable than sheep. As shepherd-author Philip Keller teaches so well in his book *A Shepherd Looks at Psalm 23,* the shepherd's rod was traditionally used to fight off *prey* and the staff was used gently to *guide* sheep along the right path, as in the phrase "your rod and your staff they comfort me" (Psalm 23:4). Jewish families we've interviewed who carefully follow dietary and lifestyle guidelines in the Scripture do not practice "rod correction"

with their children because they do not follow that interpretation of the text.

The book of Proverbs is one of poetry. It
is logical that the writer would have used a
well-known tool to form an image of authority. We believe that this is the point
made about the rod in the Psalms: Parents,
take charge of your children. When you reread the "rod verses," use the *concept of
parental authority,* rather than the concept
of beating or spanking, when you come to
the word "rod." It rings true in every instance.

While Christians and Jews believe that
the Scripture is the inspired word of God, it
is also a historical text that has been interpreted in many ways over the centuries,
sometimes incorrectly in order to support
the beliefs of the times. These "rod" verses
have been burdened with interpretations
about corporal punishment that support
human ideas. Other parts of the Bible, especially the New Testament, suggest that respect, authority, and tenderness should be
the prevailing attitudes toward children
among people of faith.

In the New Testament, Christ modified
the traditional eye-for-an-eye system of justice with his turn-the-other-cheek approach.
Christ preached gentleness, love, and understanding, and he seemed to be against any
harsh use of the rod, as stated by Paul in 1
Corinthians 4:21: "Shall I come to you with
the rod, or in love and with a gentle spirit?"
Paul went on to teach fathers about the importance of not provoking anger in their
children (which is what spanking usually
does): "Fathers, do not exasperate your
children" (Eph. 6:4), and "Fathers, do not
embitter your children, or they will be discouraged" (Col. 3:21).

In our opinion, nowhere in the Bible

does it say you must spank your child to be
a godly parent.

Spare the Rod!

There are parents who should not
spank and children who should not be
spanked. Are there factors in your history, your temperament, or your relationship with your child that put you at
risk for abusing your child? Are there
characteristics in your child that make
spanking unwise?

• Were you abused as a child?
• Do you lose control of yourself easily?
• Are you spanking more, with fewer
results?
• Are you spanking harder?
• Is spanking not working?
• Do you have a high-need child? A
strong-willed child?
• Is your child ultrasensitive?
• Is your relationship with your child
already distant?
• Are there present situations that are
making you angry, such as financial or
marital difficulties or a recent job
loss? Are there factors that are lower-
ing your own self-confidence?

If the answer to any of these queries is
yes, you would be wise to develop a
no-spanking mind-set in your home and
do your best to come up with noncor-
poral alternatives. If you find you are
unable to do this on your own, talk
with someone who can help you.

Corporal Redirection Versus Corporal Punishment

Here is an example of an alternative to spanking that physically corrects misbehavior without inflicting pain. Lauren is our family monkey; she is always climbing on things. One day Martha walked into the kitchen to see then twenty-two-month-old Lauren standing on the countertop sorting through the spice rack. (Rarely had she gotten to this level in her adventures without someone intervening.) In a rapid reflexive move, Martha swung one hand under Lauren's bottom and the other arm around her middle as she swooped her off the countertop with a firmness and swiftness that surprised them both, while saying something like "Not safe! You stay down!" Lauren happened to be bare-bottomed, so the swift, firm hand made a slightly smarting sensation on her bare skin. This registered with Lauren. She looked closely at Martha to detect anger or intent to hurt in her mother's body language. Finding none, she interpreted her removal as protection and correction rather than punishment, and she cut short her howl of protest. Martha's physical action inflicted direction, not pain. The sureness and swiftness of the movement certainly left its mark on Lauren's mind. Lauren learned, once again, that Martha is the parent and she is the child. To Lauren, Martha's bigness is not a threat but a security ("Mom can rescue me because she is big"), even though the rescues are limits to freedom that are often frustrating to Lauren. It is very important for children to get the clear message that their parents are in charge. With young children most of this impression will need to be made physically. Words alone won't work.

7. Hitting Promotes Anger — in Children and in Parents

Children often perceive physical punishment as unfair. They are more likely to rebel against spanking than against other correction techniques. Children do not think rationally like adults, but they do have an innate sense of fairness — though their standards are not the same as those of adults. This can prevent punishment from working as you hoped it would and can contribute to an angry child. Oftentimes, the sense of unfairness escalates to a feeling of humiliation. When punishment humiliates children they either rebel or withdraw. While spanking may appear to make the child afraid to repeat the misbehavior, it is more likely to make the child fear the spanker.

In our experience, and that of many who have thoroughly researched corporal punishment, some children whose behaviors are spank-controlled throughout infancy and childhood may appear outwardly compliant, but inside they are seething with anger. They feel that their personhood has been violated, and they detach themselves from a world that they perceive has been hurtful to them. They find it difficult to trust, becoming insensitive to a world that has been insensitive to them.

Parents who examine their feelings after spanking often realize that all they have accomplished is to relieve themselves of anger. The impulsive release of anger often becomes addicting, perpetuating a cycle of abusive punishment. We have found that the best way to prevent ourselves from acting on the impulse to spank is to instill in ourselves two convictions: (1) We will not spank our children, and (2) We will discipline them. Since we have decided that spanking is not an option, we must seek out better alternatives.

8. Hitting Brings Back Bad Memories

A child's memories of being spanked can scar otherwise joyful remembrances of growing up. People are more likely to recall traumatic events than pleasant ones. I grew up in a very nurturing home, but I was occasionally and, in the adults' eyes, deservedly whipped. I vividly remember the willow-branch scenes. After my wrongdoing my grandfather would tell me I was going to receive a whipping and send me to my room. I remember looking out the window, seeing him walk across the lawn and take a willow branch from the tree. Then he would come into my room and whip me across the back of my thighs with the branch. The willow branch seemed to be an effective hitting tool because it stung and made an impression upon me — physically and mentally. Although I do remember growing up in a loving home, I don't remember specific happy scenes with nearly as much detail as I remember the whipping scenes. I have always thought that one of our goals as parents is to fill our children's memory bank with hundreds, perhaps thousands, of pleasant scenes. It is amazing how the unpleasant memories of spankings can block out those positive memories.

9. Spanking Has Bad Long-Term Effects

Research has shown that spanking can leave scars deeper and more lasting than a fleeting redness of the bottom. Here is a summary of the research on the long-term effects of corporal punishment:

- In a prospective study spanning nineteen years, researchers found that children who were raised in homes with a lot of corporal punishment turned out to be more antisocial and egocentric and that physical violence became the accepted norm for these children when they became teenagers and adults.

- College students showed more psychological disturbances if they grew up in a home with less praise, more scolding, more corporal punishment, and more verbal abuse.

- A survey of 679 college students showed that those who recall being spanked as children accepted spanking as a way of discipline and intended to spank their own children. Students who were not spanked as children were significantly less accepting of the practice than those who were spanked. The spanked students also reported remembering when their parents were angry during the spanking; they remembered both the spanking and the attitude with which it was administered.

- Spanking seems to have the most negative long-term effects when it replaces positive communication between parent and child. Spanking had less damaging long-term effects if practiced in a loving home and nurturing environment.

- A study of the effects of physical punishment on children's later aggressive behavior showed that the more frequently a child was given physical punishment, the more likely it was that she would behave aggressively toward other family members and peers. Spanking caused less aggression if it was done in an overall nurturing environment and the child was always given a rational explanation of why the spanking occurred.

- A study to determine whether hand slaps had any long-term effects showed that toddlers who were punished with a light slap on the hand showed delayed exploratory development seven months later.

- Adults who received a lot of physical punishment as teenagers had a rate of spouse-beating that was four times greater than those whose parents did not hit them.

- Husbands who grew up in severely violent homes are six times more likely to beat their wives than men raised in nonviolent homes.

- More than one out of four parents who had grown up in a violent home were violent enough to risk seriously injuring their child.

- Studies of prison populations show that most violent criminals grew up in a violent home environment.

- The life histories of notorious murderers, muggers, rapists, and other violent criminals are likely to show a history of excessive physical discipline in childhood.

The evidence against spanking is overwhelming. Hundreds of studies all come to the same conclusions:

1. The more physical punishment a child receives, the more aggressive he will become.
2. The more children are spanked, the more likely that they will be abusive toward their own children.
3. Spanking plants seeds for later violent behavior.
4. Spanking doesn't work.

10. Spanking Doesn't Work

Many studies show the futility of spanking as a disciplinary technique, but none show its usefulness. In more than twenty years in pediatric practice, we have observed hundreds of families who have tried spanking and found it doesn't work. Our general impression is that parents spank less as their experience increases. Spanking doesn't work for the child, for the parents, or for society. Spanking does not promote good behavior; it creates a distance between parent and child, and it contributes to a violent society. Parents who rely on punishment as their primary mode of discipline don't grow in their knowledge of their child. It keeps them from creating better alternatives, which would help them to know their child and build a better relationship. In the process of raising our own eight children, we have also concluded that spanking doesn't work. We found ourselves spanking less and less as our experience and number of children increased. In our home, we have programmed ourselves against spanking and are committed to creating an attitude within our children, and an atmosphere within our home, that renders spanking unnecessary. Since spanking is not an option, we have been forced to come up with better alternatives. This has not only made us

When You Need Professional HELP!

Most discipline problems can be handled by just taking the time to assess the strength of your parent-child connection, using commonsense techniques, and trying one approach after another until you find what works. Yet there are times when you need outside help. Consider two different types of counselors. Consult experienced, happy parents whose advice you value. They can offer practical tips to make living with your child easier. You may need to dig more deeply into disciplining yourself in order to discipline your child. You may require the help of a therapist. Here are some red flags that mean you are at risk for disciplining unwisely.

- **Yelling.** Do you go into frequent rages that are out of control, calling your child names ("Brat," "Damn kid") and causing your child to recoil and retreat? This means that you are letting your child punch your anger buttons too easily, that you may not have control of your anger buttons, or that there are simply too many of them.

- **Mirroring unhappiness.** Do you walk around all day reflecting to your child that you are unhappy as a person and as a parent? Kids take this personally. If they bring you no joy, they must be no good. Life is a "downer."

- **Parentifying.** Are your children taking care of you instead of vice versa? Are you crying and complaining a lot and showing immature overreactions to accidents or misbehaviors? That scares children. You're supposed to be the parent, the one in control protecting them.

- **Blame shifting.** Do you unload your mistakes on your kids or your spouse? If so, children learn that the way you deal with problems is to avoid taking personal responsibility for them, and that somehow these problems are just too big for you to manage or that you don't know how to ask for help.

- **Modeling perfection.** Are you intolerant of even trivial mistakes made by yourself or your child? The child gets the message that mistakes are horrible to make. This is particularly difficult for the "sponge child," the one who soaks up your attitudes and becomes superhard on himself.

- **Spanking more.** Are slaps and straps showing up in your corrections? Are most of your interactions with your child on a negative note?

- **A fearing family.** Is your child afraid of you? Does she cringe when you raise your voice and keep a "safe" distance from you? Is your child becoming emotionally flat, fearing the consequences of expressing her emotions?

While even the most healthy parent may experience one of these red flags occasionally, if you find they are becoming a routine way of life, for the sake of yourself and your child, get professional help.

better parents, but in the long run we believe it has created more sensitive and well-behaved children.

IS THERE A SAFE WAY TO SPANK?*

By now you should realize that our position on spanking is clear: *don't*. But we are experienced enough to realize that some loving, nurturing, committed parents believe in spanking as part of their overall discipline package. We are also quite aware that regardless of our advice against spanking, some parents are going to spank their children. For these parents, the best we can hope for is to help them spank in a way that will be less abusive. Consider these suggestions.

Examine your overall parenting style. If you are generally a nurturing parent practicing the attachment styles discussed in Chapter 2, a few spankings are unlikely to damage your child or your relationship with your child — but they are unlikely to help it either. If, on the other hand, you are practicing a more restrained style of parenting, spanking will be another obstacle that prevents you from knowing your child.

Examine your relationship with your child. Do you generally feel connected to your child? Do you feel that you have a handle on why your child behaves the way she does and can anticipate the undesirable behaviors before they begin? Do you know what triggers undesirable behaviors and what fosters desirable ones? Do you see signs that your child feels close to you? Does she make eye contact? Does she show ease in approaching you, putting her arms around you, and being picked up? Does she enjoy being with you, and is she able to communicate with you? If the answer to these questions is yes, then the rare spanking is unlikely to harm your relationship. If, however, you have a distant relationship and don't feel connected to your child, physical punishment is likely to increase the distance between you.

Here is a story from a mother of two of my patients. She is an intuitive, loving parent with a strong connection to her children, and she has a huge repertoire of alternatives to spanking. "There have been a few times when we have spanked our kids, and it was when they were between three and five years old. It was three or four times for our daughter, maybe once or twice for our son. I don't like to see tantruming children flailing out of control. They need something to help them get control back. So on the few occasions that they were literally out of control we've used spanking. I can remember when one of them was throwing a tantrum, my husband said, 'I have to swat your bottom to help you stop.' It shocked our son and he was able to regain his control." Other parents would handle this differently and would not respond this way to tantrums. Yet these parents know their children and know their own tolerances for "out of control" behavior. One comment I do have is that the reason the swat worked is that it had *shock value,* meaning it was the first (or rare) occurrence. It got the child's attention because these parents saved it for the one situation they personally could not tolerate.

---

*Readers, please do not take these words out of context. We have stated that we are against spanking. This section is not to be interpreted as a license to spank, but rather it is meant for those parents who have not yet decided whether spanking belongs in their whole discipline package.

Determine where spanking fits in your overall discipline package. Do you raise your hand in the swatting position or grab the wooden spoon as a knee-jerk response the moment your child misbehaves? One way to tell you are a reflex hitter is that your child flinches anytime you raise your hand suddenly when you are near him. Reflex spanking is harmful for several reasons: It's done out of anger, you may spank harder than intended, and you don't allow yourself time to try alternatives. If you resolve to put spanking way down on the list of correction techniques, you will be motivated to use alternatives rather than immediately click into "hit mode."

Don't spank in anger. If you are an angry person given to impulsive hitting, realize you are at risk for spanking abusively and dangerously. Some children have a way of pushing "hot buttons" in adults, and some adults have very sensitive buttons. Examine your feelings during and after spanking. Do you spank to punish your child, or to vent your anger? Who's the spanking for? You or your child? Says Martha: "Previously, when I did spank our children, I never felt right about it. I didn't spank because the behavior was so bad, but because I had been inconvenienced, and I was taking it out on the child. I used to slap our first two children in anger, and as I slapped I could see in my mind's eye how I had been slapped by angry adults as a child. It was those flashbacks that made me realize how wrong I was to be hitting my child."

When you are angry, you are likely to spank too hard because you are out of control. (Your "out of controlness" traumatizes them as much as the spanking.) Spanking in anger leaves a wrong impression on children's minds. They may be so bothered by the anger in your eyes and face that they don't realize the reason or the justification for the spanking. As a result, the punishment has no teaching value. A proper disciplinary action should improve your relationship with your child by creating a feeling that the parents are fair and consistent boundary setters; the child can depend on them to be in charge when he is out of control. Spanking, especially in anger, disturbs the trust between caregiver and child. In our family, we have found the best way to avoid spanking in anger is to mentally program ourselves against spanking: We have resolved never to spank. This preprogramming against spanking will override the reflex to smack a child and give you time to think about what type of correction is best in a given situation. Programming against spanking is a sort of safety valve that keeps you from possibly hurting your child.

Do not violate your child. Removing underwear in order to spank bare skin is a humiliating invasion of personal and private space that is sexually threatening and confusing to the child. So firmly resist the traditional image of the bare-bottomed child stretched across your lap.

Should you use your open hand, paddle, or a switch to spank? Use of any of the above will not cause permanent physical harm if you avoid too much force. The one tool we definitely advise against is a wooden spoon because we have seen bodily injury result from this clublike instrument. Any spanking that leaves black-and-blue marks (bruising) is wrong, whether you have used an object or your hand. Keep your hand opened flat — a fisted hand will be too forceful and damaging. A child old enough to spank will also understand that your loving hand is holding the spanking tool. The hand-versus-object debate is meaningless to him.

Explain the spank. Spanking without an explanation contributes little to discipline.

In fact, studies have shown that calm spanking preceded by a rational explanation does less harm and more good than spanking without such reasoning. Explaining the punishment can be therapeutic for both the

The Problems with Punishment

Punishment has had an up-and-down history. In "old-fashioned" discipline, punishment was in. In fact, discipline *was* punishment. In "new-fashioned" discipline, punishment is out. It is politically incorrect even to mention the p-word in behavior books. You have only to read today's newspapers to conclude that both of these extremes are unhealthy.

The child who is *punished too much* (or too severely) behaves more out of fear of punishment or the punisher than for the satisfaction of behaving right. For this child, fear and anger become part of his personality. A distance develops between the punisher and the child, and the parent-child relationship becomes a power struggle. Sometimes the child whose behavior is punishment-controlled seems "so good." "He knows better than to get out of line. I'll ground him." This child doesn't know *better,* he only knows that punishment will occur if he misbehaves. Underneath this facade of goodness simmers an angry child ready to explode into uncontrolled behavior once the threat of punishment is lifted. If punishment overtakes the whole atmosphere in the home, fear overcomes trust and this child is at risk of becoming angry, aggressive, withdrawn, and unhappy. He is also deprived of the opportunity to be a kid, make mistakes, and realize for him-

self the natural consequences of his actions. With overpunishment a child can become so wary of misbehaving that he is unwilling to risk any behavior that could get him into trouble. He loses his spontaneity — his life will be very safe, but he will lack common sense.

The child who is *punished too little* is ill-prepared for life. Children must learn there are limits in life and "consequences" (the psychologically correct term for punishment) when boundaries are exceeded — an *if-then* lesson. If a golfer hits the ball out of bounds, she gets a penalty stroke. The police officer isn't going to give the speeder a nice psychological talk; he's going to write a ticket. Granted if we lived in an ideal society with perfect parents and perfect citizens where people are governed by their conscience alone and follow the rules simply because it's the right thing to do, punishment would not be needed. But we don't live in an ideal society and we are not perfect people. Do you drive the speed limit because it's the safe and sane thing to do, or because you don't want to get a ticket? Respect for punishment is a normal motivating force in any society, even in the foundation of society — the family. Well-meaning parents may protect their child from punishment for fear of damaging his psyche, but the child who spanker and the spankee. It can help you decide whether or not your action will be appropriate. It makes it less likely that the child will repeat the misbehavior, gives your child a chance to make a judgment about the fairness of the action, and preserves the self-image of the child by treating her as a rational person. The child will definitely feel angry and humiliated about the spanking if she feels that there is no reason for it.

The Problems with Punishment (continued)

grows up never having to face the consequences of his actions never learns responsibility. He will lack respect for authority. Yet punishment cannot be the only motivation for good behavior within the family. The child who is frequently punished doesn't develop his own inner controls. The child who is never punished never develops respect for external controls. Either way, the child and society are placed at risk.

We have learned from experience that punishment *is* part of a balanced discipline package. In the attachment approach to discipline, our goal is to create an obedient attitude within the child and a structured environment around the child so that punishment is less necessary. Yet when it is needed — and it will be — the attachment approach to discipline will help you use punishment wisely, so that it helps the child obey without becoming angry or fearful. Punishment (appropriate, not abusive) works for some strong-willed children whose self-control is always teetering on the edge; the occasional use of appropriate punishment adds just the extra boundary that is needed to motivate good behavior. It can also be a way to get a child's attention when you need to focus attention on a particular behavior. This form of discipline works best in a parent-child relationship that is based upon solid attachment. A nurturing environment and loving messages should greatly outweigh the use of punishment in the home.

Punishment must be appropriate, not abusive. Shaming, humiliating, yelling, and physical correction all do harm and no good. These are all subtle forms of abuse. Be careful not to physically overpower the child over age three with forceful restraint or emotionally overpower a child with angry, ugly looks or tones of voice. These forms of punishment produce anger and resentment, not lasting changes in behavior. For best results, set the house rules ahead of time, and be sure your child knows the consequences of breaking the rules. This keeps you from giving harsh and unfair penalties in the heat of the moment. Irrational punishment ("You're grounded for two weeks!") is usually unfair, especially if the child didn't understand the rules in the first place or wasn't given advance warning. Appropriate punishments, for example, the teaching of natural consequences, withdrawal of privileges, and use of some forms of time-out (see Chapter 13, "Discipline by Shaping Behavior: Alternatives to Spanking") teach the child external rules with a view toward the child eventually setting rules for himself.

Getting the child to understand why she is being spanked helps to clear the air of angry feelings and contributes to her gaining self-control. If during your explanation you either begin to realize that you have the facts wrong or your heart is telling you there is a better way to deal with the situation, by all means switch to another corrective action and make a mental note to give this whole thing more thought.

A child under three will not be able to understand your explanation fully; she'll just know she's being hit and it has something to do with her being bad. She's probably also too young to separate her person from her action, so she'll think she's bad even though you are telling her "That was a bad thing to do."

Ask yourself, "Is spanking working?" Evaluate your correction techniques every month or two, especially physical punishment. Which ones are working? Is your child misbehaving less? Is your relationship with your child getting better? Is your child's self-worth increasing? If the answers to all the questions are yes, then you are on the right track. If you are spanking harder and more often, this technique is obviously not working and you need to consider alternatives. If any disciplinary action is not working, drop it. You need to consider other modes of correction if you find your child is misbehaving more. Change what you're doing if the distance between you and your child is increasing.

Examine the time you spend with your child. Is much of your quality time with your child spent punishing? If this is so, you are likely to have an angry child and a weak parent-child relationship. The joys of parenting and the stages of growing up are too precious to waste on such negative interaction. Consider changing your approach; spend a lot of time with your child just having fun. Let your child help you work around the house or run errands. Let him know you enjoy his companionship. As your child realizes how much fun it is to be with you, he will translate this into behaving well — which can be fun, too.

Discipline by Shaping Behavior: Alternatives to Spanking

CAN PEOPLE CHANGE? Certainly. We all modify our behavior in one way or another over the years. Children, who are growing and developing, are more malleable than adults, though some children have strong wills that are more resistant to change. With shaping techniques, you can help the changing and maturing process along. Shaping means providing your child with cues and reinforcements that direct her toward desirable behavior. As you shape behavior, your child's personality tags along and also changes and improves. The main ways to shape a child's behavior are through the use of praise, selective ignoring, and time-outs; through teaching an understanding of consequences; through the use of motivators, reminders, and negotiation; and through the withdrawal of privileges.

PRAISE

Praise is a valuable shaper; children want to please you and keep your approval. Yet you can easily overdo it. First of all, praise the behavior, not the person. Praises like "Good girl" or "Good boy" risk misinterpretation

and are best reserved for training pets. These labels are too heavy for some children. ("If I don't do well, does that mean I'm bad?") Better is: "You did a good job cleaning your room" or "That's a good decision" or "I like the way you used lots of color in this picture." The child will see that the praise is sincere since you made the effort to be specific; it shows that you're paying attention. For quickies try "Great job!" or "Way to go!" or even "Yesss!" To avoid the "I'm valued for my performance" trap, acknowledge the act and let the child conclude the act is praiseworthy. Be realistic. If you praise every other move the child makes, he will either get addicted to praise or wonder why you are so desperate to make him feel good about himself. You don't have to praise or even acknowledge things he just does for the joy of it, for his own reasons.

Shaping through praise works well if you have a specific behavior goal that you want to reach, for example, stopping whining. Initially, you may feel like you are acknowledging nearly every pleasant word your child says ("I like your sweet voice"). Eventually, as the whining subsides, the immediate need for praise lessens (of course, a

161

Discipline Talk

A major part of discipline is learning how to talk with children. The way you talk to him teaches your child how to talk to others. Here are some talking tips we have learned with our children.

Connect before you direct. Before giving your child directions, squat to his eye level and engage him in eye-to-eye contact to get his attention. Teach him how to focus: "I need your eyes." Offer the same body language when listening to the child. Be sure not to make your eye contact so intense that your child perceives this as controlling rather than connecting.

Address the child. Open your request with the child's *name*: "Stephen, will you please . . ."

Stay brief. We use the *one-sentence rule*: Put the main directive in the opening sentence. The longer you ramble, the more likely your child is to become parent-deaf. Too much talking is a very common mistake when dialoging about an issue. It gives the child the feeling that you're not quite sure what it is you want to say. If she can keep you talking she can get you sidetracked.

Stay simple. Use short sentences with one-syllable words. Listen how kids communicate with each other and take note. When your child shows that glazed, disinterested look, you are no longer being understood.

Ask your child to repeat your request back to you. If he can't, it's too long or too complicated.

Make an offer the child can't refuse. You *can* reason with a two- or three-year-old, especially to avoid power struggles: "Lauren, get dressed so you can go outside and play." Offer a reason for your request that is to the child's advantage, and one that is difficult to refuse. This gives her a reason to move out of her power position and do what you want her to do.

Be positive. Instead of "No running," try, "Inside we walk, outside you may run."

Begin your directives with "I want." Instead of "Get down," say "I want you to get down." Instead of "Let Becky have a turn," say "I want you to let Becky have a turn now." This works well with children who want to please but don't like being ordered. By saying "I want," you give a reason for compliance rather than just an order.

Connect before you direct.

"When . . . then." "*When* you get your teeth brushed, *then* we'll begin the story." "*When* your work is finished, *then* you can play." "When," which implies that you expect obedience, works better than "if," which suggests that the child has a choice when actually you don't mean to give him one.

Legs first, mouth second. Instead of hollering "Turn off the TV. It's time for dinner!" walk into the room where your child is watching TV, join in with his interests for a few minutes, and then, during a commercial break, have him turn off the TV. Going to your child conveys you're serious about your request; otherwise children interpret this as a mere preference.

Give choices. "Do you want to put your pajamas on or brush your teeth first?" "Red shirt or blue one?"

Speak developmentally correctly. The younger the child, the shorter and simpler your comments should be. Consider your child's level of understanding. For example, a common error parents make is asking a three-year-old, "Why did you do

Discipline Talk (continued)

that?" Even most adults can't always answer that question about their behavior. Try instead, "Let's talk about what you did."

Speak socially correctly. Even a two-year-old can learn "please." Expect your child to be polite. Children shouldn't feel manners are optional. Speak to your children the way you want them to speak to you.

Speak psychologically correctly. Threats and judgmental openers are likely to put your child on the defensive. "You" messages make a child clam up. "I" messages are nonaccusing. Instead of "You'd better do this..." or "You must...," try "I would like..." or "I am so pleased when you..." Instead of "You need to clear the table," say "I need you to clear the table." Don't ask a leading question when a negative answer is not an option. "Will you please pick up your coat?" Just say "Pick up your coat, please."

Write it. Reminders can evolve into nagging so easily, especially for preteens who feel being told things put them in the slave category. Without saying a word you can communicate anything you need said. Talk with a pad and pencil. Leave humorous notes for your child. Then sit back and watch it happen.

Talk the child down. The louder your child yells, the softer you respond. Let your child ventilate while you interject timely comments: "I understand" or "Can I help?" Sometimes just having a caring listener available will wind down the tantrum. If you come in at his level, you have two tantrums to deal with. Be the adult for him.

Settle the listener. Before giving your directives, restore emotional equilibrium, otherwise you are wasting your time. Nothing sinks in when a child is an emotional wreck.

Replay your message. Toddlers need to be told a thousand times. Children under two have difficulty *internalizing* your directives. Most three-year-olds begin to internalize directives so that what you ask begins to sink in. Do less and less repeating as your child gets older. Preteens regard repetition as nagging.

Let your child complete the thought. Instead of "Don't leave your mess piled up," try "Matthew, think of where you want to store your soc-

cer stuff." Letting the child fill in the blanks is more likely to create a lasting lesson.

Use rhyme rules. "If you hit, you must sit." Get your child to repeat them.

Give likable alternatives. "You *can't* go by yourself to the park; but you *can* play in the neighbor's yard."

Encourage your child to use words instead of body. "Use your words to tell Mommy you're upset."

Give advance notice. "We are leaving soon. Say bye-bye to the toys, bye-bye to the girls...."

Open up a closed child. Carefully chosen phrases open up closed little minds and mouths. Stick to topics that you know your child gets excited about. Ask questions that require more than a yes or no. Stick to specifics. Instead of "Did you have a good day at school today?" try "What is the most fun thing you did today?"

Use "When you ... I feel ... because ..." *When you* run away from mommy in the store *I feel* worried *because* you might get lost.

Close the discussion. If a matter is really closed to discussion, say so. "I'm not changing my mind about this. Sorry." You'll save wear and tear on both you and your child. Reserve your "I mean business" tone of voice for when you do.

booster shot is needed for relapses), and you move on to shaping another behavior.

Change praises. To keep your child's attention, change the delivery of your accolades. As you pass by the open door of the picked-up room, say "Good job!" Show with body language a thumbs-up signal for the child who dresses herself. Written praises are a boon in large families. They show extra care. Private praises help, too. Leave little "Nice work" notes on pillows, "Done!" Post-its on homework, messages that convey that you noticed and that you are pleased.

As an exercise in praise giving, write down how many times you praised and how many times you criticized your child in the last twenty-four hours. We call these pull-ups and put-downs. If your pull-ups

don't significantly outnumber your put-downs, you are shaping your child in the wrong direction.

Praise genuinely. Praise loses its punch if you shower acclaim on usual and expected behavior; yet when the child who usually strikes out finally hits the ball, that's praiseworthy. Simply *acknowledge* expected behavior, rather than gushing praise. Acknowledgment is dispassionate praise that shapes a child to please himself rather than perform for approval. Don't make up fake kudos. The child will see through them and begin to suspect even your genuine praise. For example, before you praise, try to read your child's body language to see whether she feels the job is praiseworthy. If she approaches you eagerly, saying "Daddy, look at my drawing I did at school," this child

---

The Art of Complimenting

Teach your child to be comfortable giving and receiving compliments. Tell your child, "What a handsome boy you are" or "How pretty you look in that dress!" Eye and body contact during your delivery reinforces the sincerity of your acknowledgment. Make sure you're sincere. Attachment-parented children immediately see through, and shun, insincere compliments. When you hear your children complimenting one another, compliment yourself for your modeling.

Children with low self-worth have difficulty giving and receiving compliments. They are so hung up on how they imagine the receiver will take their tribute that they clam up; they feel so unworthy of any compliment that they shrug it off.

If you are like that as a person, learn to give and take a compliment yourself so that you can model this to your child. Compliment yourself: "I feel good about the sale I made today!" Acknowledge your child's praise "You're the best mommy" by saying "Thank you, honey, I like to hear that." Some parents hear these words often, yet deny the truth of their child's words by the outward response they give (sighing, gulping, frowning, shrugging, or grimacing) and by their internal guilt trip. If this is you, start believing what your child intuitively knows — you're the best parent for this child. Parental self-image directly affects a child's self-confidence and the child's ability to give and receive compliments comfortably.

Expect Good Behavior

Excessive praise will give children the message that obedience and good behavior are optional. It's better to give your child the message that he is doing *exactly what you expect,* not something out of the ordinary. Children are programmed to meet your expectations. Sometimes all that is needed for you to break a negative cycle is to expect good behavior. Treat them as if they *really are* going to choose right. When parents don't expect obedience, they generally don't get it.

external motivator. The ultimate goal of discipline is self-discipline — inner motivation. We praise good grades and have always motivated our children by planting the idea that good grades are one ticket to success. We always temper our praise with "How do you feel about your report card? We want you to get good grades mainly because it makes *you* happy." When possible, turn the focus back on the child's feelings: "You played well at the recital, bet you're relieved and proud." For best results with praise to shape behavior, set the conditions that help children know how and when to praise themselves.

deserves praise that shares her excitement. If she pulls the paper out of her schoolbag and tosses it on the kitchen table, praise may not be in order.

Avoid praises with a hidden agenda. Says Bill: "I had been on our teenager's case about dressing more modestly. One day I said, 'I like your new wardrobe.' She saw right through this, and took it as a put-down of her old wardrobe. She interpreted my comment as an attempt to manipulate what she wears. A better approach would have been more specific and more centered on her. Martha might say to her, 'That longer shirt really makes you look graceful' or 'Classy jacket — you look ready for college.' As her father, I would say, 'You look great, dear,' or just keep silent and give her an approving smile."

Problems with praise. While appropriately used praise can shape behavior, it's not the only way to reinforce good behavior. In some ways it's superficial. Praise is an

SELECTIVE IGNORING

To preserve parental sanity we run a tight ship in certain situations. In other areas we are more lax. We have learned to ignore "smallies" and concentrate on "biggies" (see discussion of smallies and biggies, page 121). A smallie is a behavior that is annoying but doesn't harm humans, animals, or

Who's in Charge?

Martha has found that on days when she is low on energy or well-being, she loses her "adultness" — she wheedles, complains, pleads, whines, even cries under stress. This is when the children have to wonder who's in charge — clearly she's not. When the parent is being mature and balanced, the question of "who's in charge" is moot — the adult naturally carries the authority and the children naturally tend to obey because they know what's expected.

property, or which even if uncorrected does not lead to a biggie. These childish irresponsibilities will self-correct with time and maturity.

Ignoring helps your child respect the limits of a parent's job description; for example, "I don't do petty arguments." One day two five-year-olds were playing in our front yard, and they got into a toy squabble. No one was getting hurt. They tried to drag Martha into the ring. She simply said "You kids are too big to act like this" and walked away. The kids got the point and settled the problem themselves.

Ignoring undesirable behaviors works best if you readily acknowledge desirable ones. The ignored interrupter learns to enter conversations with "Excuse me" once you reinforce the use of polite address. Ignore the misbehavior, not the child.

Harmless behaviors fade both as your tolerance level widens and as you avoid reactions that reinforce the child's behavior. It's helpful to gain practice in *selective ignoring* in the early years of a child's life to prepare you for the challenges yet to come — accepting teenagers with their unconventional dress and hairstyles, loud music, and moody behaviors.

TIME-OUT

Time-out is a correction strategy that works much of the time. There is a time, place, and way to make it work for you.

Time-out versus benching. Time-out is not a punishment; it seldom works when it is used that way. Used as a punishment, it is called "benching," as when a hockey player is benched in the penalty box for misconduct. Time-out calls for a break in the unde-

sirable action. It stops misbehavior and gives the older child, and parents, time to reflect. Instead of viewing it as a jail sentence, the older child should be taught to view it as a way of getting herself under control: a few minutes to reflect on what went wrong and how to make it right. Whether you call your strategy "time-out" or "benching" is often psychological semantics. The real issue is whether it works. When our four-year-old was disruptive at the dinner table, we planted him on the nearby piano bench for a few minutes. Oftentimes, just the warning "Piano bench" was enough to stop his misbehavior. In that case, we called our strategy a "reminder." Between two and three years of age, most children can understand the concept of "time-out." One day our two-and-a-half-year-old, Lauren, after being pestered by her brother, said, "Stephen pushed me — *time-out*."

Not only does time-out help children behave, it also helps parents. Time-out gives you something to do to stop a misbehavior; you gain time to plan your next move. It prevents parents from impulsively spanking. "I need time-out," revealed a mother who had been spanked as a child. She recognized that she was prone to impulsive anger and was in danger of striking her child impulsively when he "pushed her buttons." Realizing her vulnerability, she found time-out gave her a chance to cool off so she could return calm and collected to handle the conflict.

Time-out works better if it is used to shape behavior rather than punish. Picture kindergarten teacher Miss Goodchild plunking impulsive Johnny on a stool in a corner facing the wall. This doesn't do anything for Johnny except set him up as the center of attention and make him a prisoner, angry at

Time-out When You're Out

You can use time-out anywhere, as long as the place of retreat is unrewarding. For a peaceful interlude during shopping struggles, try giving your child time-out on a bench in the mall, in a boring corner in a supermarket, next to a tree in a park, or consider making an exit to your car. Put your child in the backseat while you doze for five minutes in the front. For safety's sake, be sure to keep your eye on the isolated child when using time-out in public.

the situation and at the person imposing the sentence. I can still remember the "time-outs" imposed on me at school. I was a problem child, especially in the early grades. In second grade, the teacher used what she thought was a time-out on me, but it didn't work. She would set me in the corner on the time-out stool. She was using humiliation and it backfired. It only encouraged me to continue my attention-getting antics. This teacher couldn't handle me, so I was prematurely promoted to the third grade. There I came under the firm hand of the school's best disciplinarian, Sister Mary Boniface. She gave me clear messages, making sure I knew what behavior was expected of me and what consequences would occur if I disobeyed. She also gave me a lot of attention, eye-to-eye contact with her hand on my shoulder. She showed that she genuinely cared for me as a person and was going to be sure that I learned how to control myself. When I looked as if I was about to get out of line, she would place her hand firmly on my shoulder and press hard enough that I would get the message. Of all my early disciplinarians, Sis-

ter Mary Boniface was the one I respected then and remember now.

How to Make Time-out Work for You

The following guidelines are just a starter from which you can branch out to create your own time-out style, one that works for you and your child.

Give lots of "time in." When behavioral psychologists introduced the time-out concept, it was called "time-out from positive reinforcement." Positive reinforcement means giving the child lots of positive "time in" with a connected style of parenting. Then if the child misbehaves, this positive parental input is briefly withdrawn. As a result, the child gets used to feeling right

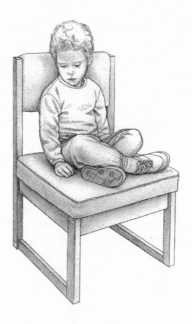

Time-out.

when acting right, and feeling not right when acting wrong. By making the connection between good behavior and good feelings the child becomes motivated to keep his act together. For time-out to work he first needs a large quantity of quality time in.

Prepare the child. Help your child connect his behavior with the time-out. Introduce time-out early, by eighteen months. Before that age, you will be using distraction and diversion to stop behaviors. Baby crawls toward the lamp. You intercept the curious explorer, carry him across the room, and sit between baby and the lamp. After some repetition baby gets the point: Certain behaviors will be immediately interrupted, so there's no point in attempting them. These baby diversions progress to toddler time-outs. In addition simply to interrupting an undesirable behavior, you now add a place to sit, such as a time-out chair. Time-out in your arms or sitting next to you is preferable if the toddler finds the chair too threatening, but you run the risk of his discovering that the way to get picked up and held is to misbehave. You can avoid this by holding your child a lot when he is behaving well — back to the concept of time in. Our grandson Andrew, at seventeen months, knew the difference between being held and time-out holding. He protested his time-out holding loud and clear. (If your toddler kicks and flails, you are only succeeding in making him angry.)

Language makes time-out easier. By two years of age most children understand what time-out means: If they misbehave it's off to the chair they go. They perceive time-out as a break in their activity, a parent-imposed (logical) consequence of their behavior. The older the child the more detailed the explanation can be. We started using official time-outs with Lauren when she was eighteen-months-old. She had witnessed many time-outs for Stephen, so when it was her turn she understood clearly what we were doing. We could tell by the gleam in her eye and her alert body language that this little ritual was a special experience, and she got into the spirit of it willingly. She also knew the ritual included an enforced (though brief) time of sitting alone. Stephen had always needed frequent reminders to stick to his time-outs, so she knew she was expected to stay seated. As soon as the novelty wore off, she was no longer amused.

Keep time-out brief. Escort your toddler to the time-out place immediately after the misbehavior. A prompt, cool, matter-of-fact approach aborts many protests. Since you set the ground rules beforehand, you need not explain, apologize, or get wishy-washy about your discipline. If your child senses uncertainty, a protest is likely to follow. Avoid yelling "I've told you no a thousand times. Now you go to your room and don't come out till I tell you to." This abusive style pushes anger buttons in the child, putting time-out into the revenge category and canceling its behavior-changing purpose. Keep the time brief — around one minute per year of age. For older children you can make the time fit the crime: "That's a five-minute time-out." When our kids were into hockey they better understood this mode of discipline: "Five minutes for pushing!"

Keep time-out quiet. This is not the time for your child to be screaming or for you to be preaching or moralizing. If there's a lesson you want your child to hear, save it for later when he'll be open to it.

No Nattering

"You're picking your nose again."
"Watch where you're going." "Late
again!" "Can't you do anything right?"
Persistent negative comments like
these, called nattering, nip away at a
child's self-worth. Studies show that
nattering does not improve behavior; it
actually worsens it. Nattering is especially defeating in children with a poor
self-image. Nattering and repeating
commands make children nervous.
Some children exhibit more than their
fair share of negative behavior, but constantly reminding them produces more
negative behavior. It is better purposely
to pick out some redeeming qualities
and concentrate on the positives ("I
like the way you stepped aside for your
sister"). You will see the negatives melt
away.

Continuing to talk, or repeating advice that you've previously given, tells
the child that you don't trust her to
carry out a simple request, such as "Put
a load of laundry in, please." If you add
a string of qualifiers, you're teaching
her you don't trust her to do it right
(*your* way). If you can't stop "advis-
ing," start writing notes.

You be the timer. "Two minutes" is meaningless to a child under three. A stove timer
or alarm clock makes a more lasting impression and helps you keep track of the time.
When the signal sounds, it simply announces that time's up. Let the child decide
his next course of action. He may still be
contemplating his behavior when the
buzzer sounds. No need to break his
thought by saying "You can come out of
time-out." He'll get the point by himself.
(See discussion of timers for sharing, pages
252–255.)

Pick the right place. You may have a des-
ignated time-out chair or stool for the toddler. A veteran mother in our practice
successfully uses the "naughty step," an idea
she gleaned from the book *The Pokey Little
Puppy's Naughty Day,* published by Golden
Books. The naughty step helps the puppy to
feel a little less "frisky" that day. For the
older child, try using her room. If you are
away from home, use any spot that removes
the child from the scene of the crime.
Oftentimes it's the actual removal of the
child from the place of misbehavior that
makes the impression rather than where, or
how long, the child sits or stands. Be sure
the time-out place doesn't have built-in rewards. To make the point, the retreat needs
to be a boring place. The TV is not on for
time-out!

**What if your child refuses to go or stay
in time-out?** Sit with her, and if necessary
keep putting her back physically and give
her the message "I'm the adult here. We are
taking time-out." If the time is short enough
and you are calm, there would be no reason for her to protest. If she screams about
it, have her sit until she's calm. If children
rebel at the negative sound of time-*out,* use
positive terms that fit the situation: "You
need a little *quiet time,*" or "*thinking
time*" or use the child's name, as in "Lauren
time."

For time-out to work for the older child,
he may need to understand it, not just that
you demand it. Try a sports model like a
basketball game on television: "Know what
the coach does when the team is falling
apart? He calls time-out. This lets the play-

ers cool off and think about how they can play a better game. That's what you need now."

This all seems so sensible, but remember, children may not think logically until around age six. If you can't sell your child on time-out, invoke your parental power. Give your child the message that he is going into time-out no matter what, so he might as well do it, get it over with, and get on with the day. For the child over five, add extra time for resistance: "Five extra minutes for protesting," announces the referee. If the child still refuses, pull out your reserves: grounding, withdrawal of privileges such as TV for the rest of the day or week — whatever has worked in the past. Give the child a choice: "You can either stay in your room for ten minutes or be bored the rest of the day."

Time-out for thought. Time-out gives your older child a chance to reflect on her deed, and it also gives you a chance to cool off and plan a strategy. While your child is in time-out, judge whether the misbehavior is a smallie that's over and done with and needs no further discipline or a biggie that needs more intensive care. If it's a biggie (for example, she hurt another person), *after* giving her a few minutes to cool off, say something like "I want you to think about what you did, how you would feel if your friend hurt you." Some children know intuitively the mental exercises to go through during time-out, but many do not. This is not a time for preaching or haranguing. Rather, matter-of-factly tell your child how you expect her to spend the time-out period. The most lasting impression is made when the child realizes the consequences of her actions on her own. That's self-discipline.

Time-out for parents. Time-out can be a retreat for mom. When our children are not really misbehaving but simply showing the childish behaviors of normal, noisy children, Martha says "I need time-out." She makes sure the children are in a safe environment and no one is getting hurt, goes into another room, ignores the noise, and regains her peace. A parent time-out also helps when you are playing a game with your child in which he is becoming a bit obnoxious. Announce that you had been having so much fun, but now you are not. "I'm going to go over and sit and read my book until you're ready to play nicely again. Let me know. I'll come back and we'll enjoy the game together."

Sometimes there are situations when your child is playing or yelling in a disturbing way, or being incessantly clingy despite the fact that you have given your maximum of "time in." Tell your child that you need some peace and quiet. Martha announces this by authoritatively stating "That's disturbing my peace." These messages help children respect the rights of others in their environment. Even parents who have learned to tune out the noise can only take so much.

Clear the air. After the time-out is over, it's over. The child has served his time and it's time to get on with the day. Convey to him that you now expect that he is ready to play nicely and quietly. Possibly orchestrate a new activity.

Parents as referees. Toddlers and young children often get very engrossed in their play. If there are a lot of children and a lot of toys in a small space, they get overstimulated and rev up into a play frenzy that gets out of control. This is not only intolerable to human eyes and ears, but it is also counterproductive to your child's play. If you sense that the play is getting out of hand, call a halt to the action before that happens or before you feel annoyed by it. Remove a few of the toys, separate the children, or change activities. It might be a time to sit the children down and read a five-minute story — a sort of halftime interlude in a boisterous game.

When several children are in a room and the behavior is deteriorating, it is often difficult to know who is the ringleader. Sometimes you simply have to separate everyone. Direct them to separate chairs, spaced out around the room, for five minutes before they can resume a calmer play activity. Sometimes it's necessary to put more space between them — one child in a time-out chair in the kitchen and another child in the living room. Though they seldom express it, children oftentimes appreciate caregivers rescuing them from themselves. They may recognize when they need relief. Once during a play frenzy, one of our children retreated from the battle and came into our room to announce "We need time-out."

HELP YOUR CHILD LEARN THAT CHOICES HAVE CONSEQUENCES

Experiencing the consequences of their choices is one of the best ways children can learn *self*-discipline. These lessons last because they come from real life. Most success in life depends on making wise choices. Being able to think ahead about the positive or negative consequences of an action and choose accordingly is a skill we want our children to learn.

Building a child's natural immunity to bad choices. Letting natural consequences teach your child to make right choices is a powerful learning tool. Experience is the best teacher: He's careless, he falls; he grabs something hot, he gets burned; he leaves his bicycle in the driveway, it gets stolen. Wise parents protect their children enough that they don't get seriously hurt but do not overprotect to the extent that a child doesn't learn the consequences of his folly. Some bruises and scrapes along the way are unavoidable and educational.

Children make unwise choices on the way to becoming responsible adults. Children must experience the consequences of their actions to learn from them. Within reason and safe limits, let your infant explore, fail, bump, and learn. Expect your preschooler to help clean up his messes. Let your school-age child experience the teacher's penalty for not completing homework by bedtime. After years of small inoculations of consequences, the child enters adolescence at least partially immunized against bad choices, having had some genuine experience with decision making. Children learn better from their own mistakes than from your preventive preaching.

Adolescence is a time when the consequences of wrong choices are serious. The child who has learned to deal with smallies is more likely to be successful with biggies. Being a wise immunizer means keeping a balance between overprotecting your child and being negligent ("Let him get hurt, he'll learn"). In the first case, the child enters adolescence with little practice at handling inevitable conflicts and risks. In the second case, the child feels no one cares. Either way, there are rough times ahead.

Sometimes the best solution is to offer your child guidance, state your opinion, and then back off and let the consequence teach your child.

Use each consequence as a teachable moment, not an opportunity to gloat. Avoid sentences that begin with "I told you so" or "If you would have listened to me...." To be sure that your child learns these little lessons of life, talk through each situation later. Replay the tape so that your child gets the point that choices count and his actions affect what happens. You want your child to realize that he is happier and his life runs more smoothly when he makes wise, though perhaps not easy, choices. Let the

consequence speak for itself. The child spills her soda and there's no more soda — without your commentary.

Use logical consequences to correct. Besides letting natural consequences teach your child, you can set up parent-made consequences tailored to have lasting learning value. Here's a logical consequence that parents in our practice tried: "Our son was four years old, and we had just moved into a new house. He had gotten a new bedroom set and was feeling very proud and grown up, enjoying his privacy and playing with his friends. It was time for the friends to leave. Our son became angry and kept slamming the door. We asked him to stop. We explained patiently why he shouldn't

Age	Child's Choice	Parent's Guidance	Consequence
1	Jumps on bed despite parents' warnings.	Redirects, cushions	"Goes boom."
2	Leaves tricycle in driveway.	Repeatedly tells child to store tricycle in garage.	Tricycle gets damaged and not replaced for a good while.
4	Overdoses on candy at party.	Advises child she will feel awful.	Develops "yucky tummy."
5	Insists on playing outside without sweater.	"It's winter outside."	Misses game to return for sweater.
6	Late for baseball practice.	"You have fifteen minutes."	Sits out next game for being late.
7	Leaves homework spread all over his floor.	"Put your schoolbooks away before bed."	Misses recess to redo homework.
10	Leaves bicycle out on the sidewalk.	"Take better care of your bike. A lot of bikes have been stolen in this area."	Bike gets stolen; next bike, he earns the money to buy.

keep slamming the door. We told him (after thirty minutes) that if this behavior continued, he would no longer enjoy the privacy of a door and Daddy would remove it. (He got this "Yeah, sure, Dad's going to take the door off" look of disbelief on his face.) For the next three days every time he got a little upset, he slammed the door. So on the fourth day he went out to play, and when he returned he found his door had been removed from the hinges. He only noticed it when he went to slam it and it was not there. A week later we put it back. Four years have passed, and he hasn't slammed the door since."

Our then ten-year-old, Erin, treasured her new bike, but now and then she would carelessly leave it overnight on the front sidewalk. On those nights the bike found its way up into the rafters of the garage and for several days she had to walk by and see it up there. This was a poignant and powerful reminder to her to care for her bike properly, and the bike slept safely in its normal place in the garage thereafter.

For the most learning value, balance negative with positive consequences: The child who frequently practices the piano gets the thrill of moving through his books quickly and receiving hearty applause at his recital. The child who consistently takes care of her bicycle merits a new one when she outgrows it. Otherwise she gets a used one or does without. The child who puts his sports equipment away in the same place each time gets the nice feeling of always being able to find his favorite bat or soccer ball.

In these examples, no amount of physical or verbal punishment could have had the lasting teaching value of natural and logical consequences. With consequences, the child makes the connection between her

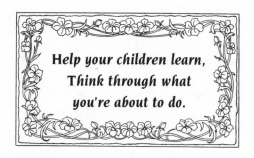

Help your children learn,
Think through what
you're about to do.

behavior and the results. You plant a lesson of life: Take responsibility for your behavior.

MOTIVATORS

Children and adults behave according to the pleasure principle: Behavior that's rewarding continues, behavior that's unrewarding ceases. While you don't have to go to the extreme of playing behavioral scientist, dangling cheese in front of little rats to direct them through the maze, you can invent creative ways to motivate desirable behavior with rewards. Motivators help family life run more smoothly: "First one in bed picks the story."

A word of caution. Prizes are a way to entice your child toward goals you've made for him. The ultimate goal is self-discipline — a child behaves because he wants to or because he knows you expect good behavior. He shouldn't expect a prize each time he behaves well. A friend who home-schooled her child until he was eight found that when he entered school, already a strong reader, motivated by the pleasure he found in reading, the reward system for reading used by the teacher was not appropriate for him. She wisely asked the teacher to not include him in that program because he would make out like a bandit. She knew his motivation would shift from reading for pleasure to reading for prizes. Ideally, reading and finishing a book is its own reward. Some children may need rewards to get them to read in the first place, but you run the risk that these children will never read for pleasure.

Still, kids are human, and humans go for that chunk of cheese. You do a job well partly because of the bonus you expect to get. If "rewards" or "bribes" offend the moralist in you, call them "motivators." An attachment-parented child is more likely to be motivated by social rewards than by prizes: "This coupon is good for one lunch date with Mommy or Daddy."

To work, a reward must be something your child likes and truly desires. Ask some leading questions to get ideas:

- "If you could do some special things with Mom or Dad, what would they be?"
- "If you could go somewhere with a friend, where would you like to go?
- "If you had a dollar, what would you buy?"

Granting privileges and rewards are discipline tools to set limits and get jobs done: "If you hurry and do a good job cleaning your room, you might get finished in time to play outside before dinner."

Rewards That Work

The best rewards are ones that children earn for their good behavior: "You're taking such good care of your train set. Let's go to the train store and get another boxcar." The natural consequences of good behavior

are not always motivating enough in themselves. Sometimes it is necessary to fabricate a reward.

Reward charts. Charts are a helpful way to motivate young children. They see their progress and participate in the daily steps toward the reward. The chart stands out as a testimony of good behavior for all to see. Charts work because they are interactive and fun. Even the business world uses charts as profit motivators. Throughout life many children will be surrounded by performance charts, so they may as well get used to seeing them in their home. Of course, there are families that won't feel comfortable with charting. Charting was fun and beneficial at a certain stage in our family. *When nothing else seems to be working,* behavioral charts can motivate a child to change a behavior. As you weed out undesirable behaviors one by one, your child gradually gets used to the feelings that come with good behavior, and these feelings become self-motivating. The need for charting lessens as your child grows, and you will need to find new clutter for your kitchen wall. In making reward charts, consider these tips:

- Follow the basic rule: KISMIF — Keep it simple, make it fun.

- Work *with* your child. Let your child help construct the chart and make daily entries.

- Construct the chart so that your child has a visual image of closing in on the reward. We have gotten good results from a "connect the dots" chart. Have your child draw a picture of what she wants. Then outline the periphery of the picture with dots an inch or so apart. With each day of successful behavior (for example, each time she remembers to take out the trash) the child connects another dot. When all the dots are connected, the child collects the prize.

- Display the chart in a high-visibility location. (We strategically place ours on the wall along the path between the kitchen table and the refrigerator.) Giving the chart a high profile and high visibility gives the child easy access, serves as a frequent reminder of the desired behavior, and lets her proudly exhibit her progress.

- Make the charts interactive: connecting dots, pasting on stickers or different colored stars, anything more interesting than a check mark.

- Charts can contain positive and negative entries, reminders of both types of behaviors. In my office I hand out charts to correct bedwetting in children older than five. The child puts a happy-face sticker on the chart for every morning he wakes up dry and a sad-face sticker on the chart for mornings he wakes up wet. If the happy faces outnumber the sad faces at the end of the week, the child gets to choose where he wants to go for lunch on Saturday.

- Keep the time until the prize is collected short. Frequent, simple rewards keep motivation high. For a toddler, use end-of-the-hour rewards; for the preschooler, end-of-the-day; for the school-age child, end-of-the-week. A month is an unreachable eternity for any child. For the preschool child, rather than setting a calendar time, refer to an event time such as "after Sunday school." Novelty wears off quickly for children. Change charts frequently.

Creative rewards. Besides charts, design your own clever motivators. Because her six-year-old's favorite toy was her dollhouse, a mother chose a piece of dollhouse furniture as a weekly reward for keeping her room tidy. She related the reward to the behavior: "When you show me you can keep your room tidy, then we'll furnish your dollhouse." She used periodic reminders: "Let's keep your room as nice as you do your dollhouse."

To keep order among the seven-to-nine-year-old boys at our twice-monthly Cub Scout meeting, we use the "good behavior candle." The object is to burn the candle all the way down so that the whole group can have a treat. At the beginning of the meeting we light the candle. The candle stays lighted until a disruption occurs. The dis-

Reward chart: When she connects all the dots, Jenny gets a cat.

rupter has to blow out the candle, and it doesn't get relit until the next meeting. The sooner the candle burns down (that is, the fewer disruptions) the sooner the boys get a prize. Consider what's going on in their impressionable minds. Each time someone snuffs out a candle, they halt the progress toward the prize. Since children do not like to delay their gratification, they're motivated to snuff out their own disruptive behavior instead.

The ticket system. Tina and her four-year-old daughter Haley were very connected.

Haley had been a high-need baby who turned into a strong-willed child. Here is how Tina channeled Haley's obstinate behavior in the right direction and had fun doing it:

Haley and I were butting heads. It seemed as if our whole day was becoming increasingly full of negatives. All the techniques I'd used before weren't working. So I tried what we fondly refer to as the ticket system. This took stress off of me as a mother; I was no longer the bad guy. I give her

---

Sometimes Humor Is the Best Discipline

In disciplining a growing child, a parent wears many costumes: You put on your policeman's cap for dangerous situations. It's serious and uncompromising. You put on your preacher's collar for morality lessons, your diplomatic tie and tails for power struggles, and your doctor's coat for healing little hurts. But the costume that will serve you best during tough discipline times is your jester's cap.

Humor surprises. Levity catches a child off guard and sparks instant attention, diffusing a power struggle before the opening shots are fired. Humor opens up closed little ears and minds. Here is how one mother turned comedienne and used humor to get cooperation from her children. Six-year-old Laurel and three-year-old Nicholas were in the middle of a squabble over a toy at the end of the day when their mother was already stressed. She had neither the time nor the energy to get out her therapist couch and delve into her children's feelings. Instead she

grabbed a big toy block and put it on her head, and her act began. "Mom is going to be a blockhead," she said. "I'm going crazy. I can't take this bickering anymore." She started being really goofy and silly. The children cracked up and everyone was laughing as the mother's antics diffused the children's quarreling. Mother then sat down with the children and said, "It's a tough time of the day. Mom is tired. I've got to get dinner ready. You're tired; you're hungry; please help me fix dinner."

Humor gets jobs done. Seven-year-old Aaron's room was a mess. Instead of "Go make your bed," his comical mother let the bed do the talking. "I walked by your bed this morning," she said, "and it cried 'Please cover me, I'm cold,'" Even for adults, humor has a way of getting jobs done. I remember well the sign in the surgeons' changing room at our local hospital: "Your mother doesn't live here."

three "free" tickets to start the day. She earns tickets for helping without being asked, for doing assigned chores, and for having a good attitude. She loses tickets for whining, complaining, and refusing to obey (which eliminated the ongoing "By the time I count to three" line that I was always using.) The tickets became like gold, and after a while she became more and more eager to please. At the end of the day, or the week, Haley got a special treat that was prearranged according to the number of coupons she had collected (fro-

zen yogurt, a movie, a hamburger, et cetera).

With Haley, it was very difficult to see the "positive" in her behavior. The ticket system forced me to catch her at being good, as opposed to just seeing the bad. I found myself saying things such as "I liked the way you smiled when you woke up this morning" or "Thank you for waiting your turn on the swing without screaming or crying." Delayed gratification was not Haley's strong suit. I would carry tickets with me everywhere we went, so

---

Sometimes Humor Is the Best Discipline (continued)

Humor protects. Three-year-old Alan had a habit of darting away from his parents, especially in parking lots. Dad decided to play the blind man's game. As they came out of a store, Dad put his hand over his eyes, gave the child the car keys, and said, "Please hold my hand and lead me to the car." Of course, he peeked a lot.

Humor disarms. Children can look at your face and realize you are going to say no to something. They are already mustering up resistance; you break through by putting on your best comic mask. Humor also helps snap a child out of regressive behavior. Here is how a mother in our practice solved this problem: Four-year-old Monica insisted on wearing a diaper because her new brother did. Mother played along with Monica's quirk by trying to put a small, newborn-size diaper on her. As they both struggled to get the diaper to fit, Monica realized how silly her whim was.

We use humor quite often to give a child a second chance to obey. Our children love videos, so we put on our "rewind" theatrics. "Matthew, please help me clear the table." "But Dad," Matthew protests. Immediately I say "Rewind!" I step back a few feet and start over, this time making a grand gesture toward Matthew, indicating the cue for his second chance. This approach usually results in both laughter and obedience.

Use humor sensitively. There are times when your child's behavior is no laughing matter. Also, children are sensitive to ridicule and sometimes take your humor as a sarcastic put-down even when you may simply be trying to bring a bit of levity to a tense situation. There are times to be serious, and there are times to be funny. Both have a place in disciplining your family. Much of your discipline will be amusing to your kids, and it's fun to have an admiring audience.

that she not only heard my words of praise but saw tangible evidence of her good behavior. This also enabled me to take them from her just as quickly to show the immediate consequence of her unacceptable behavior. Tickets helped her to understand I still loved her, that she was a good person, and that there were guidelines that needed to be followed. It helped me not to yell or feel the need to raise my voice. It was also a system my husband, Steve, could quickly pick up after a hard day's work and on weekends. Baby-sitters use it to reward Haley for cooperating.

For us, the ticket system has eliminated the need to spank. "Time-out" can be reserved for those really difficult moments when separation is best for parent and child. It has greatly lessened the power struggle that I have felt with Haley since she was very young. This system isn't easy. It's very time-consuming for the parents. Haley keeps us informed if we're slipping up on our duties. It is, however, a lot of fun and well worth the effort.

This system works so well because it helps this mother be more attentive to her child and to notice her good behavior. You might not need tickets if you could do that anyway — *parenting* takes time!

REMINDERS

"But I forgot." "But I didn't know I was supposed to." As lame as these excuses sound to adults, children do honestly forget and need reminders to keep their behavior on track.

Reminders are cues that jog the hazy memory of a busy child. They may be subtle *prompts* in the form of a look that tells the about-to-be-mischievous child, "You

know better," or a short verbal cue that turns on the child's memory: "Ah! Where does that plate belong?" Some situations call for a major reminder and follow-through that rings the child's memory bell loud and clear: "Remember what we've said about running in the street! A car could hit you! Your have to look both ways!" (See related topic, "Making Danger Discipline Stick," pages 68–71.)

Reminders are less likely to provoke a refusal or a power struggle than are outright commands. You have already painted the scene in your child's mind, he knows what you expect, and he has previously agreed to it. Reminders prompt a child to complete a behavior equation on her own. You give a clue and the child fills in the blanks. You stand over a pile of homework sprawled on the floor, then scowl disapprovingly. She gets the message and picks up the homework without you even saying a word.

Written reminders go over better with children who don't like to feel controlled. You avoid a face-off. It's up to the child to carry out the reminder in good time to avoid getting a verbal direction. A recent note on Erin's door read, "Please remove the dishes from your room before they start growing things." Frequent reminders of what's acceptable and what's not lets the child know *what is normal for your home.*

THE ART OF NEGOTIATING

Bargaining with your child doesn't compromise your authority. It strengthens it. Children respect parents who are willing to listen to them. Until they leave home children must accept your authority — that's not negotiable. But that doesn't mean you can't listen to their side of things.

Negotiating is a win-win situation that benefits parent as well as child. Parents show that they are approachable and open to another's viewpoint — a quality children become more sensitive about as they approach adolescence. In the teen years you will find that negotiating becomes your main behavior-management tool, because adolescents like to be treated as intellectual equals and expect you to respect their viewpoint. If used wisely, negotiating improves communication between parent and child. A stubborn insistence on having your own way has the opposite effect. "I just can't talk to my dad," said Jessica, a teenager whose father's attitude was "Don't confuse me with the facts, my mind is made up." Even the wishes of a seven- or eight-year-old are open to negotiation. This is a warm-up time to help you sharpen your negotiating skills for the years ahead.

Negotiating helps children develop confidence in their viewpoint and courage to stand up for their rights. Parents are the ideal persons to practice these skills on. Negotiating helps children learn fairness and respect for another's opinion even if they don't agree with it.

"Why do I have to go to bed at nine o'clock?" argued ten-year-old Margo.

"What time do you think is a good bedtime for you?" asked Father Negotiator.

"Ten o'clock," Margo suggested.

"That extra hour means a lot to you,

Holding a Family Meeting

Family meetings are good times to set *house rules.* You are relaxed and the children are more receptive. Spur-of-the-moment rules ("You're grounded!") made when you are angry are likely to be unfair and unfollowed. Getting together to sort out discipline problems is a valuable way for parents and children to express their concerns. Discipline problems that involve one child should be handled privately, but there are times when all the children get a bit lax in the self-control department and the whole family needs a reminder. Suppose your house is continually a mess. Call a family meeting and invite suggestions from the children on how to keep the house tidy. Use a chalkboard to make it more businesslike. Write down the problem and propose solutions. Put together a "kids want/parents want" list in order to set goals. To avoid chore wars, we assign each child a room to tidy. Then we know who is responsible and who to compliment. Formulate house rules for happier living. Arriving at a general consensus is better than voting, which has winners and losers. Try a suggestion box and have the children write their suggestions on little cards. You'll learn a lot about your living habits that way. I got a suggestion from my teenage daughter: "Daddy, please ask me to help instead of giving orders." You can use family councils to help a child solve a problem. Develop a share-and-care atmosphere. Make the meeting fun. Besides your living room, try other meeting places, such as a family picnic in the park. Meetings shape family behavior and are a forum in which to foster family communication.

Magic Countdowns

Many parents successfully use fun countdowns to get a toddler to cooperate. Countdowns give a child time to respond and decide that cooperating is his own idea. Suppose it's time to go and you want your child to get up off the floor so that you can put his jacket on. Tell him calmly, "I'm going to count to three and then you stand up. One, two, three. Stand up!" This gives the toddler a chance to let go of his negativity and click into the fun of your game. When countdowns work, they work like magic. If the technique doesn't work on the first or second try, use a different approach before the countdown becomes a contest of wills. Keep your countdowns positive, using a happy and animated tone of voice. Be clear about what you expect: "Give Mommy the dish" or "Let go of your sister's hair." One. Two. Three. (Keep silent between numbers.) Negative countdowns that have the air of a threat invite a challenge. "If you don't come by the time I count to three, you're going to get it." The child may call your bluff. And then you have to come through with "it." A negative approach sets the child up to disobey; he knows this is what you expect.

"Yes, I guess you are. Let's try this," Father suggested. "On school nights you must be in bed at nine o'clock and you can read in bed until nine-thirty. And on nights when you don't have school the next day you can stay up until ten o'clock."

The child thought this was acceptable; her reasoning was validated. The father achieved his goal, being sure his child got enough sleep. He knew that after five minutes of reading in bed she would probably fall asleep. As this volley went back and forth, the father was earning points with his child. The child was getting the message "I can talk to my dad. He is reasonable, and he really does care about what's good for me. My father listens, and has wise things to say."

Sometimes let your child take the lead. This is not giving in to the child or letting the child be in control; it's simply being a smart negotiator. It's a way to bring your child back to your agenda after a short excursion that satisfies his agenda.

Follow the house rules. Command and exhibit respect during negotiations. If your child starts yelling or acting disrespectful of your authority, close the discussion: "You must not talk to me in that tone, Susan. I'm the mother, you're the child, and I expect respect." This sets the tone for future negotiations. You may have to remind your child of this nonnegotiable fact of family life often during the preteen and teen years. Because of the constant haggling that children inflict on parents, it is easy to let your authority slip away. Don't! You need it to keep order in the house, and your child will need to respect authority to get along in life.

There will be situations when you don't want a discussion. You know you're right and your child is being unreasonable. (You

doesn't it? What would you do during that extra hour?"

"I could read," Margo pleaded.

"Remember how tired you are the next morning when you stay up late. You fall asleep at school," Father reminded her.

"But that was last year, Dad. I'm older now," Margo countered.

don't always have to negotiate even when he is being reasonable.) Before the child works himself up into a dither, break off the negotiations. That's the parents' prerogative. "I think that's a rotten TV program, and I've told you before why I am not going to let you watch it. I will not change my mind about this, so don't even start on me." Then walk away. Let your "no" be "no." It's OK to negotiate but never to argue. Children need to learn when parents mean business. Parents can't use this approach every time or children will see them tyrants. Be prepared to allow the child to watch other programs that are acceptable.

If used wisely, negotiation can become a valuable communication tool, helping children develop their reasoning abilities. Teach your child that negotiations work best when everyone is calm and peaceful, not in the heat of the moment. "No for now, but I'll talk it over with your dad and get back to you tonight." "I don't like the way you are talking to me. Come back later when you're feeling more peaceful." When you're not sure, or feeling pressured, decide not to decide.

WITHDRAWING PRIVILEGES

Withdrawing privileges is one of the few behavior shapers you never run out of. Kids will always want something from you. For this correction technique to have a good chance of preventing reoccurrence of a misbehavior, the child must naturally connect the privilege withdrawal with the behavior: "If you ride your tricycle into the street, you lose the use of your tricycle for the rest of the day."

Your child dawdles and misses the morning carpool, so he must walk to school. This correction technique is commonly used in adult law enforcement: You get caught driving drunk and you lose your license. But this doesn't cure your drinking problem. So you see, withdrawing privileges has its limits as a discipline technique. What does withholding television have to do with being home in time for supper? a child may wonder.

Losing privileges can work if it's part of a pre-agreed behavior-management strategy decided on during a family meeting: Parents state the behaviors they expect from their children and announce that part of the fun of being a parent is granting privileges to the children so they can have some fun, too. But if the children don't hold up their end of the bargain, the parents cannot grant those privileges. So, being home in time for supper gets you the privilege of a half hour of TV, rather than the TV time being an inalienable right of every citizen of the household. As children get older they need to learn a valuable lesson for life: With increasing privileges come increasing responsibilities.

14

BREAKING ANNOYING HABITS

THE PHRASE "BREAK A HABIT" has some biological truth to it. A child's developing brain consists of miles of electrical wires. As the child learns and grows, he makes connections between all these nerve wires, storing patterns of association. Patterns of behavior that are repeated over and over again become habits that the child performs without thinking. To break the habit, you have to put a roadblock in the nerve pathway where the habit is stored, breaking off the connection between the action and the circumstances that trigger it. It's important to break undesirable habits early before they become mannerisms — part of a child's personality — and lead to unflattering labels like "Tommy Twitch."

STEPS TO BREAKING HABITS

Here are some general steps for breaking annoying habits.

Is the habit a problem? Does this habit need breaking? Should you intervene or simply grin and bear it and let the child enjoy the habit? After all, if ignored, most habits eventually self-destruct, and if you intervene you risk pushing the child from the frying pan into the fire. To a child, a habit may be his own way of relaxing or retreating momentarily from pressures and expectations into his own world, a mini time-out, a chance to do his own thing. If you take away a harmless tension reliever, something less desirable may take its place. As a general guide, if the habit bothers the child (his thumb-sucking is causing his thumb to get infected or his teeth to become crooked) or the habit results in teasing from others or social isolation, it's time to intervene. Here's how.

Remove the trigger. What conditions set up the child to twitch, bite her nails, twirl her hair, bang her head, pick her nose, or grind her teeth? Is she bored, tired, angry, nervous? Keep a habit diary, and, as much as possible, adjust your child's environment to remove the cause. If Trudy started twitching soon after you changed day-care providers, you probably should reevaluate your choice of substitute caregivers. If your six-year-old sucks her thumb while watching TV after school, perhaps you should take her for a walk instead.

To confront or not to confront? Is it a biggie — does it physically or socially harm the child — or a smallie that is best ignored? Calling your child's attention to a smallie may intensify the habit or push him into a biggie. If it is a smallie, focus on the conditions that trigger the habit, and not on the habit itself, so you can prevent it from turning into a biggie. If it's a biggie, involve your child in the habit control. These are your child's habits, and only he can break them. Discuss the habit with your child. Inquire whether or not it bothers the child, and if so, how.

Motivate. If you decide the habit should be eliminated, make your child aware of it and involve him in the treatment. Discuss with him why it's better to lose the habit and how you and he will be partners in breaking the habit. Offering rewards along the way adds incentive.

Family habits. As little monkeys see, little monkeys do. Examine the habits of the persons of significance in your child's life. Do you bite your nails, smack your lips, tap your foot? Mrs. Daniels brought Michael in for counseling because of his twitching. In going into the family history, we found that Michael comes from a twitchy family: Uncle Joe twitches, grandmother twitches, and mother twitches. It was always considered no big deal and was played down as simply a family quirk. Since Michael was not bothered by his twitches or being teased about them, we decided that ignoring them would be the wisest therapy unless they caused Michael social embarrassment.

Relax the child. For some persons mannerisms may be a mini-relaxer, a time-out or a temporary distractor from a stressful situation. Search for stress producers in your child's life and remove as many of them as you can. Expect mannerisms to begin or intensify following a move, the absence of a parent, divorce, or any major change in the child's routine.

Offer a sub. An effective way to avoid the pathway that leads to a habit is to suggest an alternative route, a detour. If a child's fingers are busy squeezing a ball, he won't be able to suck his thumb. As soon as he is in the situation that triggers the habit or he first becomes aware that he is doing it, teach him to immediately click into the harmless alternative. For example, as soon as the nail biter feels his hands approaching his mouth, he folds his hands and twiddles his thumbs or fingers a marble in his pocket. He twists the ring on his finger or makes a hard fist and then releases the tension by shaking out the hand. Practice these alternatives. Drill, drill, drill: Urge to bite, grab marble or ring, repeat, repeat. To help your child remember, give this alternative a name such as "the sub" or "the detour." Quietly remind him, "Remember your sub."

THUMB-SUCKING

Thumbs naturally find their way into the mouths of babes and often stay there for years. Thumb-sucking is a boon to babies but bothers onlookers and dentists. So what's a poor thumb-sucker to do? Can a baby and her thumb find happiness together without public censure?

When thumb-sucking is helpful. Some babies are born thumb-suckers. Ultrasound pictures show babies sucking their thumbs in the privacy of the womb. In many babies, the need to suck is not satisfied by bottle-feeding or sometimes not even by breast-feeding alone, and they learn to suck on the ever-present thumb for comfort. In the early months, even tiny infants discover that one of life's little pleasures is right in their hands and under their noses. We consider the ability of babies to use their own body parts for comfort as a sign of emotional health, not psychological disturbance. In fact, some veteran baby comforters even help their babies find their thumbs to self-quiet. What's all the fuss about? Whose thumb is it anyway?

Some babies seem unsatisfied after bottle-feeding. They've had enough milk, but not enough sucking. One advantage of the breast is that it can still be sucked on even after the feeding part is over, so baby can get the sucking he needs without overfilling his tummy. But there are times when the breasts' owner has had enough and baby *still* needs pacifying. If you don't feel you can handle letting baby pacify on your breast, let him suck on your finger, and eventually, if he doesn't discover them on his own, you can direct his thumb or fingers into his mouth. The seemingly insatiable desire to suck is there for a reason. First, of course, it provides nourishment.

Thumbs Versus Pacifiers

Which are better, thumbs or pacifiers? Babies would vote for thumbs. They are always available, taste familiar, don't get lost in the night, and don't fall on the floor. Dentists would vote for pacifiers. Children don't use them like crowbars against their upper teeth, and they *can* be "lost" — permanently. Even for those who dislike the way "those things" obstruct the view of a baby's face, it's hard not to like the quieting effect of the silicone plug. Pacifiers are, as the name implies, peacemakers. As people who are around babies day and night, we support anything that keeps babies peaceful. Preferably this should be live caregivers, but sometimes human pacifiers need a break. As with all substitute nurturing devices, this is a question of balance. When a pacifier is used in addition to nurturing, it can be a comforting tool. If it is used instead of nurturing, it is a distance-producing device. If, when your infant cries, you find yourself reaching for the plug instead of the baby, or your baby reaches for the dummy instead of the mommy, you need to reassess your parenting. You want your baby to become attached to you, not to an inanimate sub.

If your baby is bonded to his binkie, six months is a good age to stop giving it to him. He's still young enough to learn to use his thumb (or your breast), so he will not become unglued when the plug stops showing up. As you helped your baby start this habit, you can be the one to end it. Just stop putting it in his mouth to keep him quiet. Try more attachment instead. If you are breastfeeding, let your baby pacify at your breast. Some babies think breasts are just for food because they haven't been encouraged to "hang out at mom's" until they've filled their sucking needs as well as their tummies. A baby with an ever-present plug as his way of self-soothing will become addicted to

But beyond that, sucking satisfies other important needs.

Sucking mellows the fussy baby, helping to organize the otherwise disorganized biorhythms of a newborn. Some babies need more mellowing than others. Our high-need baby was the only one of ours to suck her thumb. We thought it was sweet to see her snuggled up with her thumb while she slept. She started at three months and quit on her own at five months — a very uneventful thumb weaning. Martha was careful to breastfeed her frequently when she was awake so that the thumb did not become a substitute for the breast. Sucking at the breast is more than eating to a baby or toddler. They learn that the comforting they get helps them relax. A child who has gotten attached to her thumb will tell you she needs it to help her relax.

When Thumb-Sucking Can Be Harmful

While most mothers, for practical reasons, give infant thumb-sucking their thumbs-up approval, some dentists vote thumbs-down. While this harmless habit usually subsides in infancy, if it continues until age two it will probably go on until age four or five.

Thumbs Versus Pacifiers (continued)

always having something in his mouth. As a toddler he may not develop alternative ways to self-soothe and reconnect (he may not play quietly or ask for holding, for example). He may even be delaying or inhibiting his ability to express himself and relate socially. Once again, the plastic plug is riskier than the thumb, and the breast poses no risk at all.

What about the three-year-old who is addicted to his "paci"? Consider these tips:

- *Trade it.* If the child is old enough not to be sucking on a pacifier, he is probably smart enough to settle for a better toy. Take him to the store and make a deal with the toy salesman. Let him pick out his favorite toy. Let the child pass over the pacifier to the toy salesperson, who in turn presents the alternative.

- *Encourage the child to use his plug in private.* Mention that older children doing things that babies do bothers some adults. "If you really must use your pacifier, please use it in your room." By approaching it this way and making the pacifier less convenient to use, the child will soon wean himself.

- *Use relaxing substitutes.* Teach the child to put on a favorite tape and start singing as soon as he gets the urge to reach for the pacifier. He (probably) can't suck and sing at the same time. Keep yourself relaxed and peaceful, and offer a lot of quiet connection, such as reading books together, blowing bubbles together, "just-being" time, and so on.

- *Just say "all done" and take it away, with the explanation that it's not helping the child be a big boy or girl.* Attachment-parented children living in a peaceful home should give it up fairly easily — if you expect them to.

Habit	Motivators-Distractors	Relaxers
Thumb-sucking	Point out sore thumb. Compare sore with other thumb. Show "buck" teeth in mirror. Run fingers over protruding teeth. Busy bored hands.	Play soothing music, have cuddle time, read together (child holds book).
Nail biting	Keep hands busy. Keep both hands on book. Put hands in pockets while watching TV. Compare with unbitten nails.	Dangle hands, let fingers go limp. Lay in bathtub and let hands float. Massage hands and fingers.
Grinding teeth (clenching teeth)	Relax child before bedtime. Reduce sleep separation anxiety — sleep close to child. Show teeth damage in mirror. Run fingers over damaged teeth.	Relax jaw — let mouth drop open. Massage facial muscles. Give before-bed massage. Breathe deeply with open mouth.
Twitching and tics (blinking, facial twitching, shoulder shrugs, head jerks, forehead wrinkling, throat clearing, sniffing, neck stretching)	Remove triggers and stressors. Watch self twitch in mirror. Ignore and distract when it happens.	Practice touch relaxation: massage muscles involved at urge to twitch. Take deep breath and let muscles go limp.
Lip biting (licking, smacking)	Show child sore edges of mouth and cracked lips. Have child keep lip balm in pocket to use instead of biting.	Take deep breath, open mouth, keep tongue inside. (Sighing-type breathing can itself become a habit.)
Head banging	Remove child from banging area. Pad crib. Remove bed from wall.	Play relaxing music. Rock child in rocking chair. Carry infant in sling.
Nose picking	Show sores in nose. Relate picking with nose bleeding. Direct child to use tissues instead of finger in presence of others.	Deep breathe; teach child to stroke nose from bridge to tip, over and over slowly.
Hair pulling (eyelash plucking)	Show child pretty hair and bald spot.	Reduce stressors. Deep breathe; teach child to stroke hair or eyelid.
Throat noises (tongue clicks, clearing throat)	Video/audio-tape, replay for child to watch and hear.	Teach child how to take slow deep breaths.

Subs	Special Help
"Hide thumb" by making a fist, squeeze thumb, suck tongue.	Dental appliance, distasteful reminders — paint-on products, Band-Aid, tape, tongue-blade splint, wear mittens.
"Hide nails" by clenching fist, clasp hands together, grab sleeve, clasp chair arm-rests. Carry nail clipper in pocket, use when urge to bite is felt.	Wear mittens, manicure to keep nail and cuticle nice. Consult pediatrician for signs of damage to cuticle or infection.
Smile instead of gritting teeth — daytime. Open mouth at urge to grind. Put tongue between teeth.	Consult dentist; teeth guard appliance. Consult allergist; treat nasal allergies, environmental (bedroom) allergies.
Rotate head and stare at horizon. Tighten opposite muscles, for example, shoulders. Take a drink of water. Shrug both shoulders together.	Consult child's doctor to exclude medical causes.
Suck frozen juice bar, drink water, talk, take a deep breath.	Apply emollient to soften lips. Consult doctor if skin infected.
Dancing to music, "gentling," and physical contact.	Causes no harm and is self-limiting, but suggest child needs to learn healthier emotional releases.
Rub nose with arm; rub hand with picking finger; pick on a pocket.	Consult doctor to determine nasal irritants, humidify air; apply moisturizing ointment in nostrils. Remove allergens.
Pull hands, fingers, any safe alternative.	Consult doctor if child swallows the hair he pulls.
Talk or sing at urge to make noises.	Naturally self-limiting if ignored. Consult physician if persists.

Even then, occasional light thumb-sucking is harmless and should be ignored. Some children increase their thumb-sucking to such frequency and intensity that it becomes a social and dental problem.

Thumbs in push teeth out. In the first two to four years, don't worry about thumb and teeth not getting along. Seldom does occasional thumb-sucking harm teeth in the child under four, and it usually subsides by that age anyway. But habitual thumb-sucking at age three or four or older is a reason to start putting money aside for the orthodontist, especially if the child already has a hereditary overbite or protruding upper teeth. Or you can start thinking of ways to get that offending thumb out of the child's mouth and into his pocket. Because of the way the thumb is forced against the inside of the upper front teeth, thumb-sucking can cause overbite (buck teeth) and other dental malocclusions. If neither your child's doctor nor his dentist are worried about the thumb-sucking, you shouldn't worry either.

Oversucked thumbs get sore. Habitual sucking is hard on the skin of the thumb. Spending too much time between the moisture of the tongue and the pressure of the teeth causes oversucked thumbs to look like one long callus; others crack and bleed. Some get infected (there is a red, swollen, tender area where the thumbnail joins the skin).

Sucking becomes socially unacceptable. Toddlers don't ridicule their thumb-sucking peers because thumb-sucking is standard operating procedure for children under two. But the older the sucker the more likely she'll get teased about her thumb-in-mouth "disease." Some little thumb-suckers swallow so much air that it leads to belching and the resulting teasing about this unpleasant sound. Don't fret about a happy thumb-sucker who is gregarious and has a good self-image — this thumb will soon leave the mouth. But some suckers never show an unobstructed view of their smile; it's as if their nose has grown a fist. They prefer sucking their thumbs to relating to peers. This scene is socially difficult; the thumb and its owner may be teased continually about being a "baby."

What to Do

Like most normal but bothersome behaviors, if you did nothing but accept and ignore it, the thumb would eventually find its way into other occupations. But if the habit persists and harms the child, parents need to step in with more assertive discipline.

Satiate sucking needs. Sucking satisfies the need for attachment. A need that is filled goes away; a need that is not filled stays as a habit. If you have a "sucky baby," let her suck to her heart's content during early infancy. Breastfeed as long as possible (this is about as attached as baby can get). Let your baby suck your fingers. Allow non-nutritive sucking (sucking on an "empty" breast, finger or pacifier, or collapsible bottle nipple) after the baby's hunger is satisfied. An interesting study confirmed that babies who get their sucking needs met early seldom become habitual thumb-suckers. In 1977 researchers studied fifty children between the ages of one and seven who were habitual thumb-suckers and compared them with children who did not suck their thumbs. The studies showed that thumb-suckers tended to be bottle-fed rather than breastfed. The later the children were weaned, the less likely they were to suck their thumbs. The thumb-sucking children tended to have been fed on schedule rather than on demand. And 96 percent of the thumb-suckers had been left to fall asleep alone after having been fed. Not one of the non-thumb-suckers was left alone to fall asleep. Researchers theorize that during sleep people return to primitive reflexes, such as sucking and hand-to-mouth actions. Perhaps while falling asleep the child's primitive sucking reflex is stimulated and the sucking drive intensified. In our own pediatric practice we have noticed that babies who are nursed down to sleep and not weaned until they are ready are much less likely to become habitual thumb-suckers. Consider breastfeeding as a "suck of prevention" for habitual thumb-sucking.

Offer early alternatives to sucking. If you are blessed with a baby with a strong sucking drive, at around four months of age, instead of automatically pacifying him by sucking, try alternatives: rocking, massage, playing animated games, and singing. Babies who are worn in a sling tend to need oral pacifying less, since being worn fills the need for attachment. The earlier baby learns that there are other ways to find comfort in addition to the breast, bottle, thumb, or pacifier, the more he will seek alternatives to oral gratification later.

Keep thumbs busy. Bored little thumbs often seek their friend, the mouth, when there is nothing better to do. Busy the bored toddler. When you see the thumb heading toward the mouth, distract and redirect the child into an activity that keeps both hands busy.

Keep life calm. As your toddler gets older he will use his thumb to help himself relax. This is good. You then do what you can to keep peaceful yourself, and that will flow over into a peaceful atmosphere in the home. Model relaxing ways and your child will learn from you: quiet times, long walks, music, slow deep breathing when you feel anxious.

Show and tell. If your child is old enough for thumb-sucking to bother her teeth, she is old enough to understand why this habit harms the teeth. In front of a mirror, let your child rub her index finger over the protruding upper teeth and put her fingertip into the gap between the upper and lower teeth during a bite. Imitate a buck-toothed appearance (like Bugs Bunny), showing your child what can happen to thumb-sucked teeth. Also point out to your child that her sucked thumb does not look as nice as her other one.

Time your intervention. With thumb-sucking, wait to intervene until your child is receptive to your help. Trying to step between thumb and mouth when your child is in a negative phase is likely to result in a power struggle. Your interference will be regarded as a threat to her independence.

Offer reminders. In the thumb-sucker over four, try an adhesive bandage or tape on the thumb. A glove can remind and dissuade the nighttime thumb-sucker. For the intensive night sucker who uses his thumb on his teeth like a crowbar, I've suggested a tongue depressor taped to the thumb as a splint to keep the thumb from bending. If your child is older, talk with him about using a product that gets painted on the thumb and gives a stinging reminder when thumb meets lips. Encourage the child to paint it on himself — it's his thumb and his habit.

Suggest a competing habit. With the child over four you can use the principle of a competing habit (see page 183 for discussion of subs). Show your child how to squeeze his thumb or to make some other gesture that he enjoys instead of sucking his thumb. A trick that I've used successfully in my office is the game of hide the thumb: "As soon as you feel like sucking your thumb, wrap your fingers over your thumb into a fist." If it's a bedtime habit used to relax off to sleep, suggest hiding the thumb under the pillow and taking some slow deep breaths. The child then has something to do, which is more likely to help him stop sucking his thumb than simply telling him not to suck. He can also be shown how to suck on his tongue without the thumb inserted.

Negotiate a milestone. If your child seems to be eager to meet goals, you could give her a target date — "When you have your fourth birthday you can say goodbye to sucking your thumb!" Don't hold your breath, though. On the big day she may smile sweetly at you and say "I've changed my mind." Remember to smile sweetly back.

Consult child's dentist. When your compulsive thumb-sucker is four years of age and her teeth are reflecting the harmful habit, a dentist can fit a palatal appliance that keeps the thumb from pushing on the teeth.

Relate with people instead of the thumb. If you see your child withdrawing from group play and interacting with his thumb instead of the other children, consider the possibility that your child may need a social boost. Rather than attack the thumb-sucking, delve into the underlying problems that may hamper his social interaction. If you need some help in this department, consult a professional.

Chart-a-thumb. Once peer pressure begins, the child over ages six or seven may want to stop thumb-sucking for her own reasons. Offer to help her design a chart that she can use on her own to mark down the number of times she sucks every day. She'll be motivated to see the number get smaller and smaller. You do not have to watch her or remind her or check up on her charting.

15

Disciplining Bothersome Behaviors

INFANTS AND CHILDREN DO ANNOY-
ING THINGS, so plan to spend time
and energy correcting these behaviors
or at least modifying them. In handling
any undesirable behavior in a child, consider these general strategies:

- **Track the trigger.** Get inside your
child's mind and figure out why she is
doing what she is doing. What sets her up
for mischief? Is there a pattern to the misconduct? Is she tired, bored, hungry, or
overloaded (for example, a toddler in a
department store at suppertime)? By discovering what's behind the behavior
you'll be able to avoid it.

- **Reinforce the positive.** Young children
don't know a behavior is "good" or "bad"
until you tell them. When they get a positive response, they are motivated to continue the behavior. When they repeatedly
get a negative response, they drop it (unless the negative response is seen by
them as positive; that is, someone paid attention). This is why it is important to
reinforce desirable behavior and correct
undesirable behavior early. Otherwise
misbehavior becomes part of a child's

way of acting and is much more difficult
to change.

- **Feed flowers, pick weeds.** The conduct
of a growing child is full of undesirable
and desirable behaviors — weeds and
flowers. Given good nurturing, flowers
grow so well you hardly notice the
weeds. But often these flowers wilt at certain seasons and the weeds become more
noticeable. If you just wait until that season is over, the weeds subside and the
flowers bloom again — sometimes so
beautifully that you forget the weeds are
even there. Sometimes the weeds grow
more quickly than the flowers, and you
have to pull them out before they take
over. So with the behaviors of a growing
child. Part of disciplining a child is to
weed out the undesirables that make a
child unpleasant to live with so that the
desirables flourish and make the child a
joy to be around.

BITING, HITTING, PUSHING, KICKING

Growing teeth and hands and feet often find
their way into trouble. Toddlers often at-

tack with little awareness of the consequences of their actions. Aggressive moves hurt and should be corrected before serious harm is done to bodies and to relationships.

Why babies bite and hit. Don't take this personally. Babies do bite the hands (and the nipples) that feed them. Everything babies do revolves around their hands and mouth. The hands and mouth are their first social tools, and they practice using them. As soon as teeth erupt and hands flap, babies experiment and use these tools on different objects to see how it feels. What could be more familiar and available than parents' skin? Baby's job is to use these tools; your job is to teach him how. These early nips and slaps, as awful as they look and feel, are playful communications or at worst expressions of frustration, not aggressive, disrespectful conduct.

Aggressive biting and hitting is most common between the ages of eighteen months and two and a half years, when the child doesn't have the verbal language to communicate needs; instead he communicates through actions. Biting usually stops as the child's verbal skills grow; hitting doesn't.

Why toddlers bite and hit and push and kick. What are simply socially incorrect gestures in infants can, if unchecked, become aggressive behaviors in children. That's why you want to purge these from your baby's repertoire before they become part of the growing child. Toddlers become aggressive in order to release pent-up anger, to control a situation, to show power, or to protect their turf in a toy squabble. Some children even resort to obnoxious behavior in a desperate attempt to break through to distant parents.

What to Do

Most aggressive toddler behaviors will lessen once the child is old enough to communicate well by words instead of actions. Parents will need to correct aggression firmly to get rid of it entirely. Here are ways to keep your child from hurting others.

Consider the source. What triggers aggressive behaviors? Keep a journal (at least mental notes) identifying the correlation between how a child acts and the circumstances prompting the action. For example: "Kate bit Suzie during play group. Suzie had Kate's favorite ball. It was almost nap time. Lots of kids in a small place. Suzie is very bossy."

Child hurts parent. Face slapping is a socially incorrect gesture babies experiment with. Redirect the slapper into a socially acceptable alternative: "Give me five." Likewise, redirect nipping: "No biting. Ouchie. Hurts Mama!" (put on your unhappy face); then redirect the behavior: "Hug mama. That's nice!" (smile and hug back). Once your child's face slapping becomes an expression of frustration (for example, the toddler in your arms becomes angry and hits you because you won't let her have candy), you'll have to show her the natural consequence. Firmly but calmly announce "You may not hit" and put her down. She'll still be angry about the candy, so you can verbalize that for her. (See Chapter 5, "Taming Temper Tantrums," and "Distract and Divert," page 42.) Biting, kicking, or pushing a parent would be dealt with similarly — make her stop. Do not allow your toddler to use you as a punching bag. Give her the message that you will not let her hurt you. If you don't allow your child to hurt when he's very young, he will be less likely to let others hurt him when he's older. You will be modeling to him how to say no to being hit by, for example, holding up a hand to stop the blow but not hitting back.

Toddler hits babies. If your one-and-a-half-year-old bangs his toy hammer on the heads of other babies in the group, remove all objects that he can hit with. Show, and tell, him not to hit, and give him an alternative gesture ("Be nice, pat baby") as you gently guide his patting hand.

Don't bite back. "But the child needs to learn that biting hurts," you may reason. Yes, but there's no way your child will decide that she shouldn't bite if you bite. Try this alternative tooth-for-tooth method: Take your child aside and ask her to let you show her how teeth feel on skin. Press your child's forearm against her upper teeth as if she were biting herself, not in an angry revengeful way, but as a scientist making a point ("See, biting hurts!"). Give this lesson immediately after she bites you or someone else. You want your child to learn to sense others' feelings; don't *expect* her to show much sensitivity under age three. Briefly verbalize for the biter what she was trying to "say" with her bite.

Don't hit for hitting. Katie hits Tommy. Katie's mother (embarrassed and irritated) quickly goes over and smacks Katie on the arm, saying "Mustn't hit." Are you as confused as Katie is right now? Have you ever been driven by embarrassment or anger to do something illogical? We all have. So plan in your mind ahead of time what you will do when your child hits someone.

Child hurts child. You notice one child hits (pushes or kicks) another to get a toy. Show and tell an alternative way to get the toy. "We don't hit other people. If you want the toy, wait until your friend is finished with it or ask Mommy and I'll set the share timer. When I want something from you I don't hit you, I ask nicely." If the hitter doesn't cooperate, ask the victim to say "I'm not playing with you anymore until you say you're sorry and stop hitting." Two-year-olds may not be able to say all these words, but they'll understand them; so you say the words for them and follow through with the consequence.

Time-out the aggressor. "Biting hurts, and it's wrong to hurt. You are going to sit by me." Usually by two years of age the child can make the connection between being aggressive and the consequences. Encourage your child to say "I'm sorry." If he's not angry anymore, he might want to give a kiss or hug. (See "Teaching Your Child to Apologize," pages 244–245.)

Model nonaggression. A child who lives with aggression becomes aggressive. How do *you* communicate disappointment, handle conflicts, and get your point across? Aggression is contagious. Toddlers and young children also pick up aggressive behavior from older siblings. If the younger children see the older ones hitting each other, they conclude that's the way you treat other people. Make this a teaching experience for the older children. Point out their modeling and tell them, for their own benefit and the benefit of the little ones, to clean up their act.

Grabbing is a common aggressive behavior in toddlers and young preschoolers.

(Watch that you don't unintentionally model this by snatching things from little hands. See "Respecting Little Grabbers," page 37.) Calmly explain why he can't have the item he grabbed and ask him to hand it back to the other child or give it to you. You may have to offer a replacement for what he has to give up. If your child is about to damage something valuable, or is likely to hurt himself with an object, use a no-nonsense voice and show by your body language that you expect him to give it up immediately.

Avoid setups. At a birthday party a mother set up a scavenger hunt for a bunch of boys — inside her house, of all places. To fuel the frenzy, she offered a prize for the winner. You can imagine what happened. Both the house and the children were a wreck. They hit and shoved each other and ransacked the house in pursuit of the hidden treasures. Bruised skin and bruised feelings resulted. The moral: Avoid situations that bring out the worst in children.

Mellow a mean streak. Watch the toddler who habitually bangs toys, bashes dolls, kicks cats, and pounds on walls. While some of this acting out is normal, it can be a red flag for tension and anger. The child is at risk for treating humans this way. Besides delving into the roots of the problem, encourage more gentle play: "Hug the bear." "Pet the kitty." "Love the doll."

Reward. Children over age three respond well to rewards, such as a no-hitting chart: "Every day you are nice to your friends, put a happy face on the chart. When you have three happy faces we'll go get some ice cream."

Program self-control. Some impulsive children hit before they think. Help children over three control these impulses by suggesting substitute behaviors that the child clicks into at the first thought of hitting: "As soon as you feel like hitting, grab a pillow and pound it or go run around the yard." You can model impulse control for your child. For example, next time you feel like hitting, let your child see you think your way out of it. Grab your hand and talk to it: "Now, hand, you should not hit people." He'll pay attention, especially if he's the one you felt like hitting.

Apply double discipline. When hitting becomes disrespectful and undermines your authority, it deserves a double-dose correction from mom and dad. Six-year-old Timmy got angry and hit his mother. She immediately sat him down, looked him squarely in the eyes, and impressed on him that under no circumstances was he ever to hit his parents; that behavior was intolerable and would be firmly corrected. She sent him to his room. After this time-out they talked about his anger. Later that day she shared this incident with her husband, who had a talk with Timmy. He reinforced the seriousness of this situation and told Timmy that it would not be tolerated: "I will not allow you to hit the woman I love." This wise father got some extra mileage out of his discipline by communicating his feelings for his wife.

Supervise. It's neither fair nor safe to allow aggressive toddlers to play with potential victims in close quarters without a parent on watch. If your child is aggressive, share your concern with the other parents or teachers in the play group, and seek their help in tempering your child's aggressive behavior. Don't hesitate to tell them about the problem. You can bet they have also struggled through an aggressive stage with their own children. Your candidness shows your concern for the other children. Otherwise, aggression, especially biting, may destroy friendships. The parents of a biter are embarrassed, while the parents of the victim are angry that their child has been hurt. The biter's parents get blamed for the child's misbehavior (they are the "bad parents of a bad kid"), and the adult friendship cools.

Teachers and day-care providers also need to be vigilant in supervising the aggressive child, lest this attitude infect the whole group. In a group setting children learn what is socially acceptable behavior. If they see and feel that aggressive behavior is tolerated — especially if the biter is in the spotlight ("Watch out, he's a biter") — they pick up on this label and may try making it part of their repertoire. While the aggressor's behavior requires immediate attention, be careful not to give the other children the idea that this is the way to get attention. Be sure to find opportunities to praise the other children for their good behavior.

DRESSING DISCIPLINE

You will spend a lot of time dressing your young child. It's a lot easier to do if you don't have to wrestle him through every step. Here's how to get the job done efficiently so that you and your child enjoy it.

Plan ahead. Before buying children's clothing, dress your child in your imagination. Choose easy-to-put-on clothing, at least one size ahead, with a minimum of buttons and snaps. Look for loose, stretchy neck holes that don't catch on tender ears. Choose outfits that are easy to slip on a moving target.

Plant good dressing memories. How a child behaves during diapering sets the tone for her acceptance of dressing. (See discussion of diaper discipline, page 84.) Most children who enjoy dressing can cooperate with dressing by age one, do some self-dressing by age two and a half, and dress themselves completely by age four.

Teach as you dress. To promote cooperation, first connect at the child's eye level either by dressing your child on a bed or changing table or, more safely, kneeling on the floor. Look at her, talk, and sing. To get into the spirit, play a dressing game: "We put our right foot in./We put our left foot in./We shake them all about."

The body-parts game is an old standby to keep competing little hands busy: "Where's Daddy's nose?" Keep the child entertained by theatrics as you breeze through dressing. Sometimes, distraction techniques still the squirmer: For the two-year-old, keep special toys reserved just for dressing. Stand the older baby near a window and let him enjoy the sights while you dress him.

Sing a song about the proper sequence of dressing (to the tune of "Here We Go Round the Mulberry Bush"): "First we put on our underwear, our underwear, our underwear." Talk about what you're doing: "Where is your underwear?" "Next we put on your socks. . . ." Say the name of the clothing and show how it goes on. If your three-year-old resists being dressed, capitalize on a developmental perk of this stage — a child's love of imagination. Choose char-

Sick Child — Sick Behavior

When the body is ill, so is the child's behavior. While some sick children show model behavior, diverting their energy from troublemaking into healing, others become defiant and belligerent. Suspect illness as a hidden cause of misbehavior especially when a previously obedient child spits out a bunch of obnoxious "No"s. Undetected upper-respiratory infections (sinuses, tonsils, and ear infections) top the list of behavior-changing illnesses. Younger children with these illnesses don't tell you when it hurts. They just make everyone around them feel as miserable as they do. Sinus pressure, diminished hearing, pain, and sleep difficulties caused by these infections are the reason for misbehavior. Anemia (low red blood cell count) is another hidden cause of irritability in children. Some children whose hemoglobin is marginal when checked at the doctor's office actually have an iron deficiency that is revealed by the behavior rather than the blood count. Specialized tests are needed to detect this type of problem, dubbed iron deficiency without anemia. Many other medical problems cause changes in behavior. If your angel turns into a demon, have your child evaluated by the doctor.

acters that both of you enjoy. Here's how one mother turns entertainer and motivates her three-year-old to get his clothes on: "We become Peter Pan. We talk like Peter Pan. And we talk about how Peter Pan is getting dressed because he's going on an exciting adventure and he has to have his pants on."

When a toddler knows you want to dress him, it's a perfect chance for him to get you to play chase instead. If you have time for that, go ahead and indulge, with lots of giggling and tickling once he's caught. If you don't have time or you're not in the mood, offer him another game instead — peek-a-boo. Hold the neck hole of the shirt up to your face and peek through it at him. Then he'll come close and want to do "peek." As you slide the shirt over his head, exclaim "Peek-a-boo." Then invite him to peek-a-boo his hands and feet. By two he'll want "Me do it peek-a-boo."

Model dressing. Lay out your child's ensemble next to yours, and put the clothes on together, piece by piece. This speeds up the poky dresser. Announce a "contest" to see who can get all their clothes on first. Soon the novice dresser will be a whiz. For the beginning self-dresser (between ages three and four), help him along: "You put on your shirt and I'll button it."

Accept mismatches. Remember, a child between the ages of two and five fixes definite ideas in his mind and protests alternatives. A young child does not have an open mind. He is not being stubborn; he is developing a strong personal identity. If your child wants to wear an orange shirt and purple pants, let him, even if this violates your sense of taste. Or lay out three outfits and let your child choose. This is a smallie, not at all worth a hassle. As one mother put it, "If he dresses himself, he can wear what he pleases." Of course, she sees to it that the clothes in her son's drawers are appropriate for the season. Another mother only chooses clothing for parties and for church.

Wait about ten years and your child will probably be dressing more stylishly than you.

There are times when parents know best. Here's how a wise mother got her son properly dressed, respecting the child's will without undermining her authority:

Our three-year-old is discovering that he has a will and opinion. My job and my desire is to validate his decision-making power. When our child exerts his own will and makes a choice that is different from ours, my husband and I don't look at it as a threat to our authority. He simply wants something different than we do. Our job is to persuade him. For example, my husband was getting our child dressed. Austin wanted to wear his brand-new heavy sweater that he got for Christmas. It was about eighty degrees outside, and we were taking him to a sunny park. My husband explained that it was going to be hot, but Austin insisted on his sweater. After talking it over with him my husband said, "I have an idea. Let's take the sweater, and that way if it gets cold you'll have it to wear." Austin thought that was a great idea. His decision-making power was validated. His idea to somehow have the sweater with him was good, and so he took the sweater with him to the park. We laid it on the bench in case it got cold. In this situation my husband could have just said, "No, you're not wearing the sweater. I'm the boss. I'm the grown-up. I know what's best for you. You're not wearing that sweater on this hot day." But instead we accommodated Austin's choice, and we arrived at an agreement that worked for both of us.

Give shopping choices. Around age four, children usually care what they wear. Take your children shopping with you and let them have some choice in what you buy; for example, two of five dresses, one of three pants, and so on.

SUPERMARKET DISCIPLINE

You have to be adventurous to take a toddler grocery shopping. One young mother we know takes her three- *and* one-year-old most of the time. She says she thinks of it as a sport. To expect a curious two-year-old to be a model of obedience in a supermarket that is set up to make adults act impulsively is unrealistic, but you can create the conditions that help him behave better. Try these sane shopping tips:

- **Shop alone, or keep it short.** Unless you are a parent who enjoys shopping with kids, whenever possible leave the children at home when you have a long shopping list. Running in for a few items can be a fun activity to do together with small children, but long trips can exhaust everyone's patience.

- **Plan ahead.** Shop at the time of day when your child is on his best behavior (and you're in a good mood), which is usually in the morning. Be sure that your child enters the supermarket with a full tummy. Take along an attention-holding toy that you can tie to the cart. Take a list that is organized according to where things are in the store.

- **Contain the child.** Younger babies (and most older ones) settle happily when worn in a baby sling; otherwise, use the seat in a shopping cart and remember the safety strap. It keeps kids from standing and climbing and falling. Without the safety strap the toddler will figure out how to climb over the seat in the cart. He'll want to get out and run around or explore the carton of eggs. Keep that restraining strap on or you might as well go home.

- **Keep the assistant shopper busy.** Make your child feel useful. Depending on her age, let your child help you shop. Even a very young child can recognize the products you use regularly at home. Your child can "help you look" for the spaghetti or the oranges. From her seat she can pick the desired (unbreakable) items off the shelf. If her behavior starts to deteriorate, remind her that something more fun is just around the corner, or open the box of crackers.

- **Talk about what you're doing.** "First we'll get some lettuce for salad . . . then some bananas. . . . Who likes bananas? You do? Daddy does? . . . What kind of crackers should we buy?" Shopping conversations can help your child to practice all kinds of thinking skills. Be ready with finger games to engage your child while you wait in the checkout line.

- **Offer a snack.** Opening a box of crackers or getting a roll from the bakery has saved many a shopping trip. If you offer the same one or two eating opportunities on every trip to the supermarket, your child will know what to expect and may not clamor for other goodies.

Here's how one mother handled a supermarket tantrum:

Our five-year-old, Jason, spilled his treat all over the supermarket store and pitched a fit: "I want more! Go back and buy me more!" His pleas escalated: "Will you buy me a toy?" "You're mean." And finally, my current favorite, "You're a spit!" We wheeled over to a quiet corner of the store and I tried to reason with him, but that was completely useless. What finally did break through to him was talking about how he felt. I said, "Boy, when things like that happen to me, I get really angry. It makes me want to kick something." My "I understand how you feel" empathy caused Jason to click into a more rational mode and express his feelings: "I feel so angry about my snack that I want to throw this grocery cart out the window." "I am so upset that you won't buy me more that I want to throw all the groceries at you!" Then we began to laugh together, and within a few minutes we were able to have a reasonable dialogue and got back on the track of shopping. By the time we left the store the incident was completely forgotten. A few days later, Jason had to have a shot at the doctor's, and while waiting for his appointment he got so worked up about imagining how the shot would feel that he began crying. I replayed what worked in the supermarket and got Jason to express his feelings: "When the doctor gives me a shot, I want to give her a shot back! I want to take all the shots and put them outside so they can't give me one." By adult standards, these expressions would be ridiculous, yet by expressing these wishes, Jason felt he had some control over what was happening. He was choosing not to act on his feelings, while at the same time expressing how he felt. This gave all of us some relief.

Checkout counters are usually where most children's behavior disintegrates. At the checkout let your child help put purchases on the counter, maybe counting or naming things. Keep him busy and involved in the homestretch. You can avoid battles over candy and gum by not introducing younger ones to these delightful little packages. Try keeping your cart out of reach of temptation while you unload. When the path is clear in front of you, zip the cart right past into safer territory. Once your child knows what candy bars are you'll have to come up with a plan. Don't say yes every time he asks. He can save his own money for treats. You can discuss ahead of time if this will be a treat day. Expect the best and don't feel pressured if your child does pitch a fit at the finish line. It's important not to let your child embarrass you. If your child knows you always say no to supermarket begging, he won't do it. He can get treats at *other* times. It took us six children to figure this one out! The younger ones don't beg because Martha didn't let it get started.

TEACHING TOOTHBRUSHING

Toothbrushing must be done at least once a day. Here's how to turn a hassle into a routine.

- Start early. When your baby is between the ages of six months and a year, wrap gauze around your finger and use it to wipe the gums and new teeth as they emerge. Do this daily so that he'll be familiar with this ritual by the time he's older. Some toddlers are frightened by toothbrushing if it's started too late.

- Model good dental habits. Set your child next to you on the counter and let her watch how much fun it is to brush teeth. Give her a foamy grin. When your child

catches the spirit and grabs your toothbrush, it's time to get her own soft-bristled one. She doesn't need toothpaste yet. Kids often balk at strong-tasting paste. Some kids are fascinated with the spitting part — that's what they imitate, not the brushing.

- Don't expect children under three to clean their teeth well on their own. Your hand needs to be on the toothbrush guiding them. Begin brushing the front teeth and ease toward the molars. If you have a particularly cooperative child who enjoys toothbrushing, put your hand on hers and guide the brush in and out of all the crevices in the teeth.

- Make it a game. Announce "We're going to get the sugar bugs off" (or "the chicken, potatoes, and cookies"). Sing a song. We use an old (very old) commercial: "Brusha, brusha, brusha . . ." or "Brush, brush, brush your teeth, up and down the gums . . ." (to the tune of "Row, Row, Row Your Boat"). Children's entertainer Raffi has a great song about brushing teeth. Or talk about counting the teeth — hearing you recite numbers from one to ten in an animated way can help a child relax. (By the way, this works in the dentist's office for those early checkups.)

Take charge of the reluctant toothbrusher. Try the two-parent position, with your child lying on your laps as you sit on chairs facing each other with your knees touching. The brusher gets the best view sitting behind the child's head as she looks up at the ceiling. Initially your child may protest being held. But once he gets the message that this is a job that must be done and is nonnegotiable, he will cooperate. Be careful not to jab him in the mouth or gag him by using the toothbrush with force. Keep using a gauze-wrapped finger if he fights the brush. Keep this experience positive — it's easy to become angry and lose your patience when your child wiggles and squirms. Two-year-old Lauren cooperates when we remind her she won't get her stories until her teeth are clean. And try to be thorough. We learned this the hard way; Stephen developed a cavity in his first molar. We'd slacked off on the nightly routine because it was a hassle when we were tired.

FACILITATING A FACEWASH

In disciplining our toddlers one of our goals is to avoid hassles. One of the biggest hassles in the life of a toddler is having his face washed. We discovered a way to make this "torture" a fun time for the mom and the toddler. There is a nursery rhyme that goes "Here sits the Lord Mayor. Here sits his two men. Here sits the cock and here sits the hen. Here sit all the little chickens and here they run in. Chin chopper, chin chopper, chin chopper, chin." We use this little ditty as a finger play that is done on the child's face, starting with the child's forehead for the Lord Mayor, moving down to the two eyes for the two men. Each cheek is a cock and a hen. All the little chickens sit on the child's nose, and of course they run into his mouth. Then you finish off with the "chin chopper" verse on the child's chin. After doing this nursery rhyme with your fingers a few times and having your child thoroughly enjoying it, then the next time you go to wash his face with a washcloth you start the nursery rhyme and simply wash his face in all those areas as you say the nursery rhyme and you'll both be giggling and

the face will be clean. Many parents actually create discipline problems with their toddlers by failing to "think like a kid." If your only goal is to get the child's face washed no matter what the cost, you will wind up with a howling child and an angry, frustrated mother. You may also wind up with a child being punished for behavior that you could have facilitated toward laughter instead of anger.

WHINING

How can such an irritating sound as whining come from such adorable little people? It combines pleading, demanding, pestering, and nagging interspersed with sniffles and sobs. It escalates in pitch until either the whiner wears out (this can take a long time) or the listener wears down (this takes only a short time). Most children whine sometime between ages two and a half and four as they are trying out various voices for the effect on listeners. The reason they stick with it so long is they often find it works like a charm. Depending on the audience response, they will either go on to develop more annoying sounds or refine their tone to more pleasant speech.

Here's how to mute the whiner. Take note of what circumstances bring on the whine and keep ahead of your child. If your child whines every time you get on the phone, busy her before you make a call. If whining occurs when a child is tired or bored, correcting the circumstances will correct the whine. Oftentimes responding promptly to your child wards off a whine. The child does not have to resort to an irritating voice to get through to you.

Don't allow the whine to escalate. At the first syllable, if you suspect the whining tone of voice is coming, say "Stop! I don't listen to your whining voice" and walk away. Then turn around, look at your child, and say "But I listen to your nice voice." Or try, "This is not the whining room. If you want to whine, go to another room." Squelch whining at the first whimper, and redirect the child's voice to a more pleasant ring. Otherwise, you run the risk of letting the whine wear you down until you surrender — a concession that only prolongs the whining stage. Once the child realizes the whine will get her nowhere, it will stop. You may actually wind up giving the child what she wanted once her nice voice comes back and she can tell you her wish calmly and politely. Another way to win over a whiner is to change the subject. Keep on talking and distract the whining child into other interests: "Oh, look at this pretty flower. Let's see what it smells like." You're letting the child know that whining doesn't bother you.

If whining persists, replay for your child how unpleasant it sounds, being careful not to mock. Don't do this when you are both emotional. Do it at a calm time. Whine back: "Which do you like, Mommy's sour voice ('I don't wanna make supper') or Mommy's sweet voice ('Gosh, I'm tired. I could use some help')?" Once your child learns that whining doesn't work (and her language skills improve), whining will be a sound of the past.

CLEANING UP DIRTY WORDS

Remember your reaction the first time your four-year-old used a four-letter word? Did your mouth open with no sound coming out? Did you drop your fork at the dinner table? Did your ears turn red? To growing children toilet talk is as curious as those functions. To children words are not "dirty." They come out of children's mouths around age four.

Children pick up words and use them when they hear them frequently and when they have an effect on their audience. Kids won't know what some of the words they hear mean (for example, the "f-word"). That's why it's wise not to overreact. The stage will pass. Here's how to deal with toilet talk.

- Consider the source. A five-year-old was playing innocently near a group of older female relatives. Suddenly out came a word that silenced the crowd. As the embarrassed mother rushed to hush the little mouth, the great-aunt explained, "He talks just like his dad." Lessen your child's exposure to profanity. Clean up your own language, supervise what comes out of the mouths of your child's friends, and choose television programs carefully.

- Explain to your child, "Some words are not nice to hear. There are so many nice words, let's hear them instead." Explain that we don't use some words in certain places because these are things we don't talk about in public. "If you have to go poop at church, come and whisper in Mommy's ear. Or ask to 'go to the washroom, please.' "

- Provide alternatives. If your child uses obscenities reflexively when angry, practice alternative reactions: "Ouch! — I hit my finger." Words release tension, so model alternatives. Try the classics: "darn," "ow," "heck," "shoot," "phooey." Or use some more original epithets: "fiddlesticks," "Christopher Columbus," "Godfrey Daniel, Mother of Pearl" (from W. C. Fields).

- Ignore. Children learn what words have shock value; the more the audience reacts the more an encore is likely. After you are sure your child understands the house rules and that certain words are not allowed in public, ignore an occasional lapse. Intensify your praise for nicer alternatives.

- For older children, set the standard of language that you will allow in your home, and stick to it. If your seven-year-old comes in using the "f-word," you should sit down with him and explain exactly why it is offensive.

SOILING PANTS

You're sitting with your six-year-old son among a group of friends. Suddenly the air is not so fresh. Your eyes and nose turn toward your child, the source of this telltale smell. You're embarrassed for your child, your friends, and yourself. Your child either doesn't know, doesn't care, or represses his awareness of the odorous load.

Soiling pants, medically know as encopresis, is not unusual or abnormal. It occurs at some point after the child has been toilet trained. It is much more common in boys than in girls. It occurs more in children with a strong sense of privacy or a strong tendency to concentrate on an activity to the point that they are unwilling to stop long enough to use the toilet. But it is offensive to others. By understanding why this unpleasant problem occurs, you can help your child master his bowel habits.

When brain and bowel don't communicate. This is how I explain pants soiling to a child. The bowel, like the bladder, sends a signal to the brain. "I need emptying." (Draw a picture of the bowel below and the brain above and connect the two by an arrow, and refer to this diagram as you explain to the child.) When your bowel is full, it tells the brain it needs emptying, and the brain says "Go to the nearest toilet." (This *defecation reflex,* or urge to empty the bowel, automatically occurs in persons with healthy bowel habits.) If you listen to what your brain tells you, bowel and brain continue to talk to each other; you go to the toilet when necessary, and your pants stay clean.

But suppose you don't listen to your brain, either because you're too busy, too lazy, or you just plain can't hear what your bowel and brain say. In this case, they stop talking to each other. The bowel lets go whenever it wants to and there's poop in your pants. Usually a doughnut muscle at the opening of your bowel squeezes closed to help keep the poop inside until you can get to the toilet. Sometimes this muscle gets lazy and opens up. Sometimes you smell it before you feel it.

"If you don't listen to your bowel signals the poop gets big and hard and won't come out. This weakens the doughnut muscle around the bowel. It doesn't "feel" when the bowel is full, and you get all plugged up. It's called constipation; it feels uncomfortable. That's when you have two types of bowel movements, "hard poop" and "soft poop." The hard poop stays in your bowel and the soft poop — sometimes it's even watery — leaks around the hard poop, and you don't even feel it until it's in your pants. The longer this goes on, the harder the poop gets, the weaker the doughnut muscle gets, and the less bowel and brain talk to each other.

"So how can we keep this from happening?" you ask. (Encourage the child to answer.) First, you can always listen to what your bowel tells you. Instead of being busy and not paying attention to your body, go to the toilet as soon as your bowel says, "I'm full." Next, you can keep your poop from getting hard. Drink lots of water and juices (prune juice, pear juice). Eat fiber — prunes, whole-wheat bread, and cereals.

Busy little bowels. Keep (with your child's help) a diary of when your child soils his pants. What triggers holding on to the bowel movements and what triggers letting go? Does he poop when he is stressed in group play? Is he so engrossed in play that he ignores his bowel signals? Little boys with little bowels are forgetful. If your diary detects a correlation between play and soiling, call this connection to your child's attention. "As soon as you feel bowel pressure, go sit on the toilet. Don't hold on to it."

Embarrassed little bowels. Some children are embarrassed about toileting. Rather than let their playmates know they have to go to the toilet or ask the teacher to go to the bathroom, they ignore bowel signals; consciously or subconsciously they convince themselves — and their full bowel — that they really don't have to go. Impress upon your child that toileting is as normal and human as eating. Everyone does it. Perhaps some children can't imagine their teacher ever having to go to the bathroom.

Lazy little bowels. Some children don't want to "waste time" going to the toilet. Rather than interrupt play, expending the effort to go all the way to the toilet, get undressed, redressed, and reenter play, the child ignores his body signals. To help your child do his own toileting quickly, have simple elastic bands on pants or shorts.

Blocked little bowels. Paradoxically, the most common medical cause of pant soiling that I see in my office is constipation. This diagnosis surprises parents ("But it runs out . . ."). What soils the pants is the soft, watery stool that leaks past the hard feces. By examining your child, the doctor can tell if constipation is the culprit. Stool softeners, such as natural fiber (psyllium husks, branlike flakes, or whole flax seed, available at nutrition stores, that you sprinkle on your child's morning cereal), prune and pear juice, prune puree (if your child won't eat prunes), and two extra glasses of water each day are natural stool softeners. Remember to be patient with plugged bowels. They have been so stretched by constipation that it may take at least a month to notice improvements.

Sensitive little bowels. Explain to your child what's happening — he needs to know why he soils his pants. Probably a few of his friends also soil their pants. Explain to him that he has grown up but his bowels haven't, and you're going to help him help himself. He needs to take responsibility for his body. When his bowel and brain are giving him signals, he must listen to them. Explain to your child that sometimes if his brain is upset his bowels get upset too and don't work the way they should. If he gets tense, his bowels get tense. Avoid put-downs and criticism. Your child will get enough not-so-gentle reminders from his peers and sibs. Encopresis is embarrassing.

Children want help learning about their bodies.

When pant soiling is a choice. When older children (past age six) soil their pants by choice and not by accident, they are old enough to learn how to be responsible for cleaning their soiled pants. This increases the motivation to learn proper bowel habits. If this approach doesn't work, or works only temporarily, go to the next level of motivation. Calmly say (not at all in a punitive tone) "The next time you dirty your pants you will spend the rest of the day in your room and have whole-grain bread and water for meals." This is guaranteed to get his attention; it says you are dead serious about getting this problem fixed. You do not want him to be embarrassed anymore!!! One eight-year-old's mother who went to this level of motivation wrote this to us: "Judging by how wide and serious his eyes got when I told him the plan, I would say we definitely got our son's attention. The one comment he made was 'But that would be like prison!' He had from four P.M. on in his room, which only involved one meal. This was a welcome shortcut to having the mess go on indefinitely. This child is very focused in his activities. I saw him standing cross-legged one time, intensely holding back a bowel signal because he didn't want to lose his place in his video game! He later told me the bread tasted *very good.*" Her child actually chose "no video games for a week" over the "prison treatment" after a relapse. His memory was refreshed and so was the underwear. Breaking a habit like this won't happen overnight. The longer it has been tolerated, the longer it will take to correct. That's why it's best to deal with pants soiling as soon as you see it beginning

rather than put off dealing with it, hoping it will take care of itself.

Angry little bowels. In most children pants soiling, like bed-wetting, is a developmental nuisance, not a psychological problem. For some children, the problem lasts months or years; what lies in the pants is a symbol of emotional disturbances lying deeper inside the child, such as chronic unresolved anger or power struggles with parents. Environmental upsets (a move, divorce, illness) also upset the child's bowel habits. Seek professional help. But before you book yourself, or your child, for counseling, consult your child's doctor for a thorough physical examination. While it is safe to use the natural stool softeners mentioned above, don't use over-the-counter or prescription laxatives without your doctor's advice. Sometimes an overemphasis on bowel "treatment" calls too much attention to your child's bowel habits and may aggravate the problem. Also, take inventory of your family situation and play parent-detective to find out what disturbing factors may be triggering this offensive habit. Have a talk with your child about how you will work hard to change these factors as he works hard to control his bowel habits. Family therapy guarantees investment from all the players, and your child will respond in a healthy way to this joint effort.

NAME-CALLING

"You imbecile!" yelled fourteen-year-old Mary at her annoying seven-year-old brother, Billy. Now Billy didn't know what an "imbecile" was, but by the tone of his sister's voice he knew he didn't want to be one.

What's in a name? The point is not the word the child uses — much of the time kids don't know what the insults mean anyway. The deeper issue is insensitivity to another's feelings. Part of discipline is helping your child learn empathy. Help her imagine how the other person feels when he is called that name. Appeal to her sensitivity to her own feelings and those of others as the first step in changing the behavior. And bear in mind that a mocking voice — like saying "I love you" in a way that would make someone feel small — can be just as hurtful.

Model an apology. Even adults sometimes resort to name-calling. We've caught ourselves occasionally yelling "You're being a brat!" in frustration when a child is being willful. If your children hear a steady stream of "You're lazy" or "You're stupid," they will pick up on the habit, since it seems to be an acceptable way for parents to vent emotion. Name-calling is a put-down. It deserves an apology to build the child back up. When we hear that "brat" word come out of our mouths, we back up, hug the child, apologize, and reassure her that we think well of her. Then we talk about how we don't like what she did and go on to correct her behavior.

Pull up put-downs. To preserve the self-esteem of children, one of your jobs as house disciplinarian is to patrol your domain and stamp out put-downs. "That's dumb!" "You're a slob!" — the crippling words go on, if you let them. Point out put-downs the instant you hear them ("That's a put-down") so they'll be recognized. If your children already know that you won't tolerate put-downs in your family, they simply need a reminder, not a sermon or a tirade. One mother, Elaine, told her children how devastating these statements are, especially to younger children. She explained how calling someone an unkind name makes him angry and therefore completely unwilling to change the behavior that triggered the name-calling. She instructed: "Instead of yelling 'You're stupid' at your little brother, get down at his level, look him square in the eye, and firmly say 'That was a stupid thing to do, and I know you're smarter than that. Now help me clean up the mess.'" This not only stops the argument before it starts, it also models alternatives to name-calling for the little brother to use when playing with his friends.

Garbage in, garbage out. To mute what comes out of the mouths of children, control what goes into their ears. Certain words get into a child's memory record and seem to stick forever. Even though we carefully police our television, somehow our children managed to be exposed to Beavis and Butthead, in our opinion one of the most denigrating and potentially dangerous shows ever to get into the minds of kids — a major put-down to human intelligence. Over the next few weeks we heard "butthead" as if it were a socially acceptable form of direct address. We were ready to ban the word "butthead" just because we so heartily dislike the show. Once we stopped overreacting and realized that the actual meaning of the word to teens and kids is something like "dummy" or "oaf," the word lost its punch in our ears and we ignored it (but still banned the show itself). Eventually the word "butthead" died a slow death, at least in the confines of our home, and a new, more interesting (to them) word is now used.

In the past, one way to punish children for name-calling has been to make them write "I will not say butthead" a hundred times. We discourage this method because it plants the word even deeper into a child's memory. (After reading this section, what word do you remember the most?) A better correction would be to have the name-caller write a note of apology without using the offensive name.

GRUMBLING

Are you tired of asking your child to do something — over and over again — and all you get is a grumble? Or your child obeys, but reluctantly, protesting. Neither children nor adults always do things with a cheerful spirit, but there are ways to help children's attitudes be easier to live with.

Model cheerfulness. When your child brings you a reasonable request, give your child the message "Sure, Mary, I'm glad to please you!" — even though her request is inconvenient and you are less than thrilled about driving her to the pool for the third day in a row. Getting a "glad to do it" response makes the child happy she asked and models cheerfulness for the next time you ask the child for help.

Mirror grumbling. If your child grumbles about doing a task, help him to understand how it feels to be on the receiving end of a grumbled response. "For the next few hours I'm going to be a grumble-puss." After your child gets a grumbling response from you,

he will get the point that it's no fun to be around a crank.

Time-out the grumbler. "Johnny, I expect you to be agreeable when I ask you to do something. Go sit in the other room for five minutes and think about how grumbling makes everybody feel. When you've decided to quit grumbling, come and tell me about it. Our home would be no fun to live in if everybody grumbled."

Minimize grumble times. Nip grumbles in the bud before they become part of a child's personality. "Billy, please help Mommy set the table." "Why do I have to do everything?" Billy protests, and he clicks on his litany of complaints. At the first hint of a grumble, call it what it is: "That's a grumble. I don't want to listen to it." The use of job charts is the best way to keep track of who does what and when, so no one "always has to do everything." We have used motivational charts (see page 174) to weed out grumbles from the garden of childhood.

Cheering up the grump. Everyone is entitled to be crabby once in a while. But when it goes on and on, it's time for parents to step in. Grumpy children are no fun for themselves or others. Here's how to perk up the grouch.

Figure out why the child is grumpy. Some children are grouchy at certain times of the day. The morning grouch may need time, space, and breakfast to reenter the world after a night's sleep, or he may need a bit of careful humor to lift his still-tired spirits. The late-morning grump may be tired or hungry, a signal of the need for a nap or an early lunch. The after-school crank may need a similar tonic, an energizing snack and a brief nap to recuperate from common after-school ailments such as school-bus headache, tension buildup, or even boredom following all the stimulation of the classroom. The evening crab is probably just worn out and either needs a late-afternoon nap or an earlier bedtime. All of the above may just need to be left alone to grump for a while and nothing else. Respect that, and have as your only request that family harmony not be upset.

If your previously pleasing child suddenly turns into a grouch, suspect an illness or a recent stress in her life. If something is gnawing at her, the internal anger will affect her external mood. Time to do some listening to find the reason why your sweet child turned sour. Direct questioning will probably not work as well as just being available to listen when she's ready to talk. Connected kids usually don't wait too long to seek out a listening ear. Remember, sensitivity is what connected kids understand.

Busy the grump. A wise preschool director had a favorite motto: "Boredom is a choice." We adopted her motto when five-year-old Peter began using "I'm bored" a lot. We let Peter know that he was responsible for his own moods. If he didn't pick up the subtle hint, we'd make it more obvious: "Pete, you have lots of choices — help me with the dishes, get out your new library books or go see if your friends are playing outside." If he refused to choose something to do, we sent him off to another room to be bored on his own. One way or another, he got busy doing something he really enjoyed.

Humor the grump. Try these tactics: "Sally has a grumpy face. I sure miss the happy face. Let's see if we can paint one

on." Then stroke your child's face, pretending to color away the frown. Children like the special touch, and a laugh can loosen up the smile muscles in a tight face, which may in turn loosen up a chat about the reasons for the grumps. (This will probably not work for morning grumps.)

Don't squelch every crabby moment. Your child's emotions are a gauge of what's going on inside her. Just as you can't safely drive your car without gauges, you can't sensitively care for a child who doesn't show emotion. Let your child know, "It's OK to feel yucky. Tell us about what's bothering you, because talking about it can help you feel better." "It's OK to gripe sometimes if you don't really want to do something, but let me know how you feel using a nicer voice." "I love you even when you're grumpy. I'd rather see a real grumpy face than see a phony happy face."

Analyze the grump. Some parents tend to feel that somehow it is their fault if one of their children is not happy. Children get the message that they can expect parents to make them happy. They also learn that women (or men) expect their mates to make them happy. If you find your strings being constantly yanked by pouty, grumpy faces, call a halt. Get some counseling on how to be responsible for your own happiness. The next step is for your children to think they are responsible for you, which is very unhealthy.

ANSWERING BACK

Does your child always demand the last word? "Mary, please do the dishes." "Mom, I can't. I've got homework." "Doing the dishes is your job isn't it?" "Yes, but I have a test tomorrow." "Dishes only take ten minutes. Please be done by the time I get back." "It'll be your fault if I get an F." Some parents and children jab at each other Ping-Pong style and the conversation escalates into confrontation if neither stops to understand the other's viewpoint. Children are put on the defensive; parents feel their authority is being challenged. Nobody wins. Discussions should not become disrespectful. A respectful form of disagreement reveals that your child is willing — and comfortable — in communicating with you. Try these suggestions for the child who answers back.

Expect respect. Parents' ears are quick to pick up disrespect; keeping *your* tone respectful is not always easy, yet it is critical as a modeling tool. If you don't want your child to say "Shut up" to you, don't say it to her. Expect answering back during developmental stages when your child shows spurts of independence. Having the last word helps the child solidify her position and reaffirm her independence. Unless it's a biggie, disrespectful, or clearly done to taunt you, chalk it up to normal development. A child needs to learn how to make her point without being rude. There *is* a fine line between disrespect and spunk.

Between seven and ten years of age, part of the normal development of a child is to protect his interests. He is developing a sense of fairness. Any comment or request from you that is perceived by him as unfair will cause him naturally to go on the defensive. One day I wrongly accused Matthew of dawdling while the rest of the family was in the car waiting for him. He was quick to defend himself. The reason why he had to go back in the house was to get his shoes. This was not talking back but rather a de-

velopmentally appropriate comment from a child at a stage when he is learning a sense of social fairness. Being open to your child's defense (as long as it is respectful) conveys that you are willing to listen and respect his viewpoint. This sets the stage for opening avenues of communication with a teenager.

If things escalate into a shouting match, the talking back needs to be corrected. One day I overheard this dialogue between Martha and then eight-year-old Erin, who had talked back: "Erin, sit down. I want to talk with you," Martha said calmly. She had interrupted the battle by changing her tone of voice. The two power strugglers sat down. "I'm the mommy. You're the child. That doesn't mean I'm better than you, but I've lived a lot longer and I've learned a lot more. So I'm a bit wiser — as you will be when you're a mommy. I understand why you don't want to clean your room, but I expect you to obey." Then came a hug. Finally, Martha told Erin, "I'll help you get started."

If the talking back is becoming disrespectful and more frequent, evaluate your whole parent-child relationship. Is your child angry about something? Is a distance developing between the two of you? Have you been so preoccupied lately that your child has to shout and make a nuisance of herself to get you to listen to her? It's inventory time in the parenting business again. Here's an example. It was winter, a busy time in my pediatric practice, as well as deadline time for a book. These combined stresses left me less tolerant of the usual minor irritations that occur daily in the life of growing children.

Time-out from talking back. If you and your child are shouting at each other and a wall is going up, send your child for time-out or take time-out yourself. There's no real communication going on anyway. Announce "I need a break" or tell your child to sit down until he can talk to you respectfully. When you have both calmed down, open with an apology, if called for, to break the ice and take down the wall. Then ask to hear your child's viewpoint again (sometimes having to repeat her case lessens its importance to the child). Present your viewpoint and together arrive at a conclusion. End with a hug. Your child gets the message, without having to listen to a sermon, that disrespect from either party toward the other is counterproductive and unwise.

EXCITING THE UNMOTIVATED CHILD

Is your child becoming a couch potato? Is she not interested in any sport? Is it a chore to get her going? Does she refuse to practice her piano? From time to time most parents face the challenge of jump-starting an uninterested child.

Motivate the child from within and without. Children are either motivated from within themselves (self-motivation) or by some person or reward. Best odds for self-motivation is to allow the child to follow his own interests. To encourage a child to fire himself up you may have to resort to rewards or even bribery, along with healthy doses of praise and encouragement.

Sally's parents, sensing that she would enjoy music, encourage her to play an instrument. Sally resists, "I don't want to. I don't like to practice. I'd rather be playing outside." Eventually Sally picks an instru-

ment (piano) and agrees to lessons but still resists practicing. After a few months of lessons, her parents realize their daughter has a natural talent for the piano; still Sally is not excited. Should they drop the piano so as not to be pushy parents, or do they persist? Her parents wisely persevere. They realize how important skill development is to a child's self-esteem (see the cycle that develops between self-esteem and skill development, page 99), and they want her to enter adulthood equipped with skills for her own satisfaction. They encourage, "Sally, we love to hear you play." They really listen when she plays and often ask for encores of favorite pieces. They reward her with a new dress for her piano recital. Anticipating there will be days when it's hard to want to practice, they have a house rule — no piano, no TV. After six months of lessons, Sally masters a few longer pieces, plays them frequently, likes how they please her audience. Most importantly, she likes how she feels. She enjoys playing the piano and now practices willingly. The momentum of the child's self-motivation has taken over, so the parents back off.

"My mother made me." Every child is a storehouse of talents. What matters is how the child develops these talents into skills. That's the parents' job. Set your child up to succeed. Sometimes you have to prime the lethargic pump to get it going to the point that it runs itself. Many times adults, whose skills become their livelihood, reveal how glad they are their parents "made" them do it.

Rewards need to be immediate. I have tried the "When you're older, you'll be glad you learned how to play the piano" sermon on my kids. But to them "older" is a distant dream, outer space; they'll never be there.

This carrot is too far in front of their noses to work. Children live in, and for, the present. What worked to get two of ours over a hump was to offer a stop at the ice-cream store for a cone on the way home from lessons. If the child had practiced more than four times that week we made it a double scoop. When ice cream lost its glow after a year, we upped the ante by adding one dollar to their allowance for each extra hour of practice.

When rewards no longer work your child is ready to move on to another skill. Erin, age nine, made it clear that piano was not her passion, so we listened. She persevered to a level of competence, then we let her drop piano in favor of horseback-riding lessons. Three years later she is a very dedicated and responsible horsewoman. She still plays piano once in a while for fun or to show off to her friends.

Your child will do a task to please you or herself. She wants and needs your approval; that may be a way to fire up the unmotivated child. In no way should parents leave their children feeling parental love is conditional on their performance. Once you get the poky child going, the desire to please herself should provide the momentum to keep her going. Do not punish your child for not practicing or for not doing it well.

Beware of a sudden change. A sudden drop in interests is a red flag that something is going on inside the child or his environment that is not right: a threat to his self-esteem, loss of a friend, an overwhelming worry about school or home, or taking drugs. This is a signal that parental, or even professional, counseling is needed.

Give the child a job. The feeling that the job you are doing is worthwhile, and therefore you are worthwhile, is a valuable self-motivating tool. Janice, a creative mother, motivated her lazy five-year-old by calling her "Mommy's helper" and giving her paying jobs around the house. I have used this tool in coaching Little League baseball and as a scoutmaster. As a novice, I used the unmotivating "Get moving!" It is much easier on me and better for the child if, when I see his interest in the game or activity dwindling (as evidenced by deteriorating behavior), I give him a job in the organization. Getting perks for a good job — and good behavior — not only works for discipline, it is real life. (See related section, "Give Your Child Responsibilities," pages 103–104.)

No interest whatsoever. "But my child just isn't interested in doing anything," a desperate mother confided to us in counseling. If that's the case, suspect the underlying problem is poor self-esteem and focus on helping your child build his self-image (see suggestions for building self-esteem, pages 92–104.) Healthy self-esteem is like an internal tonic, stimulating the child to please himself and others. Be sure to ask yourself whether too much television is further sedating the child, and remember that learning an actual skill is often not seriously endeavored until ages eight, nine, or ten.

Don't rescue a child from boredom. Children have to go through boredom to get to creativity. If you never allow your child to be bored and pull himself out of it, he is much less likely to be inwardly motivated.

16

Sibling Rivalry

THREE-YEAR-OLD MOLLY'S LIFE is just perfect. She is the center of attention in the perfect love triangle: mommy, daddy, and child. She's had her parents' complete attention her whole life; she knows exactly what to expect. She has never had to share her parents with anyone.

Then into her life comes an intruder, taking her place on center stage. A star is born! The audience oohs and aahs over this newly born rival and showers him with gifts. Molly is no longer the most important member of the family. As she bids for equal time, she hears "Not now, I have to nurse the baby." When guests arrive, she gets passed over in favor of "Oh, what a beautiful baby." Her disappointment at the demotion escalates into anger at this little upstart who unseated her; she is irritated because everyone is telling her how lucky she is to have such a nice baby brother.

Many parents in this situation will try to smooth things over with adult logic. They need to realize how the situation looks through the eyes of their child. "Think on the bright side. You've gained a playmate," adults say. (Child's logic: "I've got plenty of playmates. Did I ask for another one? And this one can't even play — all he does is sleep.") "Mommy and Daddy love you just as much." ("Then why is that baby always in your arms, and I'm not?") "I need to spend more time with your baby brother because babies need mommies so much, just like you did when you were a baby." ("I'd rather still be your baby. I need a mommy too. Besides, I don't remember being a baby.") "Mommy's busy, but you and Daddy can do something special." ("Why did you need a baby? Wasn't I good enough?") "You'll get used to him, and he'll be fun to play with." ("I hate that baby. That baby ruins my fun. When can you take the baby back, Mommy?")

After months of wishful thinking, reality hits. The baby isn't going back. In fact, he's growing up, crawling, and getting into the older child's precious possessions. The child digs in to defend her turf against the enemy who by now topples her towers of blocks and captivates her playmates. Big sister spends the rest of her growing-up years competing for the family prize — her parents' attention.

INTRODUCING A NEW BABY

Some sibling strife is inevitable, though the degree depends on the ages of the two children, whether or not their personalities are compatible, and the level of sibling conflict you tolerate. An attachment-parented child will have a *much* easier time adjusting since she got what she needed when she needed it. She won't be very jealous seeing someone else get needs met. Children over age three or three-and-a-half usually welcome a new baby into the home, either with open arms or as a novelty, and sometimes these children, at least on the surface, don't seem to be jealous. They may compete more for playtime with "my" baby than for attention from you. Being verbal helps them deal with the changes. But it is not unusual for younger children to be upset for a while. (Face it: Things will never again be the same for you or your older child.) Even if you manage to "do everything right" and see very little or no hurt in your older child in the early months, once the new baby reaches eight months and can crawl, your older child will have to deal with intrusions into his space. Here's how to introduce your new baby to your older child.

What to Do

How you handle the coming blessed event and how you communicate with your older child and manage on a day-to-day basis once baby arrives can make the difference between peace and war for the two children. It's up to you as the adult to be sensitive to the inner and outer conflicts. A lot depends on how strong the connection is between you and both the children.

Make friends before birth. Tell your older child about the new baby before birth, early on or later in your pregnancy depending on her level of understanding. Show pictures of a baby in a mommy's uterus. Out of sight is out of mind to a young child, so the baby who is not born doesn't threaten her domain, though even a two-year-old may sense that mommy is preoccupied with what's beneath the bulge. Let her pat the baby, talk to the baby, and feel the baby kick. Have fun talking about and planning for the baby.

Replay the child's babyhood. Sit down with your child and page through her baby picture album. Show her what she looked like right after birth, coming home from the hospital, nursing, having her diapers changed, and so on. By replaying the child's baby events, she will be prepared for what is to come.

Foreshadow baby's coming. "When the tiny baby comes out of Mommy's uterus, Mommy's going to hold it *all* the time. Tiny babies just sleep and nurse all day long and sit in their mommy's arms. Tiny babies *really need* their mommies."

Include the child in the birth festivities. Besides encouraging him to be with mom and the new baby after the birth (if the child was not at the birth), ask for his help in planning a "birthday party." He gets to pick the cake and decorations, and to plan special presents to and from the new arrival.

Include a gift for sib. Savvy visitors who themselves have survived sibling rivalry bring along a gift for the older child when visiting the new baby. Keep a few small gifts in reserve for your young child when friends lavish presents and attention on the new baby. Let her be the one to unwrap the baby gifts and test the rattles.

Time share. Along with the uncertainty of finding where they fit into the new scheme of things, what bothers children most is sharing you with the baby. Since the concept of sharing is foreign to the child under three, and since mom is her most important "possession," it's unlikely that you'll be able to sell the child on the concept of "time shares" in mother. It sounds good to say that you'll give your older child equal amounts of your time, but in practice that's unrealistic. New babies require a lot of maintenance, and you don't have 200 percent of yourself to give (which is why we are big believers in new mothers giving themselves permission to neglect housework and chores in favor of time with baby and toddler).

You can share with your child the time you spend caring for the baby. Wear your infant in a baby sling. That gives you two free hands to play a game with your older child. While feeding baby, read a book to the sibling or just have cuddle time. Increase your time on the floor. While baby is still small, he needs to be in arms or sling, but do it on the floor, and your toddler will see your availability. As baby gets older, place him in an infant seat, or on a blanket on the floor, to watch while you play one-on-one with his big brother or sister. This entertains two kids with one parent. Try playtime for two: As baby gets a bit older, encourage the child to entertain the baby. Making faces and funny noises is something three- or four-year-olds excel at and babies love. Big, toothless grins can be an incredible ego-booster — "Hey, he *likes* me." If

you like your baby, the feeling will soon be mutual.

Remember, baby's needs *always* come first (short of life and death situations), even though your toddler can be more persistent or boisterous making her needs and wants known. Many a mother has made the mistake of not bonding appropriately with her newborn for fear of hurting the older one's feelings. If the child got what she needed as a baby, she *can* handle frustration without damage. An infant can't.

Make the sibling feel important. Give your child a job in the family organization. To pull the child out of the "I want to be a baby" blues, play up her importance to you, personally and practically. Tell her you need her help. Give her a job title. Make it fun: "You can be Mommy's helper. Get the diaper, please." "Bring the clothes for Mama." "Please grab those toys." Let him change diapers, dress baby, and bathe baby (all under supervision of course). Praise the help he gives you.

Here's how one mother handled her four-year-old's turnabout in personality after the birth of their second child. Soon after Benjamin was born, Amy seemed to go through an early childhood crisis. She reverted to bed-wetting and throwing temper tantrums. A previously happy child, Amy became sad. She talked back, was defiant, began waking at night, and made herself a general nuisance. Mom gave her a job as "mother's assistant," and even paid her for her help. After a few weeks, Amy not only became more pleasant to live with, she enjoyed her mothering skills.

Be open to sibling's feelings. Just as new parents worry about ambivalent feelings toward the baby, children dislike their angry feelings about their brother or sister and may want to hide them. Encourage your child to express her negative as well as her positive feelings. Give her an empathetic opener such as, "Sometimes I imagine you like your baby brother and sometimes you don't." Don't push, just be available. Encourage the child to *draw her feelings* about the new baby. Children often feel safer drawing what they feel. When she does tell you negative things like, "I hate that baby," resist the urge to say something like, "Oh, you don't mean that! You *love* the baby." Be glad she feels secure enough to lay her feelings out for you. If she hears you say her feelings are normal and understandable, they'll lose a lot of the initial intensity, and she'll open up more. Everyone wants to be understood and accepted.

"What's in it for me?" That's the way children think. By adult logic, children should be thrilled to have gained a live-in friend, but children in this situation are preoccupied with what they've lost. They don't see an "up" side. They've lost center stage, and the baby is too little to be fun. Mommy is no fun anymore since she's tired all the time. (Sibling rivalry comes at a bad time for parents. Just when you are exhausted from adjusting to a new baby, you have to deal with an older child undergoing a personality change.) Revive "special time," especially with dad: outings to the park, the ice-cream store, even the convenience store for bread and milk. These one-on-one outings are reserved just for the older child. The attention the child apparently has lost from mom she gains from dad. "But we tell her we love her. Doesn't that count?" Yes, but how children perceive their parents' love for them is what counts. Actions speak louder than words. Use "just-being time"

(see page 57): Your older child can sit *right next* to you as you hold baby (no need to put baby down or disturb bonding). Enjoy each other's presence with body-to-body contact. Even fifteen minutes a day can make a difference.

Protect both children's needs. "I looked around just in time to see our three-year-old hit our new baby in the head with a toy," cried a shocked new mother. Hurting the baby calls for immediate correction; safety prevails over psychology. Put on your best never-do-that-again tirade. (See the example in "Making Danger Discipline Stick," pages 68–71.) Pull out all the stops: Time-out the child (and time-out the toy, too). Control any urge to swat the child, but you must deliver firm direction. Explain how fragile babies are and that even though you understand she is feeling angry, you *will not let her hurt the baby.* Help her apologize when and if she's ready: "Pat baby's head *gently* and tell him you're sorry you hurt him."

Now that the child's feelings are out of the bag, you can address them directly; she wants you to understand her struggles. Do some verbalizing for her: "It's hard for you to see Mommy spend so much time with the baby." Then show her how to hit a soft, inanimate object like a pillow when she's angry, because it won't be hurt. Show her how she can be nice to the baby. Encourage her touches to be soft; model stroking and saying "nice." Close this memorable session with a triangle hug: parent, child, and baby. Be sure your child gets the message that she is never to do that again.

Ask your older child to tell you when she feels angry. If your older child is very young (under two), expecting her to control angry impulses around the baby is expecting too much. This is another good reason for wearing the baby as much as possible: the older one will see you as being more available to her, and you'll have baby in a safe place. Don't leave an aggressive toddler alone with the baby. She can't control herself without your help.

Sometimes older siblings want to try out baby behaviors, such as bottle- or breast-feeding. Letting the child try is the easiest way to handle this desire. Peter was weaned from Martha's breast at seventeen months. He was nearly three years old when Hayden was born. He watched closely while Martha breastfed the first day, and then he asked to nurse. He stood by the rocking chair and leaned in for a suck or two, barely got the hang of it, and wondered what the big deal was. Not to be outdone by the newcomer, he promptly asked for *two bottles*, since she had two breasts. We had to go out and buy them. He carried his two bottles around for a couple of weeks and then lost interest. Martha's not shoving him away helped with his "I hate that baby" thoughts and feelings.

New baby gets wheels. Often siblings seem to be adjusting beautifully until the baby is older. A common time for this to happen is when baby learns to crawl. Now the older one finds that nothing is safe — his towers get crashed, his best toys teethed on, his games interrupted. Some anticipatory planning is helpful. Point out that this will begin happening, and explain why babies act this way (they need to learn by exploring and they are too little to understand how to be careful) so things won't be taken personally. Teach your older one how to develop patience and the ability to plan ahead. He can set up his games at a table out of baby's reach, and he can build a

tower for baby, knowing how much fun baby has knocking it over. Point out that baby is, after all, getting more interesting.

Humor lightens the load. Six-year-old Tina, holding a lock of hair in her hands, came running to her mother complaining about her two-year-old brother: "Peter pulled a bunch of my hair out." Catching Tina by surprise, her mother suggested, "Take your lock of hair to school for show-and-tell." Tina thought this was such a funny idea that she forgot about the hair puller.

PROMOTING SIBLING HARMONY

While experts have pronounced sibling rivalry to be a normal part of family life, it doesn't have to be the norm in your family. While some adversaries are born, others are made. Full-blown, out-of-control sibling rivalry should not be considered an unavoidable consequence of having more than one child. Learning to live with a sib is the child's first lesson in getting along with other children. Here are ways to establish harmony among your children before rivalry has a chance to take root.

Raise connected sibs. The best way to prevent the older child from feeling overly jealous of the new baby is to fill the child's emotional tank in the first place. We have noticed that sibling rivalry occurs much less among attachment-parented kids. These kids enter the toddler and preschool years with qualities that partially immunize them against these germs that inflame sibling relationships: inner anger, insensitivity, and deep-rooted jealousy. Because these children have a strong sense of self and an inner peace, they are more likely to be sensitive and giving toward others — especially their new brothers or sisters. By the time a new baby arrives, the connected child is more ready to move on to relationships with others besides mom (especially dad) and doesn't mind sharing mother with a sib. Kids weaned before their time get more jealous because they feel the intruder is getting something they still need.

Yet kids are kids no matter how well-connected. Consider the rivalry that developed between four-year-old Michael, a connected child who had received the best of attachment parenting, and his one-year-old sister, Katie. At birth she had many medical problems requiring her mother to spend a lot of time at the hospital in the Intensive Care Unit, and more time doing follow-up care at home. Michael seemed to take Katie's entire first year in stride, but finally his anger got the better of him. "Why have you been misbehaving so much this week?" his mother asked. "What's wrong?" Michael asked, "When are we getting rid of Katie?" Shocked, his mother replied, "We're not!" Michael repeated, "Get rid of her! I hate her!" She asked Michael what he didn't like about his sister. He said, "She plays with all my toys." Michael's mother went on to explain how sharing is something we all have to learn: "Mommy and Daddy have to share what we have with you and Katie." She also empathized with Michael: "Sometimes little sisters are a pain to have around. You have to share your toys, your room, even your mommy and daddy." If you sense feelings in your child that need to be ventilated, draw your child out with frank empathy to see if you can uncork the built-up pressure. Having a one-year-old sister is stressful for even the most well-balanced four-year-old.

Promote sibling sensitivity. It's hard to hate and hit a person you care about and who cares for you. I don't believe siblings are born adversaries — if they have wise parents. There are four factors that set the level of sibling rivalry in your home: the temperament your children are born with — some are compatible, others clash; how *you* feel about and relate to each of your children; the structure you set up to promote sibling harmony; and how much in-fighting you allow. The first is the luck of the draw; the last three you can influence. (See discussion of temperaments, pages 281–287.)

Casually point out the advantages — both economic and social — of having a sibling. "We can buy you a really good bike because it will be passed along to your brother when you outgrow it." "We can get a bigger Lego set because you and your brother will share it." "When your brother gets bigger, you can teach him how to catch and throw."

Structure sibling relationships. This strategy settles moment-to-moment problems and establishes patterns for lifelong relationships. Help your children find constructive ways to relate to each other. This promotes desirable behavior. Give them various roles to try in relation to one another.

Try the *sib in-charge* approach. If there are several years of age difference between children, give the older one some responsibility for the younger one. Putting one child in charge of the other motivates the older one to care, and the younger one feels it. Teach the older one that he has the special job of protecting the younger one and modeling correct behavior. Keep a watch out, though, that the older siblings are capable of this. If they were not attachment-parented, they may do a lot of teasing and threatening. And don't abuse their availability.

Try the *sib as comforter* approach. When one child gets hurt, ask the other to help care for the injured one. Give your assistant a job title: "Dr. Mary, you hold Johnny's leg while I wrap it." "Please put this Band-Aid on Johnny's cut." The "doctor," by virtue of the roles she's been given, offers compassion for the patient, and the patient, who a moment ago may have yelled, "I hate you, Mary," now is on the receiving end of caring. It's hard to hate the hand that comforts you.

Try the *sib as minister* approach. This is a custom we have used in our family. If one child has a physical or emotional hurt, each sib is encouraged to offer a word of prayer to ease their brother's or sister's pain. We use a practice we call "laying on of hands:" The sib under pressure (whether it be an upcoming test, a big wish, an emotional or physical hurt) sits in the middle of the group while the family members place a hand on his arm or head or wherever the hurt is and pray for him. Often this ends with a kind thought or an offer of help.

Try the *sib as teacher* approach. "Johnny, you've been playing baseball for three years now. Would you please take Billy outside and teach him how to hit and catch?" mother asks. "Tracy, please help Ellen with her homework so I can finish mending your dress."

Encourage siblings to be *co-workers*. Set them up to cooperate. Siblings helping siblings is a strategy for lessening squabbles. Give them assignments that require cooperation and motivate them to work together: "Jimmy, would you and Johnny please clean up the garage together? If two of you do it

we can finish soon enough to catch the afternoon movie." Putting up holiday decorations, washing cars, and running lemonade stands are other sibling activities. The job gets done more quickly and with fewer hassles if the work is shared. Neither one will let the other slack off and do less work. Oftentimes, siblings discover that working together is fun. The adult in charge should keep a "bossy-submissive" relationship from developing.

Try *siblings as co-sleepers*. Sleeping side by side strengthens the bond. Children who sleep peacefully together at night usually play more peacefully together during the day. Parents have shared with us their observation that children who sleep together quarrel less.

Promote *siblings as friends*. It's interesting to us that children often get along better with their friends than with their brothers and sisters. Perhaps it's because they can choose their friends, they aren't with them as much, and they don't have to compete with friends for their parents' attention. Sometime during middle childhood (ages six through ten), impress upon your child the value of having a sibling. While some children, especially if caught up in negative feelings toward their sibs, either don't at all or only marginally appreciate their brothers and sisters, other children deeply feel the meaning of "blood relative." Even children sense that "blood is thicker than water." Watch two or more siblings close ranks and defend one another against an outsider. Brothers and sisters are a sort of live-in support system. Here's a message we give our children: "Your brothers and sisters can ultimately be your best friends. When most of your other friends have moved or drifted away, your family friends will always be there when you need them."

And if your child sees how important his aunts and uncles are to his parents, he'll believe you. If this is not the case in your family, try to avoid the pitfalls that led to this unfortunate fact. Learn your lessons carefully from the history of family trials you have experienced. Maybe even get counseling to be sure you don't repeat them. Friends come and go; siblings are forever.

Squelch fighting. Give your children clear messages as to what behavior you expect of them and how you expect them to behave toward you and each other. Let them know these expectations early, and reinforce them frequently *before* arguments become a way of life among them. Provide frequent reminders ("That's a put-down") if one sib even begins to put down the other; or give a look that says, "Don't even think about it." Nip fights at the first squabble, before they get out of hand, or you and your kids will spend years cleaning up a mess of bad feelings that could have been avoided. Devise a way of monitoring what goes on in your home when you are not there. Keep your finger on the pulse of sibling relationships. Be watchful for aggressor-victim roles. Your job is to protect your children, even from one another. Hayden was the first girl after three boys. They teased her a lot and though most of it was good natured she didn't feel it that way. One day when she was five she came to me and told me, "Nobody in this family loves me." We had a family meeting that night to raise a few consciences. The boys and Hayden are the best of friends now.

Sometimes you're just too tired to play amateur psychologist. You want to click into your police mode. Do it and don't worry about permanently damaging your child's psyche. There are times when you need to consider your psyche, too. "Just stop the behavior. That's it. End of bickering. I will not tolerate it." (Perhaps add a bit of humor.) "If you two want to fight like animals I'll build cages for you in the backyard. I'll call one of you a cat and one of you a dog, and I'll put out a little dog food for one of you and cat food for the other...."

DISCOURAGING SIBLING DISHARMONY

Besides structuring the home environment to promote harmony among siblings, you can also lessen the conditions that trigger sibling strife.

Every child is a favorite. It's unrealistic for parents to claim that they never play fa-

Help siblings play cooperatively.

Fighting in Front of Kids

Scene one: Eight-year-old Matthew and eleven-year-old Erin enter the kitchen and witness their parents venting their frustrations at each other; that is, there's a fight going on. Sparks fly. They hang around long enough to grab a snack from the pantry, then head for the garage to shoot some baskets in the driveway.

Scene two: Ten minutes later. Matthew and Erin reenter the kitchen with their antennae up and find their parents laughing together. The children are relieved and hang around awhile again, this time soaking up the conversation that lets them know how things got resolved. As you may have guessed, this is a scene from the Sears book of family struggles. Yes, the coauthors of this book fight, as do all couples. Oftentimes these fights occur where children can see and hear them. But it is possible to turn these real-life scenes into lessons for children.

Early in our parenting careers, we tried to hide our emotional outbursts from our children. Thinking they would get the wrong idea about love and marriage, we tried to put on our best behavior in front of our kids. We now know that is unrealistic and downright phony.

Parental confrontations can teach children a valuable lesson for life: People who love each other are able to express opposing opinions to each other without threatening the relationship. In stable families, mom and dad always make up. From these observations, children get the message that it's safe to express their feelings appropriately, and it's possible to "fight" without hitting or name calling, and the friendship will survive. After all, mates need to share feelings. We all disagree about how we should do things or say things sometimes. It's natural. Friends share those opinions or disappointments with each other, which sometimes gets noisy. Even the best of friends fight.

Parents, you can model fair fighting for your children, showing them how to share their feelings in ways that don't threaten relationships. Of course you would not abuse one another verbally or physically. Use "I" messages ("I feel this way") rather than "you" messages ("You are so insensitive"). Don't dredge up the past and don't drag the children into your fights. Attempt to resolve problems rather than letting them fester. Let the children see you apologize and make up.

Turning a negative scene into a positive lesson works only when parents first, by word and example, give their children the message that they are happily and eternally married. Without this stabilizer children's behavior often deteriorates following a parental battle. I once counseled an eight-year-old who became angry and depressed following a family fight. He feared that this fight signaled a divorce, which had happened recently in a classmate's family. Another child I counseled developed a school phobia. He refused to go to school, fearing his battling parents would harm each other or one wouldn't be there when he got home. A preadolescent girl once confided to me that she would never marry because her parents fought so much.

Lesson for life: If your commitment to each other is founded on love and respect, expressing your feelings will not harm your relationship. If your fights are disturbing your children, keep them private until you can get some counseling on how to fight in a constructive way.

vorites. Some parents' and some children's personalities clash; others mesh. Some children bring out the best in a parent, others push the wrong buttons. The key is not to let your children perceive this as favoritism. Better yet, make them all feel special. If your child asks you the question "Who do you love more, me or Billy?" give the politically correct answer: "I love you both in special ways." Give the comparison that love is like sunshine. Sharing the sun doesn't mean you get less, and our love shines on our children like sunshine. Mention special qualities: "You are my firstborn — no one else can be my firstborn child (or "second," or "first daughter")." Get out of the "who's best" trap. Children don't expect you to say who's better. They are only fishing for reassurance about how you feel about them.

Parents can naturally fall into playing favorites; the trick is to play favorites equally. I'm always talking about Matthew, perhaps because we've done so many things together — baseball, scouts, just "hanging out" — not to mention all the time when he was a baby (see Chapter 6, "Fathers as Disciplinarians"). I feel I know him better than the other kids. Some children respond better to parents. And certain temperaments are more of a joy to live with than others. So, the advice "don't have favorites" is an impossible goal. Perhaps it is more realistic to try to be an equal-opportunity favor giver. First, in order to do something about it, be aware that you may show favoritism. Try writing down what you like most and what you like least about each child. The things we like least in a child are often the things we least accept in ourselves.

If the list is obviously tilted to one side or the other, you have a potential problem. Do some soul-searching to determine if

these likes and dislikes affect your actions toward the child. Perhaps you need to identify the unique gifts of each child and nurture those special qualities. Look for each child's special needs, too. See if the attitudes or behaviors you dislike are biggies or smallies. If smallies, change your reactions.

Avoid comparisons. Remember, children are constantly being compared. Most of their life they will be rated on their performance — grades in school, the batting order on the baseball team, races and games among themselves. Perhaps the home is the only organization left that values the child for himself, not in comparison with others. So avoid comments like these: "Why can't you be on time like your brother?" "Your sister got such good grades. Didn't you study?" Even worse are statements like "You're just as bad as your sister." These remarks can't help your child enjoy his brothers and sisters but rather will lead him to resent them. Focus on that child's behavior. Don't use a sibling as a standard. The child will feel he can't possibly measure up, or he will deliberately choose not to. Either way you lose. Set standards for each child according to his temperament and abilities, and teach him to be happy with who he is.

Don't let kids boast or show off in your presence. "I got better grades than you did," "I have a new bike, ha ha ha." We give clear messages to our children that putdowns are prohibited in our house.

Children do not have to be treated equally. While all children are created equal, it's impossible to treat them that way all the time. In their desire to prevent sibling squabbles, parents strive to do everything the same way for all their children, whether it's buying pajamas or selecting a college. Many are hung up trying to be absolutely certain they treat their children equally. Children aren't the same; you shouldn't behave as if they were. Make moment-by-moment decisions and don't worry about the long-term consequences if you've given one child more strokes than another today. Shoot for a balanced week, not a balanced day. "Why did Jimmy get a new pair of shoes and I didn't?" quibbled Tommy. "Because his were worn out and you got a new pair of shoes last month." Don't let Jimmy flaunt his prize in front of Tommy. Children want to be treated *individually,* not equally.

Children have an innate feeling for fairness, or what they perceive as being fair. Our first two children, Jim and Bob, were two years apart. Bob, the younger, once he was old enough to compare himself with his brother, would demand equal opportunities. His standing comment on almost everything was "No fair." When Jim got married first, Bob's first comment on the wedding video was teasingly "No fair!" (Bob went on to father the first grandchild — at last he did something first!) Some children are born scorekeepers. If you try to join their game it will drive you nuts. One evening at dinner two scorekeepers counted the number of peas they had been served to be sure they got an equal number. After that we let them serve themselves. If they wanted to go through this ridiculous exercise, that was their choice. When sharing a treat, we let one child divide the piece of cake and the other gets first choice. As much as you can, try to divide chores equally among children according to their ages and capability. Be fair, when possible, but don't drive yourself crazy. Remember, you are preparing your children for life, and life does not treat people fairly or equally.

Be prepared to explain why equality doesn't mean sameness. "Daddy, why do I have to go to bed at nine o'clock when Erin gets to stay up until ten?" "Because you need more sleep." Younger sibs don't seem to grumble when the older ones have more privileges that serve their own interests. Our twelve-year-old, Erin, doesn't complain about sixteen-year-old Hayden driving because Hayden can now be her chauffeur. Explain that children get different privileges, and *more responsibilities,* as they get older. They can look forward to growing up.

Trying to give children equal amounts of time can be almost impossible. While every child certainly deserves special times with parents, the fact is that parents end up spending more time with younger children. Sometimes group therapy solves the equal-time dilemma. If we gave every child in our family equal time for a story at bedtime, we'd be reading all night. The older ones soon learn that the younger ones need more time and creativity to get them to sleep. If they want the same, they join the family bedtime story. Oftentimes we have a whole pile of kids around the bed to join in the three-year-old's story.

Humor the child into reality. "I want to be a baby too," said four-year-old Tricia. "All right," mommy played along. "You can be a baby today. What would you like to do?" "I'd like to have a bottle." She gave her a bottle (with formula, not juice!). "Yuck, this tastes awful." "What would you like to play?" "I would like to ride my tricycle." "Babies can't ride tricycles." "Can I have a peanut butter and jelly sandwich?" "Babies can't eat peanut butter and jelly sandwiches. They only eat baby food." Tricia decided that she didn't want to be a baby after all, announcing, "I think I'll just go outside and ride my tricycle."

Special occasions for one and all. We call special days "special times," not "favorite times." "Special" is not based on specific comparisons the way "favorite" is. With sensitivity and creativity you can pull up the achiever without putting down the others; don't get so hung up on equality and fairness that nobody gets to feel special. If one sib deserves special praise because of an accomplishment, prepare the other sib ahead of time: "Tonight at dinner we're going to sing congratulations to Anna for winning the race at school. It would mean a lot to her if you joined in. I expect you to." Be sure that Anna returns the praise when her brother deserves it. Birthday parties are another time when you want to draw everyone into the fun. Sometimes parents become so preoccupied with the sibling's upcoming party that they unconsciously tune out the other children. To prevent jealousy and withdrawal from the festivities, give your non-birthday child a part in the preparations: helping make the cake, wrapping presents, putting up the decorations, and even thinking up some party games. During the party, don't forget to acknowledge the sibling's help: "This game was thought up by Bobby's sister, Emily."

When to referee quarrels. When to step in as referee and when to remain a bystander is a round-by-round judgment call. Sometimes it's just play fighting. Letting children be children or giving a friendly reminder is all that is necessary. Sometimes when you intervene, it's hard to tell who is the perpetrator. The natural inclination is for parents to accuse the older child and protect the younger one. But sometimes even a one-year-old can annoy an older child by attacking his toys. Also consider, Is the quarrel bothering you? Martha's immediate fight-stopper is "You're disturbing my peace." This works because we have already planted the idea that in crowds (our family qualifies as a crowd) one respects the peace of others. If the children are in danger of hurting someone or damaging property, stop the fight.

If danger is apparent, remember, safety first, psychology second. First, separate the fighters; then, instead of being drawn into the shouting match, calm everybody down, and put your home-psychologist hat on top of your authority hat. Also, if you sense one child is victimizing the other, call a halt. Verbal abuse qualifies as fighting. You need to be particularly aware of this to prevent emotional scars. They take longer to heal than physical ones. You've already achieved your first goal, stopping the fight, and now you begin to work on your second and third: teaching children to respect one another and open up other avenues of communication, and showing them alternative ways of handling differences — valuable lessons for life. Listen to both sides: "He hit me." "No, he hit me first!" "I hate you!" "I hate you more!" Give the children time and space to vent their anger and frustration before beginning your "therapy." They are so caught up in their own emotion that they don't hear what the other is saying. Show you understand both children's viewpoints and help them hear each other by echoing their feelings: "Bob, you feel that Jim wronged you, and Jim, you feel that Bob was being unfair.... This sounds like something both of you can work out. You're big boys, and I expect you to come out of this bedroom as friends."

When the referee fumbles. Parents who had unhealthy sibling relationships growing up will find this part of their job description extremely challenging. They may even drop the ball entirely and leave the kids to fight it out between themselves. Here is another area where old wounds can continue to fester, and another generation could wind up succumbing to the ugly sores of domestic hatred and violence. If you see yourself in this condition and realize you are not able to guide your children in their relationships with one another, seek counseling to heal your own hurts so you can help your children not get caught in the same vicious cycle of out-of-control sibling rivalry.

Respect each sibling's talents. This is a difficult task. One child may have a terrific talent for music but is a bit lazy, and the parents put all their music money in that child's pot. The other child may appear to have no natural musical ability but a strong desire to play the piano simply because she wants to. Both these children deserve equal opportunity even though they do not have equal talents. On the one hand it makes sense to identify where a child's talents lie and set the conditions for them to flourish. But there are two issues here: the natural talent of the child, and the child's desire. In fact, the highly motivated but less-skilled child may learn the better lesson for life than the talented but lazy child. Also, beware of the easy trap of subtly putting down one sibling while building up the other. "Anne is the family piano player," Mother announces at a family reunion. Anne is beaming, but her highly motivated brother may get the message that piano playing is going to be Anne's role in the family, so he might as well not even try to play.

Look for ways in which you can encourage children to excel in different areas. If Rachel is a piano player, perhaps Rebecca would like to study violin. Each will have a chance to shine. They can cooperate and play duets. See to it that the family actress has as many opportunities as the family athlete. When each child is allowed and encouraged to be an individual, there is less need to compete with siblings.

Some sibling rivalry is as inevitable in families as wintertime colds. Sibling fighting should not be a disruptive part of family life. Remember, siblings relate in other ways besides fighting. One morning I was examining two-year-old Angelo for a fever. His three-and-a-half-year-old brother, Tony, concerned about his sick sib, asked, "Is he all right, Dr. Bill?" Mom commented on what a nice brother Tony was to reinforce his caring. Children can be taught to be empathetic with each other by alert parents. This is sibling sensitivity at its best.

III

DISCIPLINE FOR LIFE

Disciplining children means equipping them with the tools to succeed in life. One of the most important tools is the ability to make right choices. To do so, a child needs to develop a social sensitivity, the ability to consider how his actions will affect other people. Call it instilling values, call it developing a conscience, but whatever you call it, one of your jobs as a disciplinarian is to help your child develop an internal guidance system that steers him in the right direction when you're not there to help him make the best choice. This is discipline for life. In this part of the book we will give you the tools to help your child become morally literate. We will explore the why and how of instilling values, teaching a healthy respect for gender and for the opposite sex, and using special kinds of discipline to equip special needs children with the skills that will help them cope with their particular challenges. This guidance system, which keeps one eye on the present and the other on the future, has a proven track record for helping your child become an adult who achieves happiness with self, with a mate, and with a job.

MORALS AND MANNERS

There was a child went forth every day,
And the first object he look'd upon, that object he became,
And that object became part of him for the day or a certain part of the day,
Or for many years or stretching cycles of years.

— Walt Whitman, *Leaves of Grass*

OUR FAMILY HOBBY IS SAIL-ING, and riding the waves with kids provides hours of opportunities for teaching. One day during our weekly sailing lesson I was teaching eight-year-old Matthew the importance of proper sail trim. I used this as a chance to talk about the importance of healthy values. What I said to him went something like this: "Matthew, running your life is kind of like sailing a boat. There are rules for both. We can't change the wind or the waves, but we can decide our destination, and we must trim the sails in order to get there. If we run into a storm, we drop anchor and wait it out. Without these simple rules, the boat will drift aimlessly at the mercy of the wind and waves. We might be lucky and float safely in the right direction; more likely we would end up on the rocks. Inside you are some inner rules that keep you going in the right direction, that anchor you in rough times. These inner rules are called morals. If you follow these rules, you have a better chance of being happy. When we trim our sails just right, the boat

moves in harmony with the wind and sea. We call it being 'in the groove.' When you trim your inner guidance system right, you will feel in harmony with yourself. Matthew, you will have a smoother sail through life when you make the right choices."

RAISING A MORAL CHILD

Raising a moral child means teaching your child to live by the Golden Rule. Before your child can "treat others like you want others to treat you," he has to learn how to empathize, to be able to think through an action before doing it and to judge how the consequences of his action will affect himself and others. Therein lies the basis of a moral person.

Raise kids who care. Attachment parenting is your child's first morality lesson. Parents are the child's first morality teachers. Our own observations as well as numerous studies (see the table on page 31) conclude that attachment-parented infants are more likely to become moral children and adults. The one quality that distinguishes these children from kids raised in a detached parenting style is *sensitivity*. We view sensitivity as the *root virtue*. Plant it in your child and watch it sprout other virtues, such as self-control, compassion, and honesty. Here's how to grow a sensitive child.

When a child spends the early years with a sensitive caregiver, this little person develops an inner sense of *rightness*, a sense of well-being. In short, he feels good. Being on the receiving end of this responsive style of caring plants *trust* in the infant and, eventually, *sensitivity* in the child. The child makes these virtues part of himself. They are not something a child has, they are what the child is, *sensitive and trusting*. He has learned it is good to help and hold a person in need. He has a *capacity to care*, the ability to feel how another person feels. He will be able to consider, before he undertakes them, how his actions will affect another person.

This inner code of behavior becomes deeply rooted in connected children. As a result, they develop a healthy sense of guilt, feeling appropriately wrong when they act wrong. To a connected kid, a lie is a breach of trust. His well-being is disturbed so he will strive to preserve and restore his sense of moral balance when he slips. A connected child can truly do the right things unto others because others have done the right things for him.

Not so the unconnected kid. The child who grows up with insensitivity becomes insensitive. He has no frame of reference for how to act from his caregivers or himself. Without an inner guidance system, his values are subject to change according to his whims. He becomes a moral marshmallow.

One difference between kids who care and kids who don't is their ability to feel remorse, to be bothered by how their actions affect others. Criminologists have noticed the most significant trait shared by unconnected kids and psychopathic adults is their inability to feel remorse and empathy, and thus to take responsibility for their behavior.

A group of five-year-olds are playing and one of the children falls, scrapes her knee, and starts crying. The connected child will offer a reassuring "I'm sorry you're hurt" and show a desire to comfort. The unconnected child may say "Cry baby."

Make a moral connection. The connected toddler begins her moral development with the two fundamental qualities of sensitivity and trust. These "starter virtues" make it easier for parents to teach a toddler and preschooler the dos and don'ts of life. An astute, connected parent appropriately points out to the child what's right, what's wrong, and what's expected. The child trusts that whatever the parent says is gospel. If dad says hitting is wrong, it's wrong. If mom says comforting a hurting child is right, it's right. The parents are trusted moral authorities.

The first six years of life are a window of opportunity when a child unquestionably accepts the virtues modeled by parents. Consider what happens when the child receives even one "morality lesson" each day in the early years. For example, Ashley hurts her finger. "Let's help her feel better," you might respond. Your son takes his friend's ball. Your response: "Chris feels sad because you took his favorite ball." Or "How would you feel if Chris took *your* ball?"

Initially a child believes behaviors are

right or wrong because you tell her so, or she considers the consequences. By five years of age your child begins to *internalize* your values: What's right for you becomes right for her. Your values, virtuous or not, become part of your child.

Between ages seven and ten the child enters the age of moral reasoning. Now the child begins to act right because it is the right thing to do. By seven years of age, most children have developed their concept of "what's normal." If sensitivity, caring, po-

---

Stages of Growth for Moral Growth

Children go through stages of moral development, yet unlike physical growth, moral growth doesn't happen without some help from parents. To develop into a morally solid person, a child must be given a solid foundation at each stage.

Stage 1 — infancy. An infant does not have the capacity to moralize, other than having a sense of rightness or wrongness as those feelings apply to himself. After nine months of being nurtured in the womb, a baby enters the world expecting that nurturing will continue. Never having been hungry, baby concludes that hunger is wrong; it hurts. Never having been unattended, baby finds aloneness to be wrong; it's scary. Never out of touch, baby knows that unresponsiveness is wrong. Being in-arms, at breast, and responded to feels right! Baby feels she is the center of the world and she develops a feeling of rightness that becomes her "norm."

Stage 2 — toddlerhood. By eighteen months a sense of "otherness" begins. Toddlers learn that others share their world; others have needs and rights, too. The house he lives in has "rules" that he must learn to live by, which is frustrating.

The child does not yet have the ability to judge something as "right" or "wrong"; he is only directed by what others tell him, which competes with his internal drive to do what he wants. A child doesn't yet have the ability to realize he hurts someone when he hits. Hitting is "wrong" because parents tell him so or because he gets punished for it. Depending on how parents convey the behavior they expect, the toddler learns that obedience to adults is the norm.

Stage 3 — preschoolers (three to seven years). A major turning point in moral development occurs: The child begins to *internalize* family values. What's important to the parents becomes important to him. The six-year-old may say to a friend, "In our family we do . . ." These are the child's norms. Once these norms are incorporated into a child's self, the child's behavior can be directed by these inner rules — with frequent reminding and reinforcing from parents, of course. Later in this stage children begin to understand the concept of the Golden Rule and to consider how what they do affects other people, that others have rights and viewpoints, too, and how to be considerate. Children from three to seven years of age expect wiser people to take charge.

liteness, and empathy have been standard operating procedure in the child's home, those are his *norms,* and he operates according to them. What his parents take seriously, the child takes seriously. Up to this point, he believes his parents to be infal-

lible, so he enters middle childhood with their values as part of himself.

Along come children with other "norms," who grew up in insensitive, perhaps violent homes, with a distant parent-child relationship. Here is where the "morally con-

---

Stages of Growth for Moral Growth (continued)

They understand the roles of "child" and "adult" and need maturity from the adult. They perceive consequences and can grasp the *when-then* connection: when I misbehave, then this happens. The connected child behaves well because he has had several years of positive parental direction. The unconnected child may operate from the basis of "Whatever I do is OK as long as I don't get caught."

Stage 4 — seven to ten years. Children begin to question whether parents and teachers are infallible. Perhaps these people in charge don't know it all. They have the most respect for those adults who are fair and know how to be in charge. Authority is not threatening to the child but necessary for social living. Children believe that they should obey parents. And school-age children believe that if they break a rule they should be corrected. This strong sense of "should do" and "should not do" sets some children up to tattle.

Seven-to-ten-year-olds have a strong sense of fairness, understand the necessity of rules, and want to participate in making the rules. They begin to believe that children have opinions too, and they begin to sort out which values profit them

most — a sort of "what's in it for me" stage. Parents can use this sense of fairness and drive for equality to their advantage: "Yes, I'll drive your friends to the park if you agree to help me with the housework." These negotiations make sense to the child. This also begins the stage where children are able to internalize religious values, which concepts truly have meaning for them, and which don't.

Stage 5 — preteens and teens. These children strive to be popular. They are vulnerable to peer pressure and peer values. As they continue to sort out which values will become part of themselves and which they will discard, they may vacillate and try on different value systems to see which ones fits. This child is more capable of abstract reasoning about moral values and becomes interested in what's good for society. Children may view parents more as consultants than as powerful authority figures.

From infancy to adulthood the developing moral person progresses from *self* ("It's right because it feels right to me") to *others* ("It's right because it's what we do in our family") to *abstract* moral reasoning ("It's right because it *is* right").

nected" child shines. Because his moral code is part of him*self,* the alternative values feel strange to him. They upset his sense of well-being. He becomes morally selective, taking those values that contribute to his well-being and discarding those that don't.

Not so the morally ungrounded child. He is the product of a home where virtues are not discussed or taught and enters middle childhood like a ship without a rudder or anchor. He drifts in a sea of moral uncertainty, prey to whatever influences come along. Because he has no reference system to use as a standard, he adopts others' values or he shifts values according to what's most convenient for solving the problem of the moment. This child drifts into moral relativism: Very few things are right or wrong, black or white, but most solutions are shades of gray, and the child takes the path of least resistance or one that is most popular. This child is at risk because he lacks connection with morally grounded parents.

Model morals. A model is an example to be imitated, for better or worse. In the early years children are totally dependent on their caregivers to show the world to them. Your standards automatically become theirs, because they soak up whatever surrounds them. They make no independent judgments as to the rightness or wrongness of actions. Even if you do something you've taught them is wrong, such as hit someone, they assume you are right in what you did and that the person you hit deserved it. If they see and hear it from their parents, it's right, and they store this behavior in their impressionable minds as something worth imitating.

After six or seven years of age the child begins to make judgments about which

models are worth emulating and incorporating into his personality and which ones need to be discarded as threatening to his self. This means parents must saturate their children with healthy models in the preschool years, when children are most impressionable, so they can be discerning about models that come along later.

Healthy modeling does not imply perfect parenting; everyone blows it once in a while. It's the overall *pattern* of your behavior that becomes part of a child's self rather than the occasional goof. When your child sees you do something wrong, here's how you can get some moral mileage out of the situation. You lose your temper and a string of curse words come out of your mouth. Your mate and your child are shocked and hurt. Rather than stomping off in a huff, you sit down, take a deep breath, and you tell them how wrong you were to speak that way. The lesson you want to leave with your child is that yes, humans make mistakes, but they also *take responsibility* for correcting them.

You model life by the way you live. Everything a child sees his parents do sends a message about how seriously mom and dad believe the things they say. Children are very sensitive to hypocrisy. If you practice differently than you preach, children will learn not to take you seriously. Even trivial incidents leave an impression on little minds. The child sees a fifty-five-mile-an-hour speed limit sign and glances over to notice your speedometer reads seventy-five. This is confusing to the child searching for the meaning of right and wrong. This is situational ethics, based not on what is right and wrong but on what is convenient and expedient. Your child will pick up the way of life that she sees you living daily at home. You will inspire your child to follow

Bad Impressions

We emphasize models as one of the prime influences on child behavior. Parents need to realize that negative behaviors viewed on TV (for example, anger and violence) are easier for a child to copy than positive behaviors (say, kindness). A few examples are all that are necessary to make a lasting impression. Positive behaviors are more difficult to imitate because they require maturity and self-control. These examples need to be repeated often to sink in. Parents should not be lulled into a false sense of security because their child has seen only "a few" murders on television or gone to "only a few" violent movies. Nevertheless, you can't control everything that goes into your child's mind. To counteract the negative influences that slip in, saturate your child's mind with examples of positive behavior. Also, beware of what we term "instant replay." A child's developing mind is like a giant video library. He stores all he sees for later retrieval. If the child repeatedly witnesses graphic scenes of violence, this topic gets lots of shelf space in the library of his mind. So, years later when presented with similar circumstances, for example, a rivalry over a girlfriend, the teen or adult instantly replays the similar scene from his video library: He shoots the person who stole his girlfriend. We wonder if the criminals that go berserk (translation: "temporarily insane") and commit a hideous crime are, by reflex, replaying what they were subconsciously already programmed to do.

your example, be it a valuable or a valueless model.

Besides providing healthy models at home, screen outside influences that might leave unhealthy models in your child's mind. These include substitute caregivers, neighbors, preschool teachers, older kids, and television. Once upon a time persons of significance in a child's life came primarily from within the extended family, but in today's mobile society a child is likely to have a wider variety of models. Use these to your advantage and saturate your child's environment with persons of significance who provide healthy examples so that there is little room left for unhealthy messages.

Teach your child to think morally. Take advantage of teachable moments, ordinary events of family life that offer opportunities to talk your child through the process of moral reasoning. One day I saw two eight-year-old neighborhood kids perched on a hillside ready to toss water balloons on cars passing by below. I nabbed them before their mischief began and began this dialogue with one of the boys:

"Jason, what do you think might happen when the water balloon hits the car?" I asked.

"It would splat all over the car," Jason responded.

"Imagine if you were the driver. What do you think the driver might feel?" I said.

"I dunno," Jason mumbled.

"Do you think it might scare him?" I persisted.

"Yes, I guess so," admitted Jason.

"He might be so startled the car goes out of control; he runs up on a sidewalk and a little child goes splat. Isn't that possible?" I offered.

"I guess so," he admitted.

"You would feel pretty bad if that happened, wouldn't you?" I went on.

"Yes, I sure would," Jason agreed.

You can discuss people on TV in the same way. You notice your ten-year-old watching a questionable TV program. Sit next to her and in a nonthreatening and nonjudgmental way inquire, "Do you think what those people are doing is right?" Encourage discussion about current events: controversial public figures, newspaper headlines, social issues. Raise your children to express their opinions. Encourage lively family debates. Respect their viewpoints even if you don't agree. Studies show that children who come from families who encourage such open discussion are more likely to think "morally mature." A California study of a thousand college students looked at the relationship between the students' level of moral reasoning and their previous parenting. Students who scored high on moral reasoning came from families that encouraged open discussion of controversial topics. Other studies have shown that highly permissive parents who did not expect obedience from their children and gave inappropriate praise produced "me-firsters," children whose only thought was to satisfy themselves. And the other extreme, overcontrolling parents, produced conformist teenagers who couldn't think for themselves. In these studies, families who gave their children a voice in decisions produced teenagers who were able to reason morally. Getting children to preach to themselves becomes the most lasting morality lesson.

Let your child hear you think through the rightness or wrongness of an action. You and your child are at a store and the cashier gives you too much change back. You notice the error and share it with your child: "Oh, the cashier gave us too much money back." And then you offer a moral commentary as if thinking out loud: "This extra money does not belong to us. It would not be right to keep it. The cashier may be fined for her mistake at the end of the day, and I would feel bad if I kept the money. . . ." Your child justifies, "But Dad, everybody does it." You reply, "Does that make it right? What do *you* believe is the right thing to do? How do you think you would feel if you kept money that doesn't belong to you?" Then add, "I feel good doing the right thing and returning the money."

Know your child. Know how your child is thinking morally at each stage of development. When situations occur that require a moral decision, involve your child in them. One day our ten-year-old Erin and I saw a homeless person. Erin said, "Dad, can we stop and give him some money?" Taking her cue, I stopped the car for a teachable opportunity. Testing where she was at morally I suggested, "Maybe he should get a job." Erin answered, "Maybe he can't find one." That told me where she was. We stopped at a nearby store and bought some food for the needy person.

Morals are important to a child because they govern the choices they make. If a child is self-centered, materialistic, and lacks empathy, she will often think of her own convenience first and take the easiest route. If empathy is ingrained in her, she will make choices that make her a better person to be with and society more caring.

Know your child's friends. Parents, know the values of your child's friends because some of these will rub off onto your child. One day we witnessed the last stages of a case of childhood blackmail. Nine-year-old Matthew was playing with eight-year-old Billy, who tried to blackmail Matthew into doing something and told Matt that he would not invite him to his birthday party if he didn't do it. Matthew, a very sensitive and principled child, was visibly bothered. We used this opportunity to talk to both children. We impressed on Billy that this is not how children should treat each other. We also asked Matt how he felt being on the receiving end of the blackmail. By learning what it felt like to be treated like this, Matt's principles were reinforced. You can always get positive mileage out of negative situations. Real life provides real lessons.

In our zeal to convince our children of the wisdom of moral living, there is a bit of missionary in all of us. Yet the older children get the more they seem to tune out preaching. That's why teachable situations, such as those we mentioned above, leave more lasting lessons than anything you say.

Send your child off to school morally literate. Ground your child in your moral values day in and day out, and continue to reinforce these values as long as you have any influence on your child. You want your child to do what's right, not just what's expedient in a given situation. To do this, he must act from inner conviction built up over many years. Values don't stick if they are tacked onto the child at the last minute, like a holiday decoration, or changed like a piece of clothing, according to the fashion of the day.

Once children enter middle childhood (ages six through ten), they are on the receiving end of tremendous peer pressure. If the child does not have her own inner guidance system telling her which choice to make, she will more readily become a victim of peer pressure. Children are searching for principles. If a strong guidance system prevails at home and within children themselves, they are likely to conform to their parents' and their own inner morals. They become leaders among their peers instead of followers, setting their own course, staying on it, and swimming upstream when the prevailing current is against them.

Teaching your child right from wrong must be done with patience and care. Power or fear morality is not likely to stick because it does not become a willing part of the child's self: "If I catch you stealing again, I'll belt you even harder," yelled a dad who was determined to teach his child right and wrong by the use of fear and force. This child is more likely to spend his energy figuring out how he can avoid getting caught than in moral reasoning about the rightness or wrongness of the act.

One of the goals in raising moral children is to turn out moral citizens. The family is a mini-society where a child learns how to live with others and to respect authority. Children who operate with inner controls and not out of fear of punishment make morality a part of themselves. They have a balanced view of authority: They respect authority figures but do not accept others' values unquestioningly. If the laws are not serving the interests of the people, they'll be the ones leading the charge to throw out the lawmakers and elect new ones. Raising kids who care is the first step in maintaining a moral society.

WHY KIDS LIE — WHAT TO DO

Children lie for the same reasons adults do: to be accepted socially, to hurt someone else, or because they fear the consequences

The Age of Truth

Preschoolers usually can't (or don't want to) distinguish fact from fiction. To a four- or five-year-old, Snow White and the Seven Dwarfs exist somewhere. Most children don't begin to understand truth and falsehood until the age of seven — the age of reason. By eight or nine most children have, or should have, a sense of morality. They feel wrong when they don't tell the truth and right when they do. They understand what "lying" means and can feel "it's right to tell the truth."

of the truth. Younger children do not understand the concept of truth. Let's get into the mind of a child to understand why kids twist the truth so easily.

It's not a lie; it's fantasy. One type of childish fantasy is wishful thinking. Witness the five-year-old telling his friend about a trip to Disneyland — where he's never been. "Why, he's lying through his teeth," you think. "What's wrong with him?" He's not lying (at least by childhood standards), he's thinking wishfully — imagining what he wishes had happened. Not only does wishful thinking allow the child the luxury of living in a dream, it impresses his friends and raises his social status. "You really played with Mickey Mouse?" the admiring friends inquire. Children fabricate tall tales for other children, knowing they always have an audience of believers.

If you hear two children spinning yarns, that's innocent storytelling — not lying. This stage will pass around seven to nine years of age as imaginative thinking wanes and peers become less gullible. (If it continues past age nine, this character trait will not win friends and is probably a sign that there is an underlying problem needing attention). You can use storytelling as a teachable moment. You overhear the child's presentation of his make-believe trip to Disneyland: "We went to Disneyland for my birthday. . . ." Don't label your child a liar. That's a put-down. Instead, respect his wishful thinking: "You wish you went to Disneyland. That would be fun. Now, tell us what you really did do for your birthday." The child knows you understand and sees you are not angry. He also subtly learns there's no need to lie. Wishful thinking reveals a desire. "You want to go to Disneyland. Maybe I can help that wish come true. Let's plan a trip. . . ." It's comforting for a child to know that some dreams do come true.

Fantasy and reality. "I didn't do it. Toby did it." Who's Toby? The child's imaginary tiger friend, who broke the glass. The pre-

GUESS WHAT I SAW?

Magical thinking.

school child confuses fact and fiction. This is normal. Children often fabricate imaginary characters and enjoy living in their make-believe world. Appreciate your preschooler's creative thinking and enjoy this imaginative stage while it lasts. Play along with the child's fantasy. Sometimes children bring imaginary friends along to my office for a checkup. I place an extra chair for the invisible companion and even do a brief pretend exam. We laugh together. Adults believe that it's important to be firmly grounded in reality and to know the difference between real and pretend. But these are adult standards. To children, the world is not only what it really is but what they need or want it to be. Imaginative thinking can actually help a child cope with the real world. Children periodically retreat into their make-believe world, which they can control, as a way of coping with the adult world, which they can't control. If your child "lies" by making the fictitious friend the scapegoat ("Toby the Tiger did it"), get into your child's fantasy: "Tell me exactly how Toby broke the glass." As your child gropes for details to get himself off the hook, he will quickly reveal his part in the incident. In the meantime, ask yourself why he wanted you to think he "didn't do it." Do you tend to react to accidents or experiments too harshly?

Respect your child's creative thinking by telling him that you understand his view-

How to Tell if Your Child Is Being Dishonest

Most of the time you'll know just by your child's body language that he is not being honest. Facial expressions usually reveal truth or falsehood. Some children have a poker face that is hard to read even for the most perceptive parents. Try these detective tips: Does your child deliberately avoid looking you straight in the eye while telling the story? (This sign is especially meaningful if your child ordinarily seeks lots of eye contact). Read his body language. If he is relaxed, at peace and open, assume the truth. Children need our trust. If you expect lying you may find your child meeting your expectations; if he's innocent, he may become frustrated and angry.

Dig for details. If the more you dig the more vague your child becomes, suspect untruth. If each time he tells the story the major points are different, the story is suspect. Is he just not acting like himself? Does your child have a better motive to lie than to tell the truth? If your child is generally afraid of you, he is motivated to lie.

The same detective principles that hold true for lying are also helpful in detecting a thief. Is your child vague about how the toys found their way into his possession? Does your child have that suspicious look that an intuitive parent recognizes instantly? When the story doesn't fit or the value of the toy is beyond the child's means, suspect thievery. If your child, out of love for a parent, presents you with an expensive necklace without a credible explanation, suspect the goods are hot. Most of the time, if parents and children are connected, you'll just know — and your child will perceive that you know.

point. "It's easier if you pretend Tony broke the glass. I understand. Now tell me what really happened. I won't get angry." Help your child to see that *the truth won't hurt* — there's no need to fabricate a cover-up, because you will love and accept him no matter what he tells you.

Sometimes a recurrent theme in a child's storytelling reveals what is truly missing in her real world. A mother of a six-year-old consulted me about her child's "lying." Her daughter was telling her friends wild tales of fun things that she and her daddy were doing: fictitious yarns about trips to toy stores, airplane rides, horseback riding, and so on. The truth was she seldom saw her daddy. He traveled a lot, and because he brought his work home with him, was mentally absent while physically present at home. This child built a world of make-believe in self-defense, to protect her growing self from her loss.

Conveniently pleasing. Children want to please their parents. If they sense that lying will please, they lie, believing that's the right thing to do. Mother will ask her five-year-old, "Did you pick up your puzzles?" and will get an affirmative answer because the child wants mother to smile and say thank you. Later when mother finds the puzzles (or most of them) still spread all over the floor, she'll need to let her child know that the lie is more displeasing than the disorder. A seven-year-old will say yes to the toy question because he doesn't want to inconvenience himself at the moment and go pick up. Eventually, he'll realize mom is going to go check. He needs to discover that his tactics won't work. He is responsible for keeping his toys in order, putting them away every night before bedtime. That's a family rule.

The lie of convenience. This is a common form of lying in the older child. Lying about grades is a typical example. The parents of nine-year-old Sharon had been putting pressure on her to get good grades. Sharon thinks that their love and approval depend upon her performance, and she is afraid to tell the truth. Her C grades would displease her parents, so she tells them she made A's and B's. She justifies her fib because pleasing her parents is more important than telling the truth. Sharon felt pressured into lying. However, her deception didn't work. These wise and caring parents realized why their child lied about her grades and removed the pressure. One of the most important messages you can give a child is that love and approval is not conditional.

The truth hurts. Children develop self-protective lies out of fear of abusive punishment. Fear of punishment wipes away any guilt for not telling the truth. Children who are on the receiving end of a lot of punishment often protect themselves by becoming habitual liars. If the child believes the broken vase will merit a spanking, he reasons it's less painful to lie. The same thing happens in children who are given major punishments for minor offenses. This inappropriate correction may hinder a child's development of conscience. Children who fear punishment say anything to avoid it.

We have helped our children overcome the fear of telling the truth by making this deal: "We promise we will not get angry" — that is, punitive — "no matter what you did, if you tell us the truth, although you will have to face the consequences. However, when we find you have lied to us, the punishment will be severe." One day someone left Erin's bike in the driveway. She told me that Matthew had it last. To discover "who did it" I had to free Matt to tell the truth by assuring him I would not get angry if I heard the truth. "Matthew, the deal is I don't get angry at truth. I get angry at lies." If a child is afraid of the consequences of telling the truth, he may become a habitual liar. When he can trust you not to fly off the handle, he will be able to open up and tell you honestly what happened. Listen calmly, be fair, and help him correct his behavior. The best way to encourage children not to lie is to support them as they tell the truth.

The child who lies a lot. At some point normal childhood storytelling evolves into purposeful lying, which may become habitual. The child intends to deceive. Many of his social interactions revolve around falsehood rather than truth. The root cause is an angry child who is dissatisfied with his real life and afraid of his parents' reactions. He doesn't experience acceptance for normal clumsiness or poor judgment. He has been taught he is bad.

Seven-year-old Charlie's father disappeared from his life when he was six. To keep from acknowledging painful reality, Charlie created a make-believe world with wonderful father-son stories. Gradually he found that the world of make-believe was more comfortable than the real world. By the age of eight he was lying habitually about other things. Charlie claimed A's on his tests when he was barely passing and lied to his mother about where he went after school and about where new possessions came from. Lying became a way of life, a protection from his anger and a cover-up for his poor self-image. The cure for Charlie's lying was to help him accept

and learn to cope with his real life. Therapy allowed him to accept that his father wasn't coming back and that he hadn't caused his father to leave. It wasn't his fault. His mother learned through support counseling to spend more time with Charlie doing fun activities and listening to him. Charlie joined a soccer team and the coach took a special interest in him. Soon lying was a thing of the past.

RAISING A TRUTHFUL CHILD

By understanding why children lie at times, it is easier to understand what to do. Getting behind the deceitful words (or actions) and into the child's mind will help you practice preventive discipline. Here are ways to build a truthful child.

Practice attachment parenting. Connected children do not become habitual liars. They trust their caregivers and have such a good self-image they don't need to lie. Even the most connected child will spin a few outrageous yarns at age four, try lying on for size at seven, and try out more creative lying at ten. When you've caught your child lying once, and you've corrected her, don't automatically assume she's lying again if a similar situation arises. Give her the benefit of checking out the facts or she'll be hurt that you don't trust her.

Model truth. Create a truthful home. Just as you sense when your child is lying, children will often read their parents' untruths. If your child sees your life littered with little white lies, he learns that this is an acceptable way to avoid consequences. You may be surprised to learn the lessons in lying your child witnesses in your daily living. Consider how often you distort the truth: "Tell them I'm not here" is the way you get rid of a phone pest. You rationalize that this isn't really a lie, or perhaps it is only a "white lie," which, as opposed to a black lie, is really all right because it gets you out of an embarrassing situation. Don't ask your child to share in your lie by having him say you're not at home. (Instead, he could say "She can't come to the phone right now. May I take a message?") Don't tell your child something is "gone" when it really isn't just to make it easier for you to say he can't have any more. Sharp little eyes often see all and you haven't fooled your child at all. You've just lied to him, and he'll know that, since he knows you so well. Just say "no more now" and expect your child to accept that.

Also, don't become a partner in your child's lying. If your child didn't finish her homework because she was too tired or disorganized, don't let her convince you to write a note to the teacher saying the printer broke on the computer. These practices sanction lying and teach the child how easy it is to avoid the consequences of poor choices.

The truthful self is OK. Convince your child you like her the way she is. "I like a truthful C more than an untruthful A," you teach the youngster who marks up her real grades. The child who knows that her acceptance in the family is not conditional upon performance is less motivated to lie.

Don't label the child who lies. Avoid judgments like "You're a liar!" or "Why can't you ever tell the truth?" Children often use parental labels to define themselves. To them a bad label is better than no label at all. At least "the liar" has an

identity. A label can become a self-fulfilling prophecy. Better to say something like "This isn't like you; you're usually honest with me." Don't ask, "Are you lying?" but rather, "Is that really the truth?"

Avoid setups for lying. If your child tends to lie, confront him squarely with a misdeed rather than giving him the opportunity to lie. If you don't want to hear lies, don't ask questions. If he's standing in front of the broken cookie jar with telltale crumbs on his hands, it's ridiculous to ask if he did it. Of course he did it. Confront him.

Expect the truth. Give your child the message "I expect you to tell the truth." Children should not feel they have *choices* in this matter. Children are not intellectually ready to deal with situational ethics, which teaches: "You tell the truth when it's convenient but choose to lie when it's not." They'll get enough exposure to this kind of thinking in high school and college. When your child knows what you expect, he's likely to deliver.

When your child lies. Always correct your child for lying. Don't let him think he's getting by with it. Confront him and let him know you are disappointed. A child with a conscience will punish himself by feeling remorseful. Any further punishment would depend on each circumstance. Any natural or logical consequences should be allowed to take place. Occasional lying will happen, but habitual lying needs to receive counseling to uncover the cause.

ENCOURAGING HONESTY

Every chance you get, talk about how important "the truth" is. Don't wait until you are in the middle of a situation when what you say may be taken as preaching. Comment on broader topics, such as truth in print and advertisements, how truth keeps life simple (by avoiding the necessity of fabricating lies to cover lies), and how the truth always comes out in the end. Current events and family happenings can be analyzed from the standpoint of honesty. Talk about how truthful people are respected. Have a look at honesty themes in literature, such as "crying wolf."

Teach a child when silence is not lying. Children are delightfully honest, but sometimes at the wrong moments: "Aunt Nancy, your breath stinks" or "You really are ugly." Teach the child that if the truth hurts someone's feelings, it is not necessary to say anything. "Sometimes it's best to keep thoughts to yourself." While you don't want to squelch the candor and honesty of children, you do want to teach them to consider others' feelings. Remember the line of Thumper's from *Bambi,* "If you can't say anything nice, don't say anything at all."

Get behind the eyes of your child. "Maybe you just wanted the toy so much that you imagined that Andrew gave it to you. Shall we call him and check?" This gives your youngster a chance to come clean, or maybe Andrew *did* give it to him. You need to play detective and help him uncover the truth, for you or for him. Young children can talk themselves into believing a pretend story if that will satisfy their desires. Once a child reaches the age of seven he is better able to understand the difference between pretending and telling pretend stories that are intended to deceive.

Offer amnesty. Sometimes you know that your child has lied to you, and you wish to turn a negative experience into a moral lesson. Try offering amnesty. When our son Bob was fifteen he asked to go to a rock concert, which he rationalized would be OK because it was held at our church. We said no and told him we felt that this particular group modeled values foreign to our family. Conveniently, there was also a team curfew Bob was under because of a football game the next day. Reluctantly he agreed to forgo the concert. I had heard about the group, but I wanted firsthand observation so I could be sure of my judgment, so I went to the rock concert. A few weeks later we found out from another source that Bob had attended, too. After getting over our shock and anger (this was *way* out of character for Bob), we called a family meeting and offered "amnesty" to any misbehavior "no matter how awful." The children were allowed to get any wrongdoing off their chests. Bob confessed. Afterward he shared his relief. (We had worked hard to build consciences in our children that would bother them when they did wrong — healthy guilt.) We explained that we already knew he had gone to the concert, thus teaching Bob it's unwise to lie. If amnesty hadn't worked, we would have confronted Bob and there would have been stronger consequences. In this situation we wanted him to have the benefit of confessing voluntarily so he could experience the reward of deciding to come clean. Bob, now a father himself, fondly recalls this event.

Looking back we realize how our attitude toward something important to Bob actually pushed him to be so uncharacteristically defiant. A highly principled child from the very beginning, Bob explained he felt we were using the curfew as an excuse to deny his attendance. He was right. We had discussed this ahead of time, before we laid down the rule. We could have asked the coach for an exception or asked Bob to leave early. Bob told us afterward that the whole football team was there, flaunting the curfew. In hindsight, I should have cleared it with the coach and then arranged for us to go together, father and son, to enjoy an outing. Since this whole episode, we've watched our teens develop a wholesome discernment in their entertainment choices, and we have broadened our range of tolerance. Martha actually enjoys some of the rock music our children listen to and finds it a window into their world.

If you create the atmosphere in your home and the attitude within your child that honesty is the best policy and the child's truthful self is really the nicest person to be around, you are well on your way to building trust and avoiding dishonesty.

STEALING

Little fingers tend to be sticky, allowing objects mysteriously to find their way into little pockets. Before lamenting that you are harboring a little thief in your house, take a moment to understand why children steal and how to handle this common problem.

Why kids steal. Like lying, "stealing" is an adult term that means nothing to young children. Candy found clutched in a sticky fist after going through a checkout line or a toy car that turns up in the pocket of a four-year-old after a visit to a friend's house is not proof that your child is already a delinquent. To the preschool child, possession means ownership. In a child's morality he has a right to anything within grabbing distance. Children under age four have difficulty distinguishing between "mine" and "yours." Everything is potentially "mine." They don't know that palming a piece of candy at the grocery store is stealing until you tell them so. In the child's mind he has done no wrong until the parents pass judgment.

Many preschool children can't curb their impulses. They see the toy, feel they must have it, and take it without any judgment as to the rightness or wrongness of the action. Instead of guilt, they feel relief that their craving is satisfied. The more impulsive the child, the more likely he is to help himself to things.

Around five to seven years of age children develop a hazy notion of the wrongness of stealing. They can understand the concept of ownership and property rights. They come to terms with the reality that the whole world doesn't belong to them and begin to understand the wrongness of taking things that don't belong to them — stealing. Also, by this age the child is able to be a more clever thief. His deterrent is more the fear of adult retaliation or having to give up a "want" than an understanding of the immorality of stealing. Jimmy may recognize that it's wrong for Jason to keep the baseball cards he "borrowed," but the next day Jimmy may want to hang on to Jeff's prized cowboy pistol and bring it home at the end of the play session.

What to Do

Stopping petty stealing and teaching its wrongness may seem to some like a smallie, but learning honesty in small matters paves the way for biggies later. A child must learn to control impulses, delay gratification, and respect the rights and property of others.

Practice attachment parenting. Because connected children are more sensitive, they are better able to understand and respect the rights of others. These concepts sink in deeper and at an earlier age. Connected youngsters feel remorse when they have done wrong because they develop a finely tuned conscience sooner. It's easier to teach values to attachment-parented children. These kids have the ability to empathize and understand the effects of their actions on others. They have parents who are with their children enough to realize when they stray into these gray zones. Connected kids have an innate respect for maintaining trust between people. Lying, cheating, and stealing violate this sense of trust.

Because attachment parents know their children well, they can read facial and body language cues that reveal a child's hidden misbehavior. Because of the parent-child connection, the youngster is more likely to accept the parents' advice and values. Trusting their parents, connected kids are also more likely to come clean when confronted. They find it harder to lie about their actions because they feel wrong when they act wrong. They know that their parents can read that "suspicious look."

Lead them not into temptation. Children will take money from family members almost as though it is community property. They may even rationalize "I'll give it back when I can." Teach your children to keep their financial affairs private. Money should be kept in a locked box that is stored in a secret place. Anytime money is lent, an IOU should be required to help them remember

who owes what to whom. You should also keep your money inaccessible, except for smaller amounts in your purse or wallet that must be asked for. Sure, family members trust one another, but give children credit for being human and don't allow temptation in the path. If someone comes to us and complains, "Someone took my five dollars," we ask, "Where were you keeping it?" We don't bother detecting the perpetrator — as we said above, we know conscience is at work. And we will not be put in the position of being responsible for the safekeeping of money for those old enough to do it themselves. Siblings, after all, are not the only possible suspects. Our kids have learned the hard way that you can't trust everyone. This is in itself a good lesson for life.

Teach ownership. Toddlers have no concept of ownership. Everything belongs to a two-year-old. Between the ages of two and four a child can understand ownership (the toy belongs to someone else) but may not fully believe that the toy doesn't also belong to him. Even as young as two, begin teaching "mine" and "yours." During toddler toy squabbles the parent referee can award the toy to the rightful owner, but don't expect this concept to sink in fully until around the age of four. Look for other opportunities to reinforce the concept of ownership: "This toy belongs to Wyatt." "Here's Sarah's teddy bear." "Whose shoes are these?" As the child grasps the idea of ownership and the rights that go along with it, teach the logical conclusion that ignoring these rights is wrong.

Correct wishful ownership. When Madelaine says "Mine," her mother says, "That's Rachel's. Would *you* like a turn?" or "Beth had it first. Would *you* like to have it?," giving her ideas about both ownership and sharing. When a four-year-old brings home a friend's toy, capitalize on this teachable moment: "If Johnny took your toy, especially if it was one you really liked, you would feel very sad that your toy was missing. What would you want him to do?" The best way to teach lasting values is to draw the lessons out of a child rather than imposing them. You want the "give it back" idea to come from the child if at all possible. (See also "Sharing," pages 249–255.)

Correct the steal. Getting the thief to give back the goods sometimes requires masterful negotiating. Encouraging and helping the child to return stolen goods teaches not only that stealing is wrong but also that wrongs must be made right. If you find an empty candy wrapper, go ahead and trot the offender back to the store with payment and an apology.

Identify the trigger. Find out what prompts the child to steal. The child who steals habitually despite your teaching about honesty usually has a deep-seated problem that needs fixing. Is the child angry? Does she steal to vent the anger? Does the child need money and feel that stealing is the only way she can get what she believes she needs? Is so, offer an allowance. Give her odd jobs and pay her. Help her learn a work ethic so she can earn toys instead of stealing them. Sometimes a child who habitually steals is suffering from a poor self-image. He needs to steal to boost his worth or get attention. As in handling all behavioral problems, it's often necessary to take inventory. Does your child need more supervision? Perhaps some redefining of priorities and reconnecting with your child is in order.

Identify the child at risk to steal. Watch for these risk factors:

- poor self-esteem
- impulsiveness: strong desire, but weak control
- generally insensitive to others
- not connected
- angry
- change in family situation; for example, divorce
- generally bored
- alone a lot

If you focus on helping your child deal with these risk factors, lying and stealing should subside.

It's important to get to the bottom of stealing. If the problem behind chronic stealing and lying are uncorrected, they tend to snowball. With repeated misdeeds, the child convinces himself that stealing is not really wrong. He desensitizes himself to his own conscience and to your teachings. The child without remorse is at high risk for becoming an adult without controls. With attachment parenting, even if a child is not "caught in the act," he will punish himself sufficiently with the remorse he will feel. He won't want to repeat wrong actions often or for long.

Praise honesty. The five-year-old finds somebody's wallet and brings it to you. Praise him to the limit for his action! "Thank you for bringing Mommy the wallet you found. Now let's see if we can find out who it belongs to. I'll bet that person will be very happy you found it, just like you would feel if you lost something special and someone returned it." Avoid saying "Thank you for telling the truth." Some children may not even have thought of keeping the wallet, and you don't want to plant in their mind the option of being dishonest. Whatever praise you give, convey the message that your child did just what you expected.

CHEATING

Children cheat. But like lying and stealing "cheating" is an adult concept not well understood by the child under age seven. To an adult cheating is akin to lying or stealing. But a child who is fabricating his own rules as he grows does not yet understand why rules are inflexible. Best to translate cheating into a positive value — fairness. Even a six-year-old can understand "play fair." Teach your child that cheating is wrong because it's unfair to other children in the game. Ask him how he would feel if he played fair but his friends didn't. Notice as you play games with children from ages six to nine how they often change the rules to their favor even if they understand them in the first place. There's no problem with changing the rules as long as all the players agree before the game begins. This kind of rule change adds creativity to board (or bored) games.

The older child who cheats at school needs a good parent detective. Does the child cheat without remorse? (If so, see "Healthy Guilt," on this page.) Many times the child feels forced into cheating because of parental pressure or the spirit of competitiveness in the class. The desire to please parents with high expectations can override even the most solid conscience. The temptation to cheat is especially strong in a child with a weak self-image who equates self-worth with accomplishment. If she wins she's a winner; if she loses, she's a loser. So she must win even if she has to cheat to do

---

Healthy Guilt

One of the complaints I hear from teachers and law enforcement officers is, "Kids don't think they're doing anything wrong." Kids who don't care are operating without a healthy sense of guilt. They aren't bothered by wrongdoing. They don't care enough about themselves to feel bad when they do wrong. This is why we spend much of this book teaching parents how to raise sensitive kids. Children need to feel sad when they act bad. They need to feel remorse for wrongdoing. This is a healthy guilt that helps the child act right and correct wrong actions.

One day we heard a window break in our home. As we walked out to the front yard to see who the culprit was, eight-year-old Matthew came up to us. He had heard us calling the neighbor boy over since that boy was the only one in sight. We could see Matt was struggling to tell us he was responsible for the wild pitch. Matthew's very hard on himself when he blows it, yet the trust factor between us wouldn't allow him to hold back the truth.

---

so. This unhealthy attitude can develop if you compete with your child or if you model that winning is all that counts when playing (or working) with adults.

You can help your child avoid the temptation to cheat at school. Take care to put just the right amount of scholastic pressure on the child. Too little and she gets lazy and bored. Too much and she may give up or cheat to achieve. Try to find the balance that fits your child. We have given our children the message that good grades make you feel good and that they are one (not the only) ticket to success. We tell them that we want them to get good grades first to please themselves and second to please us. Based on how much work they were willing to do, they can achieve their own goals. We will be pleased if they sincerely do their best — no one can ask for more.

TEACHING YOUR CHILD TO APOLOGIZE

Apologizing helps your child accept responsibility for a wrong and provides a tool to make things right again. It helps the child dig himself out of the hole. It clears the air, helps heal the relationship, and gives it a new beginning. To teach your child — and yourself — the art of apologizing, try these tips:

Model apologizing. When you've acted wrongly, admit it. Apologize when you overreact: "I'm sorry I yelled at you. You didn't deserve that outburst. I've had a hard day." I've said this to my children many times. Everyone makes mistakes; that's life. Everyone apologizes; that makes life better. These are valuable lessons for a child to learn. Saying "sorry" to your child is not a sign of weakness but of strength. Even "the boss" should apologize if his or her actions are unkind. A child who has never been apologized to will feel singled out unfairly when he is made to apologize to someone else. He won't understand the apology process, and more than likely he'll refuse, turning a potentially beneficial moment into a standoff with hurt feelings.

Start young. Toddlers quickly learn to give a hug to "make it better" when they hurt

---

"Excuse Me!"

Children belch, gulp, and fart — excuse me, pass gas. Boys especially delight in showing off their body sounds (and, once older, in offending their female audience). If one unintentional belch gets laughter, you can imagine what will follow. But if these sounds meet with silence or mild disapproval from you, they will soon fizzle away. Teach children that, in company, breathing sounds (that is sneezing and coughing) are OK but digestive tract sounds are rude. When your child emits upper digestive tract sounds in your presence, look disapprovingly, and say "Excuse me." Require the older child to excuse himself. What he does when hanging around with a crowd of competitive belchers is his business. Passing gas is especially offending because of the odor accompanying the sound. As your child gets older he will learn he can control this function most of the time and do it in private. If intentional gas becomes a habit, the offender will quickly be taught by peer disgust to keep it to himself. As kids mature a bit their gut sounds diminish; these offenses will be sounds of the past.

---

someone. If you model hugs for hurts at home, he'll know just what to do. Once he's calm and ready to hug, you can verbalize a simple apology and maybe help him say it with a hug.

Forgiveness follows apologies. Apologizing and forgiving need to happen after someone gets hurt or offended. For most everyday squabbles we just tell our kids that *we* want them to "make peace" with whomever they are at odds with. It doesn't need to be a formal apology scene. We leave it up to them to figure out what "make peace" means and how to do that. Sometimes they use words, sometimes they don't. But we all know if they have or haven't. In order to live in the same house together, siblings need to be at peace with one another. Apology without forgiveness is an incomplete process. For real healing to happen the one offended needs to "drop the charges."

Stop manipulating feelings and orchestrating sincerity. Some children learn to parrot out an "Excuse me" or "I'm sorry" within a millisecond of the offense to avoid being squealed on or to get themselves off the hook quickly if parents force apologies. Parents can't force feelings; only the children know how they feel. Doing this can teach your child fake apologies, or that it is OK to be insincere, or that forgiveness has to be an instant thing, which is not real life. Depending on the ages of the children, their temperaments, the circumstances, and the emotions that may be flaring, a cooling-off period before apology will be needed. A two-year-old who just kicked his sister may need a two-minute time-out on a chair, along with a reminder that kicking hurts, before he's ready to hug her. A ten-year-old who slaps her sister for vicious teasing must deal with wounded pride before she'll be able to remember how wrong it is to slap. It's your job as a parent to make sure the apology happens so both children can start again with good feelings between them. But you cannot make it happen. What you can do is model and instruct: When people are at peace with each other they feel better inside.

WHEN YOUR CHILD INTERRUPTS

Demanding children often come between conversing adults. You're visiting with a friend, engaged in lively conversation, and a squeaky voice pipes up, "Mommy, Mommy!" You continue your adult dialogue, but the little one doesn't go away. The more you try to ignore the tug on your skirt, the more persistent he is. You want your children to grow up to be polite and considerate, not thinking they have to be the center of attention all the time, but interrupting is a children's game most adults lose. Here's how to head off the interrupter before you get pulled into the struggle. If you help your child develop more desirable behavior in situations where he might otherwise interrupt, he will eventually learn consideration for others.

Plan ahead. One afternoon we had invited TV producers to our home to plan a video on parenting. We didn't want to be interrupted, so we saturated our kids with attention all morning. By the time our guests came our children were ready to spend time on their own and leave us alone. We engaged the older children (who can understand what not interrupting means) to supervise the two- and four-year-old and play with them outside. We had a new video as a backup diversion. We wanted to make it easier for our children to leave us alone for a while.

While babies don't like the way Mom's attention is diverted by the phone, a toddler learns quickly that when she is on the phone he can do all the things she doesn't want him to do. Or it's the time the five-year-old decides to pick on a sibling. Cordless phones are a boon for busy parents. You can carry on a conversation while walking around attending to things. If you anticipate a long phone conversation, try to make your call during off-duty hours while your child is napping or after he's asleep for the night. I keep a drawer full of distracting toys (including a toy phone) in my desk to keep a toddler quiet on my lap during phone calls. If you can't or don't want to be interrupted, squat to your child's level and whisper "Shhh, I will talk to you when I'm finished talking to Aunt Nancy." Martha will often pick up a needy toddler and carry on her conversation. The toddler is happy to be held and eventually squirms to get down and run off. And don't forget praise: "Thank you for not interrupting."

Children under three can't understand what "Don't interrupt" means. You'll save yourself a lot of wasted energy by momentarily stopping your conversation, squatting to your child's level, looking him in the eyes, and finding out what he wants. A few minutes of focused attention will usually pacify the most persistent youngster.

While it's important to include your child in adult activities, it is also important that a child learn patiently to wait his turn. This is an important life skill. By age seven a child can develop a polite way to say "I have a question." Plan together how you want this to happen, to fit your family's style. Try modeling it when you need your children's attention.

TEACHING MANNERS

Every parent dreams of the polite little child who says please and thank you. After all, your child's behavior reflects on you.

Manners come easily to some children, others are social flops. Understanding the basis of good manners will help you help your child acquire them. Good manners, after all, are necessary for people to live together in this world. Gracious manners reflect a loving and considerate personality.

Expect respect. Believe it or not, you begin teaching manners at birth. The root of good manners is *respect* for another person; the root of respect is sensitivity. As we have emphasized in the early chapters of this book, sensitivity is one of the most valuable qualities you can instill in your child — and it begins in infancy. The sensitive infant will naturally become the respectful child who, because he cares for another's feelings, will become a well-mannered person if brought up by well-mannered people. His politeness will be more creative and more heartfelt than anything he could have learned from a book of etiquette. In recent years it has become socially correct to teach children to be "assertive." Being assertive is healthy as long as it doesn't override politeness and good manners.

Teach polite words early. Even two-year-olds can learn to say please and thank you. Though he doesn't yet understand the social graciousness of the words, the toddler concludes that "please" is how you ask for things and "thank you" is how you end an interaction. At least you've planted these social niceties into your child's vocabulary; later they will be used with the understanding that they make others feel good about helping you. When you ask your toddler to give you something, open with "please" and close with "thank you." Even before the child grasps the meaning of these words she

Tattling

"Mommy, Andrea was playing with your new dress yesterday. . . ." Parents are often caught up in the tattling trap. There's something unsettling, almost devious, about the motive of a "squealer." Yet some children have such a sense of rightness that they feel any impropriety must be reported. What is the parent to think? Here are some ways to sift through accusations and decide when to act and when to leave well enough alone.

Is it a smallie or biggie? For the sake of your own sanity and the better social development of your children, try not to be drawn into squabbles that are smallies. "Daddy, Daddy, Susie is using her allowance to buy cookies for her friends." That's a smallie. (It might be a nice thing to do anyway.) Don't pursue this case, but don't squelch the tattler either. Sometimes the reporter is privy to something parents need to know; you do want to hear about the biggies. If it's a smallie, let the children work it out themselves. Making a big case out of a small issue, especially when the accuracy of the charges is questionable, often causes bad feelings between the tattletale and the accused. The tattler may very well be inaccurate. Beware of a tattler who uses his tale to get even with or belittle a sibling. By the time he finds someone to listen to his story, he may have colored the facts to his liking.

Consider the source. Is the child's reporting trustworthy, or does he have a history of distorting the truth? Matthew is our family's "righteous person." No injustice goes unreported. We always respect his sincerity by listening. We are also aware that this trait of his gets him some bad press among his siblings and peers, even the ones not in trouble at the moment. We are helping Matthew lighten up a bit on being the family's Department of Justice. He gathers from our response that much of what he reports will be allowed to take care of itself. He is gradually becoming relaxed about the family foibles. When he (or any of the children) does have something big to report, we protect our informant's identity.

If five-to-eight-year-olds are constantly tattling on siblings or playmates, a good rule to use is: Unless someone is going to get hurt I don't want to hear the words *"I'm* going to tell *Mom!"* Once habitual tattlers are old enough to write, put up a tattle box and have them write it down. Mellow out the compulsive tattler so he doesn't carry this trait with him to school. His teachers will thank you.

learns they are important because mommy and daddy use them a lot and they have such nice expressions on their faces when they say these words. Children parrot these terms and understand their usefulness long before they understand their meaning.

Model manners. From age two to four, what Johnny hears, Johnny says. Let your child hear a lot of "please," "thank you," "you're welcome," and "excuse me" as you interact with people throughout the day. And address your little person with the

Shifting Blame

How often do you blame your child to get yourself off the hook? Years ago while on a shopping trip Martha lost her purse. She turned to our then six-year-old, Hayden, and said, "Hayden, if you hadn't distracted me I wouldn't have lost my purse." Martha shifted the blame to Hayden to ease the burden on herself. A wise friend who was with them rescued this child by asking her, "Hayden, do you feel this was your fault?" Hayden didn't, and the friend's intervention helped Martha realize that she was shifting blame. As parents we both tend to do this, and we often hear statements from our children such as "Why are you always trying to blame someone else?" (The answer is we are too hard on ourselves when we make mistakes and you can guess where that attitude came from). Children are easy and available scapegoats for blame-shifting, but this is too heavy a burden for them to bear. Besides, it sets a bad example.

Some parents teach young children to blame their environment for problems. They say "You bad table!" to distract the child from his crying after he runs into the table and bumps his head. Blame shifting keeps children from learning to take responsibility for their actions. Blame shifting by adults reinforces this irresponsibility.

using the name of our child: "Jim, will you do this for me?" Our children picked up on this social nicety and address us by title: "Dad, may I..." or "Mom, would you..." Our son Matthew, now nine, has made all of these language tools part of his social self. Matthew has concluded that if he times his approach at the right moment, looks me in the eye or touches my arm, addresses me as "Dad," and adds a "please" or "may I," he can get just about anything he wants. Even when I know I'm being conned, I'm a pushover for politeness. Although Matthew doesn't always get his politely presented wish, I always acknowledge his good manners.

Don't force manners. Language is a skill to be enjoyed, not forced. While it's OK to occasionally dangle a "Say please" over a child before you grant the request, don't, as in pet training, rigidly adhere to asking for the "magic word" before you give your child what he wants. The child may tire of these polite words even before he understands them. When you remind a child to say please, do so as part of good speech, not as a requirement for getting what he wants. And be sure he hears a lot of good speech from you. Overdo it while you are teaching it and he'll catch the idea faster. "Peas" with a grin shows you the child is feeling competent in his ability to communicate.

Correct politely. As a Little League baseball coach, I have learned to chew out a child — politely. When a child makes a poor play (which is to be expected), I don't rant and rave like those overreacting coaches you see on television. Instead, I keep my voice modulated, look the child straight in the eye, and put my hand on his shoulder

same politeness you do an adult. Let your child catch the flavor of polite talk.

Teach name-calling. We have always made a point of opening each request by

Acknowledge the Child

The old adage "Children should be seen and not heard" was probably coined by a childless person. Include your child in adult goings-on, especially if there are no other children present. When you and your child are in a crowd of mostly adults, tuning out your child is asking for trouble. Even a child who is usually well-behaved will click into a mind-set where she has to make a nuisance of herself in order to break through to you. Including the child teaches social skills, and acknowledging her presence shows her that she has value.

Stay connected with your child in situations that put her at risk for undesirable behavior. During a visit with other adults, keep your younger child physically close to you (or you stay close to him) and maintain frequent verbal and eye contact. Help your older child feel part of the action in the conversation so that he is less likely to get bored and wander into trouble.

during my lecture. These gestures reflect that I am correcting the child because I care, not because I am out of control. My politeness shows him that I value him and I want him to learn from mistakes so he can become a better player. The child listens. I hope someday that same player will carry on these ball-field manners when he becomes coach.

Have you ever wondered why some children are so polite? The main reason is that they are brought up in an environment that expects good manners. One day I noticed an English family entering a hotel. The father looked at his two sons, ages five and seven, and said, "Now chaps, do hold the door for the lady," which they did. I asked him why his children are so well-mannered. He replied, "We expect it."

SHARING

Children have difficulty sharing, especially young children. This is a normal part of the development process. Knowing and accepting this is the first step in helping your child grow up to be a generous person. Here's an overview of what's going on inside that possessive little mind.

Selfishness comes before sharing. The power to possess is a natural part of the child's growing awareness. During the second and third years, as the child goes from oneness with mother to being an individual, the little person works to establish an identity separate from mother. "I do it myself!" and "Mine!" scream the headlines in the toddler's tabloid. In fact, "mine" is one of the earliest words to come out of a toddler's mouth.

The growing child develops attachments to things as well as persons. This ability to form strong attachments is important for an emotionally healthy person. The one-year-old has difficulty sharing her mommy; the two-year-old has difficulty sharing her teddy bear. Some children get so attached to a toy that the raggedy old doll becomes part of the child's self. When asked to draw a picture of herself, four-year-old Hayden would always include her favorite doll — as if it were part of her body. Can you imagine convincing her to share this doll with a playmate? It was too important. She could not feel safe and secure if that doll was being handled by another child.

When to expect a child to share. True sharing implies empathy, the ability to get into another's mind and see things from his or her viewpoint. Children have difficulty with empathy under the age of six. Mostly they share because you teach them to do so. Don't expect a child less than two or two and a half to accept sharing easily. Children under two are into *parallel play* — playing alongside other children but not with them. They care about themselves and their possessions and do not think about what the other child wants or feels. But given guidance and generosity, the selfish two-year-old can become a generous three- or four-year-old. As children begin to play with each other and cooperate in their play, they begin to see the value of sharing.

Attachment-parented kids are more sensitive to others' needs, less bonded to things, thus more willing to share *and* more aware of their own need to preserve their sense of self by not sharing. It's easier to share with someone less powerful or less threatening, say, someone younger, a visitor rather than a sibling, a quiet child rather than a demanding one. Much depends on your child's temperament. Follow your child's cues in judging when he is ready to cope with sharing.

Even at four or five years of age, expect *selective sharing.* A child may reserve a few precious possessions just for himself. The child is no more likely to share his treasured teddy or tattered blanket than you would share your wedding ring or the heirloom shawl your mother gave you. Respect and protect your child's right to his own possessions. Kids know kids. At four, Matthew sized up his friend Johnny, an impulsive, curious child who would have been a natural durability tester for a toy manufacturer. Johnny explored every moving part,

pulling and twisting them; only the strongest toy could survive. Matthew recognized his friend's destructive nature and hid his valuable, breakable toys when he saw Johnny coming. We supported Matthew's wisdom.

What You Can Do

Don't force a child to share. Instead, create attitudes and an environment that encourage your child to want to share. There is power in possession. To you, they're only toys. To a child, they're valuable, prized belongings. Respect the normal possessiveness of children while encouraging sharing. Then watch how your child operates in a group play setting. You'll learn a lot about your child and what kind of guidance he'll need. If your child is a grabber, he'll discover that other kids won't play with him. If he's always a victim, he needs to learn the power of saying no. In preschool years your child naturally goes through a "what's in it for me" stage, which will progress into a more socially aware "what's in it for us" stage. Gradually — with a little help from parents — children learn that life runs more smoothly if they share.

Get connected. A child gives as he is given to. We have observed that children who received attachment parenting during the first two years are more likely to become sharing children in the years to come, for two reasons. Kids who have been on the receiving end of generosity follow the model they've been given, growing into generous persons. A child who feels right is more likely to share. An attachment-parented child is more likely to have a secure self-image. He needs fewer things to validate himself. Studying attachment-parented chil-

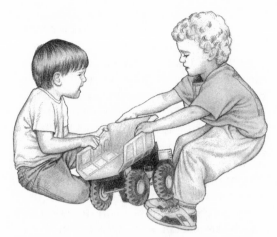

dren in our practice, we found they needed fewer attachment *objects*. They are more likely to reach for mother's hand than to cling to a blanket.

Model generosity. Monkey see, monkey do. If big monkey shares, so will little monkey. When someone asks to borrow one of your "toys," make this a teachable moment:

"Mommy is sharing her cookbook with her friend." Let your sharing shine. Share with your children: "Want some of my popcorn?" "Come sit with us — we'll make room for you." If you have several children, especially if they are close in age, there will be times when there isn't enough of you to go around. Two children can't have 100 percent of one mommy or daddy. Do the best you can to divide your time fairly. "No fair" may be the single most frequently repeated complaint of childhood. Try to be an equal opportunity parent as much as possible, while teaching your children that other factors come into play in day-to-day life.

Play games. Play "Share Daddy." Placing the two-year-old on one knee and the four-year-old on the other teaches both children to share their special person. Even a two-year-old can play "Share Your Wealth." Give your two-year-old some flowers, crackers,

Teaching kids to share.

Teaching Life Principles Through Play

A good way to model principles to a young child is through play. Games hold a child's attention, allowing lessons to sink in, in the spirit of fun. Children are more likely to remember what they have learned through play than what they've heard in your lectures. Consider the character traits that are fostered during a simple game: humor, fairness, honesty, generosity, concentration, flexibility, obedience to rules, sensitivity, and the all-American value of competitiveness. And, sorry to say, unhealthy traits such as selfishness, jealousy, lying, and cheating can also be experienced through play. Expect play time to reflect how life is to be lived, and tolerate only principled play.

blocks, or toys, and ask her to "share them with everyone in the room. Give one to big brother. Give one to Daddy." You want to convey the message that sharing is a normal way of life and that sharing spreads joy. Says Martha, "Lauren found a piece of chocolate in my purse one day. She happily ate it and then showed me a second piece she'd found. I told her that piece was for Stephen and Matthew to share and asked her to go give it to them, thinking to myself she'd just eat it on her way. I didn't bother to go with her to see the 'inevitable.' Bill later told me how cute it was when she walked up and doled out the halves, one to Stephen and one to Matthew."

When to step in. While we don't expect toddlers to be able to share, we use every opportunity we can to encourage turn-

taking. Teach your child how to communicate her needs to her friends. Say something like, "When Catherine is all done with the car, then you can ride it. Ask her *when* she will be done" or "Hold out your hand and wait; she'll give you the doll when she's ready." When a toy squabble begins, sometimes it is wise not to rush in and interfere. Give the children time and space to work it out among themselves. Stay on the sidelines and observe the struggle. If the group dynamics are going in the right direction and the children seem to be working the problem out among themselves, stay a bystander. If the situation is deteriorating, intervene. Self-directed learning—with or without a little help from caregivers—has the most lasting value.

Time-sharing. Using a timer can help you referee toy squabbles. Johnny and Jimmy are having trouble sharing the toy. You intervene by asking each one to choose a number and the one who chooses the closest number to the one you thought of gets the toy first. You then set the timer. Two minutes is about right for younger children. You can ask older ones to wait longer. When the timer goes off, the toy goes to the second child for the same amount of time (though he has probably forgotten that he wanted it). You may have to sell younger ones on the plan with an animated, simple explanation. Walk them through a cycle, starting with the older one or the one more likely to cooperate. For example, Stephen has the toy for two minutes. The buzzer goes off. Extract the toy from Stephen with talking and encouragement and hand it to Lauren, reassuring Stephen it will be his turn again when the buzzer goes off. It may take several cycles before a child can hand over the toy on her own, smiling because she knows she will get it back. A family in our practice that uses the timer idea told us that it worked so well that the older sibling runs to her mother saying, "Mom, set the timer. Suzy won't share." External and internal timers help children learn valuable lessons for later life — how to take turns and how to delay gratification.

An Rx for Crime

YOUTH ARRESTS FOR VIOLENT CRIMES ARE UP 50 PERCENT FROM 1983 TO 1992. These are the headlines from a recent FBI report on juvenile crime. The politicians' answer is to put more police on the streets; criminal psychologists suggest that putting more parents in the homes would be a more effective solution. A major reason why it's unsafe to walk the streets in most American cities can be summed up in one word — *insensitivity.* Kids don't care. Sure you can blame social conditions and erect more low-cost housing or more schools, but buildings do not make disciplined people; crime prevention should focus instead on the structure within the home. Values learned at home translate into the internal controls necessary for children to grow up to be happy and productive members of society. Many criminals lack empathy — the ability to be bothered by how their victims feel. Their anger and aggression come from non-attachment, the result of spending early years of childhood with non-nurturing caregivers. They never learned how to connect in a healthy way with important people in their lives and thus do not know how to have healthy relationships with others.

At this writing, there is a $30 billion crime bill before the U.S. Congress. That's $30 billion in addition to what the federal government already spends on crime prevention. This money would be spent primarily on increasing the number of police in urban areas. As usual, the government is funding the wrong end of the problem. Consider what would happen if one would take that $30 billion and use it to help support parents. Monetary grants would make it possible for single mothers and mothers in two-parent, low-income families to stay home with their children in the early years. They could focus on parenting, not just survival. The unskilled mothers could be given professional consultations on breastfeeding and babywearing, child development, and discipline. Parents who were themselves abused could receive counseling to prevent recurrences of these problems with their children. Mothers and fathers could be helped to connect with their children; once people are connected, empathy, self-esteem, and good discipline naturally follow. Such a pilot program, called Healthy Start, is under way in Hawaii and shows promising results toward reducing child abuse.

Somehow we must interrupt the flow of unconnected kids into the streets. Until we develop a preventive parenting approach to crime prevention, our cities will never be safe places for children or adults.

If the time routine does not work, *time-out the toy*. Put it on the shelf and explain that the toy stays there until they learn to

share it. Children may sulk for a while as the toy sits unused, but sooner or later the realization hits that it's better to share than

Growing a Conscience

Conventional wisdom says that a child doesn't have a conscience until the "age of reason," considered to be around seven years of age. Yet you begin nurturing a little conscience from birth. After watching how his models live and process thousands of choices during the early years, the child collects a large storage file of "normal behaviors," a code of how he is supposed to behave. Once the child incorporates these internal codes (his norms) as part of his growing self, it bothers him to deviate from them.

Between seven and ten years of age, a major breakthrough in moral reasoning occurs — the ability to figure out if an action is right or wrong, not because the parents said so or out of fear of punishment, but because the child knows it. This is the beginning of a true conscience. The child has internalized your values and made them his own, and now he starts gleaning others on his own. The key to conscience building is to surround the growing child with healthy choices early on so that they become such a part of himself that when he is inevitably exposed to unhealthy choices they will disturb him.

A conscience may not mature until the child is nine or ten, but it is built from birth. The child who enters the age of conscience without an internal reference file is at a disadvantage. Like a gardener who waited too late to plant crops,

parents find that values taught later in childhood may take root, but the roots are not as deep as if they had been planted in the right season.

Beginning sometime around six or seven years of age, or whenever you feel your child has the ability to understand, teach your child what a conscience is. Try what we call the "Pinocchio principle" with your child: "You will have two voices inside you, a 'do right' voice and a 'do wrong' voice. Sometimes the 'do wrong' voice is easier to listen to. It may even seem like more fun at the time; but when you choose to listen to it, you'll know it was the wrong choice because you won't feel right inside. Listen to the voice that tells you to do right. That's the one that will make you happy."

By the age of six Matthew showed the beginnings of a conscience. If I caught him beginning to fabricate an untruth, his eyes would meet mine and he would back off from his misdeed. As our eyes were engaged, he would start smiling (so would I), as if he were saying, "No, Dad, that's not really true." From the look Matthew gave me, I believe he felt that lying would breach our mutual trust, our connection. The truism "I cannot tell a lie" has some psychological basis for Matthew. He has been programmed toward truth and trust. Any deviation from his inner code disturbs his sense of well-being.

to forfeit the toy completely. They will learn to cooperate; everyone winds up winning.

Plan ahead. If your child has trouble sharing his toys and a playmate is coming over, ask the playmate's parent to send toys along. Kids can't resist toys that are new to them. Soon your child will realize that he must share his own toys in order to get his hands on his playmate's. Or if you are bringing your sharing child to the home of a nonsharing child, bring toys along. Some children develop a sense of justice at a very young age. One of our children didn't want to return to a friend's house because "he didn't share." We made this a teachable moment by praising him: "Aren't you glad you like to share? I bet kids like to come to our house."

Protect your child's interests. If your child clings to his precious possessions, respect this attachment, while still teaching him to be generous. It's normal for a child to be selfish with some toys and generous with others. Guard the prized toy. Pick it up if another child tries to snatch it. You be the scapegoat. Ease your child into sharing. Before play begins, help your child choose which toys he will share with playmates and which ones he wants to put away or reserve for himself. You may have to play referee: "This is Susie's special birthday toy; you may play with these others till she's ready to share." Respect ownership. The larger the family, the more necessary it is to arrive at a balance between respecting ownership and teaching sharing. Point out, "That's Colin's toy . . . but this one belongs to the whole family." And, of course, encourage trading. Children easily learn the concept of family toys, such as the stereo, which everyone shares. The mother of one large family with four children close in age had a policy in her house. Gifts were enjoyed by the new owner for one day before joining the pool of toys. Special toys that needed individual care were set apart in the owner's room.

Give your child opportunities to share. To encourage sharing, Janet gave four-year-old Benjamin a whole cookie with the request "Please give some of the cookie to Robin." He broke off a piece and gave it to her. It was good practice for Benjamin and, from his modeling, two-year-old Robin learned about sharing. You can teach sharing to your younger children by using the older children as models. In this case, both the teacher and the student get a lesson in generosity; Janet breathed a sigh of relief when Benjamin came through with the desired behavior.

18

Building Healthy Sexuality

HOW A CHILD LEARNS TO TREAT THE OTHER GENDER, and how children feel about their own sexuality are important parts of their self-image, and thus a part of discipline. We prefer to talk about "building healthy sexuality" rather than "teaching sex." Schools, for better or for worse, teach sex; homes model sexuality. This means not only teaching "the facts of life," but attitudes as well. To help your child develop a healthy personal sexuality, you will prepare him or her for the physical changes ahead and for the feelings that accompany these changes. Your child also needs to know about sexuality in healthy male-female relationships.

The idea of teaching children about sex creates uneasiness for many parents. They may be uncomfortable talking about sex and worry about how they come across. They don't want to cause anxiety and embarrassment for their children. The most important teaching is done not through lectures or answering questions but by example. You can always clarify facts; it's harder to fix attitudes.

Touch is the beginning of sexuality. "When do I begin teaching my child about sex?" parents ask. "At birth" is my reply. In most of your interactions you give sensual messages to your child. The earliest message is *touch*. From the moment of birth your child will know if you are a touching family. Your infant feels good giving and receiving touches. Caressing your baby's face, massaging her skin, being entranced with an eye-to-eye gaze, and having your baby at the breast and in arms instill early attitudes that the body is good. It's good to touch and be touched. As a result of the high-touch style of attachment parenting, the child gets a sensual message — be comfortable giving and receiving touches. He learns that this is one way that human beings show love for one another. Honoring the need to be touched helps a child feel comfortable about himself as a person. This is the beginning of learning to feel right as a "she" or "he."

Vive la différence. In the past, women tended babies and men tended to business. One of the richest changes in parenting over the past twenty years is that mothers and fathers are sharing child care, not in competition over "who's better" but in the growing realization that babies thrive on the *differences* in the way males and females care for them. (For a more in-depth explanation of this healthy difference, see Chapter 6, "Fathers as Disciplinarians.") Mothers and fathers hold, look at, and touch babies differently. Babies pat breasts and rub beards. Babies respond differently to male and female voices. Early on, give your infant the message that both sexes can relate to babies, and these little takers will learn to extract the best from both mother and father.

In the early years, a baby learns that mom treats him differently than dad. When both are sensitive baby benefits from this difference. Yes, baby needs mother most, but dad can be a close second. If dad is gruff, rough, and distant, this is baby's early impression of what all men are like. When baby is loved by both parents, she will see nurturing and sensitivity as normal. (See also the discussion of fathers as sexual role models, pages 88–89.)

Being different does not imply less.
Growing sexual persons, especially boys, often devalue the other sex because they think they don't perform certain tasks as well, thus ignoring the fact that everyone's skills are different. This who-is-better conflict often surfaces in middle childhood when boys and girls are in same-sex peer groups. Their natural competitiveness is self-correcting in adolescence. But parents do have to attend to their sexist remarks. One day while watching kids in a school-yard run, I remarked, "Girls sure run funny." Our fourteen-year-old daughter shot

Gender and Self-Esteem

How people view their gender reflects their self-esteem and contributes to it. Low self-esteem is likely to carry over into unhealthy sexuality; problems with sexuality are likely to weaken self-esteem. A girl needs to be glad she's a girl; a boy needs to enjoy being a boy. Convey to your children that you are happy about their gender. Children are more likely to become adults with unhealthy sexual identities if they are confused and dissatisfied with their gender as a child. This is especially true if a child picks up that her parents are disappointed with her gender. Be careful of nicknames that could subtly convey this message. We know a woman who wonders whether her father was disappointed that she was a girl. He called her "Butch," and he called her younger sister "Chuck."

back, "Boys run funny, too." She was letting me know that my comment was one-sided, sexist, and unnecessary. I apologized. Equal opportunity in school sports has helped foster mutual respect between boys and girls. When we were growing up, boys performed while girls watched and cheered. Now we see our oldest daughter performing as a cheerleader — a highly skilled and competitive sport that keeps her fit and teaches her about teamwork. All those years of soccer, softball, and gymnastics have led her to a love of doing her best. Her squad has made it to national competitions. (And there are boys on many cheer squads.)

It's important for children to learn that both genders are equally valuable. Sexual equality, used correctly, should not mean sameness but equal value, equal opportunity. It would be a dull and short-lived world if the sexes were the same. One day a couple and their four-year-old were in my office for discipline counseling. Dad dominated the conversation. Whenever mom offered an opinion, he put her down. It became obvious that the power struggle was between the sexes, not between parent and child. The child was visibly disturbed and was getting bad sexual vibes: Men devalue women. Parents, it is important to model for your children respect for the opposite sex, to build up each other in your children's presence, and to tell your children what a wonderful mother or father they have. Children who value and respect both parents are less likely to become adults who harass the other gender.

Reinforce the person more than the gender. It's normal and healthy for parents to encourage gender differences, but traditional views on what constitutes gender-appropriate behaviors are no longer in vogue. In the past, fathers have tended to reinforce more gender-specific behaviors than mothers. Dads would roughhouse with boys and play quiet games with girls. Playing more gently with a daughter conveyed to her that she was expected to be sensitive and delicate. Roughhousing with a son would encourage him to be aggressive. What was missing? Neither daughters nor sons learned how to be sensitively assertive, and the stereotypes lived on. While overemphasis on gender blending can be as unhealthy as the old stereotypes, try to *play with the child according to the child's temperament rather than the child's gender.*

Take cues from your child first as a person, second as a member of a gender. If growing children become comfortable with themselves as people, they are much more likely to be comfortable with their sexuality. I used to fall into the gender trap in my practice. In my office I would automatically greet a little boy with a hearty "give me five" but welcome a little girl with a gracious hug. I now find it more appropriate to take cues from the child and make an on-the-spot decision about whether a hand-hit or a hug is more appropriate. With my children and with my patients, I see the importance of fostering sensitive behavior in boys and encouraging assertiveness in both sexes. Tenderness and assertiveness in both sexes is a better way to have balance.

FOSTERING HEALTHY GENDER IDENTITY

By age two and a half children become aware of gender differences. They begin to identify "girls" and "boys." Girls become aware that girls have longer hair and sometimes wear dresses; boys have shorter hair and always wear pants. They see that their genitals look different and they "pee" differently. (Four-year-old brothers have been known to taunt younger sisters: "I've got a penis and you don't.") How you approach the differences in external genitalia can help play down the "who's better" problem. Say "Girls have a vulva and boys have a penis." A wise bit of teaching here can leave both genders feeling good about themselves.

From birth boys are generally more aggressive and rougher than girls, more interested in physical activities than interpersonal communication. I suspect gender behaviors are a combination of genetics and environment. Some boys dive headlong into traditionally male activities (playing with trucks, combat), some girls into traditionally female ones (playing with dolls, cooking). Most children show very individual and less gender-oriented preferences. Boys can be equally imaginative in playing house as girls can be, and girls can be just as rough-and-tumble in pretend adventure as the boys. Girls have more interesting choices when it comes to clothing, and here is where parents see a child's personal taste defy all modeling cues from her mother. The daughter whose mother is always in jeans will insist on dresses only, to her mother's amazement; the daughter whose mother prefers dresses fights tooth and nail to stay out of one, even at the tender age of three. This, of course, may have nothing to do with whether she plays creatively with dolls for hours on end or chooses to practice gravity-defying stunts most of the day. Also, gender behavior may depend on what activities parents allow. A six-year-old boy and his friend were fighting one another. Grandmother advised, "Leave them alone. Boys will be boys." The mother disagreed. "I will not allow my child to be an ill-mannered maniac just because of his sex."

MODELING HEALTHY GENDER ROLES

Children develop healthy gender identity when they have healthy gender models at home. Try to model the following attitudes for your children:

- Mom *and* dad are loving caregivers.
- Mom *and* dad are fair disciplinarians.
- Mom *and* dad respect one another.
- Mom *and* dad convey that they like their gender and their chosen roles.

A new father, grieving about not having had enough time with his father, confided to us: "He seldom held us. All I remember was seeing his back and briefcase as he left for work." Some fathers do have demanding jobs that keep them too busy. If this kind of father enjoys his work, though, he will communicate to his children that he is fulfilled in what he does "for a living," and he will also be more likely to enjoy the time he does have at home being a dad. If mom isn't resentful of dad's job, the children probably won't be either. The more mom feels abandoned and resentful of handling "solo flights," the more the kids will, too. Children benefit from seeing both parents fulfilled in their work, yet at the same time knowing "family" is more important. One very sad pitfall in the subject of work is that sometimes dad can be perceived as the more valuable parent because his worth can be measured in dollars, compared to mom, who works for "nothing" if she chooses to stay home and raise children. Women can be lured back into the marketplace, against their inner wisdom, for this same shallow rationale.

Not only do babies learn from how mom and dad care for them, but they also witness how mom and dad care for each other. It is not only healthy, but important, to show affection to your mate in front of your child. If the child sees hugs and kisses and perceives sensitivity between mates, this little sponge learns that it's good for people to show affection for one another.

The result is a child who enjoys giving and getting kisses and hugs from the people he loves. When children see one parent always putting down the other, being insensitive to or even physically abusing the other, they store these action pictures in their attitude file. They either decide that this is the wrong way for daddy to treat mommy (or vice versa) and they don't like "the way daddies are" (that is, the way men are), or they accept that strife instead of sensitivity is the normal pattern between the sexes. Either viewpoint plants unhealthy sexual attitudes and expectations in the child. How mates treat each other strongly influences how their children go on to choose and treat a mate.

CURIOUS LITTLE BODIES

We have had many phone calls from distraught parents who have gone ballistic upon opening a bedroom door and discovering two little naked bodies playing "doctor." This scene, common to all homes, pushes panic buttons in parents who wonder where they have gone wrong. Some react so strongly that the punishment leaves scars for life. To deal with this inevitable scene it helps parents to know what's normal, what's not, and what to do.

What's normal? Children are curious, especially about differences, and what could be more fascinating than different genitals? Understand this situation for what it is — normal childhood curiosity at work. It needs sensitive understanding so it won't recur. Get behind the eyes of your child. He wants to learn what the other sex looks and feels

like. The child is more interested in satisfying curiosity than in sexual arousal. You can tell innocent sexual curiosity from deviant sexual behavior by these characteristics. Innocent acts are occurring when:

- Children are young (under age ten), close in age, and know each other.
- There is mutual agreement; one child is not forcing the other.
- There is usually a gamelike atmosphere: playing "doctor" or "I'll show you mine if you show me yours."
- Secrecy is part of the game. As if sensing their parents would disapprove, children retreat into a bedroom, garage, or a private place. (This is true for deviant acts as well.)

What to do. First be prepared to compose yourself and resist the impulse to tell them they have done something "dirty" or "bad." Calmly introduce a new activity; for example, "Let's go have a snack. I'll help you get dressed." As soon as a private moment is possible (or right away if both children are yours) have a talk with your child. Convey that you are not angry. If children sense that they have done something bad or that you are angry, they will clam up. Tell your child that it's normal to be curious about another's body parts and that you understand his curiosity but that "it's not right to touch anyone else's private parts or let them touch yours. I want you to promise Mommy that you will keep your private parts private and not touch anybody else's." Let the other child's parent know how you handled the situation so he or she can do likewise.

Children can begin to learn the meaning of "private parts" early, when they are learning about other body parts. Private parts are any place that your swimming suit covers. Be aware of your own body language when addressing your child's sexuality. If your child perceives that you are uneasy about sexual matters, she may conclude this is a "bad" subject or these are "bad parts." They are good parts, but they are private parts. This will be important to convey in teaching your child about the possibility of sexual molestation. Teach your child that these special parts should not be touched or shown to anyone except mommy or daddy during a bath or dressing or to the doctor during a checkup. "If anyone touches your private parts, promise to tell Mommy or Daddy because we won't get angry. It's good to tell Mommy or Daddy if somebody touches you, even if they tell you to keep it a secret." Teach children the concept of good secrets and bad secrets. "Good secrets are never about touching someone's private parts." "Bad secrets are when somebody tells you not to tell Mommy or Daddy. You should never have secrets from Mommy or Daddy." Begin teaching the meaning of "private parts" as early as age three so that modesty becomes part of your child's growing sexuality.

To prevent recurrences of genital play, minimize opportunities. Be aware of what children are doing. Don't allow them to be unsupervised behind closed doors. We have a rule in our house that bedroom doors must always be open when friends are over — at all ages. Our teenagers have grown up with this rule and still respect our wishes on this policy. You are applying the same principles to sexuality as you do to all discipline matters: Parents set the rules and then set the conditions that make the rules easier to follow. If you sense that

Discipline and Sexuality

How a child is disciplined affects, for better or worse, his or her future attitudes toward sex. Children who receive attachment parenting learn to love and trust because they have been loved and trusted. An infant who spends many hours a day in arms and at breast learns to be comfortable touching and being touched. That child learns intimacy. The little person who grows up in a home where the mother and father respect each other and their children is likely to view sexual roles as healthy and satisfying.

The child who grows up with harsh, abusive correction may take on the abusive characteristics of the parents or unconsciously look for those qualities in a mate. The child whose expressivity is squelched by overcontrolling parents may have difficulty expressing adult sexuality or may use sex as a tool to control or be controlled by others. The child who never learned to say no may not be able to delay sexual gratification and is more likely to take what he wants without considering the cost. The most important quality of parenting — sensitivity — greatly affects sexuality. One of our goals in discipline is to help a child learn to consider how his actions will affect other people. After all, satisfying sex is basically mutual caring — the ability and desire to satisfy both one's own and another's needs.

your child is still curious, make this a teachable moment: "The body is beautiful, and let's learn more about it. Let's start with a picture book." If your four- to six-year-old wants to know where babies come from, we recommend the book *How Babies Are Made,* by Andry and Schepp (Little, Brown, 1984). Be willing to answer your child's questions *as they come up.* Keep in mind that age-appropriate answers do not have to be embarrassing for anyone. If you start out this way at age two and continue the dialogue about sex with your child, it won't be embarrassing at age sixteen either.

Be sure to report the incident to the other parents so that they can make this a teachable moment. Tell them that you understand the innocence and the normality of childish curiosity but that you want to keep it from happening again. Be open, honest, and matter-of-fact. Don't assign blame, and you won't have to worry about upsetting adult friendships.

When sex play is not normal. How do you tell when the line has been crossed from innocent childish curiosity that needs to be handled with understanding and explanations into abnormal behavior that needs serious attention? It's important for parents to know how to tell when one child is victimizing another. Here are suspicious signs:

- One child entices or forces the other into sex play.
- There is an age difference of more than four years between children.
- The sex play is not age-appropriate: for example, oral-genital contact between a six-year-old and a three-year-old.
- The event occurs more than once despite your careful intervention and supervision.

These are grounds to protect your child from another by terminating the friendship. If the sex play is between siblings, seek professional help.
- Secrecy.

What to do. For the victimizer seek professional counseling. It is often necessary to do a complete inventory of a child's self-concept, home, and school environment. If your child is the victim, replay the "private parts" talk. Be sure that your child understands that he is not bad and his body is not bad, but that it is wrong for one person to touch another's private parts. The victim may also need professional counseling.

What about denying gender and cross-dressing? Don't panic when your four-year-old son puts on his mommy's lipstick and high heels and your daughter dons her daddy's pants and suspenders. Allow some gender bending when it comes to cross-dressing. Laugh and enjoy it. This stage of curiosity and make-believe soon passes once the school-age child learns gender-appropriate dress. In one family the three-and-a-half-year-old daughter suddenly became interested in being a boy in every way she could — clothing, male identity in play, saying she'd be a daddy when she grew up. This all started when her baby brother was born. Seeking reassurance that this was normal, her mother asked her pediatrician if she should do something. She was already taking away male action hero dolls. The doctor unfortunately only worried this mother needlessly, giving her articles on sexual dysfunction in children. All she needed to do was spend time with her daughter to reassure her of her position in the family.

MASTURBATION*

Don't run to call your neighborhood psychologist when your little girl rocks on her tricycle seat or your little boy constantly has his hands in his pants. Instead stop and consider why these actions make you squirm. The very word "masturbation" gives many adults a deeply uncomfortable jolt accompanied by heavy doses of guilt. If a child pulls his ear or strokes her arm, no one notices. So why do parents ignore the little boy who pulls his ear but worry and scold when he pulls his penis? It's either because they consider genitals to be bad, mysterious, or off-limits, or they believe that genital rubbing is surely a sign of psychological disturbance. Neither of these is true.

Most children play with their genitals — expect this between ages two and six. The reason genital fondling bothers adults is that we tend to view children's actions through adult eyes. To a child, masturbation is a normal part of discovering these parts of the body and the pleasurable feelings that come from them. In exploring their bodies and during diaper changes and baths, babies discover that some parts feel more pleasurable than others. Once these areas are discovered, those little hands frequently gravitate there. To a child, massaging his or her genitals is pleasure. It is not "wrong" or "dirty." Only if a child hears these terms

from adults (or picks up on their anxiety) does she become worried and confused.

Some religions teach that masturbation is wrong. We do not intend to question this belief or value system. Adults who themselves choose not to practice masturbation for religious reasons will have to be wise in how they approach this matter with their babies and young children. There will be ample opportunity for the child as he grows older to be taught how to respect his genitals in a religious sense.

Because children aren't doing anything "wrong" when they explore or stimulate their genitals, there is no need to scold, shame, humiliate, embarrass, or punish them. Above all, avoid conveying that these are bad body parts. Later sexual hang-ups are often due to mishandling of early sexual issues by overzealous but well-meaning adults. These parents, because they themselves were shamed, frightened, and punished, may never have come to terms with their own sexuality.

When masturbation is normal. Understand that the desire to use one's body parts for pleasure is part of normal sexual development. While it is not necessary to masturbate to have a positive self-image, enjoying one's body parts contributes to developing healthy sexuality and liking one's body. So occasional genital massage is not dirty, harmful, or a signal of an underlying emotional disturbance or of problem parenting. For most kids, it's a continuing discovery and it feels good. It's as simple as that.

When masturbation becomes harmful. Genital play can become more than just a passing curiosity. When it becomes frequent and intense, the child becomes so preoccu-

---

*Some use the term "masturbation" to mean stimulating the genitals to the point of orgasm. But what constitutes childhood orgasm? By age three, children are capable of arousal by stimulating their genitals. So, strictly speaking, a three-year-old can masturbate. Some people believe the term "masturbate" is too strong for a young child and reserve this term for the adolescent who is capable of orgasm. So if you feel more comfortable with "genital play" than "masturbation," call it that, or whatever you prefer. We find it a matter of degree and use these terms: "genital play" — brief, pleasurable touches; "masturbation" — genital stimulation to the point of excitement.

pied with self-pleasure that he or she withdraws from interacting with others. As is true with any self-gratification, if the habit is an occasional departure from the routine, a quick fix for boredom or need for comfort, or an occasional release of pent-up anxiety, it's normal, a means to an end. But if the child becomes dependent on this form of self-pleasure to the degree he or she doesn't reach out in other ways to feel good, it becomes abnormal.

Medical complications from genital stimulation are rare, though in girls excessive and intense friction (rubbing of the genitals against something hard like the saddle of a toy horse) can traumatize the urinary opening, resulting in urinary tract infections. (This is less likely a problem for boys, whose urethras are longer.) Manual stimulation will not damage tissues unless the child inflicts pain on himself or herself due to the obsessive intensity generated. This is a signal to parents that some intervention is needed.

What to Do

While genital stimulation is normal behavior for a child, it bothers parents and, if excessive, can bother the child. Here are some ways to keep a common practice from becoming a harmful habit.

Not in public, please. Dear Aunt Mary is sitting in your living room and in full view four-year-old Susie climbs on the arm of the couch, wiggles around, and soon has that happy look on her face. Other faces in the room turn red. Witnessing anyone masturbating embarrasses adults. Without making judgments about her actions, quietly, matter-of-factly advise her that anything to do with her "private parts" — like going to

the bathroom — is private. Use this as a teachable moment and nicely explain that you want your child to "go do that where I can't see you; it makes people uncomfortable." Usually the child will choose to stop the activity in exchange for the privilege of staying near you. Normal social living demands that people often delay their own gratification (or repress their feelings) out of respect for the feelings of others.

Build a balanced self-esteem. Children who feel good about themselves on many

Parental Nudity in the Home

One of the earliest sexuality concepts you want your child to learn is that the body is good — all parts of it. Bathing with your baby is healthy sexual modeling. And when your toddler runs into the bathroom as you step out of the shower in your birthday suit, there's no need to dive for cover. That would convey there is something to be ashamed of. But you may wonder, until what age? As with so many aspects of discipline, take your cue from your child. Watch for signs that your child is developing a sense of modesty. When your child begins to cover up, it's time for you to cover up, too. When your child quickly crosses his hands in front of his genitals as you enter the room or carefully closes the door when he uses the toilet or is dressing, that's a modesty cue: The unclothed time of early childhood has passed. By the age of five or so most children begin reserving their bodies for private viewing, and so should parents.

fronts (home, friends, school, activities) are less likely to retreat into habitual genital stimulation. Six-year-old Tommy was going through a poor self-image stage. He wasn't getting along with parents or friends and didn't seem to fit in at school. Mother noticed Tommy had begun to spend more and more time behind closed doors in his room. One day, not knowing he was in his room, she opened the door and discovered him masturbating. She wisely shut the door immediately and walked downstairs before falling apart and calling the child's father — "I caught him doing *that.*" Rather than embarrass her son, she respected his dignity, and later, father and mother arranged to talk with Tommy together. During their discussion (*not* a confrontation) Tommy's mother referred to his penis as "your little self." Tommy's father smoothly substituted the term "penis," a word mother *and* son needed to be comfortable with. They seldom referred to the act but rather concentrated on the whole person, focusing more attention on Tommy's withdrawal from the family as the problem needing fixing than on the matter of where his hands were. In the days and weeks that followed, they helped Tommy get more comfortable in outside activities and within the family. He spent less time in his room with the door closed.

Chronically bored children often turn to their bodies for stimulation. Keep little minds and bodies active. When the boy's hands go into his pants or the little girl begins rocking, casually distract the child from the self-interest and direct him or her into other activities.

Avoid scare tactics. Here are some of the fearful myths about masturbation that years ago came from the mouths of adults:

"If you keep that up, you'll get warts on your hands."

"You'll go blind."

"Stop that. It'll make you sick."

These may have frightened children out of the habit, but they also created unwarranted guilt and damaged self-esteem, resulting in unhealthy sexual attitudes. Once children discovered that these threats were untrue, advice on other sexual matters became suspect.

Call It Like It Is

To foster a healthy sexual identity and help a child be proud of the body he or she is developing, give genitalia the proper names, beginning with naming body parts when changing your toddler's diaper. When your son grabs his penis say, "That's your penis" (instead of "thingy"). Tell your daughter, "That's your vulva" (instead of "bottom"). There is a whole vocabulary of sexual slang words, which only adds to the mysteriousness and "dirty" image. The unisex term "pee-pee" to describe an area of the body somewhere between your legs and from which urine mysteriously spurts can be confusing to a child. Girls have a vulva and a vagina; boys have a penis and a scrotum. Most children can understand and use these terms by age two and a half. Parents resort to slang words or neutral terms in order to avoid being embarrassed in public when the child starts discussing his penis or her vulva or because they never learned to be comfortable with their own body parts.

Give wise counsel. If you intervene in childhood masturbation, you must carry through with wise advice. If your child is old enough for such dialogue, try this approach: "Johnny, playing with your penis feels good and it is a good part of your body. I did this when I was your age. But too much of *this* stuff keeps you from exploring other activities that make you feel good. What are some other things you would like to do? What could we do together?" Although perhaps uncomfortable for parents, these conversations are teachable moments, healthful to the child's growing sexuality. They also strengthen your parent-child relationship.

Employ a substitute teacher. If you are uneasy about discussing sexuality with your child — and many parents are — your child is likely to sense from your body language and strained words that sex is a nasty subject. If your child is a habitual masturbator, ask the child's doctor to explore the subject as part of a checkup. Over the years hundreds of red-faced parents have asked me to take on this task. I've consented, but with reservations, because delegating an important issue to a substitute deprives the parent of the opportunity to grow in his or her role of authority and counselor. The child may feel the parent is squealing on him, although this probably won't happen if the doctor or other adviser approaches this subject as part of a normal sexuality talk rather than an accusatory confrontation. It's helpful to be able to remind the habitual masturbator: "Remember what Dr. Sears said about rubbing too hard on your vulva."

Give alternative tension releasers. I counseled a six-year-old girl, Lara, who habitually masturbated so much at bedtime that her genitals became sore, and her perceptive father rightly concluded that the habit was a tension release. We helped Lara by dealing with the cause of the tension and showing her alternative ways to relieve her anxiety. There had been a lot of recent stress in this child's life: a recent move, new school, new friends. The parents helped her work through adjusting to these changes. They gave her back rubs and a song and soothing music as she drifted off to sleep. Not only did she ease off on her masturbation, but she learned that, during tough times, parents are a valuable resource.

Discipline for Special Times and Special Children

CHILDREN WITH SPECIAL NEEDS require a special kind of discipline. Some children present unique challenges because they are *differently-abled.* By investing yourself early in your child you will not only help your child, you will develop skills you never had before. In this chapter we discuss the common special discipline circumstances. Our wish is to help you bring out the best in your child, and yourself.

DISCIPLINING THE HYPERACTIVE CHILD

By the time I saw five-year-old Ryan for counseling, he was a behavioral mess — as were his frazzled parents, Terri and Bob. Even while in her womb, Ryan had given Terri a hint that he would be a handful. He was a frequent uterus kicker and bladder thumper. Ryan had been a challenge since birth; even the nursery nurses labeled him "demanding." During his early months baby Ryan cried unless held, and Terri's description of Ryan during those days was littered with negative labels: "colicky," "fussy," "demanding," "difficult," "intense," "supersensi-

tive," "draining," and included the constant refrain "I just couldn't put him down." Unfortunately, Ryan's caring, well-meaning but desperate parents fell into the wrong crowd of baby advisers: "Leave him to cry." "You're holding him too much." "He's got to learn to soothe himself." "You're spoiling him." Bob and Terri believed it was their fault their baby acted this way; their friends' babies all seemed so content. "For his own good" Bob and Terri became less responsive to Ryan's cries.

"Don't worry. When he is able to walk and play by himself he'll be better," a friend advised. When Ryan began walking it was as if a two-legged cyclone had hit the house. He trashed every room, hurled toys, was a danger to his environment and himself. Spanking had no effect. Ryan's grandmother excused his behavior by saying "His father was like that." "He's just being a boy," advised Aunt Emma. "He'll grow out of it." Ryan didn't grow out of it. He grew into worse behavior.

"I must have told him 'no' a hundred times a day," his mother recalled. "I dreaded Ryan getting out of bed in the morning, because the chase would begin, and it didn't end until ten o'clock at night when one of us dropped from exhaustion." By three years of age, simple daily routines like dressing, brushing his teeth, and straightening up his toys became monumental chores. Ryan would flit around the house, unable to settle for more than a few moments before he was up and going again. When his parents asked Ryan three times to wait at the curb until a passing car went by, he chased the car. Other kids his age could

---

Is Your Child Hyperactive?*

Parents often wonder, "Is my child just very active, or is he a hyperactive child who needs treatment?" Here is a checklist of indicators that professional assessment is needed:

☐ Your child flits from one uncompleted activity to another, to an inappropriate degree for his age.

☐ He is easily distracted by everyday activities around the home (children running, TV).

☐ He has difficulty concentrating on a task, chore, or conversation.

☐ He is disorganized, loses toys, clothes.

☐ He is late for school, does not come home on time.

☐ He does not listen attentively, misses directions, fails to complete homework.

☐ He has difficulty standing in line or waiting for a turn during games.

☐ He often talks excessively with unconnected and irrelevant content.

☐ He has a short fuse, is easily angered or frustrated, reacts inappropriately to trivial upsets.

☐ He interrupts and blurts out answers to questions before they have been completed.

☐ He has difficulty remaining seated.

☐ He has difficulty listening to and following instructions.

☐ He has difficulty listening to an entire story, fidgets and squirms excessively.

☐ He plunges into an activity before getting all the instructions.

☐ He engages in physically dangerous activities without considering possible consequences.

☐ He has difficulty playing in groups, is bossy, aggressive

While most children show some of these signs some of the time, hyperactive children show most of them most of the time. If you checked nearly half of these boxes and your child has shown these behaviors for at least six months, consider consulting your doctor or school psychologist.

---

*ADHD is characterized by its variability from child to child, and within an individual child. Some children may show some of these features one day, and different ones the next. We have presented the most usual features of this difficulty.

sit in a circle and listen to instructions, but Ryan was always off doing his own thing. He pushed, hit, and threw toys at playmates. Ryan was seldom invited to a birthday party. The nearby park became the only place where Ryan could be contained and his parents could find some peace. Desperate to get Ryan to behave, his parents began timing him out in his room, only to find that he was spending more time "out" than "in." They tried withdrawing privileges until there was nothing else to take away.

There were periodic bright spots in Ryan's otherwise cloudy behavior. Occasionally he would have an hour or so when he could sit quietly and put a puzzle together, but the next day he would fall apart trying the same task. "Unpredictable" was added to the long list of "un"-words that described him. To complicate Ryan's behavioral problems, between the ages of two and four he suffered repeated ear infections, which contributed to his already miserable behavior.

By age four, Ryan was an angry, aggressive, belligerent, and distant child. His parents, not knowing what else to do (and perhaps, just to get a break), tried preschool. This proved to be a disaster as he acquired even more labels, including "immature," "inattentive," and "poorly socialized." Ryan couldn't complete projects, so when the other children got "special" stickers he got nothing. When the other children were enjoying themselves in a game, Ryan was in time-out. His teacher tried to help Ryan with "his problem," but she didn't know what his problem was.

As his bewildered parents sat in my office, five-year-old Ryan did everything but sit. He explored every corner, tried to take apart every piece of equipment, and when he couldn't get the hearing tester's light to turn on easily, he became frustrated and turned his attention to something else. I tried hard but couldn't connect with Ryan. As I was complimenting him for the way he

Softening the Aggressive Child

Some children have impulsive temperaments and are naturally rough-and-tumble — a double whammy that gets them tagged as "aggressive." They are not intentionally mean. They just came wired to be very physical. In pursuit of a toy, Johnny unintentionally makes contact with Billy. The smaller but scrappier Billy retaliates. Or Mary gives Susy a seemingly harmless shove that sends her teetering back into the wall. Your job is to help a child recognize this tendency to cause harm in order to control it. Point out how "Because you're stronger you have to be more careful, like Daddy is when he roughhouses with you." Help the child make an apology — even if the harm was unintentional. (See "Teaching Your Child to Apologize," pages 244–245.) Some aggressive children hug too hard. Demonstrate the difference between "bear hugs" (strong hugs) and "bunny hugs" (softer embraces). The child needs to respect his own strength and the feelings of others. It is important that parents recognize this tendency in any child who plays with their child. Redirect this behavior as early as possible, as much as possible. Children can develop psychological problems quickly if they perceive that their parents do nothing to protect them from intentional or unintentional injury from siblings or playmates.

put on my stethoscope, he was looking out the window and telling me about a lizard crawling across a red car fifty feet away. Ryan is a child who has attention deficit/hyperactivity disorder (ADHD); this is the approach I used to help Ryan.

Don't take it personally. I explained ADHD to his parents and reassured them that it was not their fault that Ryan acted this way. They were not too harsh, too lenient, or too anything. Terri seemed relieved because she was beginning to take Ryan's behavior personally; he often behaved better for teachers than he did for her, and this made her feel as if she were the problem. I explained that sometimes a child will feel free to show his problem self only in front of his mother, who is the only person in the whole world who empathizes with him. Bob then confided that Ryan had become a strain on their marriage. Bob had been feeling all along that he just needed to be treated with a firmer approach. However, he had noticed that the more he spanked Ryan the more distance developed between Ryan and him and the more Ryan gravitated toward his mother, who already felt overburdened at having to do more than her share of the correction. Terri and Bob understood that Ryan's problem had escalated into a total family problem. When I mentioned they would need some counseling, I was quick to add that although ADHD may have a biological basis and is not caused by bad parenting, the behavior of the child with ADHD improves when parents learn better ways to connect and communicate with him.

Use a team approach. Finding a solution to Ryan's problems required input from several specialists, and his parents understood that this would be a cooperative effort among Ryan, myself, his teachers, a behavioral therapist, and themselves. ADHD with behavioral problems is so complex that it's necessary to get a variety of perspectives.

What ADHD is not. Starting kindergarten had only worsened Ryan's behavior. His teacher described him as "unmanageable" and "totally off the wall." With some kids, symptoms of ADHD are not even apparent until they enter school. In classroom settings children are required to perform within certain limits and to complete tasks in a reasonable period of time. Teachers may be understandably less tolerant of disruptive behavior than parents. While parents have had five years to adjust themselves and their environment to their child's activity level, the ADHD child and his teacher are strangers, suddenly thrown into new roles that neither is equipped to handle.

It's easy to label a child with ADHD as "slow," "lazy," or "bad." But Ryan was not stupid. Like many children with ADHD, he was bright. Ryan was not lazy. He could not complete tasks because he was unable to focus on one thing for very long. This frustrated him as much as it did his parents and teachers, and as his frustration escalated, he withdrew. The less able he felt, the more his self-worth decreased. There was only one thing that made him feel better — movement. Ryan was not "bad," even though he felt that way. Here's how he got that label.

In their zeal to correct Ryan's behavior, his parents and teachers unknowingly reinforced his negative behavior. There were so many "no"s and time-outs, and so much special recognition for his bad behavior that being the bad guy became his self-image.

Labels Are Loaded

Giving a name to a condition can be a help or a hindrance. It would be easy to blame behavior on biology and overlook other problems in the home and school that will also need fixing. Labeling behavior as ADHD does not excuse obnoxious behavior; it explains it. It gives the treatment plan a starting point, relieves the guilt and stigma of the "bad child," and raises hopes for effective management. It doesn't relieve parents and child of the responsibility of consistent discipline, and oftentimes it involves a major overhaul of their lifestyle. The goal is to empower the child to be able to learn and work happily and productively for a lifetime.

His hyperactivity drove him to misbehave, the misbehavior was punished, and Ryan enjoyed the attention. (In general, hyperactive children are particularly resistant to the usual behavior-modification approach to discipline.) Over five years, what had started out as "bad behavior" became "bad Ryan," a label that Ryan adopted for himself. He expected himself to misbehave. At least it was some kind of identity.

Ryan needed connecting. Ryan was a child with a behavioral problem that needed to be fixed; yet I told his parents there was no overnight cure. Five years of conditioning had gone into forming Ryan's behavior, so it was going to take time to change both how he felt about himself and how he acted toward others. I diplomatically explained to his parents the concept of the high-need baby who goes on to become the high-need child. I reassured them

that up until now they had been doing the best they could with the advice they'd been given. But now it was time to try another approach. Ryan needed a high-touch, gentling style of parenting to counteract his built-in tendency to be impulsive and easily distracted. He needed one-on-one quiet time — back rubs, story time, soothing songs, lots of hugs, and lots of eye contact. When Ryan was out of control, his parents would need to approach him gradually. While most kids welcome a hand on the shoulder for comfort, children with ADHD often stiffen and withdraw from body contact they may perceive as controlling; thus touching them when they are upset may worsen their behavior. I told Ryan's parents that if he rejected their advances simply to stand by him and be available. I gave them suggestions for relaxation exercises to use with Ryan similar to the ones they had learned in childbirth class. Eventually Ryan would be able to use these to relax by himself ("When I feel out of control, I do this."). (See pages 275–276 for specific behavioral modifiers that compete with ADHD characteristics.) I especially impressed upon the parents the importance of using eye-to-eye contact and body language to try to connect with Ryan and help him connect with them. Basically, they were to spend the next year connecting with their son, much as an attachment parent connects with an infant.

Ryan needed behavioral therapy. The parents' main job was to focus on helping Ryan get back a sense of "good" self. His present identity was made up of negatives. Ryan needed specific positive reinforcements. If he did a certain thing, he would get a specific reward. Time-outs at school, which single him out, do not work for a child with ADHD when they reinforce his identity as "class clown" or "bad boy." I referred Ryan's parents to a behavioral therapist and a parenting course so they could learn how to practice positive reinforcement for appropriate behavior. They were to show Ryan, incident by incident, alternatives to acting impulsively and aggressively.

Ryan needed structure. For some children structure means sitting quietly in a circle holding hands; for others it's a park, and a large one at that. Ryan's parents were to make a list of the situations in which he behaved the best and try, as much as humanly possible, to structure his environment in that direction. If he played best with one playmate, they would schedule one-on-one play. They would give Ryan simple responsibilities around the house, help him complete them, and praise him for doing so. Or get him a pet, the training of which he would, with their help, be responsible for. When they had to get on Ryan's case, they were to do it in a positive way. Put a hand on his shoulder, give him eye contact, sit him in a quiet, uninteresting place, and tell him that because they loved him they were going to help him relax and think before he acted so he could control himself. The behavioral therapist also discussed this with Ryan; he learned the meaning of "control" and "focus."

Would Ryan need medication? "I hope we don't have to drug our child," his mother worried. I explained to them that none of the above treatments would work as well if Ryan could not concentrate and control his impulsive behavior in the first place. Ryan and his family could not afford another year of unhappiness. Medication can help turn the situation around more quickly by decreasing a child's impulsivity and helping him focus. (See explanation of ADHD medications, page 273.) It is usually possible to stop the medication once the parents determine how much energy they can devote to the other aspects of treatment — and it takes a *lot.*

Ryan needed monitoring. There is no set recipe for managing children with ADHD. The medication needs to be adjusted periodically, based on the child's response, and individual responses vary greatly. Behavior modification techniques work differently in different situations. For this reason, I asked the parents and Ryan's teacher to keep diaries of his behavior, of which techniques worked and which didn't, and to try to come up with ideas of their own. Ryan also needed to see progress, perhaps with a reward system or ticket system (see pages 174–178). Hyperactive children, because of their limited attention span, need frequent immediate rewards. "We'll go to a movie on Saturday" is meaningless to a child who can only relate to the next few minutes.

After our first session, Ryan's parents realized their son had been misunderstood and mislabeled. I advised them to change their expectations and to try to "set up for success." Ask him to clean up a small part of his room and give some assistance. Praise him for the result and then set another small section to clean. Ryan and his parents accomplished a lot over the next several months. After two months of using these treatments and techniques, Ryan and his parents were back in my office and I saw peace in the family. (Even my medical equipment was safe.) There was a connection between parents and child. Ryan's mother, with a tear, joyfully whispered to me, "I've always loved Ryan, but for the first

Addressing Medication Worries

I've used these medications in children with ADHD for more than twenty years. They help many children. So let me address the most common concerns and dispel some common myths.

"Can't we try something else before drugs?"

Yes, you can, and you should. ADHD medications are not the only answer to the child's (and family's) problems. If used, they are part of a whole treatment package. A child could be exposed to the best behavior modification treatment in the world, but if he can't concentrate, it won't sink in. Also, time is important to a developing child, who cannot afford to waste years waiting for behavior modification techniques slowly to have their effect. With these medicines, parents and teachers often notice that the child's behavior improves within a few days to a week, and the child's decreased impulsivity and activity and increased attention to instructions allows behavior modification to work better. Once a child is on the medication, the goal is to reduce and discontinue it as soon as possible, after behavior modification has taken hold. Many families believe the drug will cure the problem and refuse to change family systems or ways of relating to their child. Schools insist kids be medicated and then won't modify curriculums. Treatment of ADHD must be a total approach. If you decide to use drugs, they can ideally be used for six months to jump-start the changes with the addition of intense training in relaxation, sensory-motor integration, learning strategies, and revamping of parenting and educational styles.

"I worry about my child taking drugs so young."

That's a normal worry. However, there is no evidence that taking ADHD medicine predisposes a child to drug addiction. On the contrary, children who are diagnosed and treated early for ADHD are less likely to deviate into unhealthy habits later on. I believe it's unwise to withhold medication that can help a child feel and perform better. When prescribing these medications for a child, I call them "focus pills." I tell the kids, by means of a drawing, that these little pills will help their brain and their muscles listen and talk to each other so that they can think through their actions, until they learn how to focus without the pills.

"How do these drugs work? Are they safe?"

The most commonly used "focus pills," Ritalin and Dexedrine, are actually stimulants that help the child focus. They are not tranquilizers. Though generally regarded as safe, there are occasional side effects: diminished appetite, stomach aches, headaches, irritability, and trouble falling asleep. These are usually temporary. If they do last, they may subside when the dose is lowered. It's important that your child be carefully evaluated by a specialist in hyperactivity to decide if your child is indeed a candidate for these medicines. You will be given a list of objective criteria to use to determine if the medications are working so that the dosage can be adjusted appropriately. Parents should be confident concerning their own observations.

time since he was born I can honestly say I now like him."

Parents, keep in mind that not all children with attention deficit disorders (ADD) are hyperactive, at least externally. Some children are just internally inattentive and their thought processes are riddled with distractions. These children are just as misunderstood and mislabeled as the ones who are externally hyperactive. They are often called "lazy" or "immature." The behavior problems of ADD are not part of the core symptoms; they are secondary to poor academic performance, negative feedback at home and/or school, and a resultant poor self-image.

Children with ADHD are not "bad kids." Their neurological differences lead them to process instructions differently, which leads to emotional and behavioral difficulties. They are like a TV set without an antenna; things come in fuzzy. Because these children don't process requests or stick to a task like other children, they require special discipline in these areas. Here are the usual features of ADHD and the special kind of discipline that goes along with them.

Distractibility

Children with ADHD have difficulty focusing. They lose interest in most things quickly and flit from task to task, seldom completing what they begin. Much of their distractibility is internal. There are intrusions into their thought processes causing these children to lose track of where they are going. A child may decide to go upstairs

The ADHD Cycle

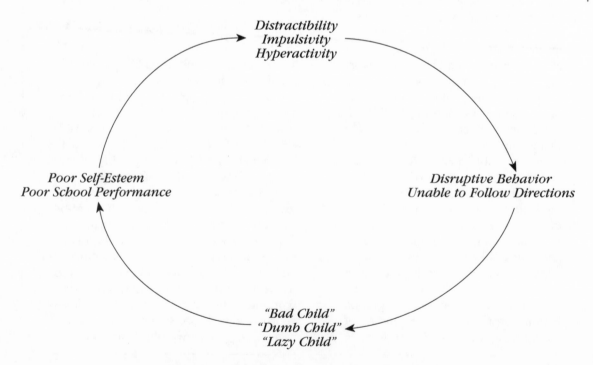

Distractibility
Impulsivity
Hyperactivity

Disruptive Behavior
Unable to Follow Directions

Poor Self-Esteem
Poor School Performance

"Bad Child"
"Dumb Child"
"Lazy Child"

A Gifted Child — A Gifted Adult

Children with ADHD are gifted children, they are just gifted differently. Their emotional development is uneven so that their undersirable behaviors often blur their special talents. They alternate quickly from inattention to hyperattention. This ability to hyperfocus may become an advantage in certain professions that require long hours of intense concentration. Also, their ability to see details and their rich imaginations bring out the creative artist in these children. The inability to handle empty time brings out a workaholic tendency in adults. Keep in mind that these children are different, not worse, than other children. The earlier you recognize that you have a child who needs to learn differently, be parented differently, and be disciplined differently, the more likely it is that this child will use these special qualities to his adult advantage.

to get a game but get sidetracked into another room; or if he makes it to his room he may forget the purpose for which he was going there. These children are hyperdistractible; they get hung up on minutiae and can't filter out irrelevant details.

Even though short attention span is characteristic of these children, they also frequently show selective *hyperattention.* They can become very engrossed in certain activities of their choosing such as TV, video games, or a computer. The child often seems so riveted on these electronic activities that he doesn't seem to hear what parents say. Because these children some-

times seem to pay attention so well, parents may feel that they really don't have ADHD. The clue that they do have a problem is their inconsistency — they can go into hyperfocus when they are engrossed by something but be highly inattentive at most other times to what others (parents, teachers, peers) feel is important. Because of short attention span and easy distractibility, children with ADHD need *management by the moment*: brief, frequent reinforcers, rewards, and reminders — the three R's of behavior modification. With these in mind, try these suggestions:

- Give eye contact when talking with your child, and require eye contact when he wants something from you. Whenever possible, don't respond to him unless he is looking at you. (See "Connect Before You Direct," page 162.)

- Have your child repeat your request. If he can't, your request is too long or too complicated. ADHD children often have poor auditory memory. Keep practicing a brief and simple way of talking with your child. Require your child to repeat back to you the *exact* request, not just to answer with a yes or a no.

- Give clear, straightforward commands. "Stop running around!" makes more of an impression on an inattentive child than "Would you please stop?" Say it only once. All kids learn their parents' time limit. ("She's a say-it-five-times mother.") Say it once and then go over and march your child through your request. If they don't understand ADHD, good parents often keep repeating their command to make it sink in. Never repeat your request over and over or get into nattering: "Did you hear me?" "How many times do I

ADHD Resources

For general information and resources on ADHD contact:

CHADD (Children and Adults with Attention Deficit Disorders)
499 Northwest 70th Avenue, Suite 308
Plantation, Florida, 33317
305-587-3700

The Rodiger Center (for sensory-motor integration training)
69 North Catalina Avenue
Pasadena, CA 91106
818-793-5626

The ADD Center (for neurofeedback training)
50 Village Centre Place
Mississauga, Ontario, Canada, L4Z1V9
905-803-8066

have to ask you?" (See related section, "No Nattering," page 169.) Constructing a word picture helps your child process your request. Describe pictorially what you ask him to do: "Imagine you are putting away your clothes in the drawer." General commands don't work with these children; keep them specific. "Clean up your room" is not a clear command. For better results try, "Put your clothes in your drawers," and after he has completed that task, "Put your toys on the shelf."

- Give your child one task at a time. Check for completion, then add another one. Don't give a string of commands: "Go upstairs, brush your teeth, put on your pajamas. . . ." ADHD children can often only process one simple request at a time. They often have trouble with sequence.

- Break up a large task, for example, homework, into small steps. Check and reward each step when completed. Minimize visual and auditory distractions in the environment. Begin the task with the child, then back off and periodically reappear to offer help and advice.

- Deliver directives personally. Instead of shouting "Go to your room," take your child there. Instead of calling "Turn off the TV," walk to the TV set and watch with him. Then, during a commercial break, turn off the TV. Instead of yelling "Come to dinner" while the child is playing with the train, go over and join in. As the train slows down, say "Oh, the train is stopping for food. Now it's time for you to stop for food, then we'll come back to the train." ADHD children are not being obstinant or defiant when they don't follow commands promptly. They just don't transition well. They have to be creatively led out of their agenda into yours.

- Use humor, body language, touch, and eye-to-eye contact to initiate and sustain attention. Most hyperactive children need a theatrical opener to get their attention, an amusing game, or a crazy antic by the parent. (See example of getting a child's attention, pages 176–177.)

- Cut out clutter; use compartmental toy shelves instead of piles of toys in a corner or in a box. The child needs order.

- Set your child up to succeed. If you predict that your child can only tolerate five minutes of an activity before disintegrating, step in at that time limit and change the setting. If your child is prone to selective hyperattention and you're planning to start dinner at six-thirty, don't let him begin watching an hourlong TV program

Homework Without Hassles

Pauline described Sam's lack of study skills: He would fidget, fall out of his chair, procrastinate, get angry and cry, anything but put pencil to paper. Because of Pauline's home business, this family's home is often cluttered, a setting that easily distracts Sam, and he is continually pestered by his two-year-old sister, who gives him no space and no peace. Exasperated, his mother often descends upon Sam with the warning that he must do his homework or he'll grow up to be a bum. Sam is now not only unfocused but unwilling. He is angry because he is being made to do the work that he doesn't want to do; he does a lot of fist pounding, which, of course, only enrages his mother so that the two of them are at each other's throats very quickly. Anger, anxiety, and clutter are not conducive to learning.

We had Sam sit at a sturdy table, free of clutter, in a room well lighted and relatively orderly. At first his body was a statue of resistance: His stiff arms and slumped-over torso revealed a child negatively programmed toward homework. So we showed him how to relax his body: "Take ten deep-down tummy breaths and blow them out nice and slowly, and relax." Then we showed him how to sit in a good posture at the table with his seat back in the chair, his feet on the floor, and his arms up on the table with his palms facing upward. As he took in the deep breaths he was to think about gradually warming up his hands. Once Sam was untensed, his resistance was gone and he was eager to get on with his work.

Sam had been set up for resistance, and Pauline had been set up for a lot of frustration. We encouraged her to find an uncluttered area, preferably in his room, where he could sit at his desk with the door shut so his sister couldn't bother him. Pauline would need to help Sam get into a relaxed frame of mind by humoring rather than hassling him. A healthy "welcome home" snack would prepare Sam and fuel his brain for think time. As for timing, Sam does better when he gets his homework out of the way right after school. (Some kids may need some outdoor exercise first.) If the subject is confusing, she would give a brief, calm explanation before leaving him alone to do his work. And she would give him a time incentive — "See if you can get it done in twenty minutes so you can go out to play."

Sam is not a stupid child; he is very able to do his work once the study environment sets him up for success, but he is a typical eight-year-old child who dislikes being hassled. Now Sam is enjoying the approval he gets from parent and teacher and the good feelings that go along with a job well done. Usually he does his homework because he wants to, not because he is forced to.

at six o'clock. He'll react violently when you turn off the set. Identify your child's areas of strength (for example, sports, art) and encourage his talent in those directions. (See discussion of carryover principle, pages 98–99.)

- Don't closet the child for homework. Keep him in view and voice range. It is tempting to put your child in a room without any visual or auditory distractions, feeling that this will help the child concentrate. While you should strive for an orderly environment, a room void of any stimuli usually is counterproductive. Either the child will find one little distractor, say, an ant, to overfocus on, or he will drive himself to internal distractions, bombarding his mind with visions of his baseball game or the movie he saw last week that keep him from focusing on the task at hand.

- Give your child responsibilities around home that he can complete, and praise the results. Children with ADHD need rewards and acknowledgment frequently. Give tangible rewards. You can usually get by with rewarding children with a happy face at the end of the day. ADHD children may need a happy face reward every five minutes during a task. (See description of ticket system for giving rewards, pages 176–178.)

Impulsiveness

Impulsiveness is what gets ADHD kids into trouble. They lack the ability to think before they act or to consider the consequences of their actions. In school and in social settings, they are labeled "disruptive." They are prone to accidents and incidents because they act on the spur of the mo-

ment. The ball runs down the driveway and the six-year-old races after it even though you have warned him many times about the danger of running into the street. He isn't being defiant or disrespectful; he is acting on impulse. He may even feel sorry that he "disobeyed" the rules of running into the street. The impulse kicked in suddenly and he followed it without thinking.

Impulsivity is what gets most children with ADHD the unfair labels "bad" or "dumb." Because ADHD is not a visible disabililty, these children do not get showered with help and empathy. Consider the child with cerebral palsy entering the class in a wheelchair. Children get to help usher the child to his proper seat. The blind child has classmates assigned to help him. The ADHD child storms into the classroom, knocks over the desks, squirms in his seat, and annoyingly taps his pencil all day long. He becomes the class nuisance, and other children withdraw from him. By finding ways to help the child deal with his impulsive nature, you can lessen the behavioral problems and boost his self-image. Try implementing the following special discipline tips for the impulsive child:

- Give the child "think before you act" drills, such as counting to five before he acts. Encourage the child to envision the consequences of an action before he acts and to explain them to you. Teach a child to imagine what the other person may feel and have him tell you. Plant in your child verbal "reminders" not to act impulsively: "Count to five." "Wait a minute." "Stop and think!" Go through drills with him so that a usual impulsive situation triggers these reminders.

- When your child is in a negative mood, give him choices, providing that all the choices are attractive to you and he gets the job done: "What do you want to do first, brush your teeth or put your pajamas on?" Choices help the child stop and think before he rushes into an action, and they help him toward an important discipline for life — becoming a decision maker. Choices help homework compliance: "Which do you want to do first, your math or your spelling?"

- Impulsive children may also be aggressive, which gets them into even more trouble. Model gentleness and foster sensitivity in your child. Consider getting the child a *sturdy* pet to care for — a dog or a rat.

- Don't spank. Children with ADHD are notoriously resistant to spanking to redirect behavior. They lack the ability to relate punishments to their actions; as a result spanking only makes them angry.

- Use the term "bad" sparingly in correcting all children. Strike it from your vocabulary entirely with ADHD children. Rather than "That's bad," try, "We don't do that." This makes him part of the "we" who know how to behave rather than the perpetual bad boy. Minimize negatives as much as possible. Instead of "Don't do this," try, "I'm going to help you remember to do it this way."

- The impulsive child and the impulsive disciplinarian are a mismatch. Your child needs time and space to redirect his interests and you need time to plan a strategy to redirect his behavior rather than immediately rushing in to stop it. Try the three-card method: Put three cards of different colors on the table and draw a face on each card, each one slightly sadder than the previous one. When your child

---

Monitoring Your Child

Sometime in the middle childhood years, be prepared for your child to question your restrictions: "Why do I always have to check in with you? I'm older now." Monitoring your child's whereabouts gives your child the message that with increasing privileges come increasing responsibilities. Also, it is polite for children to tell their parents where they are going. Monitoring is not controlling behavior. Help your children understand it's simply part of parental responsibility to monitor their activities. Expect your child to tell you where he is going, who he'll be with, what he will be doing, and what time to expect him to return. Start monitoring your child as a preteen so this is accepted as a part of life; otherwise when he's a teen he'll think you're doing it to control him and he'll turn the issue into a power struggle. Also, tell your child that parents like to know where each other are. In families, people like to know where everyone is.

---

begins a disruptive behavior, give him the first card. If he continues, he gets a second, sadder card, then the third. By that time he either has redirected himself into more constructive behavior or you have planned a better strategy.

- Impulsive children have difficulty standing in line or waiting their turn. They are prone to disrupt others' conversations. While standing in line at the movie theater or supermarket, busy the child with word games or tell stories. Eventually teach him how to busy himself with a book or a mind game (for example, he might try to think of words that start with each letter of the alphabet). During games teach him to wait his turn. You might have to structure the game so that the wait is short.

In disciplining the hyperactive child, you will feel you are catering to the child, and sometimes you may feel manipulated. Consider these discipline tricks as ways to help you enjoy living with your special child while helping him get on with life. Working with the hyperactive child teaches you that valuable negotiating skill: Meet the person where he is, and then creatively lead him to where you want him to be.

Hyperactivity

It's the quality *and* the quantity of motor activity that distinguishes hyperactivity from normally active children. Their movement often seems purposeless; they are fidgety and restless. They run into things, run over people, and climb on everything. Parents find themselves perpetually chasing their children and snatching them back from the brink of injury. The parents' job is to help these children harness excess energy and redirect it into constructive behavior. For the hyperactive child, try these discipline suggestions:

- Teach your child relaxation techniques. Teach your child to sit quietly cross-

legged style, breathe deeply, and open his hands as you massage his fingers open. To get children to breathe deeply, one helpful bit of imagery is "Imagine you've got a balloon in your tummy and you have to blow it up."

- Teach children to be aware of their body. Teach them to respect other kids' space. "Imagine there's a space around your body, and that will keep you from running into other children." While most children with ADHD don't worry about the consequences of their actions, some are just the opposite and become over-cautious.

- Provide a structured environment. The little whirlwind may trash your house if you leave a lot of clutter lying around. Living with a hyperactive child forces you to be more orderly, but don't expect your house to be as tidy as that of your neighbor who has a sit-still child. Have realistic expectations. It's unlikely that your child will sit still during circle time at preschool. You may be fortunate to get him to stay in the park. These kids, like all children, need boundaries.

- Some of these children are also verbally hyperactive, little "motor mouths." Help them to listen to other people and to take turns. If parents are also verbally hyperactive, they would have a hard time modeling language constraints to a child.

- Don't time-out the hyperactivity. The very word "out" is a negative. Keep the concept, but change the wording. Try "thinking time" or "quiet time." When the child's activity is revved up going from one destructive behavior to another, insist on "thinking time," a quiet place to ponder a more constructive activity. Short, frequent thinking times (of a few minutes each) are better than less-frequent longer ones to redirect the behavior of a hyperactive child. Because the child may already feel rejected, don't banish him to his room. Try a special chair (such as the "teddy bear" chair) in the playroom. The purpose is to get the child to sit still and think, not to be closeted. No matter what you call it, present discipline time-out like a sports time-out, as a time to rest when the hyperactive child is overwhelmed, and a time to regroup and plan a better strategy. When the going gets rough, give yourself some space. You deserve a break. Be sure your child is not in a situation where he could injure himself and then go to the bathroom with a book.

- Time-in with your child. Because hyperactive children require supervision and interactive play, try to rid your environment of intrusions. Block out a chunk of quality time, better called "focus time." Take the phone off the hook, turn off the television, and tune in to your child. Several times a day make an effort to connect with your child as you both settle down to some focus time.

Is ADHD a social disease? Like the factors determining a child's temperament (see pages 282–289), ADHD is also a nature versus nurture controversy. How much of a child's behavior comes from genes and gender, and how much is influenced by environment? While there is no doubt some children come wired biologically predisposed to hyperactivity, distractibility, and impulsivity, I believe that if they get attachment parenting, consistent discipline, and individualized schooling, many of these children can function well. They will go on to

use their drive to their adult advantage in professional life, such as in being successful on Wall Street or on Broadway. They will likely do better in sales than in accounting — choosing a career where high energy is an asset definitely helps.

Another child with ADHD may not be so lucky. He grows up in a home where attachment did not occur, nurturing is marginal, discipline is inconsistent, paternal authority is optional or absent, and the one-size-fits-all school system fails to recognize that some children must learn differently. For this child, his temperament becomes a liability and he is likely to fare poorly in society.

Could ADHD be a group of normal traits that got routed the wrong way? Is it true that ADHD occurs much less in countries other than the United States, or is it simply not as well recognized in those places? Or could ADHD be "made in America," a hectic culture that fosters early childhood independence and where cribs and cartoon violence, bottles and busy parents, day-care and divorce are accepted norms? Do we medicate our children to make them fit the system, or do we fix the system? These are questions we must wrestle with. ADHD may have a biological predisposition, but whether the child with this disorder grows up to be a creator or a criminal can be determined largely by the early parenting and social support system that child gets. We believe that the immunization against crippling ADHD is to be found in the opening three chapters of this book, rather than in the doctor's office or the pharmacy.

DISCIPLINING THE TEMPERAMENTALLY DIFFICULT CHILD (AKA THE HIGH-NEED CHILD)

The temperamentally difficult child is a challenge to live with and to discipline. The good news is that if parents pick up on their child's difficult traits early and channel them wisely, the same qualities that are likely to get the child into trouble can later work to her advantage. Each child you have will take from and give to you. Triple that for the difficult child.

Your child is special. Temperament describes the basic wiring of your child. It determines her individual behavioral style, how she acts. Temperament is neither "good" nor "bad," it just *is*. The world would be very dull (or perhaps very chaotic) if everyone were a behavioral clone. Still, some temperaments are more challenging for parents than others. How these children are disciplined can determine whether these high-need traits ultimately become an asset or a liability.

Our first three children were easy babies. They slept well at night, their needs were predictable and readily satisfied. Fortunately for us, they adjusted well to the unpredictable life of medical-training days. I remember remarking, "What's all the fuss about fussy babies. Surely parents must be exaggerating. It's not so hard to care for babies." Then along came our fourth child, Hayden, who within days after her birth caused me to retract that statement. The only schedule she knew was her own. Her cries would rally an army. The only predictable thing about her was her unpredictability. Had Hayden been our first child, we would have thought it

---

Water Therapy

A surefire solution for fussy children of any age — from the newborn with crying spells to the traumatized ten-year-old — is water therapy. Water can be soothing, relaxing, or entertaining, depending on whether the fuss is due to discomfort, agitation, or boredom. Probably the age that benefits most from water therapy is the toddler; this is when mothers would appreciate its use the most. Take a good book into the bathroom; plan on sitting there and watching your child while he plays with his water toys. Both mom and toddler get a break. With a small baby, mom can get into the water, too. These combined benefits of water therapy probably explain why a bath is a favorite bedtime routine. We counsel parents of toddlers and young children who are hard to wind down to include a nice warm soak in the bedtime routine.

---

was our fault she behaved that way, that we were doing something wrong. But she was our fourth, and by this time we had a handle on baby care. So, we learned lesson number one: *New babies fuss primarily because of their temperament and not because of your parenting abilities.*

What to call Hayden (fussy, colicky, difficult, challenging) didn't matter; what to do was the issue. Later we coined the term "high-need baby."* That was a kinder term and one that better described what she was

---

*Specific techniques on parenting high-need babies are discussed in detail in our companion book, *The Baby Book: Everything You Need to Know About Your Baby — From Birth to Age Two.*

like. I tried the term on parents who came into my office seeking consultation for handling their difficult babies. They liked it. This term was positive, uplifting, and possibly a compliment. It helped them feel good about their babies. Up until then, the labels given to these babies had been a string of negatives. Hayden grew to become a *high-need child,* and in jest we now call her a high-cost teen.

We realized our goal was to help Hayden *fit,* the tiny three-letter word that economically tells what parenting is all about. Hayden had to be taught to fit into our family, our lifestyle. In order to do this we had to adjust our parenting to her higher needs. This would help Hayden thrive and us survive. We learned lesson number two: *Disciplining a difficult child begins with mellowing the temperament of the child while improving the sensitivity of the parents.*

We identified those features of Hayden's temperament that were most trying for her and us. Next, we took the adult-in-charge approach and kept working with her until something succeeded. Hayden's intense cries mellowed as long as we carried her, so we continued to carry her. She settled well at night as long as she slept next to us, so we continued to let her sleep next to us.

She became an in-arms, at-breast, and in-our-bed baby — and she fit. Lesson number three: *High-need babies require a higher level of parenting.*

One word characterized Hayden's needs, "more." She needed more holding, more nursing, more comforting — more of everything, except sleep. Hayden opened up a whole new level of parenting to us. And as she grew, she continued to need more from us — more patience, more energy, more creativity, more anticipation, more maturity, and more nursing.

We could have closed our hearts to her, broken her spirit, made her knuckle under to our preconceived style of parenting and convinced ourselves we had fulfilled our duty to discipline her. We all would have lost this battle. We would not have fit. Hayden would not have blossomed into the sensitive leader she is today; we would not have learned the rewards of full-blown attachment parenting.

Match or mismatch? The parent-child fit, the *temperament of the pair,* influences the likelihood of discipline problems later on. Just as children come wired with different temperaments and different abilities to communicate their needs, parents also have different response levels. Some parents

For Better or Worse?

Temperament Traits	Discipline Problems (liabilities)	Personality Pluses (assets)
Strong-willed, intense, supersensitive, persistent	Obstinate, easily angered, touchy, defiant, prone to power struggles and tantrums: "I'll do it my way."	Strong leadership qualities, compassionate, empathetic, generous, assertive, determined

You can see from the above chart that the traits of temperamentally difficult children are not inherently "good" or "bad." It's what you do with them that matters.

The Need Level Concept

The ultimate goal of disciple, in fact, of all parenting, is to help babies *thrive*. The term "thriving" means more than just getting heavier and taller, it means helping the child develop to maximum potential physically, intellectually, and emotionally. While there are growth charts for height and weight, there are none for thriving. So we really never know whether or not a child is ever reaching full potential. We just do the best we can. Vital to helping your child thrive is the understanding of what we call the need level concept.

Every child comes wired with a certain level of need, and if that level is filled the child develops to her maximum potential. She thrives. For example, all babies need to be held a lot; some babies have a need to be held constantly in order to thrive. These babies usually come wired with a corresponding temperament that prompts them to complain until they get held as much as they need. These babies cry if you put them down. So these babies who have a high level of need to be held receive their very first temperament label, "demanding," or worse "fussy" or "difficult." "Demanding" may sound like a liability at first, but actually it is a positive character trait that helps this baby thrive. If a baby were endowed with high needs yet lacked the ability to communicate these needs, she would not thrive. Your baby's signals are a clue to her temperament as well as a clue to her needs. Once you recognize this you can respond accordingly.

"Our high-need baby brings out the best and the worst in me," lamented a tired mother. Another mom added, "I am tired, but never bored." The need level of the infant shapes the mother's behavior to a high level of responsiveness. Mother, sensing her baby's unique personality, makes some adjustments in order to improve the fit. The mother-child pair thrives and discipline works. If the mother is not flexible or temperaments clash, the parent and child do not bring out the best in each other.

The need level concept doesn't mean the child always takes and the parents always give. Caring for a high-need child helps her become a giver. The beauty of this approach is that the more you give, the more you get. You give your child nurturing to meet the special needs. In so doing you get skills you didn't have before, and you get a child who is responsive to your direction. You cannot choose the temperament or the capabilities of your child. But you can choose whether to meet your child's special needs. By doing so, you will enrich your own life as you become more mature.

automatically give a nurturing response appropriate to the need level of their children. Others do not find their responses so automatic, and their nurturing abilities need time to mature. When the need level of the baby and the response level of the mother match, discipline problems are less likely to occur and, if they do, are more easily solved.

The temperament of the child affects the

Framing

Some photos look better, some worse, depending on how they are framed. Whether or not a certain technique of correction has a good or bad effect on your child often depends upon how you frame it. Punishments, such as withdrawal of privileges, that are framed in anger or revenge will have a bad effect on the child. The same punishment, if framed in a genuine concern for shaping the behavior of the child for his own good, will make the point you want. Frame your correction in love and sensitivity, and whatever "method" you use is likely to leave a lasting good impression.

Putting a more likable frame on your child can change how you view him. A mother of a temperamentally difficult child told us: "Once I put a positive frame around him and quit focusing on the negatives, we got along much better." Try positive tags such as "spirited," "interesting," "challenging," "compassionate," "determined," and "sensitive." In our experience, "difficult children," if given attachment parenting and a positive frame, truly merit these compliments.

temperament of the parent. A mother of a high-need child once confided to me, "Our demanding child absolutely brings out the best and the worst in me."

Not only does the temperament of some children make them more prone to discipline problems, but parents with certain personalities are more likely to have problems disciplining. Some personalities match, others clash. A mother who has a high-strung, demanding child but is laid-back and unflappable may find discipline easier. She focuses on the biggies and doesn't waste energy on the smallies. The tense, easily bothered mother, however, will clash with the intensity of her high-need child and is very likely to find discipline difficult. Recognize when your and your child's personalities clash. The intense, overbearing parent of a laid-back child may need to lighten up a bit. The controlling parents of a compliant child need to be on guard not to manipulate her into the person they want her to be rather than the person that she is temperamentally suited to be. Similarly, the laid-back parents of a strong-willed, controlling child need to have the confidence that they are the adults. They need to think like adults, act like adults, and take charge like adults.

Difficult children need most of the discipline methods mentioned throughout this book, and they need them *more* than other children do.

Stay connected. Reread Chapter 2 of this book, on getting and staying connected to your child. It is the nature of difficult children not to want to obey directions. Instead, they regard them as a challenge. The goal of discipline is to help these children want to obey for their sake and for yours. The connected child wants to please. This child is likely to be more compliant if he receives attachment parenting; without it, he has no reason at all to go along with his parents.

Play down the negative, play up the positives. Identify the problem behaviors, those rough edges in your child's personality that need smoothing. Focusing on the

Features of High-Need Children		
Intense	*Infant*	Protests loudly if exact needs not met; reacts forcefully when not pleased; craves holding; "I just can't put her down"; "She's in high gear all the time."
	Child	Prone to temper tantrums; easily frustrated; moody, often negative.
Demanding	*Infant*	"His cries just escalate until I pick him up"; "draining"; "Needs to nurse all the time"; slow to wean; conveys a sense of urgency to his needs; quick to reject mother substitutes; not a self-soother.
	Child	Persists until she gets her way; "stubborn," strong-willed; power struggles common.
Super-Sensitive	*Infant*	Easily bothered; noises startle him easily; settles with difficulty at night; "He needs more of everything but sleep"; slow to warm up to substitute caregivers; seldom schedules regularly; awakens frequently; requires less sleep than mother.
	Child	Easily bothered and overstimulated; crumbles at slightest setback; easily distracted; "doesn't listen."
Hyperactive, Hypertonic	*Infant*	A photographer father remarked, "There's no such thing as a still shot of our baby. When I hold her I can feel the wiriness in her."
	Child	Hyperactive; impulsive; "daredevil."
Difficult to Adapt	*Infant*	Unpredictable; "What works one day doesn't work the next"; "Just as I think I have the game won, she just keeps upping the ante"; "I just can't seem to satisfy her"; Irregular feeding and sleeping.
	Child	Protests change; resists transitions: "Throws a fit when playing and it's time to leave"; protests bedtime; adjusts poorly to new situations.

negative, however, is likely to contribute to the already negative atmosphere that prevails. While helping your child fix what is wrong, acknowledge what is right. Spend more time validating the pleasant parts of her personality than commenting on the problem areas. Temperamentally difficult children are susceptible to negatives in the atmosphere that reinforce their already negative attitude. They need days full of positives: "Yes," "Great." "Thanks." "Good job." "Thumbs up."

Stay positive. It's easy for the day of a difficult child to be littered with "nos." Eventually the child picks up on the parents' negativity and either withdraws or intensifies his behavioral difficulties. It is hard to stay positive when your child is the only one in the play group that kicks the dog, but you need to remain cheerful and not get bogged down in anger and complaints. Parents who perceive their child negatively tend to use negative labels, and the child behaves accordingly. Thus "bad girl" becomes a self-fulfilling prophecy.

Don't make matters worse. Temperamentally difficult children get used to labels, to being singled out of the crowd for punishment. Soon this "specialness" becomes their identity. This doesn't improve their behavior and may make it worse. Traditional correction methods, such as time-out or withdrawing privileges, seldom work.

Diffuse anger. Nagging, yelling, and scolding intensify the oppositional behavior of the difficult child; abusive punishment, especially spanking, makes the child more difficult by making him angry. For example, if you demand that the temperamentally difficult child clean up his room, he perceives this as a challenge. The more you punish, the more he digs in and refuses to cooperate. You will eventually lose this game, so don't even start it. Once a temperamentally difficult child becomes chronically angry, you have a serious problem. Discipline must focus not only on preventing a lot of anger but also on helping your child learn mechanisms to relieve his negative feelings. (See discussion of feelings, pages 105–113.)

Different Discipline for Different Temperaments

Disciplining children with different temperaments is a matter of marketing. You have to know the little customer you are about to pitch to. This is why we emphasize that a major part of discipline is studying your child so that you can handle each situation according to the nature of the child. Here's how we approach our children when asking them to clean up their rooms. To our "take charge" child we say, "I'm going to put you in charge of the job of getting your room clean." If we tell her when and how to do it, she is likely to balk. For our "bounce and bubble" child we make a game out of it: "See if you can beat the timer in getting your room cleaned up." To our "methodical" child we appeal to his sense of duty, desire for order, and need to be industrious: "This room got out of control. Please fix it." With our "laid back" child we give enough time to anticipate doing the job and see how it can be done one step at a time: "By this evening I would like your room cleaned." Initially, approaching different children in different ways does take a lot of creativity and extra energy, but you'll gain in the long run by having more cooperation.

Run it off. Temperamentally difficult children need to release their excess energy and intense feelings in sports or any type of physical activity. Give them lots of opportunities for physical play, outdoors, if possible. Encourage them to channel their energy into running or biking. Indoors, put on some lively music and get everyone dancing and singing.

Help your child succeed. Find out your child's talents and desires. Help her learn skills, such as playing a musical instrument, excelling in a sport, or being creative in arts and crafts. Also, don't put your child into situations he can't handle. If restaurants are overwhelming, wait a year. (See related sections on how skill development improves behavior, and the "carryover principle," pages 98–99, and skill development and self-esteem, page 99.)

Increase your tolerance. Temperamentally difficult children have annoying behaviors that push parents' buttons. They seem to strike when and where you are vulnerable. Keep one step ahead. If your child waits to pester you while you are on the phone, make your calls when your child is not around. Choose your battles wisely. One evening at a Scout meeting, I heard a group of mothers discussing how they survived their strong-willed children. One mother said, "I adapted the Scout motto from 'Be prepared' to 'Be flexible.'"

Threats don't work. I asked Hayden, our high-need child, for some child's-eye viewpoints on discipline. She wrote out her comments on the correction we had used with her. On her list was "Don't threaten me. That only makes me not want to do what you want." In Hayden's logic (and she's right) she prefers to mind (meaning conform her mind to our minds) because she wants to. It needs to be her choice. Threats such as "If you're not back at a certain time I'll take away the car" take away her choice to obey. Strong-willed children

---

Nature and Nurture

Both genes and the environment influence a child's eventual personality. Temperaments are not written in stone. A child may be labeled "difficult" in one stage of development, yet because of a variety of influences and a nurturing style of parenting he *may* later mellow. To explain temperament, behavioral psychologists use a geological analogy. Some kids have natural quirks in their personality, like "fault lines," that are prone to "behavioral earthquakes." The number and magnitude of these quakes that occur depend to a large degree on the child's nurturing environment.

---

do not like to be backed into a corner. (For more tips on disciplining the difficult child, see related sections on disciplining the hyperactive child, pages 267–281; see also specific discipline techniques, pages 161–181.)

Don't take it personally. Janet and Tom consulted Martha and me about Nathan, their intense and impulsive four-year-old child who was wearing out their patience. Janet confided, "I take it personally. I feel people look at him and think he's a bad kid, the product of bad parenting. I feel hurt and angry. I'm not a bad mother. I care about Nathan very much and try my best to make him behave." We reassured Janet and Tom that Nathan's behavior was not their fault. Some kids are just difficult to manage. After listening to their description of Nathan's behavior, we suggested that he was a high-need child who would need a high level of discipline. Janet agreed, "I've always thought he has the temperament to be either a king or a criminal." We emphasized that the art of disciplining Nathan would involve striking a balance. They shouldn't squelch his personality, nor should they let him run wild. We also advised Janet and Tom to choose their advisers carefully. People who don't have a child like Nathan won't understand a child like Nathan.

DISCIPLINING THE SPECIAL NEEDS CHILD

Disciplining a child who is "differently-abled" is likely to bring out the best and the worst in a parent. Parents try to help a child make up for what's missing by increasing their love and attention, yet these kids often trigger special frustrations. Be prepared to run out of patience. We focus on Down syndrome in this section, but what we say applies equally to any cause of developmental delay. Our son Stephen has Down syndrome. Our most difficult adjustment in discipline was learning to cope with development in slow motion. Most children go through predictable stages of development. You know about when to expect which behavior and how long it will last. You know that a two-year-old's temper tantrums will diminish once the child learns to speak. Knowing this undesirable behavior lasts only a few months helps. With the developmentally disabled child, stages seem to go on forever, as do the frustrations in child and parents. For example, it may take this child a year to accomplish three months' worth of "normal" speech development. Parenting a special needs child is a tough job. The ups and downs, joys and sorrows are magnified: You rejoice at each accomplishment, worry about each new challenge.

Don't compare. Your child is special. Comparing your child to others of the same age is not fair. The real breakthrough that helped us come to terms with Stephen's "disability" was when we quit focusing on how he was different and instead started enjoying him for himself. We had to overcome our tendency to focus on his "problem" to the extent that he became a project instead of a person. "I'll become an expert on Down syndrome," I thought, "read everything, go to all the conferences, join all the support groups. We'll even write the definitive book." This didn't work. It took me two years to strike a balance. Martha's maternal drive helped her focus more on Stephen the baby than on his condition. She determined that what he needed most from us was a full dose of attachment parenting, while not denying that he had special needs that required patient parenting. We also realized that we could not let Stephen's "condition" take all of our energy away from the needs of the whole family.

Change your standards. Before a baby is even born, parents imagine what the child's life will be like: piano lessons, baseball stardom, graduating from college, and so on. Even with a normal child, you have to reconcile these dreams with reality as your child grows up. When a special needs child is born, this is a bigger task. You learn to live in the present. The milestones of the child's life are less defined and the future less predictable — though your child may surprise you! In the meantime, set your standards for your child at an appropriate level. For example, reset your anger buttons. He will do some things that exasperate you. Our then four-year-old Stephen, after watching his siblings throw floating toys into the pool, threw my pocket recorder (which contained all the notes for a chapter of this book) into the pool. In his mind, this was Daddy's toy, and it was OK to throw toys into the swimming pool. Naturally, I was angry not only at losing a three-hundred dollar recorder but about all the time it had taken to get those notes on tape. Martha reminded me that Stephen was just doing what was developmentally appropriate for him. I was the one who had behaved developmentally inappropriately. I was old enough to know not to leave the "toy" within Stephen's reach.

Different doesn't mean inferior. In children's logic, being different equates with being inferior. This feeling may be more of a problem for siblings and other kids than for the developmentally delayed child, at least in the early years. Most children measure their self-worth by how they believe others perceive them. Be sure the child's siblings don't fall into this "different equals less" trap. This is why the term "special needs children" is not only socially correct; it's a positive term, not a value judgment. In reality all children could wear this label.

Different doesn't mean fragile While it is true you have to change your expectations of a special needs child, you don't have to lower your standards of discipline! It's tempting to get lax and let special needs children get by with behaviors you wouldn't tolerate in other children. He needs to know, early on, what behavior you expect. Many parents wait too long to start behavior training. It's much harder to redirect an eighty-pound child than a thirty pounder. Like all children, this child must be taught to adjust to family routines, to obey, and to manage himself.

Attachment parenting for the special needs child. A special needs child can bring out the best and the worst in a family. David, a baby with Down syndrome, was born into a sensitive and close-communicating family. Immediately after David's birth, I had a long discussion with his parents and their six-year-old daughter, Aimee, about surviving and thriving with a special needs child. The family first had to come to terms with the normal "why us" feelings and get to the "where do we go now" level. But then I explained to these parents the *need level concept:* every baby comes with a level of need, and every family has a level of giving. By practicing attachment parenting and getting connected, the whole family would develop a sixth sense about David, a quality of caring that no book or counselor would be able to give them. With all babies, attachment parenting is highly desirable; with a special needs child it's necessary and a matter of survival.

I pointed out to them the probable pitfalls: Avoid treating David like a project. Join support groups. Learn from the real experts — parents who have thrived with their Down syndrome children. Above all, remember your vulnerability: Love for your child brings out the overwhelming desire to devote 100 percent of family energy to helping David. That leaves nothing for the rest of the family. What David needs most is support from a stable and harmonious family.

It was also necessary to involve the older sibling in these early discussions. I pointed out to Aimee that she may feel a bit left out as her parents appear to give David a lot of the energy that previously went to her, especially since she had been an only child. That didn't mean they loved her less. The parents needed to guard against Aimee feel-

One of the most empathetic and accurate portrayals of coping with Down syndrome, and true of all special needs children, was written by Emily Pearl Kingsley:

WELCOME TO HOLLAND

I am often asked to describe the experience of raising a child with a disability — to try to help people who have not shared that unique experience to understand it, to imagine how it would feel. It's like this . . .

When you're going to have a baby, it's like planning a fabulous vacation trip — to Italy. You buy a bunch of guidebooks and make your wonderful plans. The Colosseum, the Michelangelo David, the gondolas in Venice. You may learn some handy phrases in Italian. It's all very exciting.

After months of eager anticipation, the day finally arrives. You pack your bags and off you go. Several hours later, the plane lands. The stewardess comes in and says, 'Welcome to Holland.'

"Holland?!?" you say. "What do you mean, Holland? I signed up for Italy! I'm supposed to be in Italy. All my life I've dreamed of going to Italy."

But there's been a change in the flight plan. They've landed in Holland and there you must stay.

The important thing is that they haven't taken you to a horrible, disgusting, filthy place, full of pestilence, famine, and disease. It's just a different place.

So you must o out and buy new guidebooks. And you must learn a whole new language. And you will meet a whole new group of people you would never have met.

It's just a different place. It's slower-paced than Italy, less flashy than Italy. But after you've been there for a while and you catch your breath, you look around, and you begin to notice that Holland has windmills, Holland has tulips, Holland even has Rembrandts.

But everyone you know is busy coming and going from Italy, and they're all bragging about what a wonderful time they had there. And for the rest of your life, you will say, "Yes, that's where I was supposed to go. That's what I had planned."

The pain of that will never, ever, ever go away, because the loss of that dream is a very significant loss.

But if you spend your life mourning the fact that you didn't get to Italy, you may never be free to enjoy the very special, the very lovely things about Holland.

ing deprived. They involved Aimee in David's care and made sure that she got special attention unrelated to the baby. David thrived and the whole family's sensitivity level went up a notch. The parents' marriage was strengthened, and Aimee became a deeply sensitive child, which carried over into her social life outside the home.

Tips for Disciplining the Special Needs Child

The principles of discipline mentioned throughout this book apply to special needs children as well. Just apply them in a special way. Consider these points:

- Special needs children need structure appropriate for their developmental ages, not their chronological age. Watch the child, not the calendar. Try to get inside his head.

- Beware of the trap of the Overattachment syndrome. It is very easy for your whole life to revolve entirely around your special child. This is a lose-lose situation. You lose the joy of parenting and your ability to be flexible. Eventually, you will either burn out or break.

- View behaviors as signals of needs. Everything children do tells you something about what they need. This principle is particularly true with special needs children. Sharon, an autistic ten-year-old would go from child to child in her mainstream class, pinching each of her peers. Rather than extinguish this behavior by slapping her hands, the wise teacher perceived this conduct as Sharon's way of communicating. It gave her distinction: "Sharon's pinch." The teacher used the principle of *replacement behavior* to channel the pinching into worthwhile activity, while preserving the child's need to communicate. She gave her the job of passing out papers to each child in the class. Instead of pinching her classmates she could hand them a paper, and each one (with prompting from the teacher) acknowledged Sharon.

- Value the child, and don't focus on the disability. Practice attachment parenting to the highest degree you can. Feeling loved and valued from attachment parenting helps a child cope with the lack of a particular ability.

- Help your child build a sense of responsibility. There is a natural tendency to want to rush in and do things for a developmentally delayed child. The principle of "teach them how to fish rather than give them a fish" applies doubly. The sense of accomplishment from being given responsibility gives the child a sense of value and raises her self-worth.

- Give your child choices. (Be sure you like all the alternatives.) Initially, you may have to guide your child into making a choice, but just the ability to make a choice helps the child feel important. Present the choices in the child's language, which may mean using pictures, pointing, and reinforcing your verbal instructions (which may not be fully understood) with visual ones. The more you try this exercise, the more you will learn about your child's abilities, preferences, and receptive language skills at each stage of development.

As with all children, your job as parents is to arm the child with self-control tools so that eventually he can discipline himself. Instead of saying to Stephen, "Stop kicking your sister," we'd say "Stephen, control your feet."

PARENTING THE SHY CHILD

Many children are labeled "shy." If you understand what this term really means, you may decide that it's not really a negative quality at all. Shyness can be a help or a handicap to a child, depending on how it's handled.

When shyness helps a child. Shyness is a personality trait, *not a fault.* Some of the nicest people I've known are shy. These persons tend to be attentive listeners, private people who exude a welcome presence without saying a word. Shyness is what attracted me to Martha. We met at a fraternity party in my senior year in medical school. She was standing in the midst of a bunch of my boisterous frat brothers. Everyone was talking but her. She listened. Her eyes met everyone else's. She smiled and made her quiet presence felt. She wasn't outgoing, but she made all the extroverts around her comfortable. I thought, "What a nice person to be around." There was nothing flashy about her. Her body language and sweet demeanor said "She's a person who's nice to be with." I called her the next day and the rest is beautiful history.

There is no need to say apologetically, "He's shy," especially in front of your child. There is nothing wrong with being shy. Many people don't understand shyness and equate being shy with having a problem. They believe a shy child must suffer from poor self-esteem. Most of the time this label couldn't be more unfair. Many shy children

have a solid self-concept. They have an inner peace that shines. If the extroverts would be quiet long enough they would notice its glow.

Parents worry when their child clams up in a crowd. Is he just shy or is there a serious problem? Here's how to tell. A shy child with healthy self-worth makes eye-to-eye contact, is polite, and seems happy with himself. He is just quiet. His behavior is generally good. He is a nice child to be around, and people are comfortable in his presence.

Some "shy" children are deep-thinking and cautious. They are slow to warm up to strangers. They study every new person to see if the relationship is likely to be worth the effort. Shy children often have such inner peace that their shyness is one way of protecting it. Our sixth child, Matthew, is one of the most peaceful, happy children ever to live on the face of this earth. Matt is cautious in his friendships. Once he makes a friend it's for life. He is a reserved person with a lot of valuable inner stuff for others to discover. He warms up slowly to new acquaintances, but once comfortable in your presence he's charming. Matthew is just a nice child to be around. (Peter, our third child, is like this too.)

Shortly after Matthew started school, we had our first parent-teacher conference. The teacher said, "Matthew sure is shy, isn't he?" "Yes, Matt is reserved," we explained. Later in the dialogue the subject came up again: "Matt is very quiet." "Yes, he is very focused," we answered. As the discussion of Matthew continued, this teacher soon realized we saw Matthew's traits as positive. During the school year, the teacher grew to respect the quiet, peaceful, blond-haired boy in row two. Matthew was a nice student to be around.

When shyness is a handicap. In some children, shyness is the manifestation of inner problems, not inner peace. These children are more than shy; they withdraw. They avoid eye-to-eye contact and have a lot of behavioral problems. People are not comfortable in their presence. When you delve into these little persons, you discover they operate from anger and fear instead of peace and trust. You often find they have a lot to be angry about. (See "Getting a Handle on Anger," pages 118–120.)

Hiding behind the shy veil. Some older children hide behind the shy label to avoid revealing a self they don't like. It's safer not to show anything; they retreat into a protective shell. The "shy" label becomes an excuse for not developing social skills or not exercising them. The unmotivated child can use "shyness" as a defense against trying harder and as an excuse for staying at the same level of skill development. For these children, shyness is a handicap, reinforcing their weak self-esteem. To cure their shyness, you must work at building up confidence. These youngsters need parents they can trust, who discipline in a way that does not lead to internalized anger and self-dislike.

Little Miss Outward turns inward. What about the bubbly two-year-old who smiles and waves at every stranger but who at age three turns into a clam? Mothers often worry about what they did to cause such a personality reversal. The answer usually is nothing. Before age two, many children are spontaneous. They act before they think, especially in social relations. Between two and four years of age, children go through a second phase of stranger anxiety, as they become afraid of people they don't know.

I frequently experience "shy" scenes with new patients in my office. When I enter the examining room the child lowers his chin to his chest, semi-closes his eyes, puts his thumb into his mouth, and darts behind his mother, clinging to her legs, trying to hide. I make no attempt to go after the child, instead greeting the mother in an easy, friendly way. As the mother becomes comfortable relating to me, the child listens in on our socializing. Hopefully, he'll decide "He's OK with Mom, so he's OK with me." If the child doesn't reappear, I make a game out of the moment: "Where's Tommy? I sure would like to see him. I guess he isn't here. I'll come back later." I go out of the room for a moment, to give the child space, then reenter, usually to a child at ease. Social retreating is a normal stage of development. Before you apologize to your relatives, blush from embarrassment, or call a behavioral therapist, be patient. Give your child encouragement and space; he will blossom again in his own good time.

What to Do

Parents wonder what to do about their child's shyness. Is it just a passing phase? Should the child be encouraged to become more outgoing? Is there a more serious underlying problem? Here's what to do.

Hug your little blessing. First recognize that you are blessed with a sensitive, deeply caring, reserved child who is slow to warm up to strangers, approaches social relationships cautiously, but generally seems to be a happy person. Hug your quiet child. The world will be a more gentle place because of her.

The harder you pull, the more the child retreats. It's tempting to want to help the shy child. Be careful, because the more you pull, the more some children recoil. You can't force a child out of shyness. It's better to create a comfortable environment that lets his social personality develop naturally. Never label a child "shy." On hearing this a child feels something's wrong with him. He will feel more shy. If you must use words to describe your child, say he is "private" or "reserved." These are nicer terms and more accurate. Labels also affect the way others treat your child. Calling him "shy" can make others oversolicitous, as though there is something they should do to fix it. If you are going to visit Aunt Nancy and you want your quiet child to make a good first impression, avoid the temptation to say "Don't be so shy. Aunt Nancy won't bite." That's guaranteed to make him clam up. Tell the child ahead of time what's expected of him, a simple "hi" and quiet, polite behavior. Don't ask more than you can reasonably expect. Keep the attention off the child, and as he gets comfortable, trust that Aunt Nancy will come to appreciate him. Encourage your child to bring along one of his favorite activities (for example, art supplies, a board game, some cookies he helped you bake) that Aunt Nancy can use as a bridge to communication.

Don't put the little performer on the spot. The grandparents are visiting, and you can't wait to have five-year-old Johnny play the piano for them. Don't spring this request on Johnny without warning. The young pianist may run and leave you apologizing and grandmother wondering why he's so shy. Instead, privately ask your child's permission first. "You play so well

Discipline During Family Stress

Children often time their worst behavior for when parents are least able to cope. Your ability to discipline and your child's ability to receive correction weakens during times of family stress, such as during a move, illness, job change, or even rushing to get somewhere. Making nuisances of themselves may be the only way for children to break through to preoccupied parents. Regardless of how absorbed you are in your own agenda, keep connected with your kids. Talk to your kids about what's going on and what you expect of them. For example: "Mommy has an important visitor coming over and I'm feeling nervous. I expect you to be just as careful as you always are and tell me what you need." "Mommy's friend died and Mommy misses her. I like your hugs, but you don't have to stay around to make Mommy better. I'll feel less sad each day."

and Grandmother loves to hear you play. Would you please play a little piece for her?" This respects a child's comfort level with showing a skill in public. Some children are born performers; give them an audience and they're on stage. Others guard their skills cautiously and must gradually relax as they improve. At first, they are comfortable playing the piano for themselves. Next, they play for parents (because they will applaud even if the child makes mistakes). It takes a much bigger leap of faith to play Mozart for company.

The mouthy mother and the mousy child. The combination of an extroverted, domineering mother and a more reserved child is a setup for shyness. Susy, a private, polite, and approachable five-year-old, and her mother were in my office for Susy's school-entry exam. I asked Susy if she had any pains or problems she'd like to tell me about. "Susy, this is *your* special checkup," I began. As soon as Susy opened her mouth to tell me her concerns, her mother interrupted. "She feels..." said her mother, and went on to tell me in detail. I asked the child, "Susy, is that how you feel?" Within a millisecond of Susy's first syllable, mother interrupted again: "And she also..." As this became Susy's mother's checkup instead of Susy's, the previously happy little girl turned into a withdrawn little mouse, cowering more and.more as her mother's pitch escalated. Toward the end of the checkup, mom chided her daughter, "Now, Susy don't be shy, tell the doctor what bothers you." Susy clammed up during the rest of the exam, her spirit squelched by her mouthy mother. As Susy left the room with the nurse to get her immunizations, her mother leaned over to me to confide, "Doctor, she's so shy. I don't know what to do." Susy's mother, a deeply caring and committed mother, didn't intentionally override Susy's social development. She wasn't sensitively listening to her child. Susy didn't try to be shy; she was overwhelmed by her mom. This failure to listen kept Susy from developing communication skills (at least when in the presence of her mother) and her mother from learning listening skills. I suggested to the mother that if she became more reserved around Susy, Susy would become more outgoing around her. Susy's next checkup went better. Her mother sat quietly behind Susy and nodded approvingly when her child spoke.

DISCIPLINING THE FEARFUL CHILD

Helping children overcome fears not only eases their anxieties; it also provides an opportunity to build the parent-child relationship. As you and your child work through fears together, he learns to regard you as a valuable source of support.

Why children are afraid. Children do not think like adults. Most of the world is unknown to children; and they fear the unknown. The preschooler cannot decide what's OK and what's genuinely threatening. The real world can be very scary. The ability to create images, which is developed from ages two to four, opens the world of magical thinking, with its consequent fearful fantasies. This age can mentally create persons and animals, and these images can be very scary. The cute daytime dinosaur may reappear at night in fantasy form as a monster, producing the sleep disturbances so common at this age.

The ability to imagine monsters without the ability to understand they are imaginary creatures results in little persons having big fears. Fears vary from child to child. One youngster's fear is another's fascination. Some children love to play with the vacuum cleaner. Others regard it as a noisy monster that eats things. The school-age child is more afraid of changes in relationships and in health issues (for example, being hit by a car, not being able to breathe, divorce of parents, or death). Children become fearful at different ages, at different intensities, and about different things. Since we've always parented our kids to sleep, even the first few, we haven't had monsters in the bedroom, but Hayden and Erin did go through a stage where they were scared of the dark. When Matthew did not develop this fear, we wondered why. It finally did show up at a time when he was old enough for an explanation; we told him he was scared because his imagination was growing. He liked being able to understand his fear, and he grew out of it quickly.

Fear is one of the earliest emotions. With a little help from caregivers, this unpleasant feeling can be an opportunity for emotional growth. Learning to deal with fears is one of the child's earliest lessons in dealing with emotions and using outside help. Understand and support your child during these times; the closeness between you will grow.

Helping Your Child Handle Fears

First, what not to do. Don't give your child the message that it's wrong to be scared. To a growing child, this translates into "something's wrong with me." Avoid put-downs like: "Don't be afraid." "Stop being a baby." "Big boys (or girls) don't get scared." These don't put out the fears, they only drive them underground. Now the child is afraid not only of the dark; she's also afraid to tell anybody about her fear or to seek help with handling it. What began as a normal childhood problem is now chipping away at her ability to trust others. Without reinforcing your child's fears, empathize with them: "When I was a child I was afraid of a dark bedroom, too." Acknowledge your child's fears in order to help her work through them. Strike a balance. Don't ignore the

---

Fear Therapy

A fireplace accident recently frightened Lauren. As soon as the fire was "back in its place" and the screen and glass doors shut, we gathered around the fireplace and talked about how beautiful fire is when it is contained and how scary it is when it gets loose. We talked about fireplace rules and reassured Lauren that we would all be very careful to follow the rules so the fire couldn't hurt us. She did a lot of verbalizing the rest of the evening about her experience, and each time she brought it up we paid attention. She needed to tell us how the fire "might get me." Talking helped her manage the fright she'd had. Our listening helped her put it behind her.

---

fears, but don't get overinvolved in them either, or your child will play up the fear to get your attention.

When responding to children's fears, give them two messages: It's all right to be afraid; and it's good to share your fears and ask for help. Reassure your child that "Mom and Dad (or trusted adult) will keep you safe." Remember not to put down your child by saying "There's nothing to be afraid of" or "That's silly." *Never* use or create fears to discipline your child: "The boogie man will get you if you get out of bed." or "God will punish you if you talk back."

Model being unfearful. Helping your child handle fears is much easier if you are closely connected with your child. If something or someone is safe for you, then it is safe for your child. Stranger anxiety is common between the ages of one and two years. Help your child to overcome this fear by mirroring to him that this new person is OK. (See discussion of how to lessen stranger anxiety, pages 50–51.) Many a child becomes fearful of insects because he sees an adult freak out when a June bug buzzes by. Same for lightning and thunder. Try singing "My Favorite Things" during a storm to help *yourself* stay calm. Even visits to the doctor can be made less scary. Prior to your doctor visit, let your child explore a toy doctor's kit. Play doctor and go through a pretend examination so your child knows what to expect. Let the child play doctor with his pet, doll, or stuffed animal.

Always take your child's fear of caregivers seriously. Normally, familiarity lessens fear. If your child's fear at being left with a particular caregiver, even a relative, is getting more intense, change caregivers. Even if foul play seems unlikely, *give your child the benefit of the doubt.*

Bedtime fears. Nighttime is scary time for little people. Fear of the dark and of separation from parents is a double fear that keeps many children awake. Put on a night-light. Cuddle your child off to sleep with a soothing story, massage, or song. Leave relaxing tapes playing for an hour or so after she goes to sleep. Young children need these helpers because they cannot use logic to overcome their fears. (See the discussion of nighttime parenting tips, pages 131–143.) The child over age four can be helped to work through the fear of darkness. Ask her to tell you what "dark" means to her. Encourage the child to draw the fear: "Draw what your dark room feels and looks like." If you get a black sheet of paper with an or-

ange monster under the bed, you've pinpointed the fear.

The principle of *gradually increasing exposure* helps the child overcome fear of the dark. Play dark tag, beginning with the lights on in a room that preferably has a dimmer switch so that you can gradually dim the lights. Play hide-and-seek at dusk, and let the game extend into the darkness. Play follow the leader as you weave around the yard at night on an exploring expedition. Initially, hold your child's hand as you explore together. Give your child his own flashlight to keep next to his bed so that he can turn it on to shed some light onto suspicious piles of clothing that turn into "a bear" when there's only a night-light. Sometimes just knowing that he has the power to change the darkness into light is enough to quell the fear. Or just leave more light on in his room; it won't interfere with his ability to sleep. He'll start turning it off himself when he's older.

Chasing monsters out of bedrooms. "Daddy, there's a monster in my room." Here's how to get the child out of the fearful state and ease him into a sleeping one. Let him describe the monster and tell you exactly where it is. Walk around the room together, letting him share his worries. Realize that fearing monsters is a developmental stage in which the monster stands in for a frightening world. Childish fears being what they are — illogical — an explanation may not work. A more imaginative response is called for: "I'm the dad in this house and I don't allow monsters in here. He'll have to leave." Then you step into the closet and have a brief talk with the monster.

Do these kinds of responses mean that you have "caved in" to childish behavior? No, they don't. They mean you understand what that dark and shadowy room looks like to your child; your recognizing his reality by playing along shows him a way of mastering his fears. How else can a parent confront a pretend monster, if not by pretending a little!

As your child grows older the problem with joining in on fictitious fears is that you reinforce the idea that monsters really do exist. We don't believe in "chasing the monster away" once children can understand the difference between real and pretend. Tell your child matter-of-factly: "Monsters are only on drawings or TV. They aren't real. And even if they were real, Daddy wouldn't let them get in our house." Draw a monster picture and show your five- or six-year-old the difference between real and imaginary. ("Monsters are pretend. Lions are real and Daddy won't let any lions in here either.") Since we share sleep with our children, we haven't had this monster-in-the-bedroom problem ourselves. Once our kids are secure enough at night to graduate from our bedroom, they are past the age of being tricked by their imagination. Even if your child sleeps in his own room, a lovely part of his bedtime ritual could be his mom or dad lying down with him as he falls off to sleep, until he is old enough to enjoy going to sleep on his own.

Try helping your older child imagine a substitute scene: "When you dream or worry about anything scary, imagine a train at the end of your bed. Whenever you're afraid you can hop on the train, and Mommy and Daddy will be right there in the train with you. You ride around in the train for a little while with Mommy and Daddy, and then the train comes back and stops at the end of your bed. You get off, and you crawl back into bed, and by that time you'll be so tired you'll go right to sleep." Offering substitute make-believe works for the sensitive child who feels threatened at any suggestion that the monsters aren't real and that therefore you think she's dumb for even thinking about monsters. The best way to get rid of nighttime fears is to prevent them by practicing a style of nighttime parenting that helps the child feel that sleep is a pleasant state to enter and a fearless state to remain in. (See Chapter 11 "Sleep Discipline.")

Is fear fun? Fear of fantasy characters is common in the preschool child. As long as your child's favorite "scary" characters are not keeping him awake at night, bothering him at school, or making him a generally fearful person, join in the fun, and let your child enjoy fantasies. But if they are interfering with his emotional development, help him work through what is imaginary and what is real. The child under six has difficulty separating make-believe from reality.

Banish scary characters from your child's environment. Turn off scary TV shows and videos. Even better, limit TV and videos for preschoolers to very selective viewing. Beware of films and cartoons (for example, *Batman*) that were created for older children and adults. Help your child discern the difference between real and imaginary characters. Talk about how cartoons and movies are made. Use puppets to put on an act. ("See, these aren't real; they only talk with your voice or move if you pull the string.")

Be careful not to transfer your own fears to your child. For example, your toddler is climbing up on the counter. If you immediately give him the fear message, "You might fall!" or "That's dangerous!" he probably will fall. Fear can actually make risk situations more dangerous. It's best to calmly walk over to the child and assist him.

Fear Can Be a Clue

Your child's fears may be the tip of the iceberg, a clue to what your child is really worried about. I once counseled parents and their seven-year-old son about the child's fear of going to school. It turned out the child was not afraid of going to school but of leaving home. There had been a lot of divorces recently among the parents of his classmates. He feared that if he left home he might return to find a parent missing.

DISCIPLINE FOLLOWING DIVORCE

Divorce is a setup for discipline problems to surface. When parents divorce, children often blame themselves and become angry at their mother and father. They may show a complete turnabout in behavior and personality following this family upheaval. These challenges come at a time when parents are busy organizing their new lives and grieving all the losses. They are less able to cope with a child's problems. While sometimes a child's behavior actually improves following a divorce (especially when there was domestic violence preceding the divorce), more often than not it deteriorates.

It is common for preschool children to become clingy after a divorce. They are uncertain of their support base and fear the custodial parent may also take off. Expect regressive behavior, such as thumb-sucking and problems with toilet training, excessive masturbation, mood swings, aggressive behaviors, and sleep disturbances (the child fears awakening to find mommy gone too).

School-aged children are even more likely to be angry at themselves and their parents. Their school performance deteriorates, and they may form unhealthy relationships with dubious peers.

Here are some ways to discipline after divorce and reconnect with your child in the changed family setting.

Reaffirm your love and availability. Most discipline problems stem from children demanding attention and assurance that they are loved. Try to make as few changes as possible immediately following the divorce. Take one stress at a time. Try to delay moving or changing a child's school. If the previously at-home custodial parent must now work full-time, try to delay this change as long as possible. A child under age five may interpret prolonged departures as a warning that this parent likewise is going to leave.

Level with your children. Before your children fabricate their own child-centered explanation of the divorce, explain it to them yourself in language they can understand. You shouldn't dwell on the problems in the marriage. Don't run down your spouse. Give them two messages. The divorce is not their fault and "You still have a Mommy and a Daddy, and we both still love you and will take care of you." Parents divorce each other, but they never divorce their children. Then explain how family life is going to go on, what will be the same, and what will change. Uppermost in children's minds is concern about what will happen to them.

Organize the single-parent home. When parents divorce, discipline often becomes relaxed, and household routines become disorganized. If you have school-age children, call a family meeting to work out how everybody will do their fair share to make the house run smoothly. Children in single-parent families have increased responsibility; that's a fact of life. Remember, children are angry about the divorce, so ease them gently into increased responsibilities. Be supportive and set aside special times to focus on having fun with your children, as well as times to work together on household chores.

Realize the other parent will have a different discipline style. Often following a divorce what happens is that the custodial parent finds it necessary to run a tight ship, an organized home with increased responsibilities and consistent, predictable discipline, while the noncustodial parent becomes "Disneyland Daddy," all fun and games and no structure or rules. The custodial parent becomes the tough one, the noncustodial parent the fun one. Since parenting is so profoundly personal and rooted in the unconscious, there is no way divorced parents (not to mention stepparents) will be able to discipline the same way. Realizing this up front can save the parents from being continually angry with one another. Don't worry that these differences between two homes will be confusing to your child. Children are very good at sizing up people, especially parents, and they will know which set of circumstances makes them feel safer. Your child will be able to make the adjustment going from home and coming back again since children are so adaptable. This is not to say that there won't be some hassles, but as long as at least one of the parents (probably the one reading this book) has a handle on discipline, the child will feel grounded. The child will have the same attitude toward

the divorce situation as he sees his parents having. Do what you need to do to make sure that your attitude, at least, is healthy and reassuring. Counseling for single parents and stepparents is readily available. Support groups are available in communities and through churches.

CAREGIVERS AS DISCIPLINARIANS

When you turn your child over to substitute caregivers, you also turn over the job of disciplining your child. Choose subs who discipline as you do. Be especially careful when choosing someone who will be in charge of your child for many hours a week while you are at work. Choose a sub whose discipline methods you know and value. If you are looking only for the occasional babysitter, try trading child care with parents who share your philosophy of discipline. When choosing a teenage babysitter, it helps to know the correction methods his or her parents used. If your babysitter's behavior was spank-controlled as a child, she may correct your child that way.

Beware of a high-risk mismatch. Entrusting a hyperactive child to the care of a sitter with a short fuse is a risk you shouldn't take. I've seen several cases where a two-year-old's tantrum pushed anger buttons in a sitter that led to child abuse. I counseled one sorry teenager who stopped a toddler tantrum by hitting the child with a wooden spoon so hard that it caused bruising. The tantrum ignited flashbacks from her childhood when her tantrums had been squelched with a wooden spoon. Some babies have a high-pitched, irritating cry that triggers an angry response in even the most compassionate listener. Don't match a baby who has an ear-piercing cry with a sub who has a low cry tolerance.

Don't ignore the signals of caregiver-child mismatch. If your baby fears the sitter or your older child complains, take these warnings to heart and consider changing caregivers. However, watch out for the youngster playing one adult against another — a favorite pastime enjoyed by all children.

It's difficult, perhaps impossible, for a substitute caregiver to be the perfect disciplinarian. They lack your connection. When interviewing a sub, ask about discipline. Quiz her on a series of situations: "What would you do if my child had a tantrum?" "What would you do if my child were defiant?" Ask how she was corrected as a child, and try to get a feel for her overall philosophy of discipline. If her philosophy is close to yours (don't expect a perfect match), add the finishing touches by telling her specifically how you want your child corrected. Based on your knowledge of your child, walk her through specific misbehaviors she may encounter and ask her to role-play how she would handle them. Better yet, pay her to spend a few days observing, helping you, and interacting with your child. To make it easier for your fill-in, let your child know that you are transferring authority to the sitter. Tell your older child that you expect him to respect the sitter and to behave in your absence. A substitute who is overattentive may stifle a child's independence, interfere with his learning to solve his own problems, or dampen his creativity. To the other extreme is a negligent caregiver who, by placing no limits on the child, is downright dangerous. The caregiver who is appropriately attentive is a rare find. If you have discovered one, treasure her.

Closing Comments:

Putting It All Together —
A Sample Discipline Plan

B Y NOW YOU REALIZE that discipline has many facets. How do you bring them all into play when disciplining your child? While there is no one-size-fits-all approach to discipline problems, there are general guidelines that parents can use to manage discipline conflicts with their children. Here are the general guidelines that we use in our discipline counseling that apply the principles of this book to real-life situations. It can be used as a guide for analyzing the discipline problems you face in your family.

STEP ONE: SET CONDITIONS THAT FOSTER GOOD BEHAVIOR

Assess your parent-child connection.
Take inventory of your family relationships: Is the family atmosphere generally positive or negative? Is there a lot of anger in the family? What stresses are present in the marriage, in your careers, in your finances, and so on? Can you relate your child's behavior to your moods? Even in the most loving and connected families, the behavior of children deteriorates when parents are

sad or angry. What can you do to get closer to your child? Are you too busy? Are there family circumstances that are creating a distance between you and your child, for example, work or other commitments? Some situations you can change, others you may have to help your children learn to live with. Remember, think relationship first and techniques second. The goal of discipline is to help children want to obey for their own sake and for yours. Once you get connected to your child he is likely to want to please.

Give focused attention during times of good behavior. Every child has "good" times. Capitalize on these. Be especially approachable and involved during your child's best behavior times. Show how pleased you are. You want your child to figure out that he is much happier when he behaves well and his parents are happy. This motivates the child to continue wanting to please.

Have fun together. Give your child high doses of the simple pleasures of life. Pick activities that you and your child enjoy doing together, those where your child behaves his best.

Create a positive atmosphere. What do you like best about your child? What is your child good at — sports, crafts, music? What situations bring out the best and the worst in your child? Focusing on the negative is likely to contribute to the already negative atmosphere that prevails. While helping your child fix what is wrong, acknowledge what is right. Spend more time validating the pleasant parts of his personality than commenting on the problem areas. By the time discipline problems are advanced, usually a negative atmosphere prevails in the home. Children need days full of positives — "Yes!" "Great!" "Thank You." "Good job." "Thumbs-up."

Set up your child to succeed. Avoid situations that you and your child can't handle. Know your child's limits and yours. Some young children are not equipped to handle themselves in public places. Plan ahead. For now it may be easier to have a cookout in the park than go to a restaurant. Give your child paying jobs. Put him in charge of something. The child who learns to be responsible for things and other persons is more likely to take responsibility for his behavior. (See "Give Your Child Responsibilities," pages 103–104.)

Monitor your child's diet. While poor diet is not the cause of poor behavior in most children, some children show dramatic improvement in their behavior when they eat right. (See Chapter 10, "Feeding Good Behavior.")

Drop any discipline techniques that are not working and those that seem to invite conflicts. Avoid nagging. That turns off most children, especially those with strong wills. Spanking is likely to aggravate

---

Be the Adult

In the early years when you and your child are working on a discipline relationship that works, don't feel you always have to offer your child an explanation for your decision — your discipline doesn't always have to make sense to your child. Sometimes all that is necessary is giving your child the message "Because this is what I want you to do." Children expect us to be adults. That knowledge frees them to be children.

---

the already angry child. If you hit your child in anger, the child is more likely to hit others when he is angry or internalize the anger and think he is bad. Your discipline must shape the child from within. All the discipline methods, gimmicks, and professional advice are like a temporary fashion makeover. They may change how the child looks, but not how the child is inside. The effects will wear off. The best discipline methods in the world won't work unless you work on setting the conditions that foster good behavior. And, while you're doing this, be sure your child realizes that you're the trustworthy adult in charge. Convey the message to your child: "Because I love you, I'm going to help you control yourself."

STEP TWO: CORRECT THE UNDESIRABLE BEHAVIORS

Construct a behavioral profile. Here's how to analyze your child's behavioral strengths and weaknesses. Remember your goals: to help your child be likable to live with and to help him develop *self-control.* Some of your child's behavioral traits will work to his advantage. List these and figure out what situations draw them out. When is your child at his best?

In the second part of your behavioral profile, list the behaviors that bother you the most. What don't you like about your child? What situations bring out the worst in his behavior? Separate the behaviors you can live with (smallies) from the behaviors you can't (biggies). Focus on the biggies, and you'll be amazed how the smallies correct themselves. If tantrums are a biggie, identify what situations trigger tantrums and intervene early. Structure the child's environment with activities that are do-able. Try fun activities that she can handle, and keep her focused. Ignore her, walk away, or change the subject if you believe her tantrums are *manipulative.* Empathize and support tantrums caused by *frustration.*

Also, give your child activities that will mellow her impulsive tendencies. Teach her how to relax. For example, pick out the time of the day that her behavior is usually the worst (often late afternoon), and set up a special "massage time." Put on soothing music, lay her on a towel in her favorite place. (Try next to a window with the area warmed by the late-afternoon sun). Give her a soothing massage while you sing lullabies. Besides relaxing your child, this special time strengthens your connection.

Structure your child's environment. Use the information you have gleaned from your child's behavioral profile to structure the child's day so that the best behaviors have a chance to come out. For example, you notice that your child plays well in the morning, but when he's more tired during afternoon play he's likely to be too aggressive. Arrange for playmates in the morning and solo play in the afternoon. If you notice that your child plays well with Samuel, but that he and Mark fight all the time, scratch Mark as a playmate. The two boys are probably temperament mismatches. (See discussions of the importance of structure, pages 46–50 and 276.) Remember, the basis of structure is not only setting rules but creating conditions that make these rules easier to follow. Consider the *prohibit and provide* approach. Prohibit hitting and provide alternatives. When telling your child to stop hitting, give him other physical releases, such as a "give me five" slap on the palms or a ball or pillow to kick or hit. Teach him to use verbal language instead. "Nathan, use your words. Say 'That makes me mad. I don't like that.'" Teach your child to control his physical aggressiveness: "Give Daddy a 'bear hug' (a strong hug), but give Suzy a 'bunny hug' (a soft hug)." (See techniques for softening the aggressive child, pages 267–274 and 269.)

Communicate what behavior you expect. First, decide what behavior you want and just how much annoying behavior you are willing to tolerate, and stick to those guidelines. Acknowledge good behavior, catch your child in the act of being good. Try a "no-more-nos" atmosphere. Instead of telling him what you don't want him to do, offer a positive alternative. Instead of "Don't throw your truck," try "Park your truck right there on the shelf." Then show him how to do this. If he persists in throwing, tell him that toys are for playing with, not for throwing, and you *expect* him to play with the toys, not throw them. *If* he throws the toys, *then* the toys will get put away. (Carry this out matter-of-factly if he persists in his bad behavior.) Meanwhile, make sure

Make Changes Gradually

One afternoon during a counseling session, I gave a desperate mother a list of techniques to try to shape the behavior of her out-of-control five-year-old, Ashley. Upon leaving my office, the mother said, "I can't wait to try all this stuff on my daughter." I reminded this mother that behavior doesn't change overnight. If you suddenly jump in with hugs and kisses, positive reinforcement, focused attention, and so on, your child may perceive this as phony, overwhelming, and it could possibly cause her to withdraw further. Take baby steps when changing your approach to discipline. Go slowly. Ease into techniques, and wait for teachable moments to try them.

he has other opportunities for throwing, and provide soft balls that are safe for inside. Reinforce the positive behaviors with lots of smiling compliments: "Yes." "Good." "That makes me happy." As you redirect your child's behavior, teach him how to focus. Tell him, "I need your eyes," as you hold his shoulders with a firm but gentle touch and engage him in eye-to-eye contact; don't threaten or restrain him, just help him pay attention.

Try the following behavior-shaping techniques. The reasons we have saved specific discipline techniques for the very last in our plan is that they are unlikely to work without the first parts of this plan in place. Try these techniques:

- *Explain to your child the behavior-shaping partnership:* "We are going to work together so that we like living together more." Be sure your child believes there's something in it for her, that she will have more fun and you will be a happier parent. (See related story, page 103.) Be sure to convey a healthy authority so the child accepts that your job is to help her obey. Spell out specifically what you're going to do. Point out the "yes behaviors" that you expect her to do, and the benefits of good behavior. (Remember, you're trying to motivate the child from within.) Also, point out "no behaviors" that you will not tolerate and that have consequences. Be sure your child understands what you expect. With this bit of preprogramming, sometimes a simple reminder, "That's a no behavior," will redirect misbehavior before it escalates.

- *Explain the consequences.* By three to four years of age, children understand the *when-then* connection: When they obey, then living is pleasant; when they disobey, it's unpleasant. Sit with your child and go over the specific behavior you want to shape. Work on only one behavior at a time. Be sure your child understands the benefits of good behavior, and the consequences of bad. In this way, your child becomes a *partner* in his discipline: "When you play nicely with your friends, that makes me happy, then you can play longer. When you fight with your friends, then you will have to stop playing." By preplanning the rewards and consequences of good behavior, your child has, in effect, already agreed to the consequences. This saves you from lashing out with unfair punishments, such as "You can't ride your tricycle for a month." And it may ward off a tantrum. Your child makes his own behavioral choices and therefore is in control of the consequences. Children perceive this type of discipline as fair and are not likely to rebel.

- *Distract and divert.* Interrupt and redirect misbehavior before the child has a chance to get going. Distract and divert the child's attention into positive behavior: "You can't climb on the counters, but you can climb on the couch or on Daddy." You may have to shadow the child for a couple weeks and inject spur-of-the-moment reminders (see examples, page 178), redirectors (see examples, pages 42–43), and motivators (see pages 173–178) until the child gets so used to behaving the way you expect him to that he reminds himself. Remind him, "You're being anxious," or "You're getting wild," and then usher in a quick holding time to help him regain his composure. The key is to intervene *before* his behavior gets out of hand. Remember, as you are shaping your child's behavior you will have to redirect him *physically,* which means a lot of hands-on attention. Eventually, verbal requests will sink in.

- *Motivate and reward good behavior.* (See "Motivators," pages 173–178 and "Rewards That Work," pages 174–178.)

- *Time-out the child.* (See "How to Make Timeout Work for You," page 167–171.)

If your child perceives time-out as threatening or as a punishment, change his attitude by a more positive phrase substituting for the term "time-out": "special time" or "thinking time" or "Nathan time." Institute the time-out early in the situation before the child is so far gone that both parent and child are angry.

For more discipline techniques, see: "Discipline Talk," pages 162–163; "Disciplining the Hyperactive Child," pages 267–281; and "Disciplining the Temperamentally Difficult Child," pages 282–289.

Throughout this book we have taken you on a journey of disciplining your child from birth to age ten. The benefit of this approach is that disciplining your child appropriately at one stage of development makes discipline at subsequent stages easier. As your child gets older, you will notice your job description as home disciplinarian changes. Your efforts as nurturer, limit-setter, facilitator, and enforcer from birth to age six, as teacher during the next stage, and as coach and consultant during the teen years will be rewarded. You'll find that you are raising a child whom you genuinely enjoy, who is fun to be around, and who will make you proud. More importantly, your child will be proud of himself.

INDEX